THE CHAGOS ISLANDERS AND INTERNATIONAL LAW

In 1965, the UK excised the Chagos Islands from the colony of Mauritius to create the British Indian Ocean Territory (BIOT) in connection with the founding of a US military facility on the island of Diego Garcia. Consequently, the inhabitants of the Chagos Islands were secretly exiled to Mauritius, where they became chronically impoverished. This book considers the resonance of international law for the Chagos Islanders. It advances the argument that BIOT constitutes a 'Non-Self-Governing Territory' pursuant to the provisions of Chapter XI of the UN Charter and for the wider purposes of international law. In addition, the book explores the extent to which the right of self-determination, indigenous land rights and a range of obligations contained in applicable human rights treaties could support the Chagossian right to return to BIOT. However, the rights of the Chagos Islanders are premised on the assumption that the UK possesses a valid sovereignty claim over BIOT. The evidence suggests that this claim is questionable and it is disputed by Mauritius. Consequently, the Mauritian claim threatens to compromise the entitlements of the Chagos Islanders in respect of BIOT as a matter of international law. This book illustrates the ongoing problems arising from international law's endorsement of the territorial integrity of colonial units for the purpose of decolonisation at the expense of the countervailing claims of colonial self-determination by non-European peoples that inhabited the same colonial unit. The book uses the competing claims to the Chagos Islands to demonstrate the need for a more nuanced approach to the resolution of sovereignty disputes resulting from the legacy of European colonialism.

The Chagos Islanders and
International Law

Stephen Allen

·HART·
PUBLISHING
OXFORD AND PORTLAND, OREGON
2014

Published in the United Kingdom by Hart Publishing Ltd
16C Worcester Place, Oxford, OX1 2JW
Telephone: +44 (0)1865 517530
Fax: +44 (0)1865 510710
E-mail: mail@hartpub.co.uk
Website: http://www.hartpub.co.uk

Published in North America (US and Canada) by
Hart Publishing
c/o International Specialized Book Services
920 NE 58th Avenue, Suite 300
Portland, OR 97213-3786
USA
Tel: +1 503 287 3093 or toll-free: (1) 800 944 6190
Fax: +1 503 280 8832
E-mail: orders@isbs.com
Website: http://www.isbs.com

© Stephen Allen 2014

Stephen Allen has asserted his right under the Copyright, Designs and Patents Act 1988,
to be identified as the authors of this work.

Hart Publishing is an imprint of Bloomsbury Publishing plc.

British Library Cataloguing in Publication Data
Data Available

ISBN: 978-1-84946-265-5

Typeset by Hope Services, Abingdon
Printed and bound in Great Britain by
CPI Group (UK) Ltd, Croydon CR0 4YY

Acknowledgements

'The past is not dead. It is not even past.'

William Faulkner

This book evolved out of a number of papers presented at conferences and seminars including: the UK Constitutional Law Group Seminar dedicated to the Chagos litigation in 2007; the 2008 colloquium on 'The Common Law, the Royal Prerogative and Executive Legislation', Centre for Public Law at Cambridge University; and a seminar organised by the Public International Law Discussion Group at Oxford University in 2008. I also participated in an interdisciplinary conference dedicated to the Chagossian situation held in Amsterdam in 2008.

Chapter one of this book is a revised and updated version of my 'Responsibility and Redress: The Chagossian Claims in the English Courts', published in S Evers and M Kooy (eds), *Eviction from the Chagos Islands: Displacement and Struggle for Identity Against Two World Powers* (Leiden, Brill, 2011) 127–52. Chapter seven builds upon my 'Looking Beyond the *Bancoult* Cases: International Law and the Prospect of Resettling the Chagos Islands' (2007) 7 *Human Rights Law Review* (Oxford University Press) 441–82; and 'International Law and the Resettlement of the (Outer) Chagos Islands' (2008) 8 *Human Rights Law Review* 683–702.

This book has taken a long time to write and I have incurred many debts in writing it. In particular, I wish to thank Anthony Bradley, Richard Gifford, Patrick Thornberry, Rachel Murray, Tonia Novitz, Patrick Capps, David Snoxell, David Fraser and David Keane for engaging with the arguments which are developed in this book. I would also like to acknowledge the generosity of other Chagos scholars who have been instrumental in drawing attention to the Chagossian situation, especially Laura Jeffery, David Vine, Sandra Evers and Peter Sand. I am grateful to colleagues in the Law Department at Queen Mary, University of London for their encouragement and support, especially Valsamis Mitsilegas, Roger Cotterrell, Maks Del Mar, with special thanks to Malgosia Fitzmaurice. I am grateful to Richard Hart for agreeing to publish this book and for his patience when the submission deadlines came and went. Part of the book was written during my time as a visiting scholar at Suffolk University Law School in 2013. Accordingly, I would like to thank Chris Gibson for allowing me to visit and Valerie Epps for her kind support and friendship during my time in Boston. Finally, I wish to dedicate this book to Vida, and our son, Justin.

Stephen Allen
Queen Mary, University of London
March 2014

Table of Contents

Table of Cases

Table of Legislation

International Treaties and Conventions

European Union Legislation

National Legislation

France

Mauritius

United Kingdom

Introduction

IN 1965, THE UK excised the Chagos Islands from the British colony of Mauritius to create the British Indian Ocean Territory (BIOT) in connection with the founding of a US military facility on the island of Diego Garcia. Consequently, the inhabitants of the Chagos Islands – the Chagos Islanders – were secretly exiled to Mauritius, where they became chronically impoverished.[1] This book advances the argument that the BIOT constitutes a non-self-governing territory pursuant to Chapter XI of the UN Charter and for the wider purposes of international law. Further, it explores the extent to which the right of colonial self-determination; the corpus of indigenous rights; and a range of obligations contained in applicable human rights treaties could support the Chagossian right to return to the BIOT. However, the rights of the Chagos Islanders are premised on the assumption that the UK possesses sovereign authority over the BIOT. This authority is questionable and it is disputed by Mauritius in any event. The Mauritian sovereignty claim inevitably threatens to compromise the entitlements claimed by the Chagos Islanders in respect of the BIOT at the level of international law. This case study illustrates the challenges arising from international law's willingness to endorse the territorial integrity of colonial units for the purpose of decolonisation at the expense of the countervailing claims of colonial self-determination advanced by other non-European peoples that happened to inhabit the same colonial unit. To this end, the book harnesses the competing claims to the Chagos Islands to demonstrate the need for a more nuanced approach to the resolution of sovereignty disputes resulting from the legacy of European colonialism.

I. BACKGROUND

In furtherance of its Cold War policy of containing the Soviet Union, the US government negotiated an agreement with the UK government to construct a military facility on the island of Diego Garcia in the remote Chagos Archipelago, which was then part of the British colony of Mauritius.[2] The UK government

---

[1] In addition, about 500 Chagossians were transported to the Seychelles where they have endured similar experiences. See S Evers and M Kooy (eds), *Eviction from the Chagos Islands: Displacement and Struggle for Identity Against Two World Powers* (Leiden, Brill, 2011).

[2] The Chagos Archipelago consists of 56 islands spread over a total area of approximately 47.5 miles in the middle of the Indian Ocean. Diego Garcia is approximately 130 miles from the other Chagos island groups of Peros Banhos and the Salomon islands (the 'outer islands'). The island is situated 1200 miles north east of Mauritius and 1000 miles north of the island of Mahé in the Seychelles.

procured the consent of the elected representatives of Mauritian colonial government to the detachment of the Chagos Islands from Mauritius through the 1965 Lancaster House Agreement. It then enacted primary legislation, the 1965 BIOT Order in Council, to excise the Chagos Archipelago from Mauritius. The BIOT, which incorporated the Chagos Islands, was thus established. Under a 1966 US-UK treaty,[3] while the UK retained sovereignty over the BIOT, Diego Garcia was transferred to the US government for an initial period of 50 years in connection with the construction of the planned military facility. The 1966 treaty also provided that other BIOT islands could be made available to the US for defence purposes, if required. The US and UK governments covertly agreed that the entire population of the Chagos Islands would be removed before the US government took possession of Diego Garcia. Accordingly, between 1965 and 1973, against a background of UN-inspired decolonisation, the Chagos Islanders were banished from their ancestral homeland without prior consultation, consent or compensation. The vast majority were transported to Mauritius where they became chronically impoverished.[4] During the 1970s, the US facility was upgraded to a fully-fledged military base; it has since become a key site for the pursuit of US global interests, not least in its 'war on terror'.

Official documents, which are now in the public domain, show that the UK government knew that the Chagos Islands had been inhabited by the '*Ilois*' (Chagos Islanders) since at least the early-nineteenth century.[5] However, the UK government appreciated that official recognition of this permanent population would attract international legal obligations under Chapter XI of the UN Charter including the responsibility to foster full self-government for the permanent inhabitants of non-self-governing territories and to report to the United Nations on conditions and developments occurring in such territories.[6] As a result, the UK government adopted a policy of 'quiet disregard' preferring to falsify the nature of the whole population and to characterise them as contract labourers from Mauritius and the Seychelles.[7]

In 1975, Michel Vencatessen, a Chagossian who had been forced to leave Diego Garcia in 1971, instituted a private law action against the UK government for intimidation, false imprisonment and assault. In response, the UK and

[3] Exchange of Notes between the UK and US Governments concerning the Availability for Defence Purposes of the islands of Diego Garcia and the remainder of the Chagos Archipelago, and the islands of Aldabra, Farquhar, and Desroches constituting the British Indian Ocean Territory, 1 December 1966.

[4] Although figures are disputed, the available evidence suggests that the *Ilois* population stood at between 1500 and 1800 individuals immediately prior to their expulsion.

[5] *Chagos Islanders v Attorney General & HM BIOT Commissioner* [2003] EWHC QB 2222 ('*Ouseley judgment*') [41]. The term *Ilois* is French Creole for 'islanders'. It was used from the nineteenth century onwards to describe the permanent inhabitants of the Chagos islands. See J Madeley, *Diego Garcia: A Contrast to The Falklands* (London, Minority Rights Group, 1982) 12. However, in recent years, the term has taken on a pejorative meaning. This societal group now self-identify as 'Chagossians'. See *Ouseley judgment* [10].

[6] See ch 5.

[7] *R (Bancoult) v Secretary of State for Foreign and Commonwealth Affairs* ('*Bancoult 2*') [2006] EWHC 1038 (DC) [32].

Mauritian governments agreed to establish a trust fund to assist in the resettlement of the Chagossian people in Mauritius.[8] Under the Mauritian *Ilois* Trust
Fund Act 1982, a Board of Trustees were authorised to develop resettlement
programmes and distribute trust monies. However, by this time, the overwhelming majority of Chagossians were so poor that the decision was taken to distribute the fund directly in the form of cash payments. The fund was distributed
between 1344 individuals who received approximately £2700 each.[9] However,
recipients were required to renounce their claims against the UK government.[10]
In 1997, it was discovered that any exiled person born in the Chagos Islands was
a citizen of the British Dependent Territories under the British Nationality Act
1981.[11] It was therefore open to any affected Chagossian, as a Crown subject, to
institute public law proceedings against the decision to deny them the right of
abode in the Chagos Islands. The Chagossians claimed a right of abode in the
BIOT (except for Diego Garcia while the US military base remains operational).
This claim led to legal challenges against the UK government in the English
courts between 2000 and 2008.[12]

In *Bancoult 1*, Olivier Bancoult, the leader of the Chagos Refugees Group,
challenged the decision to banish the Chagossians from the BIOT. Under
section 11 of the 1965 BIOT Order in Council, the BIOT Commissioner was
empowered to legislate for BIOT's 'peace, order and good government', a standard legislative formulation used for the purpose of authorising wide discretionary powers of colonial governance. However, in the Divisional Court's view,
the Commissioner's legislative authority did not extend to the removal of the
population from the territory for reasons unrelated to it. It acknowledged that
while a colonial legislature has exclusive authority to determine the factual
requirements of 'peace, order and good government', such authority was not
unlimited.[13] Accordingly, the Court held that section 4 of the Ordinance was
ultra vires and it quashed that provision. The UK government accepted the

---

[8] The UK government contributed £4 million to the fund while the Mauritian government
pledged £1 million worth of land. The compensation was offered on the condition that the
Vencatessen proceedings were stayed. See the *Ouseley judgment* (n 5) [75].

[9] ibid, [80].

[10] The 1982 Agreement between the UK and Mauritian governments provided that compensation
in full and final settlement would be paid for 'all acts, matters and things done by or pursuant to the
BIOT Order 1965, including the closure of the plantations in the Chagos Archipelago, the departure
and removal of those living or working there, the termination of their contracts, their transfer to
and their resettlement in Mauritius'; see Madeley, *Diego Garcia* (n 5) 10.

[11] At the time of their exile, such persons were citizens of the United Kingdom and its Colonies
under the British Nationality Act 1948. By virtue of the British Nationality Act 1981, they became
British Dependent Territories Citizens. Subsequently, pursuant to the British Overseas Territories
Act 2002, they became British Overseas Territories Citizens and entitled to full British citizenship.
Since 1968 Chagossians may also claim Mauritian citizenship, see *Bancoult 2* (DC) (n 7) [43–45].

[12] The public law challenge: *R (Bancoult) v Secretary of State for Foreign and Commonwealth
Affairs* [2001] 1 QB 1067 ('*Bancoult 1*'); *R (Bancoult) v Secretary of State for Foreign and
Commonwealth Affairs* ('*Bancoult 2*') [2006] EWHC 1038 (DC); [2008] QB 365 (CA); [2008] 3 WLR
955 (HL). The private law action: *Chagos Islanders v Attorney General and HM BIOT Commissioner*
[2003] EWHC QB 2222 (HC); [2004] EWCA Civ 997 (CA).

[13] *Bancoult 1* (n 11) [55].

decision. The 1971 Ordinance was repealed and replaced by the BIOT Immigration Ordinance 2000, a piece of subordinate legislation, which allowed Chagossians to return to the BIOT (except for Diego Garcia) without permits.[14]

In 2002, a feasibility survey indicated that long-term resettlement would prove 'precarious and costly'.[15] Accordingly, the government concluded that the policy of resettlement was unfeasible. In 2004, in a volte-face, the UK government replaced the extant BIOT's Constitution and the Immigration Ordinance 2000 with two Orders in Council.[16] Together they ensured that full immigration controls over BIOT territory were reinstated. In a House of Commons debate on 7 July 2004, the Parliamentary Under-Secretary of State for Foreign and Commonwealth Affairs argued that the reintroduction of such measures was justified in order to honour UK treaty obligations.[17] Further, evidence produced in *Bancoult 2* showed that the US government vouched for the ongoing strategic value of its military facility on Diego Garcia in the 'global war on terrorism' and it claimed that resettlement to the outer Chagos Islands would compromise the base's security since it would increase the risk of terrorist infiltration and attack.[18] The 2004 Orders sought to abolish the applicant's right of abode as recognised by the Divisional Court in *Bancoult 1*. In August 2004, the applicant sought a declaration that the Orders were ultra vires. Both the Divisional Court and Court of Appeal agreed. However, by a 3/2 decision, the House of Lords decided in *Bancoult 2* that the Chagos Islanders did not enjoy a right of abode in the BIOT.[19]

II. THE CHAGOS ISLANDERS AND INTERNATIONAL LAW

This book focuses on the resonance of international law for the claims of the Chagos Islanders made in respect of the BIOT. However, the significance of international law for the Chagossian claims of a right to return to the Chagos Islands and for reparations in respect of their involuntary displacement was prompted by Chagossian litigation in the English courts. Accordingly, first, it is important to acknowledge that the international legal claims of the Chagos Islanders cannot be properly understood without acquiring a good understanding of the municipal legal claims which were advanced in the English courts and

---

[14] Pursuant to the Immigration Ordinance 2000, s 4, as discussed in ch 1.

[15] *Bancoult 2* (DC) (n 7) [84].

[16] The BIOT Constitution Order 2004; and BIOT Immigration Order 2004 were approved on 10 June 2004.

[17] *Bancoult 2* (DC) (n 7) [94].

[18] These arguments were set out in a letter from the US Assistant Secretary of State for Political-Military Affairs dated 16 November 2004 that was produced in evidence in *Bancoult 2* (DC), ibid, [96].

[19] *Bancoult 2* (HL) (n 12). The Chagos Islanders took their case to the European Court of Human Rights in connection with alleged violations of the European Convention on Human Rights. However, the Strasbourg Court ruled against them. See *Chagos Islanders v UK* (2013) 56 EHRR SE15. This case is considered in detail in ch 2.

the way in which the English courts responded to them. The English courts acknowledged, but did not engage with, the applicable principles of international law in the *Bancoult* litigation. Nonetheless, the Chagossian claims made in respect of the BIOT are not exhausted by the litigation in the English courts and it is immaterial that those courts decided that the international legal arguments advanced in *Bancoult 2* were not relevant to the determination of that litigation. Secondly, the legality of the detachment of the Chagos Islands from the British colony of Mauritius pursuant to the BIOT's creation and the history of the Mauritian-UK sovereignty dispute concerning the Chagos Islands must be fully explored before the international legal claims of the Chagos Islanders can be properly understood. In particular, these claims have been shaped by the way that the BIOT was created and by the arguments that underpin this sovereignty dispute. However, while the Chagossian claims made in respect of the Chagos Islands are bound up with Mauritian claims to the same territory, this book will show that they represent competing claims to the Chagos Islands.

As noted above, the UK government has publicly denied that the BIOT constitutes a non-self-governing territory for the purposes of the operation of Chapter XI of the UN Charter. The Mauritian government claims that the Chagos Islands remain part of its national territory for the purpose of the exercise of the right to self-determination pursuant to the provisions of the Colonial Declaration.[20] It argues that the Mauritian people constitute the unit for the purpose of the exercise of the right to self-determination and that the Chagos Islanders are merely a component part of this wider societal group.[21] In sharp contrast, this book argues that the BIOT constitutes a distinct territorial unit for the purpose of exercising the right of self-determination. It suggests that this position has been reinforced by a number of factors, including: (i) the absence of pre-colonial ties between the Chagos Islands and Mauritius; (ii) the BIOT's geographical distance from Mauritius; (iii) the Chagossian people's cultural distinctiveness; and (iv) the communal solidarity developed during the Chagossian people's exile from the BIOT and their subsequent experiences of chronic impoverishment in Mauritius.

The book advances the claim that, with regard to the BIOT, the General Assembly – the UN organ which acquired the leading role in developing and implementing the international law relating to decolonisation – made a

---

[20] The Declaration on the Granting of Independence to Colonial Countries and Peoples, UNGA Res 1514(XV), 14 December 1960 ('Colonial Declaration') provides, inter alia:

2. All people have the right to self-determination; by virtue of that right they freely determine their political status and freely pursue their economic, social and cultural development.

. . .

6. Any attempt aimed at the partial or total disruption of the national unity and the territorial integrity of a country is incompatible with the purposes and principles of the Charter of the United Nations.

[21] This approach is consistent with the positions adopted by Indonesia with regard to West Irian (West New Guinea) and India in respect of Goa. See ch 6.

mistake.[22] After the UK government informed the General Assembly's Fourth Committee, on 16 November 1965, that the BIOT had been created, the General Assembly acted quickly. It adopted resolution 2066(XX)(1965) which, declared, inter alia, that the Chagos Islands remained an inalienable part of Mauritius and it urged the UK not to dismember this colonial unit in contravention of the terms of the 1960 Colonial Declaration.[23] However, official documents, which are now in the public domain, reveal that the UK government knew that the Chagos Islands supported a permanent population during this period but it decided not to disclose this information to the General Assembly for fear that the BIOT would be classified as a non-self-governing territory and thus subject to the obligations contained in Chapter XI of the UN Charter.

UK officials were relieved when the General Assembly did not press the UK on the nature of the population which inhabited the Chagos Islands in 1965.[24] By endorsing the view that the Chagos Islands belonged to Mauritius, the General Assembly overlooked the possibility that the BIOT itself may have constituted a non-self-governing territory and, if this was established, it would not have been immune to the forces of decolonisation. Owing to the terms of the 1965 Lancaster House Agreement, the UK government knew that it could rely upon the Mauritian government not to claim that the Chagos Islands should be reverted to Mauritian sovereignty, at least for the foreseeable future.[25] The Mauritian government did not publicly challenge the provisions of the Lancaster House Agreement during the 1960s and 1970s and the General Assembly has not revisited the question of the international status of the Chagos Islands since Mauritius acceded to independence in 1968. However, regional governmental organisations have maintained the position that the Chagos Islands remain part of Mauritius and they have demanded that the Archipelago should be returned to Mauritian sovereignty.[26] The Mauritian government has also maintained such a claim since the early-1980s.[27]

[22] Its leading role was expressly acknowledged by the ICJ in the *Western Sahara Advisory Opinion* (1975) ICJ Rep 12 [59]. See ch 5.

[23] UNGA Res 2066(XX), 16 December 1965. See ch 6.

[24] PRO CO 936/947, FDW Browne to CG Eastwood, 2 February 1966 and see MM Ticu, *Chagos: Where International Law Stops* (Utrecht, Utrecht University, 2012) (on file with the author).

[25] The Lancaster House Agreement was concluded between the elected representatives of the Mauritian colonial government and the UK government in 1965. The Mauritian government was paid £3m for the detachment of the Chagos Islands from the colony of Mauritius and it provided for the conclusion of a UK–Mauritius defence treaty that would provide for Mauritius's internal and external security on the occasion of independence. There is significant evidence to suggest that the detachment of the Chagos Islands from Mauritius was the price of Mauritian independence. See ch 3.

[26] OAU Assembly of Heads of State Resolution on Diego Garcia, 4 July 1980, AHG/Res 99 (XVII). See also African Union Assembly of Heads of State Decision on Chagos Archipelago, AHG/Dec 159 (XXXVI), 12 July 2000, AU/Res1(XVI), the Assembly of the African Union, at its 16th Ordinary Session, 31 January 2011. Non Aligned Movement (NAM) adopted its resolution on the Chagos Islands at its Seventh Summit Conference in Delhi on 12 May 1983. See also the Ministerial Declaration of the Group of 77 and China at the 2012 UN Conference on Trade and Development in Doha on 23 April 2012, 13th Session, UNCTAD Doc TD/468 [20]. See ch 6.

[27] See the Comments by the Government of Mauritius to the Concluding Observations of the UN Human Rights Committee on the United Kingdom and Overseas Territories, 28 May 2002, CCPR/CO/73/UK/Add 1 and CCPR/CO/73/UKOT/Add 1. See ch 6.

The right of self-determination, as proclaimed in the 1960 Colonial Declaration, greatly enhanced the normative significance of self-determination in colonial situations. However, this book contends that it did not acquire the status of customary international law until the adoption of the Declaration on Friendly Relations in 1970.[28] As the BIOT had already been created by that time this entitlement was not binding on the UK when it detached the Chagos Islands from Mauritius and constituted the BIOT. Although this book does not endorse the Mauritian claim to the Chagos Islands it offers a different way forward: it advances the argument that the BIOT constitutes a valid non-self-governing territory and it has enjoyed this status since the moment it was created. The UK government appreciated the strength of this argument during the period when the BIOT was established. Accordingly, if it can be established that, in 1965: (i) the UK possessed the authority to dismember the Mauritian colonial unit as a matter of international law; and (ii) if the UK government had disclosed the full facts concerning the inter-generational nature of the population of the Chagos Islands to the General Assembly then, the General Assembly would have been compelled to classify the BIOT as a non-self-governing territory, pursuant to the provisions of Chapter XI of the UN Charter.[29] Nevertheless, it would not follow that the right of colonial self-determination necessarily accrued to the Chagos Islanders in 1965 as a result of the BIOT's status as a non-self-governing territory as the right had not acquired the character of customary international law by that time. Owing to the fact that the Chagos Islanders were exiled from the BIOT between 1967 and 1973 many Chagossians still inhabited the Territory when the right to colonial self-determination was rendered binding on the UK in respect of its dealings with all its remaining non-self-governing territories, via the adoption of the Declaration on Friendly Relations in 1970.

The General Assembly's standpoint regarding the international status of the Chagos Islands was substantially informed by its interpretation of the right to self-determination. This interpretation is not only constituted by the General Assembly's view of how and when self-determination became an entitlement of colonial peoples, it is also guided by the Assembly's understanding of which societal groups should be classified as colonial peoples for the purpose of exercising this right. The issue of whether the inhabitants of *all* non-self-governing territories possess the right to self-determination has been fiercely debated in situations where a colonial power has embarked on a sustained policy of settlement in colonial territories.[30] However, the argument that colonial self-determination is not an entitlement of the descendants of the colonialists is immaterial in situations where competing claims of self-determination are

---

[28] Declaration on the Principles of International Law concerning Friendly Relations and Co-operation Among States in Accordance with the Charter of the United Nations, UNGA Res 2625(XXV), 24 October 1970.

[29] It is immaterial that the true position was not revealed until the *Bancoult* litigation was heard in the English courts.

[30] In the British colonial context, good examples included the plantations on the Falkland Islands and on Gibraltar. See ch 6.

made by *different* societal groups that have been subjugated by European colonialism. But in cases where distinct colonial populations have made competing claims to the same piece of territory, the General Assembly has not always followed a consistent approach. It is important to understand why the General Assembly chose to depart from its general approach regarding the implementation of the right to colonial self-determination in a small, but significant, number of cases because it enables us to discern the weight that it attached to a range of key considerations for the purpose of bringing about decolonisation.[31] This book undertakes an examination of a range of difficult cases with the aim of offering a better understanding of the General Assembly's underlying policy preferences regarding the delivery of the right to self-determination in the colonial context.

The book argues that the General Assembly's understanding of how the right of self-determination should have been applied in the Mauritian context was compromised by three considerations. First, the UK government's failure to disclose the full facts about the inhabitants of the Chagos Islands and the General Assembly's decision to accept the UK government's statement that the Archipelago did not support a permanent population at face value meant the General Assembly's assessment of how the right to self-determination should have been implemented in the context of Mauritius was unreliable. Secondly, as discussed above, the General Assembly held the mistaken belief that the right of self-determination achieved the character of binding international law by the adoption of the Colonial Declaration and that, as a result, the UK was prohibited from dismembering the Mauritian colonial unit prior to Mauritius's accession to independence. In contrast, this book suggests that the right of colonial self-determination only achieved this status as a consequence of the adoption of the Declaration on Friendly Relations in 1970 and, up until that point, the UK retained the lawful authority to excise the Chagos Islands from Mauritius as a matter of international law. Finally, in a number of significant cases, the General Assembly has refused to countenance the prospect of sub-dividing an established non-self-governing territory in situations where distinct societal groups inhabit the same colonial unit but disagree about whether the territorial integrity of the colonial unit should be maintained in the event of decolonisation. This book suggests that – along with the disputes between the Netherlands and Indonesia over West New Guinea and between France and the Comoros regarding the island of Mayotte – the UK-Mauritian sovereignty dispute concerning the status of the Chagos Islands represents an important example of a case in which the General Assembly should have implemented the right to colonial self-determination in a contextually sensitive manner. The book contends that the General Assembly should now correct that error by recognising the BIOT as a non-self-governing territory pursuant to Chapter XI of the

---

[31] The book compares the BIOT question with the cases of territory of West New Guinea, which is now part of Indonesia, and the island of Mayotte in the Comoros Archipelago, which is administered by France. See ch 6.

UN Charter and for the wider purposes of international law. From a broader perspective, this book seeks to advance a more nuanced interpretation of the right of self-determination in the colonial context. It contends that where post-colonial identities have been imposed on separate and distinct peoples that co-existed within a single territorial unit, which was artificially created by a colonial power, such a situation may give rise to separate entitlements to exercise the right of external self-determination and outcomes that would undermine the assumption that post-colonial States are necessarily entitled to the maintenance of the territorial integrity of the colonial entities which they succeeded.[32] As a result, the book endorses the wider argument that ignoring the distinct societal identities of peoples that happened to co-exist within a given colonial unit in favour of rigid territorialised approaches to decolonisation can lead to the maintenance of an unjust peace.

---

[32] This assumption is embodied in the principle of *uti possidetis juris*. See chs 5 and 6.

1

The Chagossian Litigation in the English Courts

I. INTRODUCTION

I N 1965, THE UK excised the Chagos Islands from the colony of Mauritius to create the British Indian Ocean Territory (BIOT) in connection with the founding of a US military facility on the island of Diego Garcia. Consequently, the inhabitants of the Chagos Islands were secretly exiled to Mauritius, where they became chronically impoverished. This book focuses on the resonance of international law for the Chagos Islanders in respect of the BIOT. However, it is important to acknowledge that consideration of the significance of international law for the Chagossian claims of a right to return to the Chagos Islands and for reparation for their involuntary displacement was prompted by Chagossian litigation in the English courts. Accordingly, the applicable international law and the potential international legal claims of the Chagos Islanders cannot be properly understood without acquiring a thorough grasp of the municipal legal claims which were advanced by the Chagossians in the English courts in a series of public law and private law cases and an understanding of how the English courts responded to these claims. Against this background, this chapter examines the legal challenges brought against the UK government in the English courts to establish legal responsibility and redress for the expulsion and/or exclusion of the Chagossian people from the BIOT to Mauritius and Seychelles. In particular, it investigates the public law proceedings – the *Bancoult* litigation – which challenged the validity of the legislation which has denied the Chagossian right of abode in the outer Chagos Islands.[1] The book also discusses the attempts made to secure compensation for a number of private law wrongs perpetrated by the UK government in connection with the process of exiling the Chagossian people (the *Chagos Islanders* case).[2]

---

[1] *R (Bancoult) v Secretary of State for Foreign and Commonwealth Affairs* [2001] 1 QB 1067 ('*Bancoult 1*'); *R (Bancoult) v Secretary of State for Foreign and Commonwealth Affairs* [2006] EWHC 1038 (Divisional Court); [2008] QB 365 (Court of Appeal); [2008] 3 WLR 955; [2009] AC 454 (House of Lords) ('*Bancoult 2*').

[2] *Chagos Islanders v Attorney General and HM BIOT Commissioner* [2003] EWHC QB 2222 (High Court); [2004] EWCA Civ 997 (Court of Appeal).

II. BACKGROUND

In 1964, the US and UK governments began negotiations regarding the possibility of establishing a US military facility on the island of Diego Garcia in the remote Chagos Archipelago. The Chagos Archipelago consists of 65 islands spread over a total area of approximately 47.5 miles in the middle of the Indian Ocean. Diego Garcia is approximately 130 miles from the other Chagos island groups of Peros Banhos and the Salomon islands (the 'outer Chagos Islands'). The island is situated 1200 miles north east of Mauritius and 1000 miles north of the island of Mahé in the Seychelles. In 1965, the UK government enacted the BIOT Order in Council,[3] which excised the Chagos Islands from the British colony of Mauritius and constituted BIOT.[4] In a 1966 treaty, the UK government made Diego Garcia available to the US government for defence purposes.[5] Although the US government only required the use of one island, it was agreed that the entire Chagos Archipelago would be cleared of its inhabitants.[6] Consequently, between 1968 and 1973, the UK government covertly exiled the Chagossian people from BIOT. This process was purportedly authorised by the BIOT Commissioner. Acting in his capacity as the BIOT's colonial (subordinate) legislature, he enacted the Immigration Ordinance 1971. Section 4 provided that no person was allowed to enter BIOT or remain in the territory without a permit. Although many Chagossians had been removed by this time, the Ordinance ensured that they would be prevented from returning to the BIOT. The evacuation of Diego Garcia was completed in October 1971 and the outer Islands were emptied by May 1973. The displaced population were transported to Mauritius and the Seychelles where many of them became chronically impoverished.[7]

In 1972, the UK government agreed to pay the Mauritian government £650,000 in order to cover the costs of resettling the displaced Chagossians. However, while this sum was paid to the Mauritian government in 1972 it was not distributed to the Chagossians. By 1977, the lack of an official resettlement programme produced spiralling Chagossian debts, which led to demands for its distribution, especially from Chagossian women. The fund was distributed between 595 families in 1978. However, rampant inflation in the intervening

---

[3] SI 1965/1920. This Order in Council also included the islands of Aldabra, Desroches and Farquhar which had formerly belonged to the colony of Seychelles within the BIOT. This new British Overseas Territory came into existence on 8 November 1965. See ch 3.

[4] The 1814 Treaty of Paris ceded Mauritius and its lesser dependencies (including the Chagos Islands) to the UK.

[5] Exchange of Notes between the UK and US Governments, 1 December 1966.

[6] In a confidential agreed minute, the UK government undertook this 'administrative measure' under para 2(a) of the 1966 Treaty, ibid.

[7] D Vine, 'The Impoverishment of Displacement: Models for Documenting Human Rights Abuses and the People of Diego Garcia' (2006) 13 *Human Rights Brief* 21. Further, the displaced population included those Chagossians who were temporally outside the BIOT during the process of exile and who were subsequently prevented from returning.

period meant that the value of an already meagre sum was substantially reduced. The displaced Chagossians received paltry cash payments that did little to alleviate their suffering.[8]

In 1975, Michel Vincatassin, a Chagossian who had been forced to leave Diego Garcia in 1971, began a private law action against the UK government for a number of private law wrongs (intimidation, false imprisonment and assault) suffered during his exile. In response, in 1982, the UK and Mauritian governments agreed to establish a trust fund to assist in the resettlement of the Chagossian community in Mauritius.[9] The fund was distributed between 1344 individuals who received approximately £3300 each; in addition, some Chagossians were provided with small plots of land. The recipients were required to renounce all their claims against the UK government. In 1997, it was discovered that any exiled person born in the Chagos Islands was a British Dependent Territories citizen under the British Nationality Act 1981.[10] It was therefore open to any such person to institute public law proceedings against the decision to deny him or her the right of abode in BIOT.

III. UK PUBLIC LAW

Public law is concerned with the exercise and control of governmental power within a domestic legal system. In contrast, private law is concerned with the operation of rights and obligations created by private individuals within that legal system (the State can also be a legal person for this purpose). The UK does not have a written constitution. Constitutional law originates in the common law, a series of principles and rules made by judges when deciding cases which form the basis of English law. However, Parliament is the supreme legislative body and the common law has been superseded by Acts of Parliament (statutes), which constitute primary legislation (or via secondary legislation authorised by statute).[11] As Lord Hoffmann stated in *R (Pro-Life Association) v BBC*:

> In a society based upon the rule of law and the separation of powers, it is necessary to decide which branch of government has in any particular instance the decision-making power and what the legal limits of that power are. That is a question of law and must therefore be decided by the courts. This means that the courts themselves often

---

[8] See Mauritius Legislative Assembly, *Financial and Other Aspects of the 'Sale' of the Chagos Islands and the Resettlement of the Displaced Ilois,* Special Report of the Public Accounts Committee for the 1980 (4th) Session (Port Louis, Mauritian Government, 1981).

[9] Under the Mauritian *Ilois* Trust Fund Act 1982.

[10] Richard Gifford, Bancoult's solicitor, discovered this status as a result of research into the archives available in the Public Records Office in London. See R Gifford, 'The Chagos Islands–The Land Where Human Rights Hardly Ever Happen' (2004) *Law Social Justice and Global Development Journal*, www2.warwick.ac.uk/fac/soc/law/elj/lgd/2004_1/gifford/. At the time of their exile, such persons were citizens of the UK and its colonies under the British Nationality Act 1948.

[11] The supremacy of Parliament was a product of the constitutional settlement agreed in the aftermath of the 1688 'Glorious Revolution'.

have to decide the limits of their own decision-making power. That is inevitable. But it does not mean that their allocation of decision-making power to the other branches of government is a matter of courtesy or deference. The principles upon which decision-making powers are allocated are principles of law. The courts are the independent branch of government and the legislative and executive are, directly and indirectly, respectively, the elected branches of government. Independence makes the courts more suited to deciding some kinds of questions and being elected makes the legislature and the executive more suited to deciding others.[12]

Despite the constitutional shift in favour of Parliament, the Crown retains considerable discretionary powers (prerogative powers), notably in the areas of defence, foreign affairs and colonial governance. The UK government exercises prerogative powers on behalf of the Crown. In this regard, it legislates by enacting Orders in Council, which constitute primary legislation. Although prerogative powers can be curtailed by Parliament, if express provision is made in a statute, they remain otherwise intact. However, as the *Bancoult* litigation demonstrates, the precise scope of prerogative powers remains contested.

A colonial entity is usually constituted by an Order in Council which, among other things, empowers a colonial legislature to enact subordinate laws for the colony. While it is well-established that subordinate legislation is susceptible to judicial oversight, the English courts have refused to accept jurisdiction to review the exercise of prerogative powers in general until very recently.[13]

IV. *BANCOULT 1*

Olivier Bancoult was born in the Chagos island of Peros Banhos in 1964. In 1968, he visited Mauritius with his family for medical reasons. They were subsequently excluded from the BIOT. In *Bancoult 1*, he challenged the decision to banish the Chagossians from the BIOT. Under section 11 of the 1965 BIOT Order in Council, the BIOT Commissioner was empowered to legislate for the BIOT's 'peace, order and good government', a standard legislative formulation used for the purpose of authorising wide discretionary powers of colonial governance. However, in the Divisional Court's view, the Commissioner's legislative authority did not extend to the removal of the population from the territory for reasons unrelated to it. It acknowledged that while a colonial legislature has exclusive authority to determine the factual requirements of 'peace, order and good government', such authority was not unlimited.[14] Accordingly, the Court held that section 4 of the Ordinance was ultra vires (it was beyond the Commissioner's power to legislate in such a manner) and it quashed that provision.

---

[12] [2004] 1 AC 185 (n 2) [75–76].
[13] This was established by the House of Lords in *Council of Civil Service Unions v Minister for the Civil Service* [1985] AC 374.
[14] *Bancoult 1* (n 1) [55].

In response to the Divisional Court's decision in *Bancoult 1* the Secretary of State made the following public statement on 3 November 2000:

> I have decided to accept the Court's ruling and the Government will not be appealing. The work we are doing on the feasibility of resettling the *Ilois* [Chagossians] now takes on a new importance. We started the feasibility work a year ago and are now well underway with phase two of the study. Furthermore, we will put in place a new Immigration Ordinance which will allow the *Ilois* to return to the outer islands while observing our Treaty obligations[15]

The 1971 Ordinance was repealed and replaced by the BIOT Immigration Ordinance 2000, a piece of subordinate legislation, which allowed Chagossians to return to the BIOT (except for Diego Garcia) without permits. Specifically, section 4 of the 2000 Immigration Ordinance provided:

> (1) No person shall enter the Territory, or, being present in the Territory, shall remain there, unless he is in possession of a permit . . .
> (3) Except in respect of his entry into, or remaining in Diego Garcia, this section does not apply to any person who –
>
>> (a) is, under the British Nationality Act 1981, . . . a British Dependent Territories citizen and;
>> (b) is such a citizen by virtue of his connection with the Territory;
>
> and it also does not apply to the spouse or to the dependent child, under the age of 18 years, of such a person.

Bancoult had won, or so it appeared.

V. THE *CHAGOS ISLANDERS* CASE

English public law judgments do not attract awards of financial compensation. Accordingly, the decision in *Bancoult 1* did not result in compensation for the violations visited upon the Chagossian people by the UK government during the process of exile or for the protracted denial of their right of abode in the BIOT. Arguably, the need to secure such compensation became urgent after the right of abode was recognised as resettling the outer Islands was sure to be a costly exercise which might not attract public funding as a matter of course. In an effort to secure compensation, Chagossian representatives instituted private law proceedings – *Chagos Islanders v Attorney General and HM BIOT Commissioner* – against the government in 2002. The main causes of action were (i) misfeasance in public office (the improper performance of a lawful act); (ii) unlawful exile; and (iii) deceit (fraud). The case was heard in the High Court by Ouseley J in 2003.

At the outset, Ouseley J drew a distinction between a public law challenge concerning the validity of legislation, and a claim for compensation after a final

---

[15] 3 November 2000, quoted in *Bancoult 2* (DC) (n 1) [8].

settlement had been reached (a reference to the compensation package agreed between Chagossian representatives and the UK and Mauritian governments and administered under the Mauritian *Ilois* Trust Fund Act 1982). Consequently, Ouseley J held that the above causes of action were unavailable to the vast majority of Chagossians because they had accepted the compensation offered to them in 1982 and they 'signed' forms renouncing their private law entitlements in this respect.[16] In any event, Ouseley J decided the case in the defendants' favour.

The claimants appealed against his decision by taking the case to the Court of Appeal, which is responsible for hearing appeals from the High Court in the English legal system. However, the Court of Appeal decided to uphold Ouseley's J verdict. In particular, the Court of Appeal decided that the claim of misfeasance could not succeed because there was no evidence that ministers (or their civil servants) knew that the 1971 Immigration Ordinance was illegal at the time it was made. In fact, it was widely believed that the authority to legislate for the 'peace, order and good government' of a colony was unlimited until the contrary was held in *Bancoult 1*.[17] The deceit claim failed for the same reason.[18] Further, the Court of Appeal ruled that the claim of unlawful exile was a public law claim unknown to English private law; thus, it was not actionable in the present proceedings. Finally, the Court of Appeal upheld Ouseley's J ruling that the action was 'time-barred'. The Limitation Act 1980 established a code of time limits beyond which private law claims cannot be commenced in the English courts. For this purpose, time does not start to run until the cause of action arises, or the basis for the cause of action comes to light. Once the prescribed time limit has elapsed, a claimant is barred from instituting proceedings. Temporal restrictions on the instituting of civil claims are common in municipal legal systems as they promote certainty and prevent claimants from 'sitting' on their rights. In the present case, the Court of Appeal observed that the events which formed the basis of the case occurred during the 1960s and 1970s but that the private law action was only commenced in 2002.[19] Even it were accepted that time should not start to run at the moment of exile on the ground of unconscionability or as a result of some unspecified incapacity, the Vincatassin proceedings, which were instituted in 1975, had resulted in the disclosure of documents relating to the removal of the Chagossians from the BIOT by the UK government and a series of offers to settle the claim had been made from 1978 with the benefit of legal advice until the *Ilois* Trust Fund was established in 1982. Against this background, the Court of Appeal decided that any attempt to prevent time from running faced 'insuperable difficulties after 1983 at the

---

[16] This point was upheld on appeal (n 2) [16]. However, Chagossian representatives argue that the process of effecting renunciation was flawed and the consent of affected Chagossians was compromised as a result.

[17] ibid, [28].

[18] However, the Court of Appeal reserved its position on the question of whether the UK government had deceived the United Nations, ibid, [36–37].

[19] ibid, [43].

very latest'.[20] Accordingly, it held that the conclusion that these proceedings had been brought out of time was irresistible.

The failure of the private law action highlights the inability of the English private law regime to deliver social justice for the Chagossian people. The refusal of the High Court and the Court of Appeal to circumvent the provisions of the Limitation Act 1980 for equitable reasons occasioned technical defeat. Secondly, the application of the ordinary standard civil law rules of evidence was problematic given the oral culture that had flourished on the Chagos Islands. These difficulties were exacerbated by the transformation of personal experiences of involuntary displacement into standardised collective accounts during the years of exile.[21] The recalling of group narratives, which had not been personally experienced by Chagossians who were called as witnesses at trial undermined the probative value of their testimonies.[22] Finally, the claims of deceit and misfeasance in public office required proof that government decision-makers and representatives knew that their actions were illegal. Such claims carried heavy evidential burdens, which the claimants failed to discharge.

The appeal judges appreciated the limited utility of this process of adjudication for the Chagossians, as Sedley LJ observed in the Court of Appeal: 'It may not be too late to make return possible, but such an outcome is a function of economic resources and political will, not of adjudication'.[23] This observation suggests that the claimants' faith in English law was misplaced. The collective nature of litigation certainly diminished the cogency of some claims. For instance, the Court of Appeal noted that the decision to make the claim for unlawful exile rather than a claim for trespass to the person (physical interference), a claim well-established in English private law, was probably driven by a desire to avoid dividing the claimant group between the limited class of persons who had been physically forced to leave the BIOT and a larger class of persons whose decisions to leave may have been prompted by the policy of closing down the Islands before such coercion was used (or they had been excluded from the BIOT after having left voluntarily).[24] Secondly, as noted above, while standardised collective accounts were particularly useful in marshalling external political support for the Chagossian cause, they were ill-suited to the task of proving claims in a court of law.[25] Accordingly, the political resonance of the Chagossians' narrative conflicted with the articulation of their legal claims, a conflict which arguably brings into question their strategy of using litigation as the primary means of advancing their political cause. Finally, in the absence of the necessary political will to establish a unique legal process for effecting 'transitional

---

[20] ibid, [48].

[21] See L Jeffery, 'Historical Narrative and Legal Evidence: Judging Chagossians' High Court Testimonies' (2006) 29 *Political and Legal Anthropology Review* 228.

[22] ibid.

[23] *Chagos Islanders* case (CA) (n 2) [54].

[24] ibid, [25].

[25] Jeffery, 'Historical Narrative and Legal Evidence' (n 21) 239–40.

justice',[26] the legal processes of the ordinary courts were quite simply incapable of dealing with the substance behind the claimants' action, especially in the light of the compensation package agreed in 1982.

VI. WITHDRAWING THE PUBLIC LAW RIGHT OF ABODE

The UK government's acceptance of the Chagossian right of abode recognised in *Bancoult 1* was short-lived. A preliminary feasibility study (Phase 2A) on the question of permanent resettlement was published by the UK government on 20 June 2000. The report of the second phase of the feasibility study (Phase 2B) was published on 10 July 2002.[27] In a written statement on 15 June 2004, the Parliamentary Under-Secretary of State for Foreign and Commonwealth Affairs stated:

> anything other than short-term resettlement on a purely subsistence basis would be highly precarious and would involve expensive underwriting by the UK Government for an open-ended period – probably permanently. Accordingly, the Government considers that there would be no purpose in commissioning any further study into the feasibility of resettlement; and that it would be impossible for the Government to promote or even permit resettlement to take place. We have therefore decided to legislate to prevent it. [28]

In a policy reversal the government enacted the BIOT Constitution Order in Council 2004 and the BIOT Immigration Order in Council 2004 (the latter repealed the Immigration Ordinance 2000). Together they ensured that full immigration controls over BIOT territory were reinstated and that the displaced Chagossians had no right of abode in the BIOT. In particular, Section 9 of the Constitution Order 2004 provided:

> (1) Whereas the Territory was constituted and is set aside to be available for the defence purposes of the Government of the United Kingdom and the Government of the United States of America, no person has the right of abode in the Territory.
> (2) Accordingly, no person is entitled to enter or be present in the Territory except as authorised by or under this Order or any other law for the time being in force in the Territory.

---

[26] On the nature and scope of transitional justice, see RG Teitel, 'Transitional Justice Genealogy' (2003) 16 *Harvard Human Rights Journal* 69.

[27] *Bancoult 2* (DC) (n 1) [84]. On 10 March 2000, the BIOT Commissioner appointed independent consultants (who had previously been employed by the UK government) to investigate the feasibility of resettlement. The extent to which they were working independently has been questioned by Richard Gifford, Bancoult's solicitor. Further, there is some controversy regarding the content of the 2002 report. The UK government did not disclose the full contents of the draft report; it subsequently claimed that all copies were destroyed. See the transcript of the evidence of Richard Gifford to the Parliamentary Foreign Affairs Committee Inquiry into Good Governance in British Overseas Territories, 23 January 2008.

[28] ibid, [93].

In a parliamentary debate on 7 July 2004, the government claimed that the reintroduction of such measures was justified in order to honour the UK's treaty obligations.[29] Further, the US government vouched for the ongoing strategic value of its military base on Diego Garcia in the 'Global War on Terrorism'.[30] Accordingly, the UK government claimed that resettlement of the outer Chagos Islands would compromise the base's security since it would increase the risk of terrorist infiltration and attack.

In *R (Bancoult) v Secretary of State for Foreign and Commonwealth Affairs* ('*Bancoult 2*') the claimant sought an order that the 2004 Orders were ultra vires (beyond the lawful powers of the Sovereign in Council). A material difference between *Bancoult 1* and *Bancoult 2* was that the former concerned a challenge to subordinate legislation whereas, in the latter, the validity of primary legislation was being disputed: the claimant was challenging the legitimate scope of the Crown's prerogative power of colonial governance. Accordingly, *Bancoult 2* had profound constitutional implications. Both the Divisional Court and the Court of Appeal held that the 2004 Orders were ultra vires. However, the Secretary of State appealed to the Judicial Committee of the House of Lords. By a majority decision (3/2), it allowed the appeal.

VII. *BANCOULT 2*: THE HOUSE OF LORDS' JUDGMENT

A. Constitutional Review and Fundamental Rights

The appellant claimed that: (i) the Queen in Council's power to legislate for a ceded colony (a colony acquired derivatively by treaty) is an expression of sovereign legislative authority; (ii) alternatively, the Queen in Council could legislate without restraint in the absence of authority to the contrary; and (iii) the decision to enact the 2004 Orders was a legislative act and thus not subject to review. While he accepted that Orders in Council rank as primary legislation, Lord Hoffmann observed that, as they qualify as executive acts, they do not possess the representative quality which characterises the legislative sovereignty of the Queen in Parliament. Given that prerogative powers have not enjoyed immunity from judicial review as a matter of principle, at least since *Council of Civil Service Unions v Minister for the Civil Service*,[31] Lord Hoffmann saw 'no reason why prerogative legislation should not be subject to review'.[32] The House of Lords unanimously endorsed this position.

The appellant submitted that the legislative formulation 'peace, order and good government' did not apply to the Queen in Council's constituent powers in

---

[29] ibid, [94].
[30] ibid, [96].
[31] *Council of Civil Service Unions v Minister for the Civil Service* (n 13).
[32] *Bancoult 2* (HL) (n 1) [35].

ceded colonies because it retains full legislative power in such territories.[33] In any event, the appellant claimed that this formulation could not limit the Queen in Council's legislative authority. Lord Hoffmann observed that the legislative formulation has never been applied to non-self-governing territories. Accordingly, in his view, as the UK and its dependent territories constitute an 'undivided realm', the Queen in Council is entitled to give primacy to UK interests when legislating for a dependent territory.[34] Further, the majority decided that, as the formulation was 'apt to authorize the utmost discretion of enactment', it could not limit the Queen in Council's power to legislate in the colonial context.[35] However, Lord Mance and Lord Bingham preferred to restrict their Opinions to the question of whether the common law implied any substantive limitations upon this power.[36]

The respondent claimed that the right of abode had been established in the common law since Magna Carta (Chapter 29 provides: 'No freeman shall be taken or imprisoned . . . or exiled . . . but by lawful judgment of his peers, or by the law of the land'). As the Court of Appeal recognised that this right was 'one of the most fundamental liberties known to human beings',[37] Bancoult argued that an Order in Council could not interfere with it. However, Lord Hoffmann held that 'the right of abode is a creature of the law. The law gives it and the law may take it away'.[38] In his view, section 9 of the Constitution Order clearly abrogated any right of abode in BIOT. Lord Rodger and Lord Carswell reached the same conclusion. However, they were prepared to accept that Magna Carta was applicable and that it was arguable that the right of abode in a conquered or ceded colony was a fundamental principle of English law.[39] In this regard, they paid particular attention to Lord Mansfield's CJ sixth proposition in *Campbell v Hall* – that a Sovereign's legislative powers in conquered (or ceded) colony were subordinate to those held by a Sovereign in Parliament and that the former 'cannot make any new change contrary to fundamental principles'.[40] Nevertheless, they were concerned that the 'unspecified nature' of such fundamental principles could severely restrict a Sovereign in Council's legislative powers.[41] For them, this problem was solved by sections 2 and 3 of the Colonial Laws Validity Act 1865, which provided that no colonial law could be void

---

[33] In this respect, Lord Hoffmann relied upon *Halsbury's Laws of England* (2003) vol 6, [823], quoted at ibid, [31].

[34] ibid, [716], quoted in *Bancoult 2* (n 1) [47].

[35] *Riel v The Queen* (1885) 10 App Cas 675, 678, Lord Halsbury LC, quoted by Lord Rodger at [108].

[36] ibid, [70] and [145].

[37] *Bancoult 2* (CA) (n 1), Sedley LJ at [71]; adopted by Sir Anthony Clarke MR at [123].

[38] *Bancoult 2* (HL) (n 1) [45].

[39] ibid, [86] and [89].

[40] (1774) 1 Cowp 204, 209. That case concerned a challenge to the validity of a duty imposed on goods exported from Grenada by virtue of the Crown's prerogative power of colonial governance. Lord Mansfield CJ made six general propositions concerning the law applicable to British colonies. Considerable weight has been attached to these propositions ever since.

[41] *Bancoult 2* (HL) (n 1) [91].

because it was inconsistent with English law unless it contravened the provisions of an Act of Parliament applicable to the colony in question.[42] The 1865 Act had the effect of removing 'a fetter to repugnancy to some vague, unspecified law of natural justice'.[43] Accordingly, in their view, the 2004 Orders could not be challenged on the basis of a claim that the respondent held a fundamental right of abode in BIOT.

In contrast, Lord Bingham and Lord Mance considered the right of abode to be fundamental. They brushed aside 'the ancient and formal niceties' that prevented English law from being applied in ceded colonies as a matter of course.[44] Lord Bingham was more concerned about the contrast between the appellant's view of the entitlement belonging to the inhabitants of this non-self-governing territory and the right of abode held by British citizens in the UK.[45] Drawing upon Lord Mansfield's CJ second proposition in *Campbell v Hall* – the inhabitants of a conquered or ceded territory are entitled to the Sovereign's protection and to be universally considered as subjects – Lord Mance held that 'every British citizen has a right to enter or remain in the constitutional unit to which his or her citizenship relates'.[46] Further, he noted that, since 1965, the respondent's right was only exercisable in BIOT. Evidence of the ongoing nature of this right was gleaned from section 4(3) of the Immigration Ordinance 2000, which provided that a British Dependent Territories citizen was exempt from any applicable immigration controls by virtue of his or her connection with BIOT (with the exception of Diego Garcia).

On the question of whether the Queen in Council could abrogate this right the minority looked for guidance from the prerogative's 'previous mode of exercise'.[47] The enacting of a constitution 'with the aim of depopulating a habitable territory' was antithetical to the Queen in Council's constituent power, which was 'intended to enable the proper governance of the territory, at least among other things for the benefit of the people inhabiting it'.[48] In the circumstances, the minority found the absence of a precedent for section 9 of the Constitution Order to be dispositive.[49]

The House of Lords' decision in *Bancoult 2* provides powerful authority for the proposition that Orders in Council are amenable to judicial review.

---

[42]   ibid, [78].

[43]   Lord Rodger (n 1) [101], relying upon *Liyanage v The Queen* [1967] AC 259, 284. Lord Hoffmann at [40] and Lord Mance at [142] rejected the application of the 1865 Act on the ground that the 2004 Orders were not colonial laws.

[44]   A Tomkins, 'Magna Carta, Crown and Colonies' (2001) *Public Law* 571, 579, quoted by Lord Rodger, ibid, [80]. The laws of a ceded territory remain in force until English law is specifically extended to it, *Campbell v Hall* (n 40) 209, Lord Mansfield CJ. However, English law is applicable in settled colonies from the moment of acquisition.

[45]   *Bancoult 2* (HL) (n 1) [70].

[46]   ibid, [154].

[47]   Lord Mance, ibid, [149] relying upon *Burmah Oil Co v Lord Advocate* [1965] AC 75, 101, per Lord Reid.

[48]   *Bancoult 2* (HL) (n 1).

[49]   ibid, [157].

Nevertheless, the position of the majority casts some doubt on the practical significance that should be attached to this finding. Although Lord Hoffmann observed that Orders in Council lack the representative quality of Acts of Parliament (as the latter are made by Members of Parliament, the directly elected representatives of the British people, whereas the former are enacted by the Sovereign in Council, in practice by the government which is only indirectly elected under the British Constitution). As a result, Lord Hoffmann concluded that Orders in Council are subject to review. Nevertheless, he interpreted the Constitutional Order 2004 in the same way as if it had been an Act of Parliament. But while it is axiomatic that an Act of Parliament may abrogate constitutional (or fundamental) common law rights through clear provision;[50] it follows from the finding that Orders in Council are subject to judicial review that the position should not, prima facie, be the same for executive legislation. In *Bancoult 2* it appears that much turned on the extent to which fundamental common law rights are entrenched within the British Constitution.

The concept of fundamental principles has ebbed and flowed in English law. *Campbell v Hall* shows that their somewhat vague presence was felt during the eighteenth century. But 'the wintry asperity of authority' denied their constitutional salience before the advent of modern judicial review.[51] Nevertheless, there is undoubtedly growing judicial support for a narrow category of fundamental principles.[52] In part, this is a reflection of the changing function of judicial review in a modern constitutional democracy.[53] The courts are now more willing to play a pivotal role in the protection of constitutional values, and, under the rule of law, it is for the courts to decide the limits of their own decision-making power.[54] Further, this trend has arguably been influenced by the concept of fundamental rights, which was introduced when the European Convention of Human Rights was incorporated into English law by the Human Rights Act 1998.[55] However, at present, it may well be that the constitutional status of many principles which possess a fundamental quality remains uncertain as a matter of judicial policy.[56]

Bancoult 2 amounted to a clash of legal cultures.[57] Bancoult's case was based upon a progressive interpretation of the concept of fundamental rights coupled

---

[50] See *Hooper v Secretary of State for Work and Pensions* [2005] 1 WLR 1681.

[51] This observation was made by Laws LJ in *Bancoult 1* (n 1) [43] in reference to *Liyanage* (n 43). In *Bancoult 2* (CA), Sedley LJ noted that Lord Mansfield CJ may have been ahead of his time in his acceptance of such a category of principles, at [65].

[52] J Jowell et al, *De Smith's Judicial Review*, 6th edn (London, Sweet & Maxwell, 2007) [5-036]–[5-040]; and [11-057]–[11-067].

[53] J Jowell, 'Parliamentary Sovereignty under the New Constitutional Hypothesis' (2006) *Public Law* 562; and M Cohn, 'Judicial Activism in the House of Lords: A Composite Constitutionalist Approach' (2007) *Public Law* 95.

[54] *R (Pro-Life Association) v BBC* (n 12) [75–76], per Lord Hoffmann.

[55] See *R (Jackson) v Attorney-General* [2006] 1 AC 262, [102], per Lord Steyn.

[56] See Lord Bingham, 'The Rule of Law' (2007) 66 *Cambridge Law Journal* 67, 75–77.

[57] See J Jowell in *De Smith* (n 52) [1-027] and [1-015]–[1-036]; and TRS Allan, 'Human Rights and Judicial Review: A Critique of "Due Deference"' (2006) 65 *Cambridge Law Journal* 671.

with an established requirement that precedent be produced to authorise executive action which interferes with civil liberties (a culture of justification).[58] The appellant sought to advance the broadest possible interpretation of its ancient legislative authority in a ceded colony, which empowered it to act unless authority to the contrary was produced (a culture of authority). The Law Lords were asked to articulate their standpoints on the principle of legality by reference to their positions on constitutional values, including the contemporary parameters of judicial review.[59] The majority favoured a deferential approach to executive authority, noting that it was for Parliament, not the courts, to remedy any shortcomings in legislative processes concerning colonial governance. In contrast, the minority recognised the fundamental nature of the right of abode and accorded it constitutional significance. It also supported a culture of justification where the executive seeks to curtail important human rights. It is suggested that the minority position was more in keeping with the normative direction of English public law on this issue.[60]

B. Rationality

The appellant argued that the decision to enact the 2004 Orders was not unlawful in substance (it was neither irrational nor unreasonable in the circumstances). The test of whether a decision of a public body was made irrationally was propounded by Lord Diplock in the *Council of Civil Service Unions v Minister for the Civil Service* (that the decision was, 'so outrageous in its defiance of logic or of accepted moral standards that no sensible person who had applied his mind to the question could have arrived at it').[61] The government claimed that BIOT was constituted for defence purposes and, assessed by reference to the *Wednesbury* standard of review (that the public body's decision 'was so unreasonable that no reasonable decision-maker could have come to it'),[62] a reasonable Sovereign in Council could have reached the conclusion that the Orders should have been made. The respondent contended that where fundamental rights are threatened a high degree of scrutiny is required and compel-

---

[58] eg in *Entick v Carrington* Lord Camden CJ stated: 'If it is law it will be found in our books, If it is not found there it is not law' (1765) 19 *State Trials* 1030, 1036.

[59] The House of Lords was confronted by a similar situation (albeit in relation to the sovereignty of Parliament) in *R (Jackson) v Attorney-General* (n 55). For a discussion of the competing judicial perspectives raised in that context, see S Lakin, 'Debunking the Idea of Parliamentary Sovereignty: The Controlling Factor of Legality in the British Constitution' (2008) 28 *Oxford Journal of Legal Studies* 709, 731–34.

[60] See P Craig, 'Constitutional Foundations, the Rule of Law and Supremacy' (2003) *Public Law* 92; S Sedley, 'The Sound of Silence: Constitutional Law Without a Constitution' (1994) 10 *Law Quarterly Review* 270; and J Laws, 'Law and Democracy' (1995) *Public Law* 72.

[61] *Council of Civil Service Unions v Minister for the Civil Service* (n 13) 410.

[62] *Associated Provincial Picture Houses v Wednesbury Corp* [1948] 1 KB 223, 229–30, per Lord Greene MR.

ling justification for the abrogation of such rights must be shown.[63] However, the majority doubted whether the 2004 Orders had a 'profoundly intrusive effect' on the right of abode at the time they were made. Lord Hoffmann observed that the Chagossians had not attempted to exercise the right of abode between 2000 and 2004; and that they were unable to resettle in the absence of government sponsorship. For Lord Hoffmann, the underlying theme of the litigation was funding.[64] In his view, it was an attempt to put political pressure on the government to provide public funding for BIOT's resettlement. While the government was not under a legal obligation to provide such financial support under English law, the right of abode was 'purely symbolic' without it. It was, therefore, 'a right to protest in a particular way and not as a right to . . . live in one's homeland'.[65] Lord Rodger agreed that the decision to enact the Orders 'should be judged against the circumstances at the time it was taken'.[66] He added that the 2002 feasibility study showed that the cost of resettlement would be 'prohibitive' and US concerns regarding the security of the military base on Diego Garcia in the event of the resettlement were relevant to the decision. 'In the absence of relevant legal criteria, judges are not well placed to second-guess the balance struck by ministers on such a matter'.[67] Consequently, the 2004 Orders could not be said to be irrational.

In contrast, Lord Mance decided that the case required the application of a heightened standard of review. He noted that the prospect of resettlement was not considered to be a security threat when the Secretary of State made his statement; there was no evidence that the security risks had materially changed between 2000 and 2004; insufficient weight had been attached to Chagossian interests; and the cost of resettlement, the principal ground for denying the right of abode, was 'unconvincing' given that the government was not under a legal obligation to fund resettlement.[68] The minority adopted Sedley's LJ observation in the Court of Appeal that the logistics of resettlement were not in issue.[69] Moreover, they were of the view that the inability of a person to exercise a legal right should not serve as a reason for its withdrawing it.[70] Finally, the reason given by the government for: (i) the urgent need to enact the 2004 Orders; (ii) the decision not to publish them before their enactment; (iii) the decision not to submit them to the House of Commons' Foreign Affairs Committee for scrutiny in accordance with standard practice; and (iv) the lack of consultation with Chagossian representatives on the withdrawal of the right of abode was a fear of 'unauthorised' landings in the outer Chagos Islands. The minority considered this reason to be without foundation given the US navy's capacity to

---

[63] *R v Ministry of Defence, ex p Smith* [1996] QB 517, 554, per Lord Bingham MR.
[64] *Bancoult 2* (HL) (n 1) [55].
[65] ibid, [53].
[66] ibid, [110].
[67] ibid, [114].
[68] ibid, [168].
[69] *Bancoult 2* (CA) (n 1) [71].
[70] *Bancoult 2* (HL) (n 1) [72] and [172].

prevent such landings and the absence of any evidence to show that they were imminent.

The orthodox position is that judicial restraint is required where foreign affairs, defence considerations or the expenditure of public resources are in issue. Accordingly, an irrationality challenge concerning these areas will typically be decided by reference to the standard of *Wednesbury* unreasonableness. However, as noted above, if a court found that a fundamental right was engaged then a higher standard of review would be applied. In such a case, it would be incumbent on the decision-maker to show that the decision was reasonable.[71] The minority endorsed this position. The majority were also prepared to accept that the right of abode would possess a fundamental quality for the purpose of a challenge based on *Wednesbury* unreasonableness if the Chagossians had been in occupation of BIOT at the time the 2004 Orders were made. In other words, if the Chagossians had inhabited BIOT in 2004 all the Law Lords would have agreed that the decision to withdraw the Chagossian right of abode must satisfy the heightened standard of judicial review in keeping with Bancoult's assertion. However, in the majority's view, the absence of a population meant that the ordinary standard of review was warranted and, on this basis, a *Wednesbury* unreasonableness challenge was bound to be unsuccessful.

The particular circumstances affecting a policy decision are undeniably important and it is not for the courts to substitute their own views for those of the body charged with the task of making public decisions. Nevertheless, the courts are still under a duty to scrutinise the quality of the reasoning behind such decisions.[72] In *Bancoult 2*, the courts were confronted with a situation where the decision to enact the 2004 Orders was made: (i) without consulting the Chagossians; (ii) without materially taking their interests into account; and (iii) without the checks and balances of legislative scrutiny and political debate. Moreover, the appellant could not provide a justification for overriding these standard decision-making requirements. Even the majority acknowledged that the concerns expressed by the US regarding the security implications posed by resettlement were 'exaggerated'.[73] Further, while the majority were prepared to attach considerable weight to the fact that the Chagossians did not inhabit BIOT in 2004, it appears that no weight was attached to the reason why they were no longer in occupation. Their involuntarily displacement by the UK government should not have been used as a reason for the withdrawal of their right of abode by a successive government. In the absence of precedent, it was entirely appropriate for the courts to consider the legality of the appellant's decision to legislate by reference to a heightened standard of review.

---

[71] J Jowell in *De Smith* (n 52) [1-107].
[72] ibid, [11-015]–[11-016].
[73] *Bancoult 2* (HL) (n 1), per Lord Carswell at [132].

C. Legitimate Expectations

A legitimate expectation has been defined as:

> an expectation . . . founded on a reasonable assumption which is capable of being
> protected in public law. It enables a citizen to challenge a decision which deprives him
> of an expectation founded on a reasonable basis that his claim would be dealt with in
> a particular way.[74]

Legitimate expectations can take a number of different forms.[75] Typically, they
arise in the context of procedural fairness (eg a public body should not change
a published policy without first consulting those persons who would be affected
by that change). However, they can also manifest a substantive dimension
beyond any requirement that public bodies act in ways that are procedurally
fair. In cases where a claimant is alleging that a substantive legitimate expectation has been breached, he or she is claiming an entitlement to a particular outcome rather than that a particular process has been followed by the public body
in question. The *Bancoult* litigation gave rise to both procedural and substantive legitimate expectations. First, the UK government had changed its published
policy of permitting the Chagossians to return to the outer Chagos Islands
without consulting them (thus giving rise to a claim that the decision was procedurally unfair). Secondly, by refusing to allow the Chagossians to resettle the
outer Islands, the UK government was depriving them of a substantive benefit,
the entitlement to re-establish themselves in their ancestral homeland.

The respondent argued the Secretary of State's statement created an expectation of a substantive benefit and that the 2004 Orders, which frustrated this
expectation without good reason, were therefore an abuse of power.[76] However,
the majority decided that a substantive legitimate expectation had not been
created on the facts as the Secretary of State's statement did not constitute a
'clear, unambiguous assurance devoid of relevant qualification'.[77] Although the
statement and the decision to enact the Immigration Ordinance 2000 may have
created the impression that the Chagossians would be able to return, Lord
Hoffmann believed that the statement could not be construed as a promise that
any entitlement to return would persist, especially against the background of
the feasibility study. In any event, Lord Hoffmann decided that there had been a
sufficient change of circumstances between 2000 and 2004 to justify a change of
policy in this 'macro-political field'.[78]

---

[74] *Behluli v Secretary of State for the Home Department* [1998] Imm AR 207, per Beldam LJ at
415.

[75] See *R v Devon County Council, ex p Baker* [1995] 1 All ER 73, per Simon Brown LJ at 88–89.

[76] Relying upon *R v North and East Devon Health Authority, ex p Coughlan* [2001] QB 213.

[77] *R v Inland Revenue Commissioners, ex p MFK Underwriting Agents Ltd* [1990] 1 WLR 1545,
1569, Bingham LJ, quoted in *Bancoult 2* (HL) (n 1) [60].

[78] *R v Secretary of State for Education and Employment, ex p Begbie* [2000] 1 WLR 1115, 1131,
per Laws LJ, quoted at [60].

Both Lord Bingham and Lord Mance focused on the way the representation would have been interpreted by the Chagossians. According to Lord Bingham, the Chagossians: 'were clearly intended to think, and did, that for the foreseeable future their right to return was assured'.[79] For Lord Mance: 'The press release should be construed according to the ordinary meaning that would be attached to it by those, principally, the Chagossians and their supporters, to whom it was directed'.[80] They held that: (i) the statement amounted to a promise that the government would not challenge the decision in *Bancoult 1*; (ii) this promise was strengthened by the decision to enact the 2000 Immigration Ordinance; and (iii) the government's decision to conduct the feasibility study was concerned with the question of government funding for resettlement – it did not constitute conditional recognition of the right of abode. Lord Mance indicated that, in cases involving claims of legitimate expectations, 'the underlying principle [is] a requirement of good administration, by which public bodies ought to deal straightforwardly and consistently with the public'.[81] While departures from public promises were permissible where an assessment of relevant factors indicated that the requirements of fairness could be overridden in the public interest,[82] in Lord Mance's view, the Secretary of State's

> statement and conduct were intended and understood to resolve the long-standing controversy regarding the Chagossian right [of abode], and that it would be and in the circumstances was maladministration to go back on that resolution without any consultation and without a strong cause, which has not been shown.[83]

Accordingly, the minority decided to dismiss the appeal for a lack of vires; alternatively, they held that section 9 of the Constitution Order was unlawful by reference to the ordinary principles of judicial review.

A legitimate expectation is induced by a representation made by a public body regarding a certain course of action. However, the appeal in *Bancoult 2* raised questions about the scope of such an expectation. Lord Hoffmann focused on an objective construction of the Secretary of State's statement of 3 November 2000 while Lord Bingham and Lord Mance considered it from the respondent's perspective. In the minority's view, the statement amounted to a clear promise that the right would continue to exist for the foreseeable future. It is suggested that this approach is the correct one. The courts should examine whether the expectation was reasonably induced by the representation rather than analysing the representation's abstract meaning: neither a representation nor an expectation can be considered in isolation, their meaning is relational.

---

[79] *Bancoult 2* (HL) (n 1) [83].
[80] ibid, [174].
[81] ibid, [181–82], drawing upon *R (Nadarajah and Abdi) v Secretary of State for the Home Department* [2005] EWCA Civ 1363 [67–68], per Laws LJ.
[82] Relying upon *ex p Coughlan* (n 76) [57].
[83] *Bancoult 2* (HL) (n 1) [185].

Bancoult 2 also highlighted the difficulties affecting the concept of substantive legitimate expectations.[84] In particular, it tested the scope of the Court of Appeal's decision in the case of *Coughlan*. In that case the assurance was unqualified (a home for life in a residential care home); it had 'the character of a contract';[85] was directed at a few individuals; and involved a small financial cost. In *Bancoult 2*, the statement was a general press release. Any recognition for a right of abode in BIOT seemed to depend on foreign policy and defence considerations. The statement was directed at several thousand Chagossians and, as a matter of international law, it could require considerable public funding. Nonetheless, a representation need not be quasi-contractual in nature if the class of persons affected is a limited one.[86] And although the Chagossian community constitutes a much larger class than the affected group in *Coughlan*, it is still relatively small in public law terms.

If it is accepted that the Secretary of State's statement amounted to a promise, the central issue should have been whether there were any overriding considerations, which had arisen between 2000 and 2004, that would have allowed the Secretary of State to resile from that promise. In the case of *Coughlan*, Lord Woolf MR stated that the court would decide for itself whether any overriding considerations justified the withdrawal of a substantive benefit.[87] However, the court in the case of *Begbie* indicated that the *Wednesbury* unreasonableness test (noted above) is the most appropriate standard of review where a change of policy is made on the basis of macro-political considerations and that decision had substantial resources implications affecting a substantial section of the public.[88] As Laws LJ explained in *Begbie*:

> The more the decision challenged lies in . . . the macro-political field, the less intrusive will be the court's supervision. More than this: in that field, true abuse of power is less likely to be found, since within it changes of policy, fuelled by broad conceptions of the public interest, may more readily be accepted as taking precedence over the interests of groups which enjoyed expectations generated by an earlier policy.[89]

At first blush, it would appear that the decision to enact the 2004 Orders was based on macro-political considerations. However, a closer inspection of the facts leads to a different conclusion. First, the UK's existing treaty obligations were not in issue in *Bancoult 2* because the US government had only requested the use of a single island, Diego Garcia, for defence purposes.[90] Secondly, US

---

[84]   J Jowell, 'Beyond the Rule of Law: Towards Constitutional Judicial Review' (2008) *Public Law* 671; and J Moffett, 'Resiling from Legitimate Expectations' (2008) 13 *Judicial Review* 219.

[85]   *Coughlan* (n 76) [59], per Lord Woolf MR.

[86]   See *Begbie* (n 78) 1131, per Laws LJ.

[87]   *Coughlan* (n 76) [57].

[88]   *Begbie* (n 78) 1131, per Laws LJ. See Jowell in *De Smith* (n 52) [12-047]–[12-053]; Moffett, 'Resiling from Legitimate Expectations' (n 84) 225; and *R (Bibi) v Newham London Borough Council* [2002] 1 WLR 237.

[89]   See *Begbie* (n 78) 1131, per Laws LJ.

[90]   While, under the 1966 Exchange of Notes, the US government was entitled to require that other islands within the BIOT be made available for defence purpose, it has never sought to exercise this right, per Lord Bingham at [72(2)].

objections were only made in response to the present litigation.[91] Thirdly, as the UK government was not under an obligation to fund the cost of resettlement under English law the decision had very limited cost implications; Finally, as the UK government's international legal obligations to BIOT had not changed between 2000 and 2004 (its obligations to this non-self-governing territory had remained the same since it was created in 1965, as discussed above) any responsibility to fund resettlement under international law could not have been used to justify a change of government policy (as the government was already subject to this responsibility). While the UK government was entitled to take the US government's 'exaggerated' security concerns into account when reviewing its policy, it is far from clear that these concerns alone justified a policy reversal or gave the decision to enact the 2004 Orders its macro-political quality. In the circumstances, it is suggested that the *Wednesbury* standard was not the correct standard by which to review the legality of this decision. Had the House of Lords chosen to follow the more appropriate standard outlined by Lord Woolf in *Coughlan*, it would have been difficult for it to conclude that a change of policy was warranted on the evidence produced.

VIII. INTERNATIONAL LAW PERSPECTIVES

In *Bancoult 2*, the applicant claimed that international law was relevant to the determination of his case. In particular, he argued that the Chagos Islanders were the beneficiaries of the right to self-determination as a matter of customary international law.[92] To this end, Bancoult claimed that, as the common law had long recognised that customary international law is part of English law,[93] the UK was bound to respect this entitlement. Consequently, he argued that the removal and exclusion of the Chagos Islanders from the BIOT constituted a violation of the Chagossian right to self-determination.[94] Bancoult also asserted that the Chagos Islanders were in possession of the right of self-determination by virtue of treaty law. Article 73 of the UN Charter – which created the international legal framework through which the right to colonial self-determination emerged - established the category of non-self-governing territories. It also recognised the significance of the notion of self-government for the inhabitants of such colonial territories.[95] Further, Bancoult claimed that the right of self-

---

[91]   *Bancoult 2* (HL) (n 1), Lord Mance at [163].

[92]   Pursuant to the Declaration on the Granting of Independence to Colonial Countries and Peoples, UNGA Res 1514(XV), 14 December 1960 ('Colonial Declaration'); and Declaration on the Principles of International Law concerning Friendly Relations and Co-operation Among States in Accordance with the Charter of the United Nations, UNGA Res 2625(XXV), 24 October 1970 (the 'Declaration on Friendly Relations'). See below.

[93]   See *R v Bow Street Metropolitan Stipendiary Magistrate, ex p Pinochet Ugarte (No 3)* [2000] 1 AC 147; and *Trendtex Trading Corpn v Central Bank of Nigeria* [1977] QB 529 and following.

[94]   An argument acknowledged in *Bancoult 2* (DC) (n 1) [103].

[95]   The UN Charter, Art 73 provides:

determination had been recognised in Joint Article 1 of the International Covenants on Human Rights, which the UK had ratified and thus was applicable in relation to the BIOT.[96] Accordingly, the applicant claimed that, as the right of self-determination is a principle/rule of English law, it is unlawful for the Crown to legislate in a manner that is inconsistent with it by virtue of its prerogative powers.

At a preliminary hearing concerning *Bancoult 2*, held on 13 July 2005, Sullivan J directed that the issues of:

> whether the United Kingdom was and/or is under any obligation under (a) any treaty or (b) customary international law to respect any right of self-determination which the Chagossian people (if it existed or exists) is alleged to have or to have had and what the effect of any such obligation might be in international law [be] reserved for a further hearing if relevant.[97]

As a result, the Divisional Court in *Bancoult 2* decided not to address these issues. Moreover, in the Court of Appeal, Sedley LJ did not think 'it necessary, or perhaps wise' to address the international law arguments pleaded in the case, given 'the complex questions they throw up'.[98]

Members of the United Nations which have or assume responsibilities for the administration of territories whose peoples have not yet attained a full measure of self-government recognize the principle that the interests of the inhabitants of these territories are paramount, and accept as a sacred trust the obligation to promote to the utmost, within the system of international peace and security established by the present Charter, the well-being of the inhabitants of these territories, and to this end:

(a) to ensure, with due respect for the culture of the peoples concerned, their political, economic, social and educational advancement, their just treatment, and their protection against abuses;

(b) to develop self-government, to take due account of the political aspirations of the peoples, and to assist them in the progressive development of their free political institutions, according to the particular circumstances of each territory and its peoples and their varying stages of advancement; . . .

(e) to transmit regularly to the Secretary-General for information purposes, subject to such limitations as security and constitutional considerations may require, statistical and other information of a technical nature relation to the economic, social, and educational conditions in the territories for which they are respectively responsible

The concept of non-self-governing territories and the right to colonial self-determination and their significance in the Mauritian and Chagossian contexts are explored throughout this book.

[96] International Covenant on Civil and Political Rights 1966, 999 UNTS 171 (ICCPR); and International Covenant on Economic, Social and Cultural Rights 1966, 993 UNTS 3 (ICESCR) (1966). Joint Art 1 provides that:

(1) All peoples have the right of self-determination. By virtue of that right they freely determine their political status and freely pursue their economic, social and cultural development

(2) All peoples may, for their own ends, freely dispose of their natural wealth and resources without prejudice to any obligations arising out of international economic co-operation, based upon the principle of mutual benefit, and international law. In no case may a people be deprived of its own means of subsistence.

(3) The State Parties to the present Covenant, including those having responsibility for the administration of Non-Self-Governing and Trust Territories, shall promote the realization of the right of self-determination, and shall respect that right, in conformity with the provisions of the Charter of the United Nations.

[97] *Bancoult 2* (DC) (n 1) [106].

[98] *Bancoult 2* (CA) (n 1) [49].

During the hearing in the House of Lords, Bancoult reiterated the significance of international law for his appeal.[99] In response, the UK government acknowledged that the principles of customary international law may be incorporated into English law. However, it contended that such principles were not incorporated automatically and, specifically, that the right to self-determination had not been incorporated into English law for the purpose of the instant case.[100]

Lord Hoffmann was the only Law Lord who was prepared to address the self-determination argument directly in his Opinion and he dismissed it outright saying that:

> As for international law, I do not understand how, consistently with the well-established doctrine that it does not form part of domestic law, it can support any argument for the invalidity of a purely domestic law such as the [2004] Constitution Order.[101]

Lord Hoffmann's abrupt conclusion on this issue is premised on the assumption that the 2004 Orders had no ramifications for international law, an assumption that is clearly at odds with the BIOT's status as an undeclared non-self-governing territory. Nonetheless, Lord Hoffmann's Opinion implicitly accepted that the case exhibited a clear international legal dimension. While considering the rationality of the decision, Lord Hoffmann noted that:

> The Secretary of State is surely entitled to take into account that once a vanguard of Chagossians establishes itself on the islands in poor and barren conditions of life, there may be a claim that the United Kingdom is subject to a sacred trust under article 73 of the United Nations Charter.[102]

Lord Hoffmann's observation would have been unremarkable if the BIOT had never been inhabited. However, it is now well known that the BIOT was populated by the Chagossians from the end of the eighteenth century until 1973.[103] On 16 November 1965, the UK government quietly disregarded its Charter obligations when it incorrectly reported to the General Assembly's Fourth Committee that the BIOT's inhabitants did not constitute a permanent population and therefore it could not be classified as a non-self-governing territory.[104]

Under Article 73 of the UN Charter, States are under an international legal obligation to foster full self-government for the peoples of non-self-governing territories, an obligation that subsequently evolved into the right to colonial

---

[99] *Bancoult 2* (n 1) 474. See *R v Bow Street Metropolitan Stipendiary Magistrate, ex p Pinochet Ugarte* (n 93); and *Trendtex Trading Corpn v Central Bank of Nigeria* (n 93).

[100] *Bancoult 2* (n 1) 477. In support, see *Jones v Ministry of the Interior of the Kingdom of Saudi Arabia* [2007] 1 AC 270 and *R v Jones (Margaret)* [2007] 1 AC 136.

[101] *Bancoult 2* (HL) (n 1) [66].

[102] ibid, [55].

[103] See chs 6 and 7.

[104] See the Foreign Office documents referred to in *Bancoult 1* (n 1) [1–23]; and *Bancoult 2* (DC) (n 1) [28–34]. See chs 6 and 7.

self-determination as a matter of customary international law.[105] This obligation arose in 1965, when the BIOT was created. But while Article 73 may not
have imposed an obligation enforceable against the UK government in the
English courts, Lord Hoffmann connected it to the question of whether
Bancoult possessed a public law right of abode in relation to the BIOT as a matter of English law. Thus, while he proclaimed that the claimed right of abode in
the BIOT was merely symbolic, Lord Hoffmann understood the substantial
financial commitments that could follow from its recognition. Moreover, while
this ongoing international legal obligation may not have been binding on the
UK government as a matter of English law, nevertheless, it should have been
given weight when determining the rationality of the decision to withdraw the
right of abode. Consequently, for this reason, and the reasons discussed above,
it is very doubtful that the decision to enact section 9 of the 2004 Constitutional
Order was a reasonable one.

Notwithstanding the resonance of international law for the claims of the
Chagos Islanders the narrower question with which the English courts were
concerned in the *Bancoult* litigation was whether international law gave rise to
justiciable issues as a matter of English law. This aspect of the *Bancoult* litigation warrants an investigation into the relationship between international law
and municipal legal systems at a general level and, in particular, an examination
of the relationship between international law and English law.

IX. INTERNATIONAL LAW AND NATIONAL LAW

A. Theoretical Approaches: Dualism and Monism

Dualism adopts the standpoint that international law and national law constitute entirely separate legal systems. Accordingly, if a State adopts a dualist
approach, an international legal principle has no legal validity in its national
legal system per se. For an international legal principle to acquire legal validity
in national law it must be transformed into a national legal rule or principle
before it can have any direct legal effect. This may happen by enacting domestic
legislation or by judicial decision. The dualist approach maintains that an
impenetrable barrier exists between international law and national legal systems. It guards against the risk of national laws being determined by powers
beyond the State in question by ensuring that State representatives – the national
legislature and/or the judiciary – retain the authority to decide the content of
municipal law and the balance of constitutional responsibilities.[106]

In contrast, monism adopts the position that both international and national
legal regimes are component parts of a single overarching legal system.
Accordingly, monism holds that international law should be directly effective

---

[105] See ch 5.
[106] The dualist approach is broadly endorsed by the UK and the USA with certain qualifications.

within municipal legal regimes (albeit subject to certain qualifications). Monists criticise the distinctions that dualism draws between international law and national law.[107] In particular, they question the traditional view that the subjects of international law are different to the subjects of national law. Instead, they argue that the ultimate subjects of both international law and national law are individuals. Monism raises serious questions concerning the organisational structure of international society including the primacy of the State and the significance of State sovereignty. While it could be argued that it has had a limited practical impact thus far,[108] it represents an important ideological standpoint and there is considerable evidence to suggest that it is indicative of the normative trajectory of international law in a number of areas.[109]

B. International Law and English Law

The British Constitution maintains a firm commitment to dualism and to the doctrine of incorporation with regard to the principles of customary international law. There is considerable authority in support of the view that the principles of customary international law are part of English Law.[110] During the eighteenth century, Blackstone noted that 'the law of nations, wherever any question arises which is properly the object of its jurisdiction, is here adopted in its full extent by the common law, and is held to be part of the law of the land'.[111] More recently, in *R v Bow Street Metropolitan Stipendiary Magistrate, ex p Pinochet Ugarte (No 3)*, Lord Millet agreed that 'Customary international law is part of the common law'.[112] However, it is doubtful that customary international law becomes part of English law automatically. Lord Bingham, who gave the leading judgment in *R v Margaret Jones*, endorsed the view that customary international law 'is not a part, but is one of the sources of English law'.[113]

---

[107] See J Nijman and A Nollkaemper (eds), *New Perspectives on the Divide Between National and International Law* (Oxford, Oxford University Press, 2007); and E Denza, 'The Relationship between International Law and National Law' in M Evans (ed), *International Law*, 3rd edn (Oxford, Oxford University Press, 2010) 411.

[108] Nevertheless, a number of States, including The Netherlands, Greece and Spain, subscribe to the monist position regarding the extent to which international law is applicable within their national legal systems (subject to certain qualifications).

[109] The monist standpoint enables monists to subscribe to the idea of universal human rights. Further, it facilitates the development of international legal standards designed to address global problems.

[110] It was observed in *Buvot v Barbuit* (1737) Cas Temp Talbot 281, that: 'The Law of Nations, in its full extent is part of the law of England'. This position was subsequently endorsed by Lord Mansfield in *Triquet v Bath* (1746) 3 Burr 1478.

[111] W Blackstone, *Commentaries on the Laws of England* (1765–69) vol IV, ch 5.

[112] See *R v Bow Street Metropolitan Stipendiary Magistrate, ex p Pinochet Ugarte* (n 93) 276. Further, see *Kuwait Airways v Iraqi Airways (Nos 4 & 5)* [2002] 2 AC 883.

[113] *R v Margaret Jones* [2007] 1 AC 136 [11]. See JL Brierly, 'International Law in England' (1935) 51 *Law Quarterly Review* 24, 31; P Capps, 'The Court as Gatekeeper: Customary International Law in English Courts' (2007) 70 *Modern Law Review* 558; and P Sales and J Clement, 'International Law in Domestic Courts: The Developing Framework' (2008) 124 *Law Quarterly Review* 388.

Accordingly, the correct view seems to be that custom may only be incorporated into English law when it is permitted by the terms of the British Constitution.[114] This position allows the English courts to incorporate customary international law into English law in appropriate cases. However, it appears that the issue of incorporation may only be considered if two requirements are satisfied.[115] First, the principle in question must be well-established in customary international law. Secondly, there must be sufficient evidence that the State in question has assented to it. Regarding the first requirement, Bancoult argued that, taken together, the provisions of Article 73 of the UN Charter, the terms of the 1960 Colonial Declaration, and the 1970 Declaration on Friendly Relations have ensured that the right to self-determination has acquired the status of customary international law.[116] Regarding the second requirement, there is ample evidence to show that the UK has assented to this principle. The UK government agreed to the terms of the both Chapter XI of the UN Charter and the 1970 Declaration, which enabled the right of self-determination to acquire its international legal character of customary international law. Further, it has embraced the significance of this entitlement with regard to its policy of good governance in relation to its remaining non-self-governing territories.[117]

But while these examples demonstrate that the UK government has accepted the binding character of the right of self-determination as a matter of customary international law, it does not necessarily follow that this entitlement has been incorporated into English law as a result. During the proceedings in the House of Lord in *Bancoult 2*, the UK government questioned how the English courts could recognise the existence of such an abstract right as a matter of English law notwithstanding its recognition as an international legal entitlement. It should be acknowledged that the nature of the right to self-determination has created difficulties for adjudicative bodies. For instance, the UN Human Rights Committee which deals, inter alia, with complaints made in respect of alleged violations of the International Covenant on Civil and Political Rights,[118] does not accept complaints relating to Article 1, which is concerned with the application of the right to self-determination. However, in the *Quebec Secession* case, the Canadian Supreme Court was prepared to recognise the constitutional significance of the right to self-determination despite its conclusion that the Quebecois did not possess a unilateral right to secede from Canada as a

---

[114] *R v Margaret Jones* (n 113) [23].

[115] *R v Keyn* (1876–77) LR 2 Ex D 63.

[116] The issue of how and when the right to colonial self-determination acquired the status of customary international law is considered in detail in ch 5.

[117] See the UK government's White Paper, *Partnership for Progress and Prosperity: Britain and the Overseas Territories* (Cm 4264, 1999), which set out its vision for the development of British Overseas Territories.

[118] The quasi-judicial authority of the Human Rights Committee is only engaged in situations where a State party has ratified the Optional Protocol to the ICCPR which confers jurisdiction on the Committee to hear such complaints. The UK has not ratified this Optional Protocol. The significance of the ICCPR in the BIOT context is considered in ch 7.

matter of international law.[119] Accordingly, on one reading, this case is good authority for the reception of the right of self-determination into English law. Nevertheless, the Supreme Court's decision must be interpreted in the light of Canada's federal constitution and the extent to which the UK Constitution could be deemed to support the existence of a right to self-determination possessed by the inhabitants of a British Overseas Territory is not certain as a matter of English law.

The foundational norm of the British Constitution is the principle of parliamentary sovereignty.[120] If the UK government could participate in the creation of an international legal principle that could be directly enforced in the English courts it would create the risk that Parliament's sovereign law-making authority could be circumvented.[121] Consequently, the constitutional position remains that a treaty can only become part of English law if it has been transformed by an Act of Parliament.[122] This position was upheld by Lord Oliver in *Maclaine Watson v Department of Trade and Industry*, when he observed that:

> as a matter of constitutional law of the United Kingdom, the Royal Prerogative, whilst it embraces the making of treaties does not extend to altering the law or conferring rights upon individuals . . . without the intervention of Parliament. Treaties, as it is sometimes expressed, are not self-executing. Quite simply, a treaty is not part of English law unless and until it has been incorporated into the law by legislation.[123]

Accordingly, in the context of the *Bancoult* litigation, the relevant provisions of the UN Charter and the International Covenants could not be relied upon directly as their provisions concerning the application of the entitlement of self-determination with regard to non-self-governing territories have not been transformed by statute for the purpose of rendering the right to self-determination a principle of English law. Nonetheless, while an un-enacted treaty cannot create directly enforceable rights and obligations under English law there is a presumption that Parliament intends to legislate in a way that is consistent with the UK's international legal obligations. Accordingly, the courts endeavour to interpret English law in a way that does not conflict with the UK's international legal

---

[119] *Quebec Secession Case* [1998] 2 SCR 217. The court held that, in general, the right of self-determination is an internal right that to be exercised by groups within the confines of a State. See J Crawford, 'State Practice and International Law in relation to Secession' (1998) 69 *British Yearbook of International Law* 85.

[120] *R (Jackson) v Attorney-General* [2006] (n 55).

[121] Not only would this violate the democratic principle given Parliament's representative nature, it would undermine the ancient common law principle that that only Parliament has the authority to make the law of the land (unless the area in question is subject to the exercise of the royal prerogative).

[122] See *The Parlement Belge* (1879–80) LR 5 PD 197.

[123] [1990] 2 AC 418, 500. Also see *A v Secretary of State for the Home Department* [2006] AC 221, where Lord Bingham accepted that: 'a treaty, even if ratified by the UK, has no binding force in the domestic law of this country unless it is given effect by statute or expresses principles of customary international law', at 254–55.

obligations, wherever possible.[124] While the *Bancoult* litigation concerned a challenge to the exercise of the royal prerogative it could be argued that legislation enacted under the auspices of the prerogative should likewise by construed in a way that would not offend the UK's international obligations, unless compelling evidence was adduced to the contrary.

C. The Fitzmaurice Compromise

Although they adopt very different positions regarding the reach of international law both monism and dualism accept that international law and national legal regimes exist on the same legal plane. Dualism erects a barrier between international law and national law but it accepts that international legal rights and/or obligations can be transposed into national law by the appropriate constitutional mechanisms. In contrast, monism, adopts a holistic approach, which disregards normative barriers between national and international law. The conceptual approach originally developed by Gerald Fitzmaurice rejects the idea that international law and national legal regimes exist on the same conceptual plane.[125] Instead, Fitzmaurice argued that the relationship between international law and national legal systems should be considered from the perspective of conflicting legal obligations that exist on different legal planes. Consequently, if a State enacts municipal legislation, or if national courts uphold municipal legal rules and principles that conflict with an international legal obligation that is binding on that State, while the legislation, or the rules and principles recognised by the courts, will be valid at the level of national law, the State may nevertheless incur international responsibility for violating the applicable provisions of international law. Accordingly, in such a situation, the conflict may be viewed as a dispute between different obligations owed by the State rather than as a clash of legal regimes which exist on the same conceptual plane. The 'Fitzmaurice Compromise' has attracted considerable support because it reflects the pragmatic reality of the relationship between national legal systems and international law.[126] While it is possible that a State would be prepared to bear the burden of international responsibility for national legislation, or judicial

---

[124] See *Derbyshire CC v Times Newspapers* [1992] 3 WLR 28. Nevertheless, it should be noted that this is only a rule of construction. If a statute clearly contradicts international law the courts are bound to give effect to the will of Parliament regardless of whether international responsibility is engaged. See *R v Secretary of State for the Home Department, ex p Brind* [1991] 1 AC 696.

[125] See G Fitzmaurice, 'The General Principles of International Law Considered from the Standpoint of the Rule of Law' (1957) 92 *Rec de Cours* pt II 68–99.

[126] eg the assumptions which underpin the 'Fitzmaurice Compromise' are clearly apparent in the provisions of the 1969 Vienna Convention on the Law of Treaties. eg Art 27 provides that: 'A party may not invoke the provisions of its internal law as justification for its failure to perform a treaty'. Further, Art 46(1) provides that: 'A State may not invoke the fact that its consent to be bound by a treaty has been expressed in violation of a provision of its internal law regarding competence to conclude treaties as invalidating its consent unless that violation was manifest and concerned a rule of its internal law of fundamental importance'. See *Cameroon v Nigeria* (2002) ICJ Rep 303.

decisions, that violate international law, Fitzmaurice's conceptual approach assumes that, once the disparity between international law and national law becomes apparent in a given area, the State in question would change its municipal law so that it accords with the position adopted by international law in order to minimise its international liability. However, it should be acknowledged that, in the event of a dispute arising, this approach to the relationship between national legal systems and international law presupposes that: (i) international jurisdiction arises in relation to the dispute in question (ie international law seeks to regulate the contested matter); and (ii); the international legal principles are binding on the State in issue.

On this reading, the Chagossian claims made in respect of the BIOT are not exhausted by the Chagossian litigation in the English courts and it matters not that those courts decided that the international legal arguments advanced in *Bancoult 2*, were not considered to be relevant to the determination of that case by those judicial authorities. Accordingly, if it can be shown, as a matter of international law, that: (i) the right to self-determination is applicable in the Chagossian context; and (ii) it is binding on the UK in respect of the BIOT, it follows that, in principle, the UK is under an international legal obligation to facilitate the exercise of this right by the Chagossian people irrespective of the position adopted by English law on this issue.

The following chapters explore the extent to which these two conditions can be satisfied. Further, the resonance of international law for the Chagos Islanders cannot be properly understood without first examining the circumstances surrounding the BIOT's creation. In particular, the legality of the detachment of the Chagos Islands from the British colony of Mauritius for the purpose of establishing the BIOT must be fully examined along with the history of the Mauritian-UK sovereignty dispute over Chagos Islands. The Chagossian claims are shaped by the origins of the BIOT question. Accordingly, at the level of international law, Chagossian claims in respect of the BIOT are bound up with Mauritian claims to the same territory as a matter of international law.

X. CONCLUSION

The House of Lords' decision to review primary legislation enacted by the Sovereign in Council under its prerogative powers in *Bancoult 2* was a profound constitutional moment. Notwithstanding this development, *Bancoult 2* demonstrated the continuing uncertainty surrounding status of fundamental rights within English law.[127] While the majority were reluctant to engage on this constitutional issue, the willingness of the lower courts and the minority in the House of Lords to recognise the right of abode in the BIOT as a fundamental

---

[127] Also see M Elliott and A Perreau-Saussine, 'Pyrrhic Public Law: Bancoult and the Sources, Status and Content of Common Law Limitations on Prerogative Power' (2009) 52 *Public Law* 697.

right is consistent with the normative direction of English public law on this issue. Regarding the application of the ordinary principles of judicial review – ie whether the decision to enact the 2004 Orders was not unreasonable or procedurally flawed – the majority's temporal assessment of the respondent's right of abode in the BIOT conditioned its view of the reasonableness of the government's decision to enact the Orders. By taking 2004 as the relevant date for assessing the UK government's decision to enact the Orders the majority had a different view of whether the Orders were unreasonable from that of the minority, which considered 1965 to be the critical date for this purpose. Consequently, the majority denied the right's fundamental quality, thereby justifying a less intrusive standard of review (the *Wednesbury* unreasonableness test). Given the nature of the right; the history surrounding its protracted denial; the lack of compelling reasons for its withdrawal; and the UK government's existing international legal obligations to this non-self-governing territory the decision's rationality should have been determined by reference to a heightened standard of review, which would surely have favoured the respondent.

In 2004 a petition was lodged at the European Court of Human Rights alleging a number of violations of the European Convention on Human Rights arising out of the *Chagos Islanders* case.[128] It alleged breaches of Article 3 (inhuman and degrading treatment); Article 6 (absence of fair trial); Article 8 (respect for family and private life); Article 13 (lack of an effective national law remedy); and Article 1 of Protocol 1 to the Convention (violation of property rights). However, the petition was deferred pending the final resolution of the *Bancoult* litigation. The petition was revived and revised in the light of the House of Lords' decision in *Bancoult 2*. This combined European case was heard by the Strasbourg Court in 2012 and judgment was entered on 11 December 2012.[129] The *Chagos Islanders v UK* case will be considered in detail in the next chapter. However, at this stage, it is worth noting that the case turned on the issue of whether the UK's jurisdiction was engaged for the purpose of applying the European Convention in respect of the BIOT.[130] In essence, the UK government's argument was that the Convention only applies in the relation to the combined European territory of Contracting States – the *espace de juridique* – unless the responsible Contracting State has specifically extended the Convention to the Overseas Territory in question. More generally, the European Convention exists within a wider framework of international law and the European Court has often relied upon the relevant principles of international law in connection with the task of interpreting Convention rights and obligations. In particular, the Court's jurisprudence in relation to the concept of jurisdiction for the purpose

---

[128] *Chagos Islanders v UK* (2013) 56 EHRR SE15. The statement of facts and questions in this case was drawn up by the Court's Judge Rapporteur on 20 February 2009 [2009] ECHR 410.
[129] ibid.
[130] ECHR, Art 1 provides: 'The High Contracting Parties shall secure to everyone within their jurisdiction the rights and freedoms defined in Section I of this Convention'. Art 56 of the Convention gives State parties the discretion to extend the Convention to its dependent territories. However, the UK has never formally extended its ratification to the BIOT.

of the Convention's application has been largely informed by the doctrine of State jurisdiction at the level of international law.[131] Given this book's interest in the Chagossian litigation in the English courts and its principal focus on the international law applicable in relation to the BIOT, it seems sensible to examine the way in which the Strasbourg Court – this important site for connecting municipal and international legal orders in the areas addressed by the European Convention – approached the issue of whether the UK's jurisdiction was engaged for the purpose of applying the Convention in respect of the BIOT before turning to consider the wider issues of sovereignty and self-determination in the Chagossian context.

---

[131] See esp *Bankovic v Belgium* (2001) 44 EHRR SE5; *Al-Skeini and Others v UK* (2011) 53 EHRR 18. These cases are discussed in ch 2.

2

The Chagos Islanders and the European Convention on Human Rights: Extra-territoriality and the Concept of State Jurisdiction

I. INTRODUCTION

IN 2004, A petition, the *Chagos Islanders v UK*, was lodged at the European Court of Human Rights alleging a number of violations of the European Convention on Human Rights (ECHR) arising out of the private law litigation in the *Chagos Islanders v Attorney General and HM BIOT Commissioner* case.[1] The petition was deferred pending the final resolution of the public law challenge made in the *Bancoult* litigation. It was revived and amended in the light of the decision of the House of Lords in *Bancoult 2*.[2] The amended petition alleged breaches of Article 3 (inhuman and degrading treatment); Article 6 (the absence of a fair trial); Article 8 (respect for family and private life); Article 13 (lack of an effective national law remedy); and Article 1 of Protocol 1 to the Convention (the violation of property rights). However, before the alleged substantive violations of the Convention could be determined, the Strasbourg Court had to decide whether the UK's jurisdiction was engaged in respect of the BIOT for the purpose of applying the European Convention to that British Overseas Territory. Accordingly, the *Chagos Islanders* case turned on the preliminary issue of whether State jurisdiction had been established on the facts.[3] In the absence of a finding of jurisdiction, the case would be held to be inadmissible and the UK could not be held responsible for any violations of the Convention claimed by the Chagos Islanders.

---

[1] *Chagos Islanders v UK* (2013) 56 EHRR SE15. The statement of facts and questions in this case was drawn up by the Court's Judge Rapporteur on 20 February 2009, [2009] ECHR 410.
[2] *R (Bancoult) v Secretary of State for Foreign and Commonwealth Affairs* ('*Bancoult 2*') [2008] 3 WLR 955.
[3] *Chagos Islanders v UK* (n 1).

II. STATE JURISDICTION AND ARTICLE 1
OF THE EUROPEAN CONVENTION

It is well-established that a State is entitled to exercise its jurisdiction in respect of territory over which it exercises sovereign authority.[4] However, a State's sovereignty is limited by the sovereignty of other States as a result of the principle of sovereign equality.[5] Consequently, in the *SS Lotus* case, the Permanent Court of International Justice (PCIJ) stated that:

> Now the first and foremost restriction imposed by international law upon a State is that . . . it may not exercise its power in any form in the territory of another State. In this sense jurisdiction is certainly territorial; it cannot be exercised by a State outside its territory[6]

Thus, while a State is entitled to exercise its jurisdiction within its national territory, it has no right to exercise jurisdiction within the territory of another State. Nevertheless, a State's jurisdiction is not necessarily limited to its own national territory. States may exercise extra-territorial jurisdiction by reference to a number of established principles of international law.[7] But although claims of State jurisdiction are mediated by international law, a State must claim jurisdiction and such claims are typically made by a State in its municipal legislation. This prescriptive form of jurisdiction was famously stated in the *Lotus* case where the PCIJ observed that:

> Far from laying down a general prohibition to the effect that States may not extend the application of their laws and the jurisdiction of their courts to persons, property and acts outside their territory, [international law] leaves them in this respect a wide measure of discretion.[8]

The notion of State jurisdiction is addressed in Article 1 of the ECHR. It provides that: 'The High Contracting Parties shall secure to everyone within their jurisdiction the rights and freedoms defined in Section I of this Convention'. According to the European Court of Human Rights in *Al-Skeini v UK*:

> 'Jurisdiction' under art.1 is a threshold criterion. The exercise of jurisdiction is a necessary condition for a contracting state to be able to be held responsible for acts or

---

[4] See *The Legal Consequences of the Construction of a Wall in the Occupied Palestinian Territory Case* (2004) ICJ Rep 136 [109].

[5] The principle of sovereign equality is recognised in Art 2(1), UN Charter, which provides that: 'The Organisation is based on the principle of sovereign equality of all its Members'. It was further elaborated in the Declaration on the Principles of International Law concerning Friendly Relations and Co-operation Among States in Accordance with the Charter of the United Nations, UNGA Res 2625(XXV), 24 October 1970.

[6] *SS Lotus* case *(France/Turkey)* (1927) PCIJ Rep Ser A No 10, 18–19.

[7] Five principles of State jurisdiction in international law have been identified: territorial; nationality; universal; protective; and passive personality. See the Harvard Research Draft Convention on Criminal Jurisdiction (1935) 29 *American Journal of International Law Supplement* 443.

[8] *SS Lotus* case (n 6) 19.

omissions imputable to it which give rise to an allegation of the infringement of rights and freedoms set forth in the Convention.[9]

Consequently, State jurisdiction activates both the human rights expressed in the Convention for individuals who come within the jurisdiction of a Contracting State and the corresponding Convention obligations which are binding on that State in a given situation. Nevertheless, it is notable that Article 1 does not address the issue of the territorial parameters of jurisdiction for the purpose of applying the European Convention. In *Bankovic v Belgium and Others*, the European Court of Human Rights observed that the European Convention is 'a constitutional instrument of *European* public order' which operates 'in an essentially regional context and notably in the legal space (*espace juridique*) of the Contracting States'.[10] Further, it noted that the Convention 'was not designed to be applied throughout the world, even in respect of the conduct of the Contracting States'.[11] Consequently, in general, the Court indicated that a violation would have to occur within the Convention's legal space for the responsibility of a Contracting State to arise.[12] Moreover, according to the Court in *Bankovic*:

> Article 1 of the Convention must be considered to reflect this ordinary and essentially territorial notion of jurisdiction, other bases of jurisdiction being exceptional and requiring special justification in the particular circumstances of each case.[13]

It is clear from the above passage that the Strasbourg Court's view of the concept of State jurisdiction for the purpose of applying the European Convention was heavily influenced by the concept of State jurisdiction as it has been developed in international law.[14]

The decision of the European Court of Human Rights in *Al-Skeini* seems to have clarified the principles which underpin the notion of State jurisdiction under Article 1 where the Convention's extra-territorial application is in issue.[15] The case turned on whether the UK's jurisdiction was engaged for the acts and/ or omissions of British military forces during their occupation of Southern Iraq in 2003. Specifically, a number of Iraqi civilians were killed in the area of Basra: either they were shot in the streets or they died as a result of torture and one

---

[9] *Al-Skeini and Others v UK* (2011) 53 EHRR 18 [130]. This is consistent with the Court's established jurisprudence see *Bankovic v Belgium* (2001) 44 EHRR SE5 [65]. For a useful discussion of jurisdiction as a threshold criterion, see S Besson, 'The Extraterritoriality of the European Convention on Human Rights: Why Human Rights Depend on Jurisdiction and What Jurisdiction Amounts to' (2012) 25 *Leiden Journal of International Law* 857, 862–64.

[10] ibid, [80].

[11] *Bankovic* (n 9). See also *Loizidou v Turkey (Merits)* (1997) 23 EHRR 513 [78].

[12] Subject to Art 56 of the Convention which gives State parties the discretion to extend the Convention to its dependent territories. See below.

[13] *Bankovic* (n 9) [61].

[14] The extent to which these two approaches areas are comparable has been questioned by commentators. See eg M Milanovic, *Extraterritorial Application of Human Rights Treaties: Law, Principles and Policy* (Oxford, Oxford University Press, 2011) 21–30.

[15] *Al-Skeini* (n 9) [130–42].

Iraqi was killed in a British military prison. In *Al-Skeini*, a Grand Chamber of the Court confirmed that a prerequisite for a finding of State jurisdiction remains that a Contracting State must exercise 'some of the public powers normally to be exercised by a sovereign government' in a particular situation.[16] Further, in *Al-Skeini*, the Court decided that, if a Contracting State exercises such public powers in a setting that is beyond its national territory, its jurisdiction may be engaged for alleged violations of the Convention by reference to two distinct approaches. First, State jurisdiction may arise where a Contracting State has 'effective control of the relevant territory and its inhabitants' (the spatial mode of jurisdiction).[17] Alternatively, a Contracting State's jurisdiction may be established where its agents exercise 'authority and control' over the affected individual or individuals (the personal mode of jurisdiction).[18] Accordingly, in general, an alleged victim of a violation of the Convention, as established by either mode, will have come within the jurisdiction of that Contracting State for the purpose of Article 1 of the Convention.

In *Al-Skeini*, the Court considered the notion of *espace de juridique*, which was developed in *Bankovic*.[19] First, in keeping with its established jurisprudence, the Court upheld the drafters' political assumption that the Convention is a constitutional instrument of European public order.[20] It also reaffirmed the territorial assumption that a Contracting State's jurisdiction would *normally* be engaged, under Article 1, for violations of the Convention that have allegedly been committed either within its national territory or within the national territory of another Contracting State.[21] Nevertheless, in *Al-Skeini*, the Court expressly stated that a Contracting State's jurisdiction may be engaged beyond the collective territory of the member States of the Council of Europe, in exceptional circumstances.[22] This position is consistent with the Court's previous jurisprudence, which indicated that the Convention could be applied extraterritorially, albeit on an exceptional basis.[23] It has been suggested that the European Court's decision in *Al-Skeini* has cleared the way for the development of a broader conception of State jurisdiction based on spatial grounds.[24]

---

[16] ibid, [135]. Echoing its standpoint in the earlier case of *Bankovic* (n 9) [71].

[17] ibid, [138–39]; *Bankovic* (n 9); and *Loizidou v Turkey (Preliminary Objections)* (1995) 20 EHRR 99 [75].

[18] *Bankovic* (n 9) [71]; *Al-Skeini* (n 9) [136–37].

[19] *Al-Skeini* (n 9) [141–42].

[20] Regarding the Convention's drafting history, see L Moor and AWB Simpson, 'Ghosts of Colonialism in the European Convention on Human Rights' (2005) 76 *British Yearbook of International Law* 121, 132–50.

[21] *Al-Skeini* (n 9) [131].

[22] ibid, [142].

[23] ibid, [142]. This position was also evident in earlier cases: see *Issa and Others v Turkey* (2005) 41 EHRR 27 and *Ocalan v Turkey* (2005) 41 EHRR 45. It has been suggested that this position was implicit in *Bankovic*; see R Wilde, 'Legal "Black Hole" Extraterritorial State Action and International Treaty Law on Civil and Political Rights' (2004-05) 26 *Michigan Journal of International Law* 739, 795–97.

[24] See M Milanovic, '*Al-Skeini* and *Al-Jedda* in Strasbourg' (2012) 23 *European Journal of International Law* 121.

However, it is possible that the significance of the decision has been overstated in this respect. Indeed support for a more modest conception of the notion of State jurisdiction under Article 1 has been confirmed by the Strasbourg Court in the *Chagos Islanders* case.[25]

The *Chagos Islanders* case was concerned with the issue of whether the UK's jurisdiction was engaged for the purpose of applying the European Convention to the British Indian Ocean Territory (the BIOT), an Overseas Territory for which the UK bears international responsibility.[26] Although the European Convention was designed with a view to being applied within the European context, Article 63 of the Convention established a system whereby a Contracting State could extend the application of the Convention to a Territory for which it bears international responsibility, on a voluntary basis.

Article 63 was renumbered as Article 56 by the Eleventh Protocol.[27] Article 56 provides:

1 Any State may at the time of its ratification or at any time thereafter declare by notification addressed to the Secretary General of the Council of Europe that the present Convention shall, subject to paragraph 4 of this Article, extend to all or any of the territories for whose international relations it is responsible.

2 The Convention shall extend to the territory or territories named in the notification as from the thirtieth day after the receipt of this notification by the Secretary General of the Council of Europe.

3 The provisions of this Convention shall be applied in such territories with due regard, however, to local requirements.

4 Any State which has made a declaration in accordance with paragraph 1 of this article may at any time thereafter declare on behalf of one or more of the territories to which the declaration relates that it accepts the competence of the Court to receive applications from individuals, non-governmental organisations or groups of individuals as provided by Article 34 of the Convention.

Article 63 did not expressly identify the territories to which it may be applied. However, during the Convention's drafting process, it was widely understood that Article 1 governed the notion of State jurisdiction in relation to the metropolitan territories of the Contracting States while Article 63 addressed the issue of the jurisdiction of Contracting States in respect of those non-metropolitan territories for which each Contracting State bore international responsibility.[28] It is clear from the Convention's drafting history that Article 63 was developed as a colonial application clause. In 1961, this understanding was confirmed by the

---

[25] *Chagos Islanders v UK* (n 1).

[26] The British Overseas Territories Act 2002, s 1(1)(a) identifies 14 British Overseas Territories, which are listed in the British Nationality Act 1981, sch 6. For a discussion of the terminology relating to these colonial territories, see I Hendry and S Dickson, *British Overseas Territories Law* (Oxford, Hart Publishing, 2011) 2–3.

[27] The text of Art 56(4) was a revised version of Art 63(4). Art 56 is commonly referred to as the territorial application clause.

[28] Moor and Simpson, 'Ghosts of Colonialism in the European Convention on Human Rights' (n 20) 144–46.

European Commission in *X v Belgium*. In this early case, the Commission decided that the European Convention had no application in relation to the Belgian Congo because Belgium had not made a declaration, under Article 63 of the Convention, extending the Convention to that non-metropolitan territory for which it bore international responsibility.[29]

Nonetheless, this understanding did not extend to the precise relationship between Article 1 and Article 63(56). Did the existence of a voluntary system of extension via declaration pursuant to Article 63 mean that the jurisdiction of a Contracting State could only be established in relation to its national territory via Article 1? Or could a Contracting State's jurisdiction be engaged, under Article 1, beyond its national territory in certain circumstances? Moor and Simpson identified a number of interpretations of the effect of Article 63(56). For the present purpose, the most significant interpretation is that Article 63(56) enables a Contracting State to exclude the application of the European Convention in relation to a non-metropolitan territory that would otherwise come within its jurisdiction under Article 1 of the Convention.[30] This interpretation is in keeping with the established presumption that a treaty applies to all the territories over which a State exercises sovereignty.[31] But while this presumption was subsequently enshrined in Article 29 of the Vienna Convention on the Law of Treaties 1969,[32] it is unclear whether it had crystallised into a recognised principle of customary international law at the time the European Convention was concluded.[33] Consequently, the nature of the Convention and its drafting history appeared to indicate that it would not necessarily extend to all those territories for which each Contracting State was responsible.[34] However, the fact that Article 1 did not manifest an explicit territorial dimension meant that this remained a moot point during the Convention's early years.

It was not long before the legal institutions of the Council of Europe had to address the question of the precise relationship between Article 1 and Article 63(56). In *Cyprus v Turkey*, Turkey argued that Article 1 applied in relation to metropolitan territories only.[35] As a result, it claimed that the notion of State jurisdiction under that provision was restricted to the national territory of a Contracting State and that Article 63 applied in relation to non-metropolitan

---

[29] *X v Belgium* (1961) ECHR Yearbook 260. The position that Art 56 applies only in relation to non-metropolitan territories was confirmed more recently in *Ilascu and Others v Moldova and Russia* (2005) 40 EHRR 1030.

[30] Moor and Simpson (n 20) 126–32.

[31] ibid, 132 and Milanovic, 'Al-Skeini and Al-Jedda in Strasbourg' (n 14) 14–15.

[32] The Vienna Convention on the Law of Treaties 1969, Art 29 provides: 'Unless a different intention appears from the treaty or is otherwise established, a treaty is binding upon each party in respect of its entire territory'.

[33] See Moor and Simpson (n 20) 137.

[34] ibid, 144–47. Hendry and Dickson argue that the UK has adopted a general practice of not extending treaty commitments to its Overseas Territories. Accordingly they claim that the UK established has established a 'different intention' and that treaties concluded by the UK do not automatically apply to British Overseas Territories. See Hendry and Dickson, *British Overseas Territories Law* (n 26) 255–56.

[35] *Cyprus v Turkey* (1976) 4 EHRR 482.

territories. The Commission rejected this argument. It decided that Turkey's jurisdiction was engaged, under Article 1 of the Convention, for the acts and omissions of its military forces in connection with their occupation of Northern Cyprus. This conclusion was justified on the ground that Turkey was exercising authority and control over persons located in an area that was beyond Turkey's national territory (ie in a non-metropolitan territory). This early extra-territorial decision suggests that the relationship between Article 1 and Article 63 was not considered to be restrictive or exclusive in nature.

Nevertheless, in *Bui Van Thanh and Others v UK*, the Commission was faced with the reverse situation.[36] In that case, the applicants claimed that the UK's jurisdiction was engaged in respect of alleged violations of the European Convention committed in Hong Kong, even though the UK government had not made a declaration extending the Convention to that British Overseas Territory, pursuant to Article 63 of the Convention. The Commission concluded that the UK's jurisdiction was not engaged under Article 1 of the Convention in the absence of such a declaration.[37] Accordingly, in *Bui Van Thanh*, the Commission appeared to endorse the relational argument advanced by Turkey in the earlier case of *Cyprus v Turkey*, albeit indirectly. Thus, while the decision does not support the view that the Convention has no application beyond a Contracting State's national territory, it endorsed the view that State jurisdiction cannot be established in respect of an Overseas Territory, for which a Contracting State bears international responsibility, if the responsible State has not made a declaration under Article 63/56 of the Convention. At this stage in the evolution of the combined jurisprudence of the Commission and Court, the orthodox position appears to have been that if a Contracting State had not made a declaration extending the Convention to a given Overseas Territory pursuant to Article 63, the Convention could have no application in respect of that Territory.

This orthodox interpretation of Article 63/56 was endorsed more recently by the European Court of Human Rights in *Quark Fishing v UK*.[38] The case concerned a dispute which arose in the South Georgia and the South Sandwich Islands (SGSSI), a British Overseas Territory. The UK government had made a declaration under Article 63/56 which extended the European Convention to the SGSSI. However, it had not made a declaration extending Article 1 of Protocol 1 to the Convention to the SGSSI, in accordance with Article 4 of Protocol 1, which was drafted in similar terms to Article 63/56.[39] The question for the

---

[36] *Bui Van Thanh v UK* (1990) 65 *European Commission Decisions and Reports* 330.
[37] ibid.
[38] *Quark Fishing Company v UK* (2007) 44 EHRR SE4, 70.
[39] The ECHR, Protocol 1, Art 4 provides that:

Any High Contracting Party may at the time of signature or ratification or at any time thereafter communicate to the Secretary General of the Council of Europe a declaration stating the extent to which it undertakes that the provisions of the present Protocol shall apply to such of the territories for the international relations of which it is responsible as are named therein. Any High Contracting Party which has communicated a declaration in virtue of the preceding paragraph

Strasbourg Court in this case was whether Protocol 1 to the Convention applied in respect of the SGSSI. In answering that question the European Court observed that:

> Since there is no dispute as to the status of South Georgia and the South Sandwich Islands as a territory for whose international relations the United Kingdom is responsible within the meaning of Article 56, the Court finds that the Convention and Protocol cannot apply unless expressly extended by declaration. The fact that the United Kingdom has extended the Convention itself to the territory gives no ground for finding that Protocol No.1 must also apply or for the Court to require the United Kingdom somehow to justify its failure to extend that Protocol. There is no obligation under the Convention for any contracting state to ratify any particular protocol or to give reasons for its decisions in that regard concerning its national jurisdictions. Still less can there be any such obligation as regards the territories falling under the scope of Art.56 of the Convention.[40]

The Court was sympathetic to the applicant's contention that the 'territorial application' clause was anachronistic but it felt that its hands were tied. In its view, interpretation could only go so far and the Court could not rewrite the Convention's provisions – the system created by Article 63/56 could only be changed by amending the Convention itself.[41]

III. *AL-SKEINI* AND THE RELATIONSHIP
BETWEEN ARTICLE 1 AND ARTICLE 56 ECHR

The European Court's decision to reconceptualise the notion of State jurisdiction under Article 1 in *Al-Skeini* afforded it the opportunity to re-evaluate its view of the relationship between Article 1 and Article 56 of the Convention in the context of the spatial concept of State jurisdiction. The Court addressed the relationship between Article 1 and Article 56 directly in paragraph 140 of its judgment:

> The 'effective control' principle of jurisdiction . . . does not replace the system of declarations under art.56 of the Convention (formerly art.63) which the states decided, when drafting the Convention, to apply to territories overseas for whose international relations they were responsible. Article 56(1) provides a mechanism whereby any state may decide to extend the application of the Convention, 'with due regard . . . to local requirements', to all or any of the territories for whose international relations it is responsible. The existence of this mechanism, which was included in the Convention for historical reasons, cannot be interpreted in present conditions as limiting the scope of the term 'jurisdiction' in art.1. The situations covered by the 'effective control'

may from time to time communicate a further declaration modifying the terms of any former declaration or terminating the application of the provisions of this Protocol in respect of any territory.

[40] *Quark Fishing Company v UK* (2007) (n 38) 73.
[41] ibid, 73.

principle are clearly separate and distinct from circumstances where a contracting state has not, through a declaration under art.56, extended the Convention or any of its Protocols to an overseas territory for whose international relations it is responsible.

This paragraph has been viewed by some commentators as a signal of a move towards a more progressive interpretation of the Convention's extra-territorial reach, one which would render the colonial application clause, contained in Article 56, largely obsolete. In particular, Milanovic has suggested that: 'In para. 140 the Court attempted to end the difficult problem of the colonial clause in Art. 56 by saying that it is really no longer relevant to the application of Art. 1'.[42] The sentence in paragraph 140 which seems to support Milanovic's interpretation provides that: 'The existence of [the Article 56(63)] mechanism, which was included in the Convention for historical reasons, cannot be interpreted *in present conditions* as limiting the scope of the term "jurisdiction" in Article 1.'[43] If a temporal construction of this sentence is adopted it would appear that the Strasbourg Court in *Al-Skeini* distinguished between, on the one hand, the Article 56 system of declarations, which was created to address the question of the Convention's application to those colonial territories that still belonged to the Contracting States when the Convention was being drafted and, on the other, the contemporary post-colonial world where colonial possessions are considered to be objectionable and anachronistic. On this reading, the view that Article 56 can no longer represent an obstacle to an expansive and general interpretation of Article 1 in the extra-territorial context, must be correct.

However, it is suggested that the temporal construction of paragraph 140 is not sustainable in view of the Court's endorsement of the Article 56 system of declarations in the rest of paragraph 140. In this respect, it is clear that the Court was not trying to supplant and replace the Article 56 system with a more comprehensive interpretation of the effective control test of State jurisdiction pursuant to Article 1 of the Convention. The words 'in present conditions' in the above-mentioned sentence must be read as a reference to the factual circumstances under consideration in *Al-Skeini* rather than as a temporal counterpoint to the historical justification for the colonial application clause. Any other construction of this sentence would render the rest of paragraph 140 meaningless. The meaning and importance of this paragraph of the *Al-Skeini* judgment was vital to the Strasbourg Court's decision in the *Chagos Islanders* case.

IV. THE *CHAGOS ISLANDERS v UK* CASE

Before the alleged substantive violations of the Convention could be determined in the *Chagos Islanders* case, the question of whether the UK's jurisdiction was engaged for the purpose of applying the Convention to the BIOT had to be

[42] Milanovic (n 24) 129.
[43] Emphasis added.

decided, no Article 63/56 declaration having been made by the UK government in respect of the BIOT. The question for the Strasbourg Court in the *Chagos Islanders* case was whether the position adopted in *Quark Fishing* was still tenable in the light of the Court's decision in *Al-Skeini*.

In the *Chagos Islanders* case, the applicants claimed that paragraph 140 of the *Al-Skeini* judgment confirmed that Article 56 could not be viewed as limiting the scope of State jurisdiction, expressed in Article 1 of the Convention. They argued that the UK's jurisdiction was engaged under the Convention by reference to both the spatial and the personal modes of jurisdiction, as recognised in *Al-Skeini*. The applicants claimed that the UK government exercised effective territorial control over the BIOT during the relevant period. Accordingly, they argued that it was responsible for all the acts and omissions of the officials and agents of the BIOT administration *and* the acts and omissions of the UK's officials and agents. Alternatively, the applicants claimed that, as the BIOT was under the direct authority and control of the UK government, it was only nominally governed by the BIOT Commissioner. Consequently, the UK was responsible for all the acts and omissions of its own officials and agents in respect of the BIOT.

In response, the UK government argued that a Contracting State's jurisdiction for the purpose of applying the Convention to an Overseas Territory, for which it was internationally responsible, could only be established if a declaration had been made in respect of that Territory pursuant to Article 56 of the Convention. It reminded the Court that no such declaration had been made in respect of the BIOT. It claimed that such a position was in keeping with the Court's decision in *Quark Fishing*.[44] Consequently, the UK government claimed that, in *Al-Skeini*, the Court had not deviated from its previous jurisprudence. It relied on paragraph 140 of the *Al-Skeini* judgment in support of the contention that, in that case, the Strasbourg Court had not intended to replace the Article 56 system of declarations with a broad effective control test of State jurisdiction under Article 1 of the Convention.

In the *Chagos Islanders* case, the Court addressed the issue of the proper interpretation of paragraph 140 of the *Al-Skeini* judgment. It observed that, in that paragraph, the Court in *Al-Skeini* was responding to the UK government's argument that it would be absurd if Article 56 allowed a Contracting State to choose whether or not to extend the Convention to an Overseas Territory, for which it bears international responsibility, but that it had no choice about the Convention's application in respect of an area over which it only exercised temporary control as the result of military action.[45] It is important to note that, if this argument had been successful, the UK's jurisdiction could not have been

---

[44] *Quark Fishing Company v UK* (n 38) 73.
[45] *Chagos Islanders v UK* (n 1) [73]. Lord Brown agreed with the UK government's argument in the House of Lords. See *R (Al-Skeini and Others) v Secretary of State for Defence* [2008] 1 AC 153 [113].

engaged for the acts and omissions of its military forces in Southern Iraq during the relevant period. However, in *Al-Skeini*, the Court was not prepared to accept the UK government's argument regarding the correct relationship between Article 1 and Article 56. This information helps to put paragraph 140 of the *Al-Skeini* judgment into its proper context. It confirms that, in *Al-Skeini*, the Court was not providing an assessment of the temporal significance of Article 56. Instead, it was saying that Article 56 could not be used as a way of restricting the scope of State jurisdiction under Article 1 in general terms. Accordingly, it is clear that the sentence of paragraph 140 highlighted above was concerned with the factual circumstances prevailing in *Al-Skeini* rather than with contemporary viewpoint regarding the abhorrence of colonial possessions and thus, by implication, the necessary obsolescence of Article 56 of the Convention.

In the *Chagos Islanders* case, the Court noted that the applicants were arguing that it would be odd if a Contracting State's jurisdiction could be engaged anywhere in the world for a violation of the European Convention committed by its own officials/agents or where a violation is alleged to have occurred in a territorial unit which it effectively controlled, *except for* in situations where a Convention violation has occurred in an Overseas Territory for which the Contracting State bears international responsibility.[46] The applicants submitted that this would be a strange outcome given that Contracting States typically govern their Overseas Territories effectively. The Court accepted that Contracting States generally exercise authority and control over their Overseas Territories.[47] Further, it appreciated that the decision in *Al-Skeini* meant that, but for Article 56 of the Convention, a Contracting State's jurisdiction may be engaged under Article 1 of the Convention in connection with a violation allegedly committed in respect of an Overseas Territory for which it bears international responsibility. However, it noted that, if the notion of State jurisdiction under Article 1 is reduced to a factual assessment about the level of control exercised over a territorial unit by a Contracting State then Article 56 would be rendered redundant, in principle.[48]

Against this background, in the *Chagos Islanders* case, the Court held that *Quark Fishing* had not been wrongly decided, not least because the reasoning of that decision was adopted by the Grand Chamber in *Al-Skeini*.[49] Further, it reaffirmed that situations covered by the effective control test are 'clearly separate and distinct' from the sphere of operation of the system of declarations contained in Article 56.[50] It also appeared to indicate that the effective control test for State jurisdiction under Article 1 is confined to situations where a Contracting State exercises effective control of an area beyond its national

---

[46] *Chagos Islanders v UK* (n 1) [73].
[47] ibid, [75].
[48] ibid.
[49] ibid, [73]; and *Al-Skeini* (n 9) [140].
[50] *Chagos Islanders v UK* (n 1) [73]; and *Al-Skeini* (n 9) [140].

territory as a result of lawful or unlawful military action.[51] However, in this respect, the Court was simply reiterating the position it had adopted in *Loizidou v Turkey (Preliminary Objections)*, where that Court noted:

> Bearing in mind the object and purpose of the Convention, the responsibility of a Contracting Party may also arise when as a consequence of military action – whether lawful or unlawful – it exercises effective control of an area outside its national territory. The obligation to secure, in such an area, the rights and freedoms set out in the Convention, derives from the fact of such control whether it be exercised directly, through its armed forces, or through a subordinate local administration.[52]

The fact that the Court did not contemplate the possibility that the spatial approach to State jurisdiction might be applicable beyond the military context may be seen as significant. Nonetheless, the general approach adopted by the Court in the *Chagos Islanders* case demonstrated that the Grand Chamber in *Al-Skeini* was not endorsing a more expansive interpretation of the notion of State jurisdiction under Article 1 for the purpose of the Convention's extra-territorial application on spatial grounds. To this end, it expressly confirmed that, in general, the two *Al-Skeini* tests for extra-territorial State jurisdiction under Article 1 of the Convention do not trump the provisions of Article 56. Specifically, in paragraph 74 of its judgment, it stated that:

> Anachronistic as colonial remnants may be, the meaning of Article 56 is plain on its face and it cannot be ignored merely because of a perceived need to right an injustice. Article 56 remains a provision of the Convention which is in force and cannot be abrogated at will by the Court in order to reach a purportedly desirable result.

Nevertheless, in a tantalising manoeuvre, the Court raised the possibility that, in exceptional circumstances, the *Al-Skeini* tests for a finding of extra-territorial State jurisdiction might be applicable in the absence of an Article 56 declaration extending the Convention to a given Overseas Territory.[53] But, having raised the question, the Court was not prepared to answer it. In relation to the BIOT, it decided that the *Chagos Islanders* case would have failed on its merits, in any event.[54] Specifically, the Court concluded that the applicants had lost their victim status under Article 13 of the Convention as a result of the compensation that they had already received and/or the judicial determination of their complaints by the English courts pursuant to Article 6 of the Convention.[55]

The question of whether exceptional circumstances warranted the Convention's extra-territorial application in relation to the events complained about in the *Chagos Islanders* case should have been considered irrespective of whether the case would have succeeded on its merits. A given individual can

---

[51] *Chagos Islanders v UK* (n 1) [70].
[52] See eg *Loizidou v Turkey (Preliminary Objections)* (n 17) [62].
[53] *Chagos Islanders v UK* (n 1) [75].
[54] ibid, [76].
[55] See ch 1.

only possess human rights, as guaranteed by the European Convention, if it can be shown that he or she comes within the jurisdiction of a Contracting State under Article 1 of the Convention. If the threshold requirement of jurisdiction can be established the next step is to determine whether that individual's Convention rights have, in fact, been violated. In contrast, in the *Chagos Islanders* case, the European Court decided that the State party's jurisdiction was not engaged because any rights that the Chagos Islanders may have possessed had been undermined by the summary conclusion that they had lost their status as victims. This approach overlooks the staged approach ordinarily followed by courts when determining cases. The preliminary issue of whether the UK's jurisdiction had been engaged under Article 1 of the Convention should have been considered first. If it could have been established, on the facts, that the UK's jurisdiction had been engaged under Article 1 then it would follow that the Chagos Islanders possessed Convention rights and the UK was subject to the corresponding Convention obligations in respect of the BIOT. The question of whether exceptional circumstances would have justified a finding of State jurisdiction should have been considered as part of the assessment of whether the applicants' case was admissible. If the *Chagos Islanders* case was held to be admissible then the Court was under a duty to determine whether the human rights of the Chagos Islanders had been violated. While courts often consider questions of admissibility and merits together they do not usually consider them in reverse. In refusing to consider whether the UK's jurisdiction was established in relation to the BIOT, under Article 1, in respect of the claims made against it by the Chagos Islanders, the European Court was engaging in a blatant act of backwards reasoning. Consequently, it can be argued that the decision in this case perpetuates the confusion in the Court's jurisprudence concerning the circumstances in which the Convention's extra-territorial reach is legitimate. In particular, it demonstrates the Court's lack of confidence in principles, which it developed in a number cases over a considerable period of time, and which were recently clarified and reinforced in *Al-Skeini*, to regulate the notion of State jurisdiction for the purpose of applying the Convention on an extra-territorial basis. Further, it is important to draw attention to the fact that the meagre level of compensation paid to Chagossians was offered long after they were exiled to Mauritius. Accordingly, the fact that the chronically impoverished Chagossians took the money cannot be construed as a validation of the UK's involuntary displacement of the BIOT's permanent population and it should not be used as a justification for withholding the benefit of the rights contained in the Convention from the Chagos Islanders in this context.

In the light of the above and given that the Court accepted that, in principle, the Convention could apply to an Overseas Territory, in exceptional circumstances, in respect of a given Overseas Territory – in the absence of a declaration of extension made under Article 56 – the question of which of the bases for State jurisdiction, under Article 1 of the Convention, would be applicable in such a situation should be considered.

V. THE GOVERNANCE OF BRITISH OVERSEAS TERRITORIES

However, before addressing the question of which of the bases for State jurisdiction, under Article 1 of the Convention, would be applicable in relation to an Overseas Territory belonging to a Contracting State it is useful to consider the governance of British Overseas Territories in general terms. To this end, it is helpful to draw a distinction between those British Overseas Territories which are sparsely populated or not inhabited on a permanent basis and those British Overseas Territories that support more substantial populations. Regarding the former category, the BIOT, the SGSSI, the British Antarctic Territory (BAT) and the Sovereign Base Areas in Cyprus (SBAs) are not inhabited on a permanent basis.[56] The BIOT, SGSSI, BAT and SBAs are non-autonomous constitutional units with governmental and legislative authority for each Overseas Territory being vested in a non-resident Commissioner who acts, constitutionally, in accordance with the instruction of the UK government in relation to the exercise of all or some of their constitutional responsibilities.[57] Pitcairn Island supports a tiny permanent population of approximately 50 individuals. The permanent inhabitants of Pitcairn Island lack a meaningful degree of constitutional autonomy. It is governed by a non-resident Governor who retains considerable legislative authority and is not bound to consult with the Island Council before enacting legislation for this Overseas Territory.[58]

In a 1999 White Paper, *Partnership for Progress and Prosperity: Britain and the Overseas Territories*, the UK government set out its vision for the development of British Overseas Territories.[59] It stated that policy would be based on four principles: (i) constitutionality; (ii) autonomy; (iii) self-determination; and (iv) economic development.[60] The promotion of good governance in British Overseas Territories was reiterated in a 2006 White Paper, *Active Diplomacy for a Changing World*.[61] This White Paper identified the security and good government of British Overseas Territories as one of its strategic priorities. It stated that one of the ways in which this strategic priority would be satisfied was by ensuring that the UK meets its international legal obligations to its Overseas Territories.[62] Writing in

---

[56] The BIOT's permanent population was involuntarily displaced by the UK government and its colonial officials and agents between 1965 and 1973.

[57] See Moor and Simpson (n 20) 160–64.

[58] A new constitution was established by the Pitcairn Constitution Order in Council 2010. See T Angelo and R Kessbohm, 'The New Constitution of Pitcairn: A Primer' (2009) 7 *New Zealand Yearbook of International Law* 285.

[59] (Cm 4264, 1999).

[60] These principles were identified in the foreword written by then Foreign Secretary, Robin Cook, ibid, 4–5.

[61] (Cm 6762, 2006).

[62] ibid, 39. The UK government issued a set of Departmental Strategic Objectives for the period 2008–11, in which the relationship between the UK and its Overseas Territories was not mentioned. The current position of the UK government in respect of British Overseas Territories is set out in its 2012 White Paper, *The Overseas Territories: Security, Success and Sustainability* (Cm 8374, 2012).

2006, Moor and Simpson doubted whether the guiding principles concerning the good governance of British Overseas Territories set in the 1999 White Paper could be satisfied in relation to the BIOT, SGSSI, BAT or SBAs which they labelled 'British Non-Autonomous Overseas Territories' (BNOTs).[63] The lack of political autonomy in such Territories is significant for the purpose of establishing State jurisdiction under Article 1 of the European Convention both with regard to the State agent authority and control approach and the effective territorial control approach.

VI. THE PERSONAL AND SPATIAL MODES OF STATE JURISDICTION

In the *Chagos Islanders* case, the applicants' case appeared to manifest a preference in favour of the State agent authority and control test for jurisdiction. This may have stemmed from the narrow interpretation of the effective control test adopted in *Loizidou v Turkey (Preliminary Objections)*, where the Court tied the notion of effective control to situations of involving the lawful or unlawful use of military action.[64] Further, the Chagos Islanders' apparent preference for the personal mode of jurisdiction may have reflected the fact that although, in *Al-Skeini*, the Court endorsed the effective control test as a legitimate basis for a finding of extra-territorial State jurisdiction, it chose to apply the State agent authority and control test, on the facts.[65] In addition, it may be significant that, in the *Chagos Islanders* case, the Court seemed to respond to the applicants' case by reference to the State agent authority and control test of jurisdiction when it noted that: 'Contracting States generally did, and do, *exercise authority and control* over their overseas territories'.[66]

The potential significance of the authority and control approach to State jurisdiction in relation to the Overseas Territories was noted in *Loizidou v Turkey (Preliminary Objections)* where the Court reflected upon the scope of Article 63 (now Article 56). Specifically, it observed that:

> Article 63 concerns a decision by a Contracting Party to assume full responsibility under the Convention for all the acts of public authorities in respect of a territory for whose international relations it is responsible.[67]

This formulation does not deny the possibility that extra-territorial State jurisdiction could not arise for *specific* acts undertaken in respect of a given Overseas Territory by the officials/agents of the responsible Contracting State by reference to the authority and control test (as opposed to *all* the acts undertaken by a local administration).[68] However, it is suggested that the value of this test as a

---

[63] Moor and Simpson (n 20) 163–64.
[64] *Loizidou v Turkey (Preliminary Objections)* (n 17).
[65] *Al-Skeini* (n 9).
[66] *Chagos Islanders v UK* (n 1) [75]. Emphasis added.
[67] *Loizidou v Turkey (Preliminary Objections)* (n 17) [88].
[68] Moor and Simpson (n 20) 182.

means of establishing the jurisdiction of a Contracting State for the acts and/or omissions of its own agents and officials in relation to one of its Overseas Territories is open to question.

The State agent authority and control approach to State jurisdiction, under Article 1 of the Convention, imputes jurisdiction to a Contracting State for the acts and/or omissions of its own officials/agents. The adoption of this approach to State jurisdiction in relation to Overseas Territories would ensure that jurisdiction, pursuant to Article 1, could only arise in highly exceptional circumstances. Consequently, the Article 56 system of declarations would remain generally intact as an Overseas Territory will, typically, have its own specially devised constitutional arrangements and its own officials/agents. Accordingly, the jurisdiction of a Contracting State would not be engaged for the conduct of the officials/agents of the local administration of an Overseas Territory, *unless* an Article 56 declaration had been made in respect of that Territory. The State agent authority and control test for jurisdiction under Article 1 would allow the Article 56 system of declarations to be circumvented only when the officials/ agents of the responsible Contracting State exercised direct authority and control over a particular Overseas Territory.

While there is some merit in the above approach, it is suggested that it does not reflect the close relationship that exists between a Contracting State and an Overseas Territory for which it bears international responsibility. Two points are worth making in this regard. First, the State agent authority and control approach does not acknowledge the fact that the governmental institutions of an Overseas Territory are created by the municipal legislative mechanisms of the responsible Contracting State. Secondly, this approach fails to attach sufficient weight to the fact that Overseas Territories will usually be directly controlled by the government of that Contracting State, notwithstanding the distinct formal constitutional arrangements made for such an Overseas Territory by the responsible State. It should be acknowledged that the constitutional arrangements made for any Overseas Territory are liable to be *sui generis* and the integrity of any such arrangements must be evaluated on a case by case basis. However, in relation to the four BNOTs identified above (and also with regard to Pitcairn), there can be no doubt that these Overseas Territories are hollow constitutional entities that possesses no meaningful political autonomy and have no separate governmental existence from the Contracting State that exercises sovereignty over it.

In relation to these Overseas Territories, the State agent authority and control approach is under-inclusive. In general, it allows for a formal constitutional distinction to be drawn between the officials/agents of the responsible Contracting State and the nominal officials/agents of the local administration of a given Overseas Territory. Although the authority and control approach enables this constitutional separation to be set aside in exceptional circumstances, it upholds the validity of this distinction in general terms. Therefore, while this approach maintains the overall integrity of the Article 56 system of declarations, it does not reflect the constitutional reality that Overseas Territories are, invariably, effectively governed by the Contracting State that exercises sovereignty over them.

However, the adoption of a spatial approach to State jurisdiction in respect of a Contracting State's Overseas Territories also appears to be problematic. While, in *Al-Skeini*, the Court confirmed that a Contracting State's jurisdiction can be engaged beyond the combined metropolitan territory of the Member States of the Council of Europe, it held that such a finding can only be justified in exceptional circumstances.[69] In *Al-Skeini*, the European Court observed that, in general: 'It is a question of fact whether a contracting state exercises effective control over an area outside its own territory'.[70] Although, in *Al-Skeini*, the Court was careful to distinguish between situations where the general spatial test of State jurisdiction would apply and the operation of the system of declarations created by Article 63/56 vis-a-vis Overseas Territories, the resonance of the effective territorial control approach cannot be ignored in the context of Overseas Territories, as a matter of principle. As noted above, a particular difficulty in applying the effective control test of State jurisdiction to Overseas Territories arises from the constitutional reality that Contracting States invariably control their Overseas Territories effectively.[71] Accordingly, if the effective control approach could be applied in relation to Overseas Territories it would seem to be *over-inclusive*. It would attribute jurisdiction to a responsible Contracting State for *all* the acts and omissions of officials/agents within a given Overseas Territory (ie for both the officials/agents of the local territorial administration and the officials/agents of the responsible Contracting State). Consequently, in this context, the spatial test of State jurisdiction would ignore the *formal* constitutional separation that exists between the Contracting State and an Overseas Territory.[72] As a result, if the jurisdiction of a Contracting State could be engaged, under Article 1 of the Convention, in relation to an Overseas Territory, on spatial grounds, the exceptional nature of the Convention's extra-territorial application would be lost in favour of the general application of an effective territorial control test, which would render the system of declarations contained in Article 56 redundant in turn.

The issue of the Convention's application to those Overseas Territories belonging to Contracting States can be cast as a contest about the relative importance attached to values of formalism and effectiveness. From a formalist standpoint, a valid constitutional distinction exists between the Contracting State and the Overseas Territory for which it bears international responsibility, a distinction that emanates from the municipal law of the responsible State. This distinction is especially significant in relation to the non-autonomous

---

[69] *Al-Skeini* (n 9) [131] and [142].

[70] ibid, [139].

[71] ibid, [140].

[72] It is accepted that this formal separation would have been created by the municipal law of the responsible Contracting State in any event.

British Overseas Territories, identified above. Moreover, the constitutional order created for that Overseas Territory is invariably the product of the municipal legislative processes of that State. Consequently, in general, the governmental and legislative arrangements made for an Overseas Territory leave no doubt that the Contracting State exercises authority over such a Territory. This position is reinforced by international law, which recognises that a Contracting State exercises sovereignty over its Overseas Territories. However, as discussed above, the formalist approach ignores the extent to which the responsible Contracting State effectively controls its Overseas Territories. In the British context, the value of effectiveness is especially significant in relation to those Territories that lack any political autonomy and which are controlled more or less directly by the UK government.

The balance between formalism and effectiveness may have been weighted in favour of the former in the period before *Loizidou* was decided by the European Court. However, it has looked increasingly untenable since that decision. Further, any justification for clinging to a formalist interpretation of the Convention's extra-territorial reach, at least as far as Overseas Territories are concerned, has been shattered, in principle, by the Strasbourg Court's decision in *Al-Skeini*. This argument remains valid notwithstanding the Court's general endorsement of the continuing significance of the Article 56 system of declarations in relation to those Overseas Territories which still belong to the Contracting States. The Court's recognition, in *Al-Skeini*, that State jurisdiction under Article 1 of the Convention is triggered – thereby potentially giving rise to a finding of State responsibility – in any situation where a Contracting State exercises the public powers normally exercisable by a sovereign government and where Convention rights are violated by reference to either the personal or spatial modes of jurisdiction. This approach shifts the balance decisively in favour of the value of effectiveness. The ramifications of this shift in relation to those Overseas Territories, which belong to the Contracting States, are obvious regardless of the provisions found in Article 56 of the Convention.

VII. DIVIDING AND TAILORING CONVENTION OBLIGATIONS IN THE EXTRA-TERRITORIAL CONTEXT

An established standpoint of international human rights law is that all human rights are indivisible and interdependent: specific human rights contribute to an overall package of rights which protect and promote the human dignity of all individuals and groups of individuals.[73] However, this holistic approach may have negative ramifications in certain situations because it suggests that the cor-

---

[73] The Vienna Declaration and Programme of Action was the product of the UN World Conference on Human Rights (1993), which involved 171 States and a significant number on non-governmental organisations. It was subsequently endorsed by UNGA Res 48/121 (1993). See (1993) 32 *International Legal Materials* 1661

responding obligations owed by States must be, likewise, indivisible and inter-dependent.[74] In principle, a State must be able to satisfy *all* the obligations which are binding upon it under a treaty to which it is a party in situations where the corresponding human rights have been triggered. It follows that if, in a given extra-territorial situation, a Contracting State cannot satisfy *all* the obligations that it owes to those individuals who are within its jurisdiction, under Article 1 of the European Convention, it is not under a duty to meet *any* of the obligations imposed upon it by virtue of the Convention.[75]

In general, international human rights law distinguishes between negative and positive obligations. A State may be subject to a negative obligation to refrain from interfering with the rights of an individual who comes within its jurisdiction. For example, a State might be under an obligation to prevent its officials and agents from violating the prohibition on torture of an individual, pursuant to Article 3 of the Convention.[76] This negative obligation relates directly to the conduct of the State itself via its officials/agents. In contrast, positive obligations impose a duty on the responsible State to secure the Convention rights of all those individuals who come within its jurisdiction. For instance, a responsible Contracting State must protect the individuals who are within its jurisdiction from torture committed by other private individuals and third parties. In short, the responsible State must create the environment in which the right to not to suffer torture is protected in general terms for those individuals who come within its jurisdiction.[77] Positive obligations presuppose that a Contracting State has the capacity to establish the institutional structures required to meet its positive obligations in a particular setting irrespective of whether it has, in fact, put such measures in place.[78] Consequently, it is important to appreciate that, when positive obligations are imposed on a State, an additional criterion of whether it is feasible for the Contracting State to meet such obligations does not arise.[79]

In *Bankovic*, the European Court of Human Rights indicated that Convention rights could *not* be divided and tailored in relation to the specific acts which led to the violations of the Convention alleged in that case.[80] Consequently, under Article 1, in order for the jurisdiction of the Contracting States, which participated in the NATO aerial bombing campaign of the Federal Republic of Yugoslavia, to have been engaged on the facts of *Bankovic*, they would have needed to be in a position to be able to satisfy both the negative and the positive

---

[74] Milanovic (n 14) 57.

[75] See *Bankovic* (n 9) [75] and following.

[76] The ECHR, Art 3(1) provides that: 'No one shall be subjected to torture or to inhuman or degrading treatment or punishment'.

[77] See Milanovic (n 14) 46. See also the *Genocide Convention* case *(Bosnia and Herzegovina v Serbia and Montenegro)* (2007) ICJ Rep 43.

[78] The European Convention does not expressly distinguish between negative and positive obligations. However, this distinction has been assumed and the Court in *Al-Skeini* endorsed this assumption; see below.

[79] See Besson, 'The Extraterritoriality of the European Convention on Human Rights' (n 9) 868.

[80] See *Bankovic* (n 9) [75] and Milanovic (n 14) 57.

obligations contained in the Convention in that particular extra-territorial context. As the Contracting States involved in this campaign were not in a position to meet all the obligations contained in the Convention it could not be said that they were exercising the public powers normally exercisable by a sovereign government in that situation. Accordingly, the Court concluded that the jurisdiction of the Contracting States involved in the bombing campaign was not engaged under Article 1 of the Convention.

However, in *Al-Skeini*, the Court expressly reversed the approach adopted in *Bankovic*. At paragraph 137 of its judgment, it stated:

> It is clear that, whenever the state through its agents exercises control and authority over an individual, and thus jurisdiction, the state is under an obligation under art.1 to secure to that individual the rights and freedoms under s.1 of the Convention that are relevant to the situation of that individual. In this sense, therefore, the Convention rights can be 'divided and tailored' (compare Bankovic . . . para. 75).

Therefore, in *Al-Skeini*, the Court held that a distinction could be drawn between negative and positive obligations, at least where the State agent authority and control basis of jurisdiction is being applied. Accordingly, in such a situation, the responsible Contracting State could be under an obligation to satisfy its negative obligations under the Convention without being under a duty to secure the positive obligations contained in the Convention as well.

In relation to the spatial basis for jurisdiction under Article 1, in *Loizidou v Turkey (Preliminary Objections)*, the Court decided that Turkey's effective overall control of Northern Cyprus meant that it was subject to both the positive and the negative obligations imposed by the Convention in respect of that territory.[81] Accordingly, Turkey's jurisdiction was engaged not only in respect of any violations carried out by its own officials/agents but also in respect of any violations of the Convention committed in Northern Cyprus, the area which it controlled as a result of military occupation.

In contrast to the approach it adopted for the purpose of applying the personal mode of jurisdiction, the European Court in *Al-Skeini* recognised that if a Contracting State effectively controlled an area then the obligations contained in the Convention could *not* be divided and tailored. Consequently, where jurisdiction could be established on spatial grounds, both the Convention's negative and positive obligations would be imposed on the responsible Contracting State. The Court made this point clear in its judgment:

> Another exception to the principle that jurisdiction under art.1 is limited to a state's own territory occurs when, as a consequence of lawful or unlawful military action, a contracting state exercises effective control of an area outside that national territory. The obligation to secure, in such an area, the rights and freedoms set out in the Convention, derives from the fact of such control, whether it be exercised directly, through the Contracting state's own armed forces, or through a subordinate local administration. Where the fact of such domination over the territory is established, it

---

[81] See *Loizidou v Turkey (Preliminary Objections)* (n 17) [62], quoted above.

is not necessary to determine whether the contracting state exercises detailed control over the policies and actions of the subordinate local administration. The fact that the local administration survives as a result of the contracting state's military and other support entails that state's responsibility for its policies and actions. The *controlling state has the responsibility under art.1 to secure, within the area under its control, the entire range of substantive rights set out in the Convention* and those additional Protocols which it has ratified. It will be liable for any violations of those rights.[82]

The Court's jurisprudence reveals a significant difference between the personal and spatial bases for jurisdiction under Article 1 of the European Convention. Rather than being separate routes to the same range of entitlements, it appears that any of the substantive rights contained in the Convention may be claimed where a responsible State effectively controls the territorial unit in issue. This position clearly enhances the appeal of the spatial approach to establishing State jurisdiction under Article 1, especially in relation to violations of the Convention which are alleged to have occurred in an Overseas Territory belonging to a Contracting State.

VIII. THE NORMATIVE FOUNDATIONS OF THE CONVENTION'S EXTRA-TERRITORIAL APPLICATION

The relationship between Article 1 and Article 56 of the Convention should be re-evaluated in order to place the notion of State jurisdiction on firmer normative foundations. In particular, the question of whether the extra-territorial reach of the Convention should be exceptional – at least in relation to a Contracting State's Overseas Territories – should be reconsidered. As noted above, in both *Bankovic* and *Al-Skeini*, the Strasbourg Court confirmed that the European Convention can only be applied extra-territorially in exceptional circumstances. One reason for this requirement is that the notion of State jurisdiction contained in Article 1 of the Convention presupposes the existence of a normative relationship between a Contracting State, on the one hand, and the individual alleging that his or her Convention rights have been violated, on the other. It has been observed that Raz's conception of authority supports this interpretation of the notion of State jurisdiction.[83] A Contracting State can be viewed as a de facto political and legal authority that provides its subjects with normative guidance by issuing directives which are accompanied by corresponding appeals for compliance.[84] Individuals qualify as subjects because, in general,

---

[82] *Al-Skeini* (n 9) [138]. Emphasis added.

[83] J Raz, 'The Problem of Authority: Revisiting the Service Conception' (2006) 90 *Minnesota Law Review* 1003. Besson refers to Raz's *Ethics in the Public Domain: Essays in the Morality of Law and Politics* (1995) to make the same point (n 9) 865. I have used Raz's service conception of authority in relation to the UK jurisdiction over the Pitcairn Islands, another British Overseas Territory. See S Allen, 'The Pitcairn Prosecutions and the Rule of Law' (2012) 75 *Modern Law Review* 1150.

[84] Raz, 'The Problem of Authority: Revisiting the Service Conception' (n 83) 1017 and Besson (n 9) 865.

they are located within a Contracting State's national territory.[85] However, as discussed above, the notion of State jurisdiction under Article 1 of the Convention is not confined to the national territory of a Contracting State.[86] In this regard, given that the responsible State exercises territorial sovereignty over its Overseas Territories as a matter of international law, it is clear that the inhabitants of an Overseas Territory are in an analogous position to those individuals situated in a Contracting State's national territory.

According to Raz, a claim made by a de facto political and legal authority is not the same thing as the exercise of coercive power because it amounts to a normative claim which is founded on an appeal to legitimacy.[87] As noted above, invariably, a State makes a claim of authority and, thus, a claim of jurisdiction, by reference to its own municipal law. Further, as the officials/agents of a State are products of its municipal legal system, their acts and omissions must be interpreted as legal forms of conduct irrespective of whether or not their acts or omissions are deemed to be ultra vires.[88] Besson argues that, with regard to the notion of State jurisdiction contained in Article 1 of the European Convention, the political and legal circumstances that create a normative relationship between an authority and its subjects can be established where a Contracting State exercises effective overall control over a range of interdependent stakes in a normative fashion.[89] That is why a Contracting State must exercise some or all of the public powers normally exercisable by a sovereign government in a given situation in order for its jurisdiction to be engaged under the Convention.[90] This requirement amounts to a significant constraint on the extra-territorial application of the European Convention. A Contracting State will not typically have created the political and legal environment that would give rise to a normative relationship between itself and an individual (or a group of individuals) located beyond its national territory. The absence of such a normative relationship explains why, in *Bankovic*, the actions of the Contracting States involved in the bombing campaign against the Federal Republic of Yugoslavia did not result in a finding that their jurisdiction had been engaged for the purpose of Article 1 of the Convention. By reaffirming the requirement that a Contracting State must be exercising the public powers normally exercisable by a sovereign government in such a situation, the Court in *Al-Skeini* reiterated the normative basis of State jurisdiction. It re-established the need for a political and legal relationship to exist between a Contracting State (authority) and the addressees of its normative guidance (subjects) before a finding of State jurisdiction can be made under Article 1 of the Convention.[91]

---

[85] Individuals could qualify as subjects by other routes, including by virtue of their nationality. See the bases of jurisdiction identified above.

[86] See Besson (n 9) 862–63. See *Bankovic* (n 9) [61] and [67]; and *Al-Skeini* (n 9) [131].

[87] Raz (n 83) 1005 and Besson (n 9) 865.

[88] This legal status derives from the fact that such officials/agents are authorised to represent the State by lawfully organised constitutional arrangements; Besson (n 9) 865.

[89] ibid, 866.

[90] See *Bankovic* (n 9) [71]; and Besson (n 9) 866.

[91] See *Al-Skeini* (n 9) [149]; and Besson (n 9) 866.

In sharp contrast, the constitutional and legislative arrangements made by a Contracting State for its Overseas Territories *do* create the political and legal circumstances which enable normative relationships to be developed between an authority (the responsible Contracting State) and its subjects (the inhabitants of a given Overseas Territory). However, it should be acknowledged that such normative relationships are mediated through constitutional arrangements which have been devised for an Overseas Territory by the responsible State.[92] This raises the important question of whether the creation of such subordinate constitutional legal orders represents an exercise of State jurisdiction by the responsible State. If a State is deemed to create a separate constitutional regime which establishes a distinct municipal legal order for an Overseas Territory, for which it is internationally responsible, it would be possible to argue that the governance of such a Territory cannot be attributed to that State. Consequently, it could be argued that its jurisdiction would not be engaged pursuant to Article 1 of the European Convention for the acts and omissions of an Overseas Territory's local administration. However, if an Overseas Territory is not endowed with the governmental arrangements that enable its inhabitants to engage in meaningful representative government, it is inconceivable that such an Overseas Territory could be said to have a separate government which is distinct from the government of the responsible Contracting State. Accordingly, on this view, the jurisdiction of a Contracting State should be engaged in relation to the governance of its Overseas Territories, in principle.

IX. CONSTITUENT AND LEGISLATIVE AUTHORITY IN BRITISH OVERSEAS TERRITORIES

The view that each British Overseas Territory has a government which is separate from the government of the UK was considered by the House of Lords in *Quark Fishing*.[93] This case concerned a challenge to the lawfulness of a decision to withhold the grant of a fishing licence in respect of the South Georgia and the South Sandwich Islands (SGSSI). The decision was made by the SGSSI Commissioner, acting on the instruction of the Crown, which was acting in accordance with the advice given to it by the UK Foreign Secretary, pursuant to section 5(1) of the SGSSI Order in Council 1985, which established the SGSSI's constitutional framework. A central question in this case was in what capacity was the Crown discharging its constitutional responsibilities in respect of the SGSSI? If it was acting in right of the UK, the Crown would constitute a UK public authority for the purpose of applying the Human Rights Act 1998 and a

---

[92] eg in the UK context, British Overseas Territories are constitutionally separate from the UK and from one another. See Hendry and Dickson (n 26) 22–27.

[93] R *(Quark Fishing Ltd) v Secretary of State for Foreign and Commonwealth Affairs* [2006] 1 AC 529 (HL). See A Twomey, 'Responsible Government and the Divisibility of the Crown' (2008) *Public Law* 742.

challenge to the decision would be permissible under UK law.[94] However, if the Crown was acting in right of the SGSSI, UK law would be inapplicable and the decision could not be so challenged.

The House of Lords decided that, in discharging its constitutional responsibilities in respect of the SGSSI, the Crown was acting in right of SGSSI, not in right of the UK. It held that this outcome was justified by the doctrine of the divisibility of the Crown, which holds that the Crown has distinct constitutional rights and obligations in relation to each and every Territory of which it is sovereign.[95] Consequently, the SGSSI not only had a government that was separate from the UK government,[96] the municipal law applicable in that territory was not UK law; instead, it was the separate municipal legal order created by the 1985 SGSSI Order. It is worth noting that, under the constitutional regime created by the 1985 Order, the SGSSI is governed by a non-resident Commissioner who acts on the instructions of the Crown via the recommendations of the UK Foreign Secretary. It has no permanent inhabitants and thus no representative government. The only way that the SGSSI could be said to possess responsible government would be by virtue of the fact that the UK Foreign Secretary is accountable to the UK Parliament for the advice that he or she has given to the Crown.[97] Accordingly, from a doctrinal standpoint, it has been suggested that the Crown acts in respect of the SGSSI, in its capacity as the Crown of the UK even though it is discharging its constitutional responsibilities in respect of the SGSSI.[98]

The House of Lords subsequently revised its interpretation of the doctrine of the divisibility of the Crown in *Bancoult 2*.[99] Lord Hoffmann admitted that the conclusion that the Crown necessarily acts in right of a particular British Overseas Territory when it legislates for such a territory by Order in Council was incorrect.[100] Specifically, he observed that:

> Her Majesty exercises her powers of prerogative legislation for a non-self-governing colony on the advice of her ministers in the United Kingdom and will act in the

---

[94] The Human Rights Act 1998, s 6(1) provides that: 'It is unlawful for a public authority to act in a way which is incompatible with a Convention right'. Under s 7(1): 'A person who claims that a public authority has acted (or proposes to act) in a way which is made unlawful by section 6(1) may (a) bring proceedings against the authority under this Act in the appropriate court or tribunal, or (b) rely on the Convention right or rights concerned in any legal proceedings'.

[95] However, Finnis was highly critical of this interpretation of constitutional theory and practice. See J Finnis, 'Common Law Constraints: Whose Common Good Counts?' (2008) University of Oxford Law Faculty Legal Studies Research Paper Series, Working Paper No 10/2008 [17–19].

[96] However, it should be noted that the existence of separate governments is not indicative of independence. See the judgment of Kerr LJ in the Court of Appeal in *R v Secretary of State for Foreign and Commonwealth Affairs, ex p Indian Association of Alberta* [1982] QB 892 and the House of Lords in *Quark Fishing* (n 93) [72].

[97] This was the conclusion of reached by Baroness Hale in the House of Lords, at [94] and see Twomey, 'Responsible Government and the Divisibility of the Crown' (n 93) 746.

[98] See Twomey (n 93) 760–61.

[99] See *Bancoult 2* (HL) (n 2).

[100] ibid, [48].

interests of her undivided realm, including both the United Kingdom and the colony: see Halsbury's *Laws of England* (4th ed 2003 reissue) vol 6, para 716:

> 'The United Kingdom and its dependent territories within Her Majesty's domin-ions form one realm having one undivided Crown . . . To the extent that a depend-ency has responsible government, the Crown's representative in the dependency acts on the advice of local ministers responsible to the local legislature, but in respect of any dependency of the United Kingdom (that is, of any British overseas territory) acts of Her Majesty herself are performed only on the advice of the United Kingdom government.'[101]

Further, Lord Hoffmann observed a consequence of the legislative notion of the Crown's undivided realm was that:

> Her Majesty in Council is . . . entitled to legislate for a colony in the interests of the United Kingdom. No doubt she is also required to take into account the interests of the colony . . . but there seems to me no doubt that in the event of a conflict of inter-est, she is entitled, on the advice of Her United Kingdom ministers, to prefer the inter-ests of the United Kingdom.[102]

It follows from the notion of the Crown's undivided realm of the UK and its Overseas Territories that British Overseas Territories have no distinct sover-eignty of their own. According to Hendry and Dickson:

> Self-evidently, it is through the retention of legislative and executive powers and, where considered necessary or expedient, the exercise of those powers in the interests of the United Kingdom, or the United Kingdom and its overseas territories as a whole, that the United Kingdom maintains ultimate control of the British overseas territo-ries, for which the United Kingdom Government is responsible.[103]

Finnis developed the notion of the undivided realm further by connecting it to the concept of the 'common good'. In his view:

> [Orders in Council] are acts of the UK Government in the exercise of its responsibility for the common good – the peace, order and good government – of the United Kingdom and all its dependencies . . . The legal doctrine that there is one undivided realm and Crown of the United Kingdom and its dependent territories corresponds to the moral and political reality that the common good of each part is dependent on the common good of the whole. If the UK is conquered or subverted or economically ruined or impoverished, the common good of each dependent territory is more or less radically affected, presumptively for the worse.[104]

The Crown in Council possesses original constituent authority in respect of the BIOT pursuant to the royal prerogative and therefore the BIOT Order 1965, the BIOT Constitution Order 2004 and the BIOT Immigration Order 2004 all

---

[101] ibid, [47].
[102] ibid, [47–49]. See also the Opinions of the other Law Lords, at [114], [120] and [132] on this issue.
[103] Hendry and Dickson (n 26) 24.
[104] Finnis, 'Common Law Constraints' (n 95) [20].

constitute primary legislation.[105] Moreover, in *Bancoult 2*, the House of Lords unanimously held that Orders in Council are amenable to judicial review in the UK courts according to the established grounds for review.[106] Consequently, any constitutional or legislative regime created for the BIOT by Order in Council finds its source in the UK municipal legal system.[107] In other words, the source of the constitutional framework created for the BIOT is UK law even though such constitutional arrangements have no direct application within the UK itself. The same reasoning can be extended to all British Overseas Territories.[108] Therefore, although British Overseas Territories are constitutionally separate and distinct from the UK,[109] the authority of the Crown to enact Orders in Council for the purpose of establishing the constitutional order of an Overseas Territory, or to enact primary legislation for that Territory, represents an exercise of the UK's jurisdiction over such a Territory as a matter of UK municipal law.[110] This position is consistent with the notion of the Crown's undivided realm and also with the fact that the UK exercises sovereignty over its Overseas Territories as a matter of international law.

X. SUBORDINATE LEGISLATIVE AUTHORITY

In contrast to the Crown in Council's constituent authority in respect of the BIOT and its capacity to enact primary legislation for that Overseas Territory, the BIOT Commissioner, as a subordinate legislature, exercises his or her authority in right of the BIOT only. Nevertheless, the Divisional Court in *Bancoult 1* confirmed that subordinate colonial legislation is subject to judicial review in the UK courts. As a result, the 1971 Ordinance was susceptible to judicial review. As Laws LJ stated in that case:

> Indeed, I have to say that the Crown's reliance on the proposition that the Ordinance is a legal creature of the government of BIOT which must be taken to possess a separate and distinct sovereignty of its own, such that the Queen's courts sitting here in London have nothing to do with the matter, represents in my judgment an abject

[105] This was confirmed by the House of Lords in *Bancoult 2* (n 2) [34].
[106] ibid,[35].
[107] Moreover, any such arrangements may be amended or repealed by the legislative mechanisms of the UK legal system.
[108] See Twomey (n 93) 762–63, in respect of the SGSSI. It is important to note that the constituent power differs in respect of different British Overseas Territories. In certain Territories the constitutional framework has been created or supplemented by Acts of the UK Parliament whereas in others, such as the BIOT, the constituent authority is retained by the Crown by virtue of the royal prerogative. See Hendry and Dickson (n 26) 14–19.
[109] See Hendry and Dickson (n 26) 9–11.
[110] This position is also consistent with the notion of State jurisdiction as a matter of international law. However, it is interesting to note that the European Commission in its earlier decision in *X v Belgium* (1961) considered that Belgium's exercise of municipal law jurisdiction over the Congo did not bring that colonial territory within Belgium's jurisdiction under Art 1 for the purpose of the Convention's extra-territorial application. The Commission held that a declaration of extension pursuant to Art 63 would be required for a Contracting State's jurisdiction to be engaged.

surrender of substance to form. Nothing is plainer, from the history of events which I have recounted by reference to the contemporary documents, that the making of the Ordinance and its critical provision – s.4 – were done on the orders or at the direction of Her Majesty's Ministers here, Her Ministers in right of the government of the United Kingdom. That government had entered into obligations and understandings with the Americans; not with the government of BIOT. The government of BIOT, indeed, was itself a very creature of those understandings. If the applicant in these proceedings had sought to sue in the BIOT courts, the reply might have been that those courts had no authority to control the Secretary of State sitting in Whitehall; and it would have been a true reply.[111]

It would seem to follow, from the decision of the House of Lords in *Quark Fishing*, on the interpretation of the revised view of the doctrine of the Crown's undivided realm as expressed by the House of Lords in *Bancoult 2*, that if, in legislating for the BIOT, the Crown acts in right of the UK rather than in right of the BIOT – or in right of a combination thereof – that the UK Human Rights Act 1998 should apply in respect of the BIOT.

Against this background, it should be acknowledged that English law is incorporated into BIOT law by general reference via the BIOT Courts Ordinance 1983. In particular, Clause 3(1) provides:

the law to be applied as part of the law of the Territory shall be the law of England as from time to time in force in England and the rules of equity as from time to time applied in England. Provided that the said law of England shall apply in the territory only so far as it is applicable and suitable to local circumstances, and shall be construed with such modifications, adaptations, qualifications and exceptions as local circumstances render necessary.

However, the House of Lords decided in *Bancoult 2* that although English law is a source of 'BIOT law' the UK Human Rights Act 1998 does not apply to the BIOT. As Lord Hoffmann explained:

the [Human Rights] Act defines Convention rights (in section 21(1)) as rights under the Convention 'as it has effect for the time being in relation to the United Kingdom'. BIOT is not part of the United Kingdom.[112]

Consequently, the European Convention does not apply to the BIOT via the Human Rights Act because the 1998 Act has not been extended to the BIOT. However, the fact that the European Convention does not apply to the BIOT through the UK's municipal legislative mechanisms – ie that it does not apply *indirectly* via the inter-territoriality legislative route – would not necessarily prevent the European Convention from being applied to the BIOT *directly* given the Strasbourg Court's decision in *Al-Skeini* which confirmed the Convention's extra-territorial application, pursuant to Article 1, in exceptional circumstances.

---

[111] *R (Bancoult) v Secretary of State for Foreign and Commonwealth Affairs* [2001] 1 QB 1067 ('*Bancoult 1*') [128].

[112] *Bancoult 2* (HL) (n 2) [65].

XI. THE OBJECT AND PURPOSE OF
ARTICLE 63/56 OF THE EUROPEAN CONVENTION

It is necessary to consider whether Article 63/56 of the European Convention constitutes a general barrier to a finding of State jurisdiction, under Article 1, with regard to violations of the Convention allegedly committed in respect an Overseas Territory for which a Contracting State is responsible. It is apparent from the Convention's *travaux* that the UK government insisted on the inclusion of a territorial application clause in the Convention when it was being drafted.[113] It argued that such a clause would promote responsible self-government in those colonial territories belonging to the Contracting States on the ground that decisions regarding the extension of the European Convention to a given Overseas Territory should be made by the local territorial administration in the interests of its local inhabitants rather than by the responsible Contracting State.[114] To this end, it indicated that a British constitutional practice had emerged to reflect this policy so that a multilateral treaty would not be extended to a British Overseas Territory unless and until the local government had been consulted and its consent had been secured. British negotiators succeeded in persuading the other Contracting States of the need for a territorial application clause on the basis that it represented a means of protecting the political autonomy of their Overseas Territories.[115]

However, Moor and Simpson argued that the rationale for the territorial application clause contained in Article 63(56) does not extend to situations where an Overseas Territory is directly controlled by the officials/agents of the responsible Contracting State. Specifically, they contended that:

> Voluntary extension presupposes the possibility of consulting with a local governmental institution possessing some significant degree of autonomy . . . If the reality of the matter is that such a body does not exist, or exists only in symbolic form, logic dictates that such a provision is rendered irrelevant. If a state's central government can, without consultation or approval by any local democratic institution, extend or not extend the Convention to a territory, then to deny that such a territory is 'within the jurisdiction' under Article 1 is untenable if the interpretation of the Convention is related to its object and purpose.[116]

Moor and Simpson suggested that the authority and control approach is an appropriate test of State jurisdiction in those Overseas Territories which are sparsely inhabited, or lacking in permanent inhabitants, as they are, in fact, non-autonomous constitutional units.[117]

---

[113] Moor and Simpson (n 20) 140–43.
[114] ibid, 138–41. See also B Miltner, 'Revisiting Extraterritoriality After *Al-Skeini*: The ECHR and Its Lessons' (2012) 33 *Michigan Journal of International Law* 693.
[115] This position is supported by the *travaux* of the Convention; see Moor and Simpson (n 20) 143–44.
[116] ibid, 188.
[117] ibid, 188.

Since it was created on 8 November 1965, pursuant to the BIOT Order in Council 1965, on the occasion of the detachment of the Chagos Islands from the British colony of Mauritius, the BIOT has been directly controlled by the officials/agents of the UK, the responsible Contracting State. As noted above, the authority and control argument was advanced by the applicants in the *Chagos Islanders* case. They claimed that although a formal BIOT administration exists, in practice, the BIOT Commissioner only governs this British Overseas Territory in accordance with the instructions of the UK government. Consequently, the BIOT does not constitute a de facto separate constitutional unit. Further, from the moment it was created until the Chagos Islanders were removed and/or prevented from returning to the BIOT, the Chagos Islanders never possessed any political autonomy in relation to the BIOT. Further, Article 63/56 is inapplicable to the BIOT because to conclude otherwise would be to ignore the object and purpose of this provision, as evident from the Convention's drafting history. This argument was advanced by the applicants in the *Chagos Islanders* case. However, it was not accepted by the European Court in that case. It decided that the meaning of Article 56 was plain: the provision must be interpreted literally so as to apply to all the Overseas Territories belonging to Contracting States.[118]

In the circumstances, it is worth considering the proper interpretation of Article 56 in greater detail. Article 31 of the Vienna Convention on the Law of Treaties 1969 codified existing customary international law regarding the interpretation of treaties. It provides that: 'A treaty shall be interpreted in good faith in accordance with the ordinary meaning to be given to the terms of the treaty in their context and in the light of its object and purpose'. Further, Article 32 of the Vienna Convention permits courts to refer to a treaty's *travaux*, in order to confirm the meaning of a particular interpretation arrived through the application of Article 31. Moreover, Article 32 can also be used to determine the meaning of a particular provision when such an interpretation is otherwise ambiguous or obscure; or if it leads to a manifestly absurd or unreasonable result.

While the meaning of Article 56 is clear, prima facie, the line of authorities, culminating in the European Court's decision in *Al-Skeini*, which have facilitated the Convention's extra-territorial application, cast doubt on the continuing value of a literal interpretation of this provision. At the very least, recent developments should have prompted the Strasbourg Court to consider the object and purpose of Article 56/63 when reaching its decision in the *Chagos Islanders* case. Moreover, the textual interpretation of Article 56 favoured by the European Court in the *Chagos Islanders* case should be contrasted with the purposive approach adopted by the Strasbourg Court regarding the interpretation of the Convention's provisions in general. The Court has often proclaimed that the Convention is a 'living instrument' that must keep pace with the values of the constituent societies of the Contracting States. Arguably, nowhere in the

---

[118] See *Chagos Islanders v UK* (n 1) [74].

Court's jurisprudence is the purposive approach to interpretation more apparent than in the way the Convention's extra-territorial application has evolved. A literal interpretation of Article 1 could result in the Convention having no extra-territorial application given that the drafters assumed that the Convention was limited to the metropolitan territories belonging to the Contracting States, with the caveat that the Convention could be extended to their Overseas Territories on a voluntary basis under Article 63/56.[119] The absence of an express reference to the scope of State jurisdiction in Article 1, coupled with the nature of the Convention itself, lends weight to the argument that the intention of the Contracting States was clear: the Convention was designed to be instrument of European public order.

To what extent would a purposive interpretation of Article 56 have helped the applicants in the *Chagos Islanders* case? The Chagossians were the permanent inhabitants of the Chagos Islands from at least the early-nineteenth century onwards.[120] They were involuntarily displaced by the UK government and its colonial officials and agents between 1965 and 1973. The BIOT has had no permanent inhabitants since it was cleared in 1973. Accordingly, how could the BIOT Constitutional Order 2004, which established the BIOT's current constitutional order, have created a normative relationship between the UK and the Chagossians for the purpose of engaging the UK's jurisdiction under Article 1 of the European Convention in respect of the BIOT?

As noted previously, the BIOT was created by the BIOT Order 1965. The constitutional arrangements made under the 1965 Order confirmed the existence of a normative relationship between the UK (authority) and the Chagos Islanders (subjects) as a matter of UK law. At the time of their removal from the BIOT, the Chagos Islanders were citizens of the United Kingdom and its colonies under the British Nationality Act 1948. They possessed a right of abode in respect of the BIOT. As Lord Mance observed, in the House of Lords in *Bancoult 2*, 'every British citizen has a right to enter or remain in the constitutional unit to which his or her citizenship relates'.[121] Further, he noted that since 1965, the right of abode possessed by the Chagos Islanders was only exercisable in relation to the BIOT. The normative relationship between the UK and the Chagos Islanders was recognised as an ongoing one in subsequent primary and secondary legislation. Their status as 'belongers' of the BIOT was the reason why the BIOT Commissioner enacted the 1971 BIOT Immigration Ordinance. The Chagos Islanders became British Dependent Territories Citizens by virtue of the British Nationality Act 1981. Further, section 4(3) of the BIOT Immigration Ordinance 2000 provided that a citizen of the British Dependent Territories was exempt from any immigration controls concerning the BIOT by virtue of his or her connection with that Territory (with the exception of the island of Diego Garcia). Further, the Chagos Islanders became British Overseas Territories

---

[119]   See Moor and Simpson (n 20) 127.
[120]   See ch 7 for full details about the settlement of the Chagos Islands.
[121]   Lord Mance in *Bancoult 2* (HL) (n 2) [154].

Citizens and entitled to full British citizenship pursuant to the British Overseas Territories Act 2002. Moreover, the ongoing nature of the normative relationship between the UK and the Chagos Islanders was the reason for enacting the BIOT Constitution Order 2004 and the BIOT Immigration Order 2004. Consequently, the normative relationship which was established as a matter of UK law via the BIOT Order 1965 has been maintained ever since through primary and subordinate legislation, despite the absence of a permanent population in the BIOT since 1973.

The European Court appreciated, in the *Chagos Islanders* case, that the jurisdiction of a Contracting State could be established, under Article 1 of the Convention, in respect of an Overseas Territory, for which it is responsible, in exceptional circumstances. However, it is suggested that the question of whether a Contracting State's jurisdiction is engaged, under Article 1, for violations of the European Convention committed in one of its Overseas Territories, should be reconsidered at a more fundamental level given the wider ramifications of the European Court's decision in *Al-Skeini* concerning the Convention's extra-territorial application. Against this background, it is suggested that, in principle, the level of control generally exercised by a responsible Contracting State over its Overseas Territories is comparable to the level of control required for a finding of State jurisdiction, under Article 1 of the Convention, according to the spatial mode of jurisdiction, as recognised in the European Court's jurisprudence. The validity of this comparison is apparent from a survey of the key cases which were instrumental in the development of the effective territorial control test.

In *Loizidou v Turkey* and *Cyprus v Turkey* the European Court decided that Turkey's jurisdiction was engaged under Article 1 of the European Convention because it exercised effective control over Northern Cyprus. In *Loizidou v Turkey (Preliminary Objections)*, the European Court was willing to find that Turkey's jurisdiction was engaged, under Article 1 of the Convention, in respect of conduct occurring outside of its national territory as a result of its military occupation of Northern Cyprus.[122] In *Loizidou v Turkey (Merits)* the Court elaborated on the scope of the effective control test it had developed in its decision in the *Preliminary Objections* phase of this case.[123] In the context of Northern Cyprus, the Court made it clear that Turkey was not only responsible for the conduct of its own soldiers and officials according to the authority and control test. It presumed that Turkey was also be responsible for the policies of the local administration in Northern Cyprus, the 'Turkish Republic of Northern Cyprus' (TRNC), as a result of the fact that Turkey exercised overall effective control of this area. In the Court's own words:

> It is not necessary to determine whether, as the applicant and the Government of Cyprus have suggested, Turkey actually exercises detailed control over the policies and

---

[122] *Loizidou v Turkey (Preliminary Objections)* (n 17).
[123] ibid.

actions of the authorities of the 'TRNC'. It is obvious from the large number of troops engaged in active duties in northern Cyprus that her army exercises effective overall control over that part of the island. Such control, according to the relevant test and in the circumstances of the case, entails her responsibility for the policies and actions of the 'TRNC'. Those affected by such policies or actions therefore come within the 'jurisdiction' of Turkey for the purposes of Article 1 of the Convention. Her obligation to secure to the applicant the rights and freedoms set out in the Convention therefore extends to the northern part of Cyprus.[124]

This position was reiterated by the Court in *Cyprus v Turkey*:

However, it is to be observed that the Court's reasoning is framed in terms of a broad statement of principle as regards Turkey's general responsibility under the Convention for the policies and actions of the 'TRNC' authorities. Having effective overall control over northern Cyprus, its responsibility cannot be confined to the acts of its own soldiers or officials in northern Cyprus but must also be engaged by virtue of the acts of the local administration which survives by virtue of Turkish military and other support. It follows that, in terms of Article 1 of the Convention, Turkey's 'jurisdiction' must be considered to extend to securing the entire range of substantive rights set out in the Convention and those additional Protocols which she has ratified, and that violations of those rights are imputable to Turkey.[125]

In this paragraph, the Court was reflecting on the relationship between a Contracting State, which effectively controls a territorial unit, and the local territorial administration which survives only as a result of the military and other support offered to it by the Contracting State. In *Ilascu v Moldova and Russia*,[126] the Court decided that Russia's jurisdiction was engaged under Article 1 in respect of violations of the Convention committed in the 'Republic of Transdniestria' which constituted part of Moldova's national territory. Interestingly, the Court indicated that Russia's jurisdiction could be engaged even though it did not effectively control the territory in issue. According to the Court, in order to establish jurisdiction under Article 1 of the Convention, it was sufficient that the regime in Transdniestria 'survives by virtue of the military, economic, financial and political support given to it by the Russian Federation'.[127]

Against this background, in *Al-Skeini*, the European Court concluded that:

It is a question of fact whether a contracting state exercises effective control over an area outside its own territory. In determining whether effective control exists, the Court will primarily have reference to the strength of the state's military presence in the area. Other indicators may also be relevant, such as the extent to which its military, economic and political support for the local subordinate administration provides it with influence and control over the region.[128]

---

[124] ibid, [56].
[125] *Cyprus v Turkey* (2002) 35 EHRR 30, [77].
[126] *Ilascu v Moldova and Russia* (2005) 40 EHRR 1030.
[127] ibid, [392].
[128] *Al-Skeini* (n 9) [139] (footnotes omitted).

As previously stated, it is important to appreciate that the European Court in *Al-Skeini* distinguished between situations encompassed by the effective territorial control test and the sphere of operation of the systems of declarations contained in Article 56 of the Convention. Nevertheless, in principle, the level of control which Turkey exercises over Northern Cyprus is comparable with the level control maintained by the UK government and its agents in respect of the BIOT.[129] This is not to suggest that the actions of the Turkish State in Northern Cyprus are comparable to the constitutional arrangements made by a Contracting State for one of its Overseas Territories for all intents and purposes. However, it would be absurd if, as a result of an accident of (colonial) history, human rights protection is afforded under the European Convention in some Overseas Territories for which a Contracting State is responsible but not in other Overseas Territories over which it exercises sovereignty.

The claim that the decision as to whether to extend the Convention (and any ratified Protocols) to a given Overseas Territory is purely a voluntary matter for the responsible Contracting State, pursuant to Article 63/56, has become increasingly untenable in a post-colonial world. The decision of the European Court in *Al-Skeini* has significantly weakened any justification for a general interpretation of the territorial application clause contained in Article 56. In particular, it could be argued that the principled endorsement of the Convention's extra-territorial application in *Al-Skeini*, where the conditions set out in the Court's judgment are satisfied, has undermined the blanket interpretation of Article 56, as such an approach creates the risk of a manifestly absurd or unreasonable outcome, especially in relation to non-autonomous Overseas Territories. As a result, it is suggested that the approach endorsed in *Al-Skeini* requires the Court to have recourse to the Convention's *travaux* in order to determine the object and purpose of Article 63/56 in cases where it is alleged that the Convention has been violated in respect of an Overseas Territory for which a Contracting State is responsible.

The spatial mode of jurisdiction closely resembles the basis for jurisdiction that would be applicable if a violation of the Convention had occurred in the national territory of the responsible Contracting State, where State jurisdiction would ordinarily be presumed. Therefore, the level of overall effective control exercised by a Contracting State in relation to its Overseas Territories – especially in relation to those Overseas Territories which are the most susceptible to the direction of the government of the responsible Contracting State – should generate a presumption that is comparable to the presumption which operates in relation to the national territory of a Contracting State for the purpose of establishing State jurisdiction under Article 1. In principle, such a presumption would not be problematic as the responsible Contracting State would be presumed to possess State jurisdiction over that Overseas Territory as a matter of international law anyway. Further, it is also consistent with the territorial

---

[129] See Moor and Simpson (n 20) 190.

interpretation of jurisdiction endorsed by the Grand Chamber in *Bankovic*.[130] Not only is this position supported by the Northern Cyprus cases it is strengthened by the decisions in *Ilascu* and *Al-Skeini*. In addition, a significant advantage of the effective control approach to State jurisdiction in relation to Overseas Territories arises from the fact that the Court in *Al-Skeini* confirmed that if a Contracting State exercises effective overall control of an area then it is under a duty to satisfy both the positive and negative obligations contained in the Convention in that particular context.

As the suggested interpretation of Article 56 would be most appropriate where an Overseas Territory could be shown to be non-autonomous, the operation of the system of declaration would remain generally intact. As discussed above, such an interpretation of Article 56 would be in keeping with its object and purpose, as apparent from the Convention's *travaux*. Moreover, this approach is justified by the normative relationship that exists between a responsible Contracting State and the inhabitants of an Overseas Territory. The Chagos Islanders are not currently in occupation of the BIOT. However, as discussed above, they constitute the permanent population of that Territory and this normative relationship has been maintained in both primary and secondary UK legislation. Accordingly, Article 56 should not constitute a general barrier to a finding of State jurisdiction under Article 1 in relation to an Overseas Territory which belongs to a Contracting State. There is no reason why exceptional circumstances should be required in order for a Contracting State's jurisdiction to be engaged in response to allegations of violations of the Convention made in respect of an Overseas Territory for which it is responsible. If a Contracting State maintains a claim of sovereign authority over its Overseas Territories then, in principle, the European Convention should apply to them. While this standpoint does not necessarily render Article 56 redundant it does point to a change in the way that this provision has been interpreted thus far. Specifically, rather than endorsing a blanket interpretation which holds that the Convention can have no application to an Overseas Territory – in the absence of a declaration made by a Contracting State which has extended the Convention to that Territory – the Court should support an interpretation that *only requires* such a declaration to be made when an Overseas Territory possesses local democratic governmental institutions and decision-making processes that evidence a degree of political autonomy from the responsible Contracting State in a manner that is in keeping with the object and purpose of Article 56 as apparent from the Convention's *travaux*.

XII. CONCLUSION

This chapter considered whether Article 63/56, which established a voluntary system of declarations, which allowed a Contracting State to extend the

---

[130] ibid, 189.

European Convention to those Overseas Territories, for which it bears international responsibility, presents a general barrier to a finding of State jurisdiction under Article 1 of the Convention, or whether this provision could be interpreted in such a way that the jurisdiction of a Contracting State would be engaged in response to alleged violations of the Convention occurring in an Overseas Territory, in the absence of an Article 56 declaration being made in respect of that Territory. Four interrelated general arguments were advanced in this chapter. First, it claimed that Article 56/63 should not be viewed as a barrier to the Convention's extra-territorial application with regard to a Contracting State's Overseas Territories, particularly where the Overseas Territory in question constitutes a non-autonomous unit. It was suggested that such an interpretation accords with the object and purpose of Article 56/63, as apparent from the Convention's *travaux*. Secondly, a normative relationship exists between a Contracting State and the inhabitants of an Overseas Territory for which it bears international responsibility and such a relationship is created by the municipal legal system of the responsible State. Thirdly, in principle, the constitutional arrangements for an Overseas Territory should be viewed as representing an exercise of State jurisdiction under Article 1 of the European Convention because the responsible Contracting State invariably exercises some or all of the public powers normally exercisable by a sovereign government in respect of that Overseas Territory. Finally, as a consequence of the above arguments, the jurisdiction of a Contracting State may be engaged in a concrete case either by reference to the State agent authority and control approach (the personal mode of jurisdiction) or the effective territorial control approach (the spatial mode of jurisdiction). It is suggested that the latter approach is to be preferred given that a responsible State will typically govern its Overseas Territories effectively and it will exercise sovereignty over them as a matter of international law in any event. Moreover, the spatial approach is justifiable in relation to Overseas Territories because it is comparable to the jurisdictional approach that would be presumed in relation to a Contracting State's national territory.

The Strasbourg Court's view that any rights that the Chagos Islanders may have possessed in respect of the BIOT had been lost because they had received a (meagre) level of compensation is questionable because any such compensation only related to any private law rights that the Chagossians had in respect of the BIOT. These reparations did not undermine any public law entitlements which they may have possessed in relation to that Overseas Territory and this conclusion was the basis on which the *Bancoult* litigation had progressed through the English courts. Further, more significantly given the nature and extent of the present enquiry, the Chagos Islanders did not sign away any entitlements that they held by virtue of being the permanent inhabitants of this non-self-governing territory pursuant to the provisions of Chapter XI of the UN Charter and the right to colonial self-determination as a matter of international law.

The legality of the detachment of the Chagos Islands from the British colony of Mauritius pursuant to the BIOT's creation must be considered in detail and the history of the Mauritian-UK sovereignty dispute over Chagos Islands must be fully explored before the international legal claims of the Chagos Islanders can be properly understood. The Chagossian claims are premised and shaped by the history of BIOT's creation and the arguments which underpin this sovereignty dispute Accordingly, at the level of international law, Chagossian claims in respect of the BIOT are bound up with Mauritian claims to the same territory as a matter of international law. If it can be shown, as a matter of international law, that: (i) the right to self-determination is applicable in the Chagossian context; and (ii) it is binding on the UK in respect of the BIOT, it follows that the UK is under an international legal obligation to facilitate the exercise of this right by the Chagossian people irrespective of the position adopted by English law on this issue. The following chapters of this book explore the extent to which these two conditions can be satisfied in this context and the ramifications of such an outcome for the Chagos Islanders.

3

Detaching the Chagos Islands from Mauritius: The 1965 Mauritian Constitutional Conference and the Making of the Lancaster House Agreement

I. INTRODUCTION

THIS CHAPTER EXAMINES the proceedings of the intergovernmental Constitutional Conference on the future of Mauritius, which was held in London in September 1965, and its role in the detachment of the Chagos Islands from the colony of Mauritius. The Conference resulted in a change of UK government policy in favour of Mauritian independence. It also produced the Lancaster House Agreement, in which the elected representatives of the Mauritian colonial government agreed to the detachment of the Chagos Islands from Mauritius for the purpose of establishing a US military facility on the island of Diego Garcia. The chapter analyses the relationship between the UK government's support for Mauritian independence and the preparedness of Mauritian political leaders to consent to the dismemberment of the Mauritian colonial unit so that the British Indian Ocean Territory (BIOT) could be created. More generally, the chapter establishes the historical and political context in which the Chagos Islands were detached from Mauritius in order to facilitate a reliable assessment of the legality of that process from the perspective of international law.

II. COLONIAL ACQUISITION IN THE MAURITIAN CONTEXT

The island of Mauritius is located approximately 550 miles to the east of Madagascar in the Indian Ocean. It remained uninhabited, and unclaimed, by any state, entity or societal group until the arrival of a succession of European colonial powers.[1] The Netherlands first claimed sovereignty over Mauritius in 1598 but, after a number of failed attempts to establish a viable settlement there it abandoned its claim in 1710.[2] France subsequently claimed sovereignty over Mauritius (*Isle de France*) and established a successful settlement on the island in 1721. During this period, France also claimed sovereignty over a number of islands located in the Indian Ocean, including Reunion, Rodrigues and the Seychelles.

The Chagos Archipelago consists of 56 islands spread across a total area of approximately 47.5 square miles in the middle of the Indian Ocean. It is situated about 1200 miles north east of Mauritius and 1000 miles north of the island of Mahé in the Seychelles. Diego Garcia, the principal island, has a land mass of approximately 11 square miles. It is located about 130 miles from the other major Chagos island groups of Peros Banhos and the Salomon islands. The archipelago also includes the Egmont Islands, Trois Freres, Danger Island and Eagle Island.[3] The Chagos Islands were first sighted and mapped by Portuguese explorers during the sixteenth century; however, Portugal made no effort to claim or settle the Islands.[4] France claimed sovereignty over the uninhabited Chagos Archipelago in the late-eighteenth century: in 1776, two French settlers were granted a fishing concession relating to Diego Garcia by the French colonial government in Mauritius on the condition that they accept sufferers of leprosy from Mauritius.[5] In 1783, Pierre Le Normand was granted a concession by the French colonial government in Mauritius to establish a coconut plantation on Diego Garcia.[6] The other Chagos island groups of Peros Banhos and the Salomon Islands were settled in 1813.[7] During this period, the French colonial government began leasing land to Franco-Mauritian companies for the development of coconut plantations in the Chagos Archipelago. Slaves were brought from Madagascar and Mozambique to work on these plantations and a thriving copra industry was quickly established.[8]

As part of the wider conflict with Napoleonic France, British military forces occupied Mauritius in 1810 and the island and its dependent territories were

[1] For general historical background, see PJ Barnwell and A Toussaint, *A Short Study of Mauritius* (London, Longmans, 1949) and R Scott, *Limuria: The Lesser Dependencies of Mauritius* (London, Oxford University Press, 1961).

[2] D Vine, 'From the Birth of the *Ilois* to the "Footprint of Freedom": A History of the Chagos and the Chagossians' in S Evers and M Kooy (eds), *Eviction from the Chagos Islands: Displacement and Struggle for Identity Against Two World Powers* (Leiden, Brill, 2011) 1, 13.

[3] Mauritian Legislative Assembly, 'Report of the Select Committee on the Excision of the Chagos Archipelago (No 2 of 1983)' (Port Louis, Mauritius, Mauritian Legislative Assembly, 1983) (The 'Excision Report') 2–3.

[4] Vine, 'From the Birth of the *Ilois* to the "Footprint of Freedom" ' (n 2) 13.

[5] See J Madeley, *Diego Garcia: A Contrast to The Falklands,* Report No 54 (London, Minority Rights Group, 1982) 3.

[6] Vine (n 2) 14. See also D Vine, S Wojciech Sokolowski and P Harvey, *Dérasiné: The Expulsion and Impoverishment of the Chagossian People* (11 April 2005) (on file with the author) 89.

[7] See Vine, Wojciech Sokolowski and Harvey's *Dérasiné* report (n 6).

[8] See Vine (n 2) 11.

ceded to the UK by France under the Treaty of Paris in 1814.[9] The treaty did not expressly transfer sovereignty over the Chagos Archipelago to the UK but both parties assumed that this was the case.[10] A subsequent geographical survey conducted in 1826 by the British Governor of Mauritius prompted the British government to make a formal claim to the Chagos Islands, which was not challenged by France. The Chagos Islands were administered as a lesser dependency of the British colony of Mauritius from that time onwards. During the nineteenth century, the other dependencies of Mauritius included the Seychelles, Rodrigues, Agalega and St Brandon. In 1903, the Seychelles was detached from Mauritius and reconstituted as a separate British colony.

III. BRITISH COLONIAL WITHDRAWAL AND THE PROSPECT OF A US MILITARY FACILITY ON DIEGO GARCIA

The political humiliation caused by the 1956 Suez Crisis forced the British government to re-evaluate its role in the world. In July 1961, as a direct consequence of the growing financial constraints placed upon it, the British government informed the US government of its plan to withdraw its military presence from the Indian Ocean.[11] The US government was concerned that such a withdrawal could be exploited by the Soviet Union and it was anxious to find the most effective way to fill the anticipated power vacuum in the region.[12]

US imperialism did not conform to the territorial model of colonialism, which was favoured by European powers during the eighteenth and nineteenth centuries. In part, the US government's antipathy for classical forms of colonialism stemmed from its revolutionary origins. However, more significantly, its reluctance to replace the declining European colonial powers flowed from sheer pragmatism. The US government wanted to pursue its foreign policy objectives without being encumbered by the financial costs of territorial administration and the political restrictions which were associated with governing non-self-governing territories during the UN era. One of the US government's favoured strategies for projecting its power beyond its national territory was known as 'off-shoring'.[13] The US government began to embrace a policy of establishing military bases on foreign soil during the Second World War. This approach

---

[9] Under Art 8 of the Treaty, 'the colonies which were possessed by France on 1 January 1792 . . . and of the Isle of France and its Dependencies, especially Rodrigues and Seychelles, which several Colonies and Possessions His Most Christian Majesty cedes in full right and sovereignty to His Britannic Majesty', 30 May 1814.

[10] See D Snoxell, 'Expulsion from Chagos: Regaining Paradise' (2008) 36 *Journal of Imperial and Commonwealth History* 119, 120.

[11] CINCPACFLT, *memorandum to CINCPAC*, 13 August 1964, NHC:00 Files, 1964, Box 20, 11000/1A, Tab-B. See also D Vine, *Island of Shame: The Secret History of the US Military Base on Diego Garcia* (Princeton, Princeton University Press, 2009) 70.

[12] Vine, *Island of Shame* (n 11) 59 and 70.

[13] See K Raustiala, *Does the Constitution Follow the Flag?* (New York, Oxford University Press, 2009) 112–13.

provided it with considerable freedom of action without incurring the costs typically associated with sovereign authority in such situations. Nevertheless, this policy typically required the US government to observe certain restrictions, which were either imposed upon it by the host State or by other geopolitical conditions affecting the territory in which the base was situated. These jurisdictional limitations led the US government to settle on a 'strategic island policy' in the aftermath of the Second World War.[14] This policy was premised on the identification of geographically remote islands that were strategically significant from a military perspective and which were either uninhabited or sparsely inhabited territories. When such territories were inhabited, the US government would endeavour to ensure the prompt removal of their inhabitants so that they would not interfere with the operation of the planned military purpose to which the island, or islands, were to be put.[15]

In 1962, in response to the UK government's declared policy of colonial withdrawal, the UK and the US governments began to discuss the prospect of finding a joint military facility in the Indian Ocean.[16] Formal discussions began in February 1964.[17] On the issue of establishing a joint military facility in the Indian Ocean, the British Foreign Office, Colonial Office and the Ministry of Defence spoke with a single voice. A memorandum of 23 April 1964 recorded that, in the Indian Ocean, British defence:

> efforts were deployed less in the defence of British interests than in support of the United States, the Commonwealth and the free world. By persuading the United States to associate themselves with Britain . . . Our burden might be reduced. United States initiative in Indian Ocean should be welcomed.[18]

A joint UK/US survey of a number of small uninhabited (or sparsely inhabited) islands attached to the British colonies of the Seychelles and Mauritius was scheduled to be undertaken in 1964. On 20 October 1964, in connection with this survey, the British government expressed the view that:

> It would be unacceptable to both the British and the American defence authorities if facilities of the kind proposed were in any way to be subject to the political control of ministers of a newly emergent independent state (Mauritius is expected to become independent sometime after 1966) . . . it is hoped that the Mauritius Government may agree to the islands being detached and directly administered by Britain.[19]

---

[14] ibid. See also Vine (n 11) 56–68.

[15] A good example of this is the removal of the inhabitants of Bikini Atoll. For an overview of this process, see Vine (n 11) 63–64.

[16] ibid, 70.

[17] J Chan-Low, 'The Making of the Chagos Affair: Myths and Reality' in S Evers and M Kooy (eds), *Eviction from the Chagos Islands: Displacement and Struggle for Identity Against Two World Powers* (Leiden, Brill, 2011) 71.

[18] CCP Heathcote-Smith, PRO FCO 32/484/1: *Chronology of Events Leading to Establishment of BIOT*, 13 December 1968. See also Chan-Low, 'The Making of the Chagos Affair' (n 17) 69.

[19] Chan-Low (n 17) 77. Also quoted by Laws LJ in R *(Bancoult) v Secretary of State for Foreign and Commonwealth Affairs* [2001] 1 QB 1067 ('*Bancoult 1*') [11].

Against this background, the UK government indicated that it would be prepared to detach any chosen island, or islands, from the established colonial unit or units to satisfy the US government's requirements. Diego Garcia in the remote Chagos Islands, which were attached to the British colony of Mauritius, became the preferred location.[20] The US government insisted that it wanted the entire Chagos Archipelago under its 'exclusive control (without local inhabitants)'.[21] The planned military facility was referred to as an 'austere naval communications station' and the view that Diego Garcia would be used as a site for 'certain limited facilities' remained the UK government's public position throughout the 1960s.[22] However, the US and UK governments shared an understanding that a much more substantial military base would be constructed in due course, in keeping with the long-term objective of filling the strategic gap that would be created as a result of the UK's planned colonial withdrawal.[23]

Under the 1964 Mauritian Constitution, the colonial government of Mauritius was vested in the British Governor who governed with a Council of Ministers and an elected Legislative Assembly. The Governor appointed a Premier, who was drawn from the Mauritian Legislative Assembly. The Council of Ministers was comprised of no more than 15 nominated members, including the Mauritian Premier and the Chief Secretary to the Council. The other members of the Council were selected from the members of the Legislative Assembly by the Governor, acting on the advice of the Premier. On 29 June 1964, ahead of the joint Anglo–American survey, the British Governor of Mauritius consulted with the Mauritian Premier, Seewoosagar Ramgoolam, about the prospect of establishing a defensive communications facility in the Chagos Islands.[24] While Ramgoolam was receptive to this idea of establishing such a facility he made it clear that he would not agree to the detachment of any islands from Mauritius.[25] The Mauritian Council of Ministers was advised of the planned survey on 13 July 1964, although the possibility of any islands being detached from Mauritius was not raised on that occasion.[26] The planned survey was carried out in July

---

[20] TNA PRO 22 February 1965 'Defence Interests in the Indian Ocean' – Memorandum by the Foreign Secretary, Defence Secretary and the Commonwealth Secretary, FO 371/184522 Z4/12/G and see JC De l'Estrac and T Prayag, *Next Year in Diego Garcia* (Mauritius, Edition Le Printemps, 2011) 12.

[21] See Vine (n 11) 78.

[22] See the UK government's announcement in the House of Commons on 5 April 1965. TNA PRO 21 April 1965, 'Defence Interests in Indian Ocean' – Telegram from Commonwealth Relations Office to British High Commissions, FO 37/184523 Z4/36 in De l'Estrac and Prayag, *Next Year in Diego Garcia* (n 20) 16–17.

[23] See 'Defence Interests in the Indian Ocean' – Memorandum by the Foreign Secretary, Defence Secretary and the Commonwealth Secretary (n 20) and De l'Estrac and Prayag (n 20) 12. For details of the phased development of the US military base on Diego Garcia, see the 1983 Excision Report (n 3) 6–7. For a detailed account of the upgrading of the military facility on Diego Garcia, see PH Sand, *United States and Britain in Diego Garcia* (New York, Palgrave, 2009) ch 3.

[24] Heathcote-Smith, *Chronology of Events Leading to Establishment of BIOT* (n 18), about the events on 29 June 1964 and see Chan-Low (n 17) 70 and the 1983 Excision Report (n 3) 21.

[25] See Vine (n 11) 70.

[26] ibid, 70.

and August 1964 and its report was published on 23 September 1964. It concluded that Diego Garcia was a suitable location for the proposed military facility and it confirmed that it was possible to effect the 'removal, resettlement and redeployment of the civil population of any island required for military purpose'.[27]

An official in the UK Foreign Office subsequently clarified the common policy of the UK and US governments during this period regarding the detachment of the Chagos Islands from the British colony of Mauritius and certain islands from the British colony of the Seychelles in order to create the British Indian Ocean Territory (BIOT). According to the official correspondence:

> The primary objective in acquiring these islands from Mauritius and Seychelles . . . was to ensure that Her Majesty's government had full title to, and control over, these islands so that they could be used for the construction of defence facilities without hindrance or political agitation and so that when a particular island would be needed for the construction of British or United States defence facilities Britain or the United States should be able to clear it of its current population. The Americans in particular attach great importance to this freedom of manoeuvre, divorced from the normal considerations applying to a populated dependent territory.[28]

In 1964, it was agreed that the UK government would meet the financial costs of detaching the selected islands from their respective colonial units (and the associated costs of resettling any inhabitants) while the US would meet the financial costs of constructing and operating the military facility on Diego Garcia.[29] However, the UK Cabinet subsequently changed its position on this issue in response to further information, which had come to light since the original agreement was made. As a result, the UK Foreign Office advised the US government that:

> it is now clear that in each case the islands are legally part of the territory of the colony concerned. Generous compensation will, therefore, be necessary to secure the acceptance of the proposals by the local governments (which we regard as fundamental) for the constitutional detachment of the islands concerned.[30]

On 12 April 1965, the UK Cabinet endorsed the establishment of a US austere communications facility on Diego Garcia; the detachment of the Chagos Islands from the colony of Mauritius and the islands of Aldabra, Desroches and Farquhar from the colony of the Seychelles; to resettle the affected inhabitants of any such islands; and to compensate any private interests adversely affected

---

[27] PRO CO 1036/1332: Report by R Newton, 23 September 1964. Chan-Low (n 17) 71.

[28] UK Foreign Office, 'Steering Committee on International Organisations Presentation of British Indian Ocean Territory in the United Nations' 8 September 1966 [10–11], quoted in Vine (n 11) 78.

[29] US Embassy London: telegram to Secretary of State, 3 March 1964, enclosure, 'US Defence Interests in the Indian Ocean' NARA:RG 59/250/6/56/3/4, Subject-Numeric Files 1964-1966, Box 1638: 2–3. See also Vine (n 11) 78.

[30] PRO 30 April 1965. *Defence Facilities in the Indian Ocean – a Telegram from the Foreign Office to Washington*, FO 371/184523 Z4/44. See De l'Estrac and Prayag (n 20) 58.

by the implementation of this policy.[31] In the light of new information regarding the constitutional implications of this strategy, the Cabinet also decided that a financial contribution to the costs of detachment should be sought from the US government as it anticipated that substantial levels of compensation would have to be offered to the governments of Mauritius and the Seychelles in return for their consent to the detachment of the identified islands from their respective national territories. After a period of negotiation, on 24 June 1965, the US government agreed to meet half the costs incurred by the British government in bringing about the creation of the BIOT. However, in order to keep the arrangement secret from the US Congress and the UK Parliament, it offered the UK government a discount on the British contribution to the research and development costs incurred in respect of the Polaris nuclear missile programme, a discount equivalent to the value of $14 million.[32]

On 2 June 1965, the UK Cabinet's Defence and Overseas Policy Committee (DOP) decided that the agreement of the Mauritian and the Seychelles governments should be sought and obtained as soon as practicable.[33] The Seychelles government agreed to the detachment of the islands of Aldabra, Desroches and Farquhar from its colonial territory. In return, the UK government undertook to build an international airport on the island of Mahé. The cost of construction was approximately £6 million. The UK government also offered to compensate private landowners affected by the detachment of these islands from the Seychelles.[34] On 3 July 1965, the Mauritian Council of Ministers was informed of the plan to excise the Chagos Islands from Mauritius in connection with the establishment of the planned US military facility on Diego Garcia.[35] The Mauritian Council refused to agree to the detachment of the Chagos Islands from Mauritius on that occasion. Nevertheless, it indicated that it was prepared to grant a lease of the Chagos Islands at a substantial annual rent on condition that Mauritian rights in respect of fishing, navigation, air routes and mineral resources were recognised during the period of the lease. In addition, the Council demanded the conclusion of a defence treaty between Mauritius and the UK government that would guarantee Mauritius's internal and external security in the event of Mauritian independence.[36]

The UK Foreign Office and Ministry of Defence were opposed to the idea of negotiating a defence treaty with Mauritius, particularly one that sought to guarantee both internal and external security for Mauritius in the event of

---

[31] Heathcote-Smith (n 18) and see Chan-Low (n 17) 74.
[32] See Heathcote-Smith (n 18); Vine (n 11) 83 and 87; Chan-Low (n 17) 74 and Snoxell, 'Expulsion from Chagos' (n 10).
[33] Chan-Low (n 17) 74.
[34] Heathcote-Smith (n 18) and Chan-Low (n 17) 74. The islands were never evacuated and they reverted to the Seychelles on its accession to independence on 29 June 1976. The Seychelles were admitted to UN membership via UNGA Res 31/1, 21 September 1976.
[35] See Chan-Low (n 17) 74.
[36] ibid, 74 and Heathcote-Smith (n 18).

independence.[37] Both departments were concerned that such treaty commitments would be contrary to the British government's declared strategy of colonial and military withdrawal from the Indian Ocean. However, at that time, the position adopted by the Mauritian Council of Ministers did not unduly trouble the Foreign Office. Foreign Office officials were of the view that the Chagos Islands could be excised from the colony of Mauritius unilaterally by Order in Council, if necessary, and the boundaries of Mauritius could be redrawn under the Colonial Boundaries Act 1895. Consequently, the Foreign Office argued that there was no need to obtain the agreement of the Mauritian government or to offer compensation in return for any such agreement.[38] In contrast, the Colonial Office was far more anxious about the political consequences of failing to secure the agreement of the elected representatives of the Mauritian government to the detachment of the Chagos Islands from the established colonial unit. In particular, it was concerned about the United Nations monitoring processes undertaken by the Special Committee on the Situation with Regard to the Implementation of the Declaration on the Granting of Independence to Colonial Countries and Peoples (known as 'C24') regarding developments in respect of non-self-governing territories.[39] This concern was heightened by the wider processes of decolonisation that had gathered considerable momentum throughout the 1960s.[40]

Against this background, the political wisdom of detaching the Chagos Islands from Mauritius unilaterally was highly questionable. As a result, the UK government was prepared to give some ground. The Foreign Office and the Ministry of Defence withdrew their opposition to the conclusion of a UK–Mauritian defence treaty, if this was the price to be paid for the detachment of the Chagos Islands from Mauritius.[41] As a result, in a DOP meeting of 30 August 1965, the Prime Minister indicated that a UK–Mauritian defence treaty would be favourably considered.[42] During this period, the UK government was being pressured by the US government regarding the progress made towards the creation of the BIOT. The next series of meetings between the UK and US government concerning the establishment of the military facility on Diego Garcia were scheduled to be held on 23–24 September 1965.[43] Consequently, the British government felt that a concrete plan of action regarding the detachment of the Chagos Islands from Mauritius had to be in place as a matter of urgency.

[37] See Chan-Low (n 17) 75.
[38] PRO CO 1036/133: Trafford Smith to Anderson, 13 July 1965 and Chan-Low (n 17) 71.
[39] This Committee was established in the aftermath of the Colonial Declaration by UNGA Res 1654 (XVI), 27 November 1961. It succeeded the Special Committee on Information from Non-Self-Governing Territories (established by GA Res 146(II), 3 November 1947 and renamed by UNGA Res 569(VI), 18 January 1952). Mauritius and the Seychelles were identified as non-self-governing territories by the UK in 1946; see UNGA Res 66(1)(1946).
[40] See Chan-Low (n 17) 71 and see ch 5.
[41] PRO CAB 148/22 COPD (65): *Memo by Secretaries of State for Defence and Foreign Affairs*, 26 August 1965 and Chan-Low (n 17) 75.
[42] DOP minutes, 37th meeting, 30 August 1965, and see Chan-Low (n 17) 75.
[43] Chan-Low (n 17) 76.

Nevertheless, in a meeting on 16 September 1965, the DOP was reassured by Anthony Greenwood, the Colonial Secretary, that he would be able to resolve the matter imminently with the Mauritian ministers, who were then in London to attend the inter-governmental Mauritian Constitutional Conference.[44]

IV. THE 1965 MAURITIAN CONSTITUTIONAL CONFERENCE AND THE LANCASTER HOUSE AGREEMENT

As noted above, by the early 1960s, the UK government was intent on making a strategic withdrawal from its remaining colonies situated to the east of Aden. However, with regard to Mauritius, it was concerned that 'withdrawal would lead to violent upheaval' as a result of latent tensions which existed at the time between the ethnic groups which inhabited Mauritius.[45] This factor, coupled with the lack of discernible nationalistic sentiment during the early 1960s, informed the UK government's view that independence was unrealistic for Mauritius at that time.[46] Instead it maintained that the best solution would be some form of continuing colonial association between the UK and Mauritius, at least for the foreseeable future. Nevertheless, as the decade progressed, the prospect of independence became a pressing issue in Mauritian domestic politics. The Mauritian Labour Party (MLP), which was supported by the Hindu majority on the island, favoured independence. In contrast, the party of the threatened established Franco–Mauritian elite, the Parti Mauricien Social Democrate (PMSD), endorsed a policy of continuing association with the UK. This position attracted a significant degree of supported from the African–Creole group, which was also concerned about the ramifications of a Hindu government gaining power in a newly independent Mauritius.[47] Consequently, by the mid-1960s, the question of Mauritius's future status became a major political issue on the island. Against this background, the UK government decided to arrange an intergovernmental Constitutional Conference to discuss the future status of Mauritius. The Conference was scheduled to be held at Lancaster House in London in September 1965.

In the lead up to the Conference, the position of the UK government remained that association was the best option in the circumstances.[48] In May 1965, Anthony Greenwood, the Colonial Secretary, expressed a preference for a policy of 'association with Great Britain as the long term objective of the

[44] PRO CAB 48/18 DOP, 39th Meeting, 16 September 1965 and see Chan-Low (n 17) 76.

[45] CO 1036/331: *Future Constitutional Development of Colonies*, CO print, May 1957 and see Chan-Low (n 17) 64.

[46] This was the view of the British Governor of Mauritius in 1957, CO 1036/331: Scott to Macpherson, 6 February 1958 and Chan-Low (n 17) 64.

[47] For details of the ethnic divisions in Mauritius during this period, see S De Smith, 'Mauritius: Constitutionalism in a Plural Society' (1968) 31 *Modern Law Review* 601, 603.

[48] In April 1965, Greenwood expressed the view that 'independence is not desirable for Mauritius in the near future', PRO CO 1036/1084: Notes of Meeting on 15 April 1965, Colonial Office, and Chan-Low (n 17) 67.

constitutional evolution of Mauritius' and he declared that he intended to advocate such a policy during the September conference.[49] From the UK government's perspective, this policy was vindicated by the onset of violence between the Hindu and African–Creole groups. These instances of ethnic conflict led the British Governor of Mauritius to declare a state of emergency between May and August 1965, which necessitated the dispatching of British troops from Aden to keep the peace in Mauritius.[50]

The Mauritian Constitutional Conference was convened at Lancaster House in London on 7 September 1965. It was chaired by the Colonial Secretary and the Mauritian delegation included representatives of the main five Mauritian political parties, which were, at that time, participating in a coalition government (as well as the two independent members of the Mauritian Council of Ministers). According to the Colonial Secretary, the aim of the Conference was: 'to reach agreement on the ultimate status of Mauritius, the time of accession to it, whether accession should be preceded by consultation with the people and, if so in what form'.[51] The MLP, then the largest of the political parties in Mauritius, advocated a policy of independence. In this regard, it was supported by two other political parties that attended the Conference – the Independence Forward Bloc and the Muslim Committee of Action. The PMSD, the second largest party, remained resolutely opposed to independence. As noted above, it preferred the development of constitutional measures that would permit continuing association between Mauritius and the UK. In any event, the PMSD demanded a referendum on the question of constitutional reform whereas the MLP favoured the determination of constitutional arrangements through ordinary electoral processes.

During the course of the Constitutional Conference the representatives of the MLP and the PMSD were both acutely aware of the UK government's favoured constitutional solution. Duval, a leading PMSD representative, observed that: 'the British seemed to be in favour of the proposals of the PMSD though they did not state it openly and at one point it was expected that these proposals would be accepted'.[52] Further, Harold Walter, a representative of the MLP, expressed the view that: 'at one time during the conference, the British authorities tended to agree to the claim of the [PMSD] for a referendum'.[53] However, by the end of the Constitutional Conference, on 24 September 1965, the UK government had committed itself to a policy of independence for Mauritius. In the final communiqué, the Colonial Secretary announced that the UK government had decided to: 'take the necessary steps to declare Mauritius independent after a period of six months full internal self-government if a resolution asking for

[49]   ibid and Chan-Low (n 17) 67.
[50]   See HC Deb 18 May 1965, vol 712, col 200-1W. The state of emergency was lifted on 1 August 1965. See HC Deb 4 August 1965, vol 717, col 356-7W.
[51]   See 'Report of the Mauritian Constitutional Conference – September 1965 – Sessional Paper No 6 of 1965', 1; and the 1983 Excision Report (n 3) 7.
[52]   See 1983 Excision Report (n 3) 14 and Chan-Low (n 17) 62.
[53]   See 1983 Excision Report (n 3) 12.

this was passed by a simple majority of the new assembly'.[54] This outcome raises the question of what happened, during the period in which Constitutional Conference was held, to cause the UK government to reverse its position on the question of Mauritius's final status.

As the Constitutional Conference progressed it became clear to the Colonial Secretary that the Mauritian political parties were not prepared to compromise on the question of Mauritius's final status.[55] It was at this point that Greenwood decided to raise the question of the detachment of Chagos Islands from Mauritius. As noted earlier, the Colonial Secretary had reassured the UK Cabinet's DOP that the issue of the military facility on Diego Garcia would be resolved during the Mauritian delegation's visit to London and he was under obvious pressure to achieve an outcome favourable to the UK and US governments.[56] In such circumstances, the Colonial Secretary adjourned the Conference and invited the Mauritian delegates to discuss the question of Diego Garcia with him and his officials at the Colonial Office. The representatives of the PMSD refused to attend the meeting as they felt that they did not have a mandate to discuss this matter.[57] However, the other Mauritian delegates accepted Greenwood's invitation and the meeting took place on 20 September 1965. The minutes of this meeting show that the Mauritian Premier, Ramgoolam, 'said firmly that Mauritian government was not interested in excision and would stand out for 99 year lease'.[58] In this meeting, Ramgoolam proposed that a rent should be paid of £7 million per annum for the first 20 years of the lease and £2 million per annum thereafter. He suggested an alternative way forward would be for the UK government to grant Mauritius its independence and then allow it to negotiate directly with the US and UK governments regarding the detachment of the Chagos Islands from Mauritius.[59]

Later on the same day, Greenwood had a meeting with the UK Prime Minister, Harold Wilson, to discuss the way forward given the demands of the Mauritian political leaders. A private meeting between Wilson and the Mauritian Premier was arranged for the morning of 23 September 1965. Prior to the meeting, Wilson received briefings from a number of different sources in the British government. In a note, Greenwood wrote:

---

[54] ibid, 8, quoting from 'Report of the Mauritian Constitutional Conference – September 1965 – Sessional Paper No 6 of 1965' (n 51) 4.

[55] This was confirmed in his briefing note to Wilson (see below).

[56] DOP minutes, 39th Meeting, 16 September 1965 (n 44) and Chan-Low (n 17) 76.

[57] See 1983 Excision Report (n 3) 14.

[58] Mauritius Defence Issues, Record of a meeting in the Colonial Office, FO 371/184528 Z4/169, 20 September 1965; and PRO 1036/1253, Record of a meeting held in Lancaster House at 2.30pm on Thursday 23 September 1965. See Heathcote-Smith (n 18); Chan-Low (n 17) 77; and De l'Estrac and Prayag (n 20) 55.

[59] TNA PRO 20 September 1965, Letter and Note for the Record from JO Wright, Prime Minister's Office to JW Stacpoole, Colonial Office. TNA PRO September 1965, Record of a conversation between the Prime Minister [Harold Wilson] and the Premier of Mauritius Sir Seewoodsagur Ramgoolam, at Downing Street, FO 371/184528 Z4/172. See also De l'Estrac and Prayag (n 20) 53.

I am glad you are seeing Ramgoolam because the Conference is a difficult one and I am anxious that the bases issue should not make it even harder to get a Constitutional settlement than it is already. I hope that we shall be as generous as possible and I am sure that we should not seem to be trading Independence for detachment of the Islands. That would put us in a bad light at home and abroad and would sour our relations with the new state. And it would not accord well with the line you and I have taken about the Aden base (which has been well received even in the Committee of 24). Agreement is therefore desirable and agreement would be easier if Ramgoolam could be assured that:

(a) We would retrocede the Islands if the need for them vanished, and
(b) We were prepared to give not merely financial compensation (I would think £5,000,000 would be reasonable but so far the D.O.P. have only approved £3,000,000) but a defence agreement and an undertaking to consult together if a serious internal security situation arose in Mauritius.

The ideal would be for us to be able to announce that the Mauritius Government had agreed that the Islands should be made available to the U.K. government to enable them to fulfil their defence commitments in the area.[60]

In addition, the Prime Minister was briefed that:

Heading: Mauritius. Sir Seewoosagar Ramgoolam is coming to see you at 10.00 tomorrow morning. The object is to frighten him with hope: hope that he might get independence[.] Fright lest he might not unless he is sensible about the detachment of the Chagos Archipelago. I attach a brief prepared by the Colonial Office, which the ministries of Defence and the Foreign Office are on the whole content. [. . .] I also attach a minute from the Colonial Secretary, which has not been circulated to his colleagues [. . .]. In it, the Colonial Secretary rehearsed arguments with which you are familiar but which have not been generally accepted by ministers[61]

This brief was accompanied by a separate note from the Colonial Office. It expressed the view that little would come about of the ongoing constitutional conference because:

The gap between the parties . . . will not be closed by negotiation. HMG will have to impose a solution . . . The Secretary of State's mind is moving towards a decision in favour of independence . . . as the right solution, rather than a referendum to choose between independence and free association[62]

The note also included some biographical information on Sir Seewoosagar Ramgoolam. In particular, it advised the British Prime Minister that the Mauritian Premier was: 'Getting old. Realises he must get independence soon or it will be too late for his personal career. Rather status-conscious. Responds to flattery'.[63]

---

[60]   PRO PREM 13/3320.
[61]   JO Wright, 22 September 1965, ibid.
[62]   This unattributed note from the Colonial Office formed part of the Prime Minister's briefing for his meeting of 23rd September with the Mauritian Premier. It subsequently was filed in the PRO PREM 13/3320, n 60.
[63]   ibid.

At 10 am on 23 September 1965, the Mauritian Premier met with the UK Prime Minister. According to the minutes of this meeting, Wilson informed Ramgoolam that he:

> wished to discuss with Sir Seewoosagur a matter which was not strictly speaking within the Colonial Secretary's sphere: it was the Defence problem and in particular the question of the detachment of Diego Garcia. This was of course a completely separate matter and not bound up with the question of Independence. It was, however, a very important matter for the British position East of Suez. Britain was at present undertaking a very comprehensive Defence Review, but we were very concerned to play our proper role not only in Commonwealth Defence but also to bear our share of peace-keeping under the United Nations: we had already made certain pledges to the United Nations for this purpose.

> Sir Seewoosagur Ramgoolam said that he and his colleagues wished to be helpful.

> The Prime Minister went on to say that he had heard that some of the Premier's colleagues, perhaps having heard that the United States was also interested in these defence arrangements, and seeing that the United States was a very rich country, were perhaps raising their bids rather high. There were two points that he would like to make on this. First, while Diego Garcia is important, it was not all that important; and faced with unreasonableness the United States would probably not go on with it [. . .] As for Diego Garcia, it was a purely historical accident that it was administered by Mauritius. Its links with Mauritius were very slight. In answer to a question, Sir Seewoosagur Ramgoolam affirmed that the inhabitants of Diego Garcia did not send elected representatives to the Mauritius Parliament. Sir Seewoosagur reaffirmed that he and his colleagues were very ready to play their part. The Prime Minister went on to say that, in theory, there were a number of possibilities. The Premier and his colleagues could return to Mauritius either with Independence or without it. On the Defence point, Diego Garcia could either be detached by order [sic] in Council or with the agreement of the Premier and his colleagues. The best solution of all might be Independence and detachment by agreement, although he could not of course commit the Colonial Secretary at this point. Sir Seewoosagur Ramgoolam said that he was convinced that the question of Diego Garcia was a matter of detail; there was no difficulty in principle.[64]

When the Constitutional Conference reconvened on the afternoon of 23 September, Duval, a representative of the PMSD, observed that the Colonial Secretary's position regarding the final status of Mauritius had radically changed. During that session, Greenwood ruled out the possibility of a referendum on the future status of Mauritius and he came down firmly and openly in favour of independence for Mauritius. This volte face led Duval to conclude that 'some sort of blackmailing had taken place'.[65] The representatives of the PMSD decided to withdraw from the Conference in protest at this sudden decision. Nonetheless, the remaining leaders of the three political parties participating in the Mauritian coalition government proceeded to reach an agreement

---

[64] n 60.
[65] See 1983 Excision Report (n 3) 14.

in principle regarding the detachment of the Chagos Islands from Mauritius.[66] The minutes of this meeting contain the terms of the Lancaster House Agreement.[67]

V. THE LANCASTER HOUSE AGREEMENT

The material conditions of the Lancaster House Agreement were as follows:

1. Negotiations regarding a defence agreement between the UK and Mauritius would be undertaken.
2. In the event of independence, an understanding would exist between the UK and Mauritian governments that they would consult together in the event of a difficult internal security situation arising in Mauritius.
3. Compensation totalling up to £3 million should be paid to the Mauritian government (over and above direct compensation to landowners and the cost of resettling others affected in the Chagos Islands).
4. The UK government would use their good offices with the US government to ensure that the following facilities in the Chagos Islands would remain available to the Mauritian government as far as practicable:

   (a) navigational and meteorological facilities;
   (b) fishing rights; and
   (c) use of an airstrip for in the event of emergency landings.

5. If the need for the facilities on Chagos Islands should disappear the islands should be returned to Mauritius.
6. The benefit of any minerals or oil discovered in or near the Chagos Islands should be reverted to the Mauritian government.[68]

The issue of the detachment of the Chagos Islands from Mauritius was formally considered by the Mauritian Council of Ministers in its meeting of 5 November 1965.[69] A memorandum, written by the Chief Secretary to the Council, containing the terms of the Lancaster House Agreement, was prepared in advance of the meeting.[70] However, it added an express term that had previously been assumed by both sides, namely that 'the Chagos Archipelago should be detached from Mauritius and placed under British sovereignty by Order in

---

[66] ibid, 23.

[67] The minutes of this meeting were approved by Ramgoolam (Mauritian Premier and Leader of the Labour Party); Bissoondoyal (Minister for Local Government & Development and Leader of the Independence Forward Bloc); and Mohamed (Minister for Social Security and Leader of the Muslim Committee of Action) on 6 October 1965. See 1983 Excision Report (n 3) app L, 58.

[68] See 1983 Excision Report (n 3) app K, 57.

[69] ibid, app N, 61. An Order in Council is a form of UK primary legislation enacted by virtue of the royal prerogative: see ch 1. It should not be confused with the decisions of the Mauritian Council of Ministers.

[70] 4 November 1965. ibid, app M, 59–60.

Council'.[71] The Council of Ministers approved the terms of the modified Lancaster House Agreement on this occasion.[72] Nevertheless, according to the minutes of this meeting,

> Council decided that the Secretary of State should be informed of their agreement that the British government should take the necessary legal steps to detach the Chagos Archipelago on the conditions enumerated on the understanding that the British government has agreed that [in relation to the condition regarding the reversion of the Chagos Islands to Mauritian sovereignty] there would be no question of sale or transfer to a third party nor of any payment or financial obligation on the part of Mauritius as a condition of the return

In response to this query, in a telegram dated 19 November 1965, the Colonial Secretary stated:

> the assurance can be given provided it is made clear that a decision about the need to retain the islands must rest entirely with the United Kingdom Government and that it would not (repeat not) be open to the Government of Mauritius to raise the matter, or press for the return of the islands on its own initiative.[73]

In the meantime, the BIOT was created by the enacting of the UK British Indian Ocean Territory Order in Council on 8 November 1965.[74] The Sovereign in Council had the authority to make such an Order by virtue of the Colonial Boundaries Act 1895.[75] Specifically, section 3 of the Order provided that:

> As from the date of this Order –
>
> (a) the Chagos Archipelago, being islands which immediately before the date of this Order were included in the Dependencies of Mauritius, and
> (b) the Farquhar Islands, the Aldabra Group and the Island of Desroches, being islands which immediately before the date of this Order were part of the Colony of Seychelles,
>
> shall together form a separate colony which shall be known as the British Indian Ocean Territory.

The creation of the BIOT was announced by the British government in the UK House of Commons on 10 November 1965 in the following terms:

> With the agreement of the Governments of Mauritius and the Seychelles new arrangements for the administration of certain islands were introduced by an Order in Council made on the 8th November. The islands are the Chagos Archipelago, some 1,200 miles north-east of Mauritius, and Aldabra, Farquhar and Desroches in the Western Indian Ocean. Their populations are approximately 1,000, 100, 172 and 112 respectively. The Chagos Archipelago was formerly administered by the Government

---

[71] ibid, app M, 59–60.
[72] ibid, apps O and P, 62–63.
[73] ibid, app R, 65.
[74] The British Indian Ocean Territory Order in Council 1965, SI 1965/1920.
[75] See *R (Bancoult) v Secretary of State for Foreign and Commonwealth Affairs* [2001] 1 QB 1067 ('*Bancoult 1*') [2].

of Mauritius and the other three islands by that of the Seychelles. The islands will be called the British Indian Ocean Territory and will be administered by a Commissioner. It is intended that the islands will be available for the construction of defence facilities by the British and U.S. Government, but no firm plans have yet been made by either Government. Compensation will be paid as appropriate.[76]

This section examined the proceedings of the 1965 Mauritian Constitutional Conference, which resulted in a volte face regarding the British governmental policy on the question of Mauritius's final status. Further, it sought to establish the issue of whether the UK government's decision to grant Mauritian independence was closely connected to the willingness of Mauritian political leaders to give their consent to the terms of the Lancaster House Agreement, which provided for the detachment of the Chagos Islands from Mauritius pursuant to the plan to establish a US military facility on Diego Garcia. The next part of this chapter considers the available evidence, including pertinent British official documents, which are now in the public domain, and the findings of the Mauritian Legislative Assembly's 1983 inquiry into the excision of the Chagos Islands from Mauritius in order to assess the extent to which there was, in fact, a causal connection between Mauritian independence and the dismemberment of the Mauritian colonial unit.

VI. ASSESSING THE RELATIONSHIP BETWEEN THE DETACHMENT OF THE CHAGOS ISLANDS AND MAURITIAN INDEPENDENCE

On 21 July 1982, the Mauritian Legislative Assembly established a select committee to conduct an investigation into the circumstances surrounding the excision of the Chagos Islands from Mauritius. In its 1983 Report on the Excision of the Chagos Islands, the Select Committee tied together the UK government's decision to grant Mauritian independence with the detachment of the Chagos Islands from the colony of Mauritius.[77] The Committee's report was also highly critical of the failure of the elected representatives of the Mauritian government to appreciate the significance of the establishment of the US military facility on Diego Garcia. The report catalogued the growing media concern, both in Mauritius and around the world, about this planned facility before it observed that:

> It is a matter of regret therefore, that none of the political parties which, at that time, formed part of the Coalition Government, did not think it fit to allay the fears of the population. Hence, the Select Committee strongly condemns the passive attitude of the political class represented in the then all-party Government and which formed part of the Mauritian delegation which attended the Constitutional Conference of

[76] See the Excision Report (n 3) app U, 68.
[77] The Select Committee observed that: 'the genesis of the whole transaction is intimately connected with the constitutional issue then under consideration', see the 1983 Excision Report (n 3) 9 [23].

September 1965. Their silence, in the light of such repeated warnings from responsible sectors of public opinion, bordered, in the Committee's judgment, on connivance.[78]

The Committee resolved 'to denounce the then Council of Ministers which did not hesitate to agree to the detachment of the [Chagos] Islands'.[79] However, the Committee was convinced that the UK government presented the political leaders of Mauritius with a choice between independence and the excision of the Chagos Islands. It reached the conclusion that, if the elected representatives of the Mauritian government had not given their consent to the detachment of the Chagos islands from the colony of Mauritius the prospect of independence would have been substantially delayed. The Committee held that such a choice was consistent with 'the most elementary definition of blackmailing'.[80] Consequently, it decided that the evidence which was available at that time cast doubt over the validity of the agreement to detach the Chagos Islands from the colony of Mauritius as a matter of international law.[81]

However, in the evidence he gave to the Select Committee, Ramgoolam, who was the Mauritian Premier during the material period, made it clear that, he was determined to achieve independence for Mauritius, during the 1965 Constitutional Conference, at any cost.[82] In particular, Ramgoolam stated that:

> a request was made to me. I had to see which was better – to seek out a portion of our territory of which very few people knew and independence. I thought that independence was much more primordial and more important than the excision of the island which is very far from here, and which we had never visited, which we could never visit . . . If I had to choose between independence and the ceding of Diego Garcia I would have done again the same thing.[83]

Further, in its 1983 report, the Select Committee stated that Ramgoolam: 'maintained that the choice he made between the independence of Mauritius and the excision of the archipelago was a most judicious one'.[84] Accordingly, it recorded that he 'refused to describe the deal as a blackmail'.[85]

In sharp contrast, the willingness of the British government to conclude a UK–Mauritian defence agreement, covering both internal and external security in the event of independence, made a much greater impression on the Mauritian

---

[78] ibid, 32.
[79] ibid, 35.
[80] ibid, 36.
[81] For this purpose the 1983 report relied upon the provisions of Declaration on the Granting of Independence to Colonial Countries and Peoples, UNGA Res 1514 (XV), 14 December 1960, ('Colonial Declaration'), which proclaimed that all colonial peoples possess the right to self-determination (para 2). The report alluded to para 5, which decried the imposition of conditions and/or reservations regarding the achievement of independence and para 6, which prohibits the dismemberment of a territorial integrity of colonial units in advance of independence. See ch 5 for further discussion of the application of the right to colonial self-determination in the Mauritian context.
[82] See the 1983 Excision Report (n 3) 22 [36].
[83] ibid, 22.
[84] ibid, 10.
[85] ibid, 36.

delegates at the 1965 Constitutional Conference than the loss of sovereignty over the Chagos Islands. On this issue, the 1983 report summarised the evidence provided to it by Veerasamy Ringadoo, one of the MLP's representatives at the 1965 Conference. According to the report, Ringadoo:

> did not object to the principle of the excision as he felt that, been given the defence agreement entered into with Great Britain [. . .] – a decision which had the unanimous support of all political parties present at Lancaster House, most particularly in view of the social situation which had deteriorated in Mauritius – the United Kingdom Government should be given the means to honour such agreement.[86]

On the issue of the proposed defence treaty, the final communiqué of the 1965 Constitutional Conference stated that:

> In the course of the Conference, it became clear that all parties wanted Mauritius to continue her collaboration with Britain in matters of defence; and Her Majesty's Government agreed that they would be willing in principle to negotiate with the Mauritius Government, before independence, the terms of a defence agreement which would be signed and come into effect immediately after independence. Her Majesty's Government envisage that such an agreement might provide that, in the event of an external threat to either country, the two governments would consult together to decide what action was necessary for mutual defence. There would also be joint consultation on any request from the Mauritius Government in the event of a threat to the internal security of Mauritius. Such an agreement would contain provisions under which on the one hand the British Government would undertake to assist in the provision of training for, and the secondment of trained personnel to, the Mauritius Police and Security forces: and on the other hand, the Mauritius Government would agree to the continued enjoyment by Britain of existing rights and facilities in HMS Mauritius and at Plaisance Airfield.[87]

A UK–Mauritian defence treaty, addressing both internal and external aspects of the security situation in Mauritius, was subsequently concluded. It was signed in 1968 and came into effect on Mauritian independence on 12 March 1968.[88] Mauritius's political elite was reminded of the importance of such a treaty by the resumption of ethnic violence on the eve of independence. Rioting, which began in January 1968, prompted the British Governor of Mauritius to declare a state of emergency extending to the whole island. British troops were again dispatched to Mauritius to keep the peace.[89] The state of emergency remained in place until independence and it was maintained, under different constitutional arrangements, by the new government of Mauritius after independence.[90]

---

[86] ibid, 11. It should be recalled that the PMSD did not participate in the session of the Constitutional Conference at which the Lancaster House Agreement was concluded.

[87] See 'Report of the Mauritian Constitutional Conference – September 1965 – Sessional Paper No 6 of 1965' (n 51) 5. Also see the 1983 Excision Report (n 3) 8 [23].

[88] FCO 32/315. The treaty remained in force until 1975.

[89] HC Deb 23 January 1968, vol 757 col 216–21.

[90] The rioting led to 27 deaths and the cancellation of a planned royal visit to mark Mauritius's accession to independence, HC Deb 8 March 1968, vol 760, col 838–41.

The available evidence suggests that *none* of the Mauritian political parties were deeply troubled by the prospective detachment of the Chagos Islands from the colony of Mauritius. Even the PMSD, which withdrew from the coalition government ostensibly in protest at the transaction, was not against the idea of transferring the Chagos Islands to British sovereignty, in principle. Instead the PMSD representatives were of the view that the level of compensation that had been offered by the British government was inadequate.[91] Consequently, the PMSD did not escape from criticism in the Select Committee's 1983 Excision Report.[92] The report castigated the political wisdom of the Mauritian political leaders during the 1960s. However, it is apparent that the 1983 report evinces a degree of political bias against senior figures in the MLP, which was the predominant force in Mauritian domestic politics in the lead up to Mauritian independence (with the support of the other political parties that favoured independence). The MLP became the party of government in Mauritius from the moment of independence until it was ousted from power, in 1982. Against this background, it may be no coincidence that the election of a new government prompted a reassessment of the circumstances surrounding the detachment of the Chagos Islands from Mauritius.[93]

Regardless of the motivation for the investigation into the circumstances surrounding the excision of the Chagos Islands from Mauritius, by the 1980s, Mauritian politics had entered a new phase. The perspective of the Mauritian political elite during the period leading up to independence was very different from the view of the Mauritian politicians who were in office during the 1980s, when the Select Committee was carrying out its work. For the former group, the prospect of independence and the need to maintain public order in Mauritius far outweighed concerns about the remote small Chagos Archipelago. As Chan-Low correctly points out:

> For the Mauritian political class, grappling with ethnic tensions that flared up into deadly interethnic rioting, living in a country deep in the throes of an acute crisis of underdevelopment, the Diego Garcia affair and [the] fate of the Ilois was a matter of detail.[94]

In contrast, by the 1980s, Mauritius had survived the trauma of independence and had established itself as a viable post-colonial State. Opinions in Mauritius about the value of the post-independence defence arrangements negotiated as a consequence of the agreement to detach the Chagos Islands from Mauritius had

[91] This point was made by the British Governor in a telegram to the Colonial Secretary dated 5 November 1965. See Excision Report (n 3), app O, 62. The PMSD resigned from the coalition government after the Mauritian Council of Ministers meeting held on 5 November 1965.
[92] See 1983 Excision Report (n 3) 33–34.
[93] In the 1982, an alliance between the Movement Militant Mauricien (MMM), a Marxist political party, which was committed to fighting colonialism, and the Mauritian Socialist Party won the general election and they formed a coalition government. However, another general election was called in 1983. A coalition government was formed by the Mauritian Labour Party, the PMSD and the Militant Social Movement.
[94] Chan-Low (n 17) 61.

clearly altered with the passage of time and with the subsiding of fratricidal struggles. Against this background, it is not surprising that a new generation of political leaders wanted to re-evaluate Mauritius's post-colonial entitlements as a matter of international law.

The different positions of Mauritian political leaders during the two periods were central to the observations made by David Snoxell, the former High Commissioner to Mauritius, in a foreword to De l'Estrac and Prayag's book, *Next Year in Diego Garcia*:

> Hindsight can set things in a different context from the one prevailing at the time. The daily pressures on political leaders of a small country, lacking in natural resources, as it approaches independence make the choices more difficult and fateful. I suggest that most politicians of the 1960s would have reached the same conclusions and made the same choice. It could be argued that Mauritius might have extracted a better deal from the UK and the US but there really was only one choice. Under its own law Britain could have gone ahead with the excision of the Chagos Islands, without the agreement of the Council of Ministers, though if at all possible the Foreign Office wanted to avoid that situation.[95]

Snoxell's assessment of the predicament of Mauritius's political leaders during the mid-1960s is justified. However, it is suggested that the absence of choice as a matter of UK constitutional law (colonial law) is not the pivotal issue regarding the legality of the excise of the Chagos Islands from Mauritius. Instead, the central issue remains, whether such a 'choice' should have been offered to the elected representatives of the colony of Mauritius by the British government given the obligations that the UK owed to this non-self-governing territory as a matter of international law.[96]

The strain between the established Mauritian political elite and the next generation of Mauritian politicians became increasingly apparent from the mid-1970s onwards. The issue of the detachment of the Chagos Islands became increasingly controversial in Mauritius when the Movement Militant Mauricien, a Marxist political party, which was committed to fighting all forms of colonialism, became a major force in Mauritian politics.[97] Although the re-evaluation of the legitimacy of the detachment of the Chagos Islands was most apparent in the work of the Select Committee on the Excision of the Chagos Archipelago it was also evident in other political initiatives pursued in the Mauritian Legislative Assembly during the 1980s. In 1980, the Public Accounts Committee of the Legislative Assembly conducted an investigation into the 'Financial and other aspects of the "Sale" of the Chagos Islands and the Resettlement of the

[95] Snoxell in De l'Estrac and Prayag (n 20) 5.

[96] See ch 6.

[97] See R Aldrich and J Connell, *The Last Colonies* (Cambridge, Cambridge University Press, 1998) 180; and AS Simmons, *Modern Mauritius: The Politics of Decolonization* (Bloomington, Indiana University Press, 1982). In the 1976 general election, the MMM won the most seats in the Legislative Assembly but a coalition government was formed between the Mauritian Labour Party, the Muslim Committee for Action and the PMSD which enabled Ramgoolam to remain as the Mauritian Premier.

Displaced *Ilois*'.[98] The Committee noted that the £3 million paid by the British government, in connection with the detachment of the Chagos Islands from Mauritius, was credited to the Mauritian government's capital revenue account in the financial year 1965/66. According to the Accountant General's financial report for that financial year, the transaction was identified as item L IV/4 – 'Sale of the Chagos Islands'.[99] The Committee sought to investigate whether there was any significance attached to the use of the word 'sale' regarding the labelling of this transaction. In its Special Report, the Committee stated that it was unable to obtain any further information in order to clarify this matter or to establish how the figure of £3 million was arrived at. Nevertheless, in an annex to its report, the Committee reproduced an extract from the debate held in the Mauritian Legislative Assembly on 14 December 1965 regarding the creation of the BIOT. Specifically, the representative of the Mauritian government, Guy Forget, stated that, as the UK retained the authority to detach the Chagos Islands from Mauritius by Order in Council, the Mauritian government was of the opinion that there was 'no question of insisting on a minimum amount of compensation' and, as a result, 'the question of the sale or hire of the Chagos Archipelago has not arisen'.[100] In the circumstances, it is difficult to conclude that any weight should be attached to the bureaucratic decision to label this transaction a 'sale'. Nevertheless, from a political perspective, the decision could be used in support of a narrative of collusion on the part of the Mauritian government. Secondly, in 1980, the Movement Militant Mauricien sponsored an amendment to the Mauritian Constitution so that it would include a claim that the Chagos Islands form part of Mauritius.[101] The amendment was vigorously debated in the Mauritian Legislative Assembly. However, it failed to attract the requisite support on that occasion.[102] In particular, it was resisted by the Mauritian government itself which maintained that, under the terms of the 1965 Lancaster House Agreement, the UK had a valid claim to the Chagos Islands and it exercised sovereignty over them.[103]

---

[98] See Mauritius Legislative Assembly, *Financial and Other Aspects of the 'Sale' of the Chagos Islands and the Resettlement of the Displaced Ilois,* Special Report of the Public Accounts Committee for the 1980 (4th) Session, Mauritius Legislative Assembly (Port Louis, Mauritian Government, 1981).

[99] ibid, 1.

[100] ibid, 9 (Annex 1).

[101] See the Mauritian National Assembly debate, 26 June 1980, Mauritius Hansard 3415. See MM Ticu, *Chagos: Where International Law Stops* (Utrecht, Utrecht University, 2012) (on file with the author) 51.

[102] Parliamentary debate in the Mauritian National Assembly, 26 June 1980, Mauritius Hansard at 3416. See Ticu, *Chagos: Where International Law Stops* (n 101) 51.

[103] See Ramgoolam's statement dated 27 June 1980 in de l'Estrac and Prayag (n 20), 138. The Mauritian Constitution was only amended to include a claim to the Chagos Islands in 1991. See Art 111 of the Constitution of the Republic of Mauritius, as amended by Act No 48 of 17 December 1991, Legal Supplement to the Government Gazette of Mauritius No 131 (23 December 1991) 231; see GH Flanz (ed), Constitutions of the Countries of the World 12 (Dobbs Ferry/NY, Oceana, 1998) 81, 95.

It is important not to lose sight of the diplomatic manoeuvrings of the UK government when dealing with the US government regarding the constitutional requirements for detaching the Chagos Islands from the colony of Mauritius. As noted above, the British government advised the US government that as 'the islands are legally part of the territory of the colony concerned' the need to reach agreement with the elected representatives of the Mauritian government was considered to be 'fundamental for the constitutional detachment of the islands concerned'.[104] Further, while the British government was eager to endorse the planned US military facility on Diego Garcia and the detachment of certain islands from Mauritius and the Seychelles it maintained to the US government that the agreement of the two local governments involved was 'essential'.[105] De l'Estrac harnesses these official sources in support of his claim that: 'the United Kingdom could not "constitutionally" excise the Chagos Archipelago from the Mauritian territory without the consent of Mauritius'.[106] However, in this respect, De l'Estrac makes the mistake of taking the statements of the UK government at face value. At the time that these statements were made the UK government was trying to get the US government to make a financial contribution to the costs of detaching the Chagos Islands from Mauritius and the Seychelles.[107] As noted above, this strategy was adopted by the UK Cabinet on 12 April 1965. The significance of the financial implications of the UK government's policy was apparent from a brief to the British Foreign Secretary in advance of his meeting with representatives of the US government. In this brief, Edward Peck, the Assistant Under-Secretary of State, advised that:

> if we do not settle quickly (which must mean generously) agitation in the colonies against 'dismemberment' and 'foreign bases' (fomented from the outside) would have time to build up to serious proportions, particularly in Mauritius where the political balance in a multiracial society is easily upset.[108]

Accordingly, it was in the interests of the British government to exaggerate the obstacles it was confronting with regard to the detachment of the Chagos Islands from Mauritius and to overstate the legal requirements that such a process involved. As noted above, the US government eventually agreed to contribute up to half the costs of detaching the Chagos Islands from Mauritius. In any event, the UK government must have appreciated that, as the Chagos Islands

---

[104]   PRO 30 April 1965. 'Defence Facilities in the Indian Ocean' – Telegram from Foreign Office to British Embassy in Washington (n 30).
[105]   PRO 15 June 1965, 'Defence Interests in Indian Ocean': Brief by the Commonwealth Office (n 20) and see De l'Estrac and Prayag (n 20) 22.
[106]   De l'Estrac and Prayag (n 20) 57.
[107]   As noted above, it was originally agreed that the UK government would bear the full costs of detaching the identified islands from their respective colonial units. US Embassy London, telegram to Secretary of State, 3 March 1964, enclosure 'US Defence Interests in the Indian Ocean' (n 29) 2–3 and Vine (n 11) 78.
[108]   TNA PRO 7 May 1965. 'Defence Facilities in the Indian Ocean: Briefing for the Secretary of State's discussion with Mr Rusk (USA)'. FO 371/184523 Z4/64/G. See also De l'Estrac and Prayag (n 20) 22.

would remain under UK sovereignty once the US military facility on Diego Garcia had been built, it would have to mediate between the US authorities and the government of an independent Mauritius. In the circumstances, the agreement of the elected representatives of the Mauritian government would have appealed to the UK government irrespective of the constitutional requirements regarding the excise of the Chagos Islands from the colony of Mauritius.

The diplomatic manoeuvrings of the British government were also apparent in its dealings with the elected representatives of the Mauritian government. As noted above, Greenwood, the Colonial Secretary, informed the Mauritian political leaders that the Chagos Islands could be detached from Mauritius unilaterally by Order in Council, if necessary. This position was also impressed upon the Mauritian Premier by the UK Prime Minister in their private meeting on 23 September 1965. Moreover, Wilson indicated to Ramgoolam that Diego Garcia was not 'all that important; and faced with unreasonableness the United States would probably not go on with it'.[109] However, the official record reveals that nothing could have been further from the truth. The planned military facility on Diego Garcia was of fundamental importance to the UK government and the US government was putting it under immense pressure to take the necessary steps to detach the Chagos Islands from Mauritius at the time that Wilson made this statement. Clearly, in this respect and in the veiled threat to excise the Chagos Islands unilaterally if the agreement of the Mauritian political leadership was not forthcoming both elements of the negotiating strategy were being pursued by the British government in order to achieve its political goals of the detachment of the Chagos Islands from Mauritius; the creation of the BIOT; and the establishment of the planned US military facility on Diego Garcia with the minimum amount of political aggravation and financial expenditure.

It is possible to challenge the view that a shift in the UK government's policy in respect of Mauritius, from favouring a position of continuing association to a straightforward endorsement of independence, can only be explained by reference to the need for a US military facility on Diego Garcia. Official documents, now available in the public domain, support the view that the Colonial Secretary's change of position was influenced by discussions with participants in the 1965 Constitutional Conference. In official correspondence to the Governor of Mauritius, Greenwood stated that independence: 'was conceded because the overwhelming majority of the delegates at the Constitutional Conference came down in favour of it and because the decision seemed to me in any case to be the right one'.[110] The available evidence may give us cause to be sceptical about the veracity of this statement, especially given the PMSD's ongoing resistance to independence during the Conference. However, it is worth remembering that the British government's wider policy preference was to withdraw from its remaining colonial territories in the Indian Ocean. The granting

---

[109] Minutes of meeting on 23 September 1965 (n 58).
[110] PRO CO 1036/1253: Greenwood to Rennie, 15 December 1965 and Chan-Low (n 17) 68.

of independence to Mauritius was entirely consistent with this broader strategy. As discussed above, the option of independence was not pursued by the UK government during the early-1960s because of real concerns about the risk of ethnic violence in the event of a British withdrawal from Mauritius. However, by the mid-1960s, demands for independence had been made by a majority of the Mauritian political parties. While ethnic tensions were an ongoing concern in such a highly stratified society, the UK government concluded that such tensions would have been a continuing feature of Mauritian society even if a policy of ongoing association was implemented on the island. Ultimately, it appears as though the British government realised that such concerns could not present an obstacle to independence. This is reflected in the Colonial Secretary's statement made in the final communiqué of the 1965 London Conference:

> as between independence and some form of continuing association with Britain, the parties concerned have maintained their opposing views, and although both systems have many features in common I see no possibility of reconciling them. I was urged to agree that a referendum should be held to decide between independence and association. I concluded however that the main effect of a referendum would be to prolong the current uncertainty and political controversy in a way which could only harden and deepen communal divisions and rivalries. In this situation, and after careful study of all the factors involved, Her Majesty's Government have reached the conclusion that it is right that Mauritius should be independent and take her place among the sovereign nations of the world.[111]

However, despite the obvious pragmatism of the UK government's ultimate position on the question of Mauritius's independence the available evidence strongly suggests that a deal was made between the elected representatives of the Mauritian government and senior figures in the UK government – independence was granted in return for the detachment of the Chagos Islands. The view, in Mauritius, that such a deal had been struck was reported to the Colonial Office by John Rennie, the British Governor of Mauritius, on 11 November 1965.[112] Moreover, this view was subsequently confirmed by internal correspondence within the British government itself. In 1967, in the context of a discussion about Mauritian independence, an official in the Colonial Office reported that, regarding the promise of independence:

> I am told that it was a cabinet decision that this undertaking should be given and that in addition, Her Majesty's decision to come out publicly in favour of independence for Mauritius was part of the deal between our present Prime Minister and the Premier of Mauritius regarding the detachment of certain Mauritian dependencies for BIOT.[113]

Consequently, there is cogent evidence in support of the conclusion that there was a deal between the British government and the elected representatives of the

---

[111] See 'Report of the Mauritian Constitutional Conference – September 1965 – Sessional Paper No 6 of 1965' (n 51) 4; and see 1983 Excision Report (n 3) 8 [22].
[112] PRO CO 1036/1084: Rennie for OAG, 23 September 1965 and Chan-Low (n 17) 78.
[113] PRO CO 1036/268: Minute on file: Terry to Fairclough, 14 February 1967 and Chan-Low (n 17) 79.

colony of Mauritius. Moreover, it appears that there was an absence of a mean-ingful choice on the part of the Mauritian political leadership regarding the terms of the bargain.[114]

It could be argued that the UK government was in a comparable position, vis-a-vis the US government, regarding the establishment of the planned military facility on Diego Garcia, to that of the elected representatives of the Mauritian government vis-a-vis the UK government, in respect of the excision of the Chagos Islands from Mauritius. After the political and financial humiliation caused by the Suez Crisis, the UK could no longer afford to maintain an empire. Nevertheless, the British government was anxious to avoid the creation of a political and military vacuum in the Indian Ocean during the height of the Cold War and to avoid the prospect of further embarrassment that would be occa-sioned by its declining political and military power in the absence of a close association with the United States. The US government was insistent about the terms on which the military facility on Diego Garcia would be constructed and developed and it placed the UK government under considerable pressure throughout the process of detaching the Chagos Islands from Mauritius. In the circumstances, similar arguments about the difficult situation confronting the Mauritian political leaders in the mid-1960s could be applied to the British political leaders during this period as well. However, while there were some sim-ilarities between the UK and Mauritian governments, the material difference between them was that the UK government had a meaningful choice. It may not have been a very palatable one but it was undoubtedly a choice. The UK could have granted Mauritius its independence first and then the UK and/or the US government could have negotiated with the government of a newly independent Mauritian State regarding the detachment of the Chagos Islands from Mauritius. On 14 August 1965, the Indian government had indicated to the UK government that it would not be opposed to such a potential arrangement.[115] Moreover, as noted above, this way forward was also suggested by the Mauritian Premier to the Colonial Secretary when the possibility of detaching the Chagos Islands from Mauritius was raised in their meeting at the Colonial Office on 20 September 1965.[116] Clearly, if Mauritius was granted its independence before negotiations were instituted then the US government and/or the UK government could not dictate the terms of any agreement to transfer sovereignty over the Chagos Islands. Undoubtedly, the arrangement would have been significantly more costly but there would seem to be no reason why Mauritius should bear the burden of defending the 'free world' disproportionately. The long-term benefits of an agreement freely concluded between sovereign States are glaringly obvious. Any such agreement would manifest a higher degree of political

[114] This issue is explored in the next chapter.
[115] TNA PRO 28 July 1965 'Defence facilities in the Indian Ocean – reactions of Governments to notification by HMRR'. FO 371/184526 Z4/122. See De l'Estrac and Prayag (n 20) 42.
[116] See Heathcote-Smith (n 18); the 1983 Excision Report (n 3); Chan-Low (n 17) 77; De l'Estrac and Prayag (n 20) 55.

legitimacy and there would be some truth in the hollow claim that has been advanced by the UK government – that the agreement of the elected representatives of the Mauritian government to detach the Chagos Islands from Mauritius represents an act of self-determination rather than an abuse of it.[117] However, such an enlightened strategy was not pursued and, given the conditions of the Cold War and the imperialist mindsets of the UK and US governments, it was never likely to be.

VII. CONCLUSION

This chapter considered the impact of the UK government's planned colonial withdrawal from the Indian Ocean on the US government's regional military policy, which culminated in the Anglo-American initiative to establish a US military facility on the island of Diego Garcia in the Chagos Archipelago. It analysed the way in which this strategy was implemented and it paid particular attention to the way in which the UK government negotiated the obstacles to the detachment of the Chagos islands from the colony of Mauritius in order to facilitate the creation of the BIOT. The chapter also examined the proceedings of the 1965 Mauritian Constitutional Conference, which resulted in a startling shift in British governmental policy, away from a firm commitment to ongoing colonial association to outright support for Mauritian independence. This Conference also produced the Lancaster House Agreement through which the elected representatives of the Mauritian colonial government agreed to the excision of the Chagos Islands from Mauritius. The chapter analysed the extent to which the decision to grant Mauritius its independence was linked to the dismemberment of the Mauritian colonial unit and, more specifically, whether the consent of Mauritian political leaders to the terms of the Lancaster House Agreement amounted to the cost of Mauritian independence. To this end, this chapter also drew on a range of sources, including the official documents of the British government and the 1983 report of the Select Committee of the Mauritian Legislative Assembly on the excision of the Chagos Islands from Mauritius, in order to determine the extent to which there was, in fact, a causal connection between the granting of Mauritian independence and the cleaving of the Mauritian colonial unit. The available evidence strongly suggests that Mauritian independence was granted in return for the detachment of the Chagos Islands from Mauritius.

There is little doubt that, as a matter of UK law, the UK government had the authority to legislate, by Order in Council, to detach the Chagos Islands from the colony of Mauritius. However, the more important question is whether the UK government had the legal authority to dismember one of its non-self-

---

[117] TP Lynch, 'Diego Garcia: Competing Claims to a Strategic Isle' (1984) 16 *Case Western Reserve Journal of International Law* 101, 110.

governing territories as a matter of international law during the period of widespread decolonisation. The UK's decision to procure the consent of the elected representatives of the Mauritian colonial government to the excision of the Chagos Islands from the Mauritian colonial unit via the 1965 Lancaster House Agreement gives rise to a number of questions including: what status did the 1965 Agreement possess, if any, as a matter of international law? Further, did the elected representatives of the colonial government of Mauritius have a degree of international legal personality for the purpose of concluding the Lancaster House Agreement? These are questions will be considered in the next chapter.

4

The 1965 Lancaster House Agreement and International Law

I. INTRODUCTION

THE LAST CHAPTER discussed the circumstances surrounding the 1965 Lancaster House Agreement through which the Chagos Islands were detached from the colony of Mauritius. The available evidence strongly suggests that the conclusion of the 1965 Agreement was a condition of the grant of Mauritian independence by the UK. The previous chapter also foreshadowed the argument that the elected representatives of the Mauritian colonial government possessed a degree of international legal personality, which enabled them to conclude the 1965 Agreement. This chapter examines the issue of international legal personality in this context and it analyses the status of the 1965 Lancaster House Agreement as a matter of international law. In particular, it considers whether the connection between the grant of independence and the detachment of the Chagos Islands from Mauritius had the effect of rendering the 1965 Agreement invalid on the ground that the elected representatives of the Mauritian colonial government were coerced into making the Lancaster House Agreement and that their consent to its terms was compromised as a result.

The next section examines the development of the doctrine of coercion in relation to the conclusion of treaties in international law. It pays particular attention to the doctrine's association with the threat or use of force, both as a matter of customary international law and in treaty law. Further, it assesses the resistance, from developed States, to the progressive development of the doctrine of coercion in international law with specific reference to the use of political and economic forms of duress in the context of the conclusion of treaties. Consequently, the chapter highlights the fundamental tension that evolved in international law between the development of a narrow conception of coercion, which ties coercion to forms of military aggression, and a broader normative commitment to the idea that treaties must be the product of freely given consent and that a treaty may be declared invalid if consent has been vitiated as a result of the application of duress during its conclusion. Accordingly, this second section explores the consequences for international law of the argument that, if international law recognises the existence of a causal relationship between the use of coercion and compromised consent, the particular form that the coercive pressure takes should be immaterial for the purpose of determining its legal validity. The third part of this chapter considers whether a broader conception of coercion in international law has emerged in modern international law, one that encompasses political and economic forms of duress as well as instances of military aggression. Specifically, it considers whether such a conception of duress has been recognised as a general principle of law in municipal legal systems and whether such a principle has been transposed into international law by virtue of Article 38(1)(c) of the ICJ Statute, which enumerates the sources of international law. In addition, this part examines the evidential barriers that confront the application of a broader interpretation of the doctrine of coercion in international law. Consequently, this section assesses the extent to which an expansive doctrine of coercion could be used to determine the legal validity of the 1965 Lancaster House Agreement. The penultimate part of this chapter addresses the issue of whether colonial entities possessed international legal personality and treaty-making capacity as a matter of international law. It then turns to consider the related issues of whether, in this context, the elected representatives of the Mauritian colonial government possessed international legal personality for the purpose of concluding the 1965 Lancaster House Agreement and whether the 1965 Agreement constituted a treaty as a matter of customary international law. This section also considers the implications of the conclusion of the Lancaster House Agreement for the relationship between international law and municipal law in the colonial context. Prima facie, the 1965 Agreement would appear to be the product of UK municipal law. However, the 1965 Agreement may also be viewed as an agreement made between an administering State and a non-self-governing territory, which was intended to have legal effect after Mauritius had acceded to independence. But as the available evidence indicates that the detachment of the Chagos Islands from Mauritius was a condition of Mauritian independence it could be argued that the question of the validity of the Lancaster House Agreement should not be treated as a matter that falls exclusively within the UK's exclusive jurisdiction.

II. THE DOCTRINE AND THE DEVELOPMENT OF THE TREATY LAW

The preamble of the 1969 Vienna Convention on the Law of Treaties recognises the fundamental importance of the principles of freedom of consent, good faith and *pacta sunt servanda* for the law of treaties. The notion that agreements should be honoured (*pacta sunt servanda*), which is enshrined in Article 26 of the Vienna Convention,[1] has attracted the overwhelming approval of international lawyers through the centuries,[2] and it has been widely accepted as one of

---

[1] The Vienna Convention on the Law of Treaties (VCLT), Art 26 provides that: 'Every treaty in force is binding upon the parties to it and must be performed in good faith'.

[2] See HG De Jong, 'Coercion in the Conclusion of Treaties' (1982) 15 *Netherlands Yearbook of International Law* 209. See also I Detter, 'The Problem of Unequal Treaties' (1966) 15 *International and Comparative Law Quarterly* 1069.

the foundational principles of the international legal system itself. Further, the connection between treaties and private law contracts has long been recognised.[3] In particular, freedom of consent and good faith were widely considered to be essential to both forms of agreement during the Roman era and this understanding was transposed into early international law.[4] But while the legitimacy provided by these principles remained significant in relation to international treaties, the function of consent presented a range of practical problems for international law. One enduring problem flowed from the fact that the threat or use of force was not considered to be unlawful in international law until the conclusion of the Kellogg-Briand Pact in 1928.[5] Moreover, a general prohibition on the threat or use of force was not established until the advent of the UN Charter.[6] Consequently, until then, it was not unlawful to threaten the use of force as a means of coercing a State or entity into concluding a treaty. Accordingly, until relatively recently, international law tolerated blatant instances of coercion in relation to the conclusion of treaties that had no parallel in municipal legal systems with regard to the conclusion of private law contracts.[7]

Against this background, in 1949, the UN International Law Commission began work on the codification the law of treaties, which culminated in the production of a draft Convention on the Law of Treaties in 1966.[8] Regarding the grounds for invalidating a treaty, the members of the Commission agreed that, given the general prohibition on the threat or use of force in modern international law, treaties concluded as a result of the threat or use of force would be unlawful and void ab initio as a matter of customary international law.[9] As a

---

[3] F Lauterpacht (ed), *Hersch Lauterpacht, International Law: Collected Papers*, vol 1 (Cambridge, Cambridge University Press, 1970) 351–52.

[4] See De Jong, 'Coercion in the Conclusion of Treaties' (n 2).

[5] (1929) UKTS 29, Cm 3410; 94 LNTS 57.

[6] The UN Charter, Art 2(4) provides that: 'All Members shall refrain in their international relations from the threat or use of force against the territorial integrity or political independence of any State, or in any other manner inconsistent with the Purposes of the United Nations'. In the *Case Concerning Military and Paramilitary Activities in and Against Nicaragua (Nicaragua/United States)* (1986) ICJ Rep 14, the ICJ noted that a parallel principle on the prohibition on the threat or use of force had evolved in customary international law. This customary principle was included in principle 1 of the Declaration on the Principles of International Law concerning Friendly Relations and Co-operation Among States in Accordance with the Charter of the United Nations, UNGA Res 2625(XXV)(1970), 24 October 1970. It declares that: 'Every State has the duty to refrain in its international relations from the threat or use of force against the territorial integrity or political independence of any State'.

[7] Peace treaties represent a good example of a situation where coercion is used as a means of compelling a State to conclude an unfavourable treaty. See De Jong (n 2) 222 and, more generally, Detter, 'The Problem of Unequal Treaties' (n 2).

[8] In resolution 174(II)(1947), the UN General Assembly established the International Law Commission with the aim of undertaking studies 'to encourage the progressive development of international law and its codification'.

[9] See the *International Law Commission Yearbook* (1966), vol II, 246–47, quoted in DJ Harris, *Cases and Materials on International Law*, 7th edn (London, Sweet & Maxwell, 2010) 691–92. For commentary on the proceedings of the Vienna Conference, see C Murphy, 'Economic Duress and Unequal Treaties' (1970–1971) 11 *Virginia Journal of International Law* 51.

result, the final version of the Commission's Article 49 of the draft Convention provided that: 'A treaty is void if its conclusion has been procured by the threat or use of force in violation of the principles of the Charter of the United Nations'.[10] However, during the drafting process, a significant number of the Commission's members – principally the representatives of socialist and developing States – argued that the doctrine of coercion should be extended to encompass economic and political forms of duress as well as instances of military aggression. While this disagreement was mentioned in the Special Rapporteur's 1966 report to the UN General Assembly, the Commission decided not to reformulate the draft provision.[11]

The question of the parameters of the doctrine of coercion in international law was raised during the 1968/69 Vienna Conference on the Law of Treaties. A proposed amendment to Article 49 of the draft Convention on the Law of Treaties was sponsored by Afghanistan and supported by a total of 19 developing and socialist States.[12] The amendment proposed that: 'a treaty is void if its conclusion has been procured by the threat or use of force including economic or political pressure in violation of the principles of the Charter of the United Nations'.[13] Many non-European States and political entities had experienced the subtle ways in which the colonial powers had used improper pressure in order to conclude agreements that were disadvantageous to the non-European party during the colonial period.[14] Consequently, during the sessions of the Vienna Conference in 1968/69, the representatives of the developing States were concerned about the ways in which powerful developed States could use political and economic pressure in a coercive manner to bring about the conclusion of treaties that were unfavourable to developing States in the post-colonial era. In response to this proposed amendment to draft Article 49, the representatives of developed States argued that a conception of coercion, which encompassed political and economic forms of pressure, would substantially weaken the principle of *pacta sunt servanda*.[15] They claimed that such a revised approach would allow States to discard their treaty obligations as soon as they became onerous or disadvantageous. In particular, the representatives of the governments of Canada and the United States made impassioned defences of the established customary international law position.[16] They claimed that any treaty could be vulnerable to the charge that a party's consent was vitiated as a result of the application of some form of political or economic pressure. Accordingly, they argued that such a development would threaten the predominance of the

---

[10] See Murphy, 'Economic Duress and Unequal Treaties' (n 9) 54
[11] ibid, 56.
[12] ibid, 57–58.
[13] ibid, 58–59.
[14] See Detter (n 2). On the colonial encounter more generally, see A Anghie, *Imperialism, Sovereignty and the Making of International Law* (Cambridge, Cambridge University Press, 2004).
[15] See Murphy (n 9) 58–59.
[16] ibid, 58–59.

treaty as a source of international law to the detriment of the international community of States as a whole.[17]

While the issue of the legitimate scope of the doctrine of coercion in international law inspired vigorous debate during the Vienna Conference between developed States and developing/socialist States, their differences of opinion were eventually accommodated by the adoption of a Declaration, which endorsed a prohibition on the use of political or economic coercion in relation to the conclusion of treaties. This compromise enabled the participating States to reach agreement on the grounds upon which a treaty could be invalidated for the purpose of the Convention. The final version of draft Article 49 was adopted and renumbered at the Plenary Session of the Vienna Conference in 1969. As a result, Article 52 of the Vienna Convention on the Law of Treaties provided that:

> A treaty is void if it is conclusion has been procured by the threat or use of force in violation of the principles of international law embodied in the Charter of the United Nations.

In contrast, the Declaration on the Prohibition of Military, Political or Economic Coercion in the Conclusion of Treaties provided that:

> *The United Nations Conference on the Law of Treaties,*
>
> *Upholding* the principle that every treaty in force is binding upon the parties to it and must be performed by them in good faith,
>
> *Reaffirming* the principle of the sovereign equality of States,
>
> *Convinced* that States must have complete freedom in performing any act relating to the conclusion of a treaty,
>
> *Deploring* the fact that in the past States have sometimes been forced to conclude treaties under pressure exerted in various forms by other States,
>
> *Desiring* to ensure that in the future no such pressure will be exerted in any form by any State in connexion with the conclusion of a treaty,
>
> 1. *Solemnly condemns* the threat or use of pressure in any form, whether military, political, or economic, by any State in order to coerce another State to perform any act relating to the conclusion of a treaty in violation of the principles of the sovereign equality of States and freedom of consent,
>
> 2. *Decides* that the present Declaration shall form part of the Final Act of the Conference on the Law of Treaties.

The Declaration forms part of the Final Act of the Vienna Conference. However, it is not a binding international instrument per se. It is clear from the text that the Declaration's aim was to contribute to the progressive development of international law rather than as a means of confirming the content of *lex lata* regard-

---

[17] ibid, 58–59.

ing the doctrine of coercion in customary international law. Villiger, in his authoritative commentary on the Vienna Convention on the Law of Treaties, points out that the language used in both the preamble and the main body of the Declaration are not indicative of the creation of international legal obligations for States.[18] The preamble to the Declaration expressed a desire to prevent coercive agreements being concluded in the future. Moreover, it does not state that treaties entered into as a result of the use of political or economic coercion are concluded in violation of international law; rather, the first paragraph of the Declaration condemns the use of such forms of improper pressure.[19] Accordingly, it is clear that the customary international law position was codified in Article 52 of the Vienna Convention. Villiger suggests that the Declaration's value is limited to an interpretative guide to Article 52 of the Vienna Convention';[20] however, such a viewpoint is unduly narrow. It is important to recall that the Declaration was produced as a result of a compromise between developed States and developing/socialist States regarding the general effect of the use of coercion in the context of the conclusion of treaties. Consequently, the Declaration's provisions were designed to extend the doctrine of coercion beyond instances where force is threatened or used to procure the conclusion of a treaty.

Shaw suggests that the provisions of the Declaration have not achieved the status of binding international law;[21] consequently, he assumed that the Declaration remains a 'soft law' international instrument. Nevertheless, Shaw's interpretation is based on the fact that the Declaration's provisions were not included in the Vienna Convention on Law of Treaties and not to the extent to which the international community of States has supported the Declaration's provisions in the period since it was adopted.[22] Villiger accepts that the Declaration's provisions have the capacity to crystallise into customary international law.[23] However, it appears that there is insufficient evidence of the necessary *opinio juris* and State practice in support of the introduction of a new principle of customary international law concerning the doctrine of coercion in relation to the conclusion of treaties.[24] As a result, the established customary international law position regarding the use of coercion in this context remains the principle that was codified in Article 52 of the Vienna Convention on the Law of Treaties.[25] The coincidence of treaty law and customary international

[18] ME Villiger, *Commentary on the 1969 Vienna Convention on the Law of Treaties* (Leiden, Brill, 2009) 653–54.
[19] ibid, 653–54. See also L Caflisch, 'Unequal Treaties' (1992) 35 *German Yearbook of International Law* 52, 73–75.
[20] Villiger, *Commentary on the 1969 Vienna Convention on the Law of Treaties* (n 18) 657.
[21] MN Shaw, *International Law*, 6th edn (Cambridge, Cambridge University Press, 2008) 943.
[22] This is also the position of Caflisch, 'Unequal Treaties' (n 19) 73–75.
[23] Villiger (n 18) 656.
[24] The requirements for the formation of customary international law are discussed in the next chapter.
[25] See also VCLT, Art 51, which provides that: 'The expression of a State's consent to be bound by a treaty which has been procured by the coercion of its representative through acts or threats directed against him shall be without any legal effect'.

law on this issue was confirmed in the 1981 *Dubai-Sharjah Border Arbitration* case.[26] It has been suggested that this principle derives its customary international law status from its nexus with the prohibition on the threat or use of force rather than from an independent doctrine of coercion in international law.[27] Accordingly, it would appear that no separate and distinct principle of customary international law regarding the effect of coercion in the context of the conclusion of treaties existed during the period when the 1965 Lancaster House Agreement was concluded. However, does such a conclusion mean that a broader conception of the principle of coercion in such situations was unknown to international law at the moment when the Chagos Islands were detached from the British colony of Mauritius?

III. THE RELATIONSHIP BETWEEN COERCION AND CONSENT IN THE CONCLUSION OF TREATIES

In *American Independent Oil Company Case v Kuwait* (the *Aminoil* case),[28] the company claimed that it was pressured into an agreement with the government of Kuwait and that its consent to the agreement was vitiated as a result.[29] The arbitral tribunal accepted, in principle, that the threat of having the company's operations in Kuwait closed down would amount to strong economic pressure and that such a form of pressure could be equated to duress since it would deprive the company's consent of its full effect.[30] However, on the facts, the tribunal decided, that: 'the whole conduct of the company shows that the pressure it was under was not of a kind to inhibit its freedom of choice'.[31] It was led to this conclusion by evidence that company had not protested against instances where the government of Kuwait had breached the agreement. The tribunal concluded that the company had acquiesced in the conduct of the government of Kuwait;[32] consequently, it decided that the company had lost its entitlement to claim to duress. The tribunal's view was captured in the following observation: 'In truth, the company made a choice; disagreeable as certain demands might be, it is considered that it was better to accede to them because it was still possible to live with them.'[33]

It should be acknowledged that, in principle, companies do not possess international legal personality and that agreements between multinational companies and the governments of States do not necessarily have the status of treaties as a matter of international law. A good example of this standpoint is apparent

---

[26] *Dubai-Sharjah Border Arbitration* case (1981) 91 ILR 543, 569. This case is discussed in detail below.

[27] Villiger (n 18) 649 [20] and De Jong (n 2) 246.

[28] *Aminoil v Kuwait* (1982) 21 International Legal Materials 976.

[29] ibid, [40].

[30] ibid, [41].

[31] ibid, [44].

[32] ibid, [42–44]

[33] ibid, [44].

from the ICJ's decision in the *Anglo-Iranian Oil Company case*.[34] In this case, the ICJ observed that the agreement between the Anglo-Iranian Oil Company and the Iranian government was, 'nothing more than a concessionary contract between a government and a foreign corporation'.[35] Nevertheless, it is clear from subsequent decisions by international tribunals, such as the *Texaco v Libya Case*, that such contracts may be 'internationalised' by the agreement of the parties.[36] Consequently, in cases where the parties have agreed that international law shall be the applicable law for the purpose of a given agreement between the government of the State and a non-State actor, in the event of a dispute, the decisions of international tribunals are determined by reference to international law. Moreover, arbitral awards in such cases have proved to be a valuable source of jurisprudence concerning the principles of international law relating to international agreements, notwithstanding their hybrid nature.

The *Aminoil* case is potentially significant for the present purpose for a number of reasons. First, the case did not involve the threat or use of force, as recognised by international law. As a result, the conception of coercion considered in that case did not fall within the scope of the customary international law principle, which was enshrined in Article 52 of the Vienna Convention. However, in the *Aminoil* case, the tribunal implicitly accepted the existence of a broader conception of coercion as a matter of international law. This conception was grounded in a contextual determination of whether there was an absence of choice on the facts of the case. In this regard, the tribunal drew on the principle of coercion as it has been recognised in the field of contract law by municipal legal systems. Further, in his commentary on the Vienna Convention on the Law of Treaties, Villiger harnesses the *Aminoil* case as a reliable authority for the proposition that, as a matter of international law, there must be a causal relationship between the coercion used by a stronger party to procure the consent of a weaker party to enter into a treaty and that the coercion must be sufficient to ensure that the treaty would not have been concluded otherwise.[37] It could be argued that, as the *Aminoil* case was concerned with an agreement between the government of a State and a non-State actor, the decision has very little resonance for the international law relating to the use of coercion in the context of the conclusion of treaties. Nevertheless, it is suggested that the decision remains important for at least two reasons. First, the Tribunal's discussion of the notion of coercion was determined by reference to international law because this was the applicable law as determined by the agreement. Secondly, Villiger in his authoritative work on the Vienna Convention considers the *Aminoil* case as an important authority regarding the basic need for a causal relationship between the coercion used and the consent procured.

---

[34] *Anglo-Iranian Oil Company* case (1952) ICJ Rep 93.
[35] ibid, 112.
[36] *Texaco v Libya* case (1978) 17 International Legal Materials 1. See cl 28 of the Agreement, discussed in the award, at [40–47].
[37] Villiger (n 18) 645–46.

The requirement of the presence of a causal relationship between the coercion and the consent with regard to the conclusion of a treaty in international law is indicative of the fundamental role that consent performs in relation to the validity of agreements and the legitimacy that it confers on the foundational principle of *pacta sunt servanda*. In general, municipal legal systems assume that contracts are concluded on the basis of freely given consent. When it is established that a party has been coerced into concluding a contract then it is deemed to be void (or voidable).[38] The notion of coercion as a lack of consent is a central element of contract law in municipal legal systems. Moreover, as noted above, during the early period of international law's development, it was widely assumed that the conception of coercion applied to private law contracts and international treaties given that both these forms of agreement had their origins in Roman law.[39] However, the fact that the threat or use of force was not prohibited in international law until the UN era meant that international lawyers lost sight of the significance of this parallel over time.

In his *Private Law Sources and Analogies of International Law*, Lauterpacht emphasised that consent was a vital element in the conception of both international treaties and private law contracts alike.[40] In his view: 'It is believed that the lack of analogy of treaties and contracts so far as it was occasioned by the admissibility of duress cannot survive in an organised community of nations.'[41] However, at that time, Lauterpacht was clearly focused on challenging the lawfulness of the threat or use of force in international law rather than on advancing the argument that coercion was founded on the absence of consent and that this could vitiate the consent secured during the process of concluding a treaty. Nevertheless, Lauterpacht viewed the inconsistency between coercion in spheres of international law and municipal law as a normative anomaly which was a consequence of the immaturity of the international legal system and he believed that it would disappear as international law developed.[42]

But, as discussed above, neither the International Law Commission nor the international community of States, during the proceedings at the Vienna Conference, decided to endorse a binding freestanding doctrine of coercion in relation to the conclusion of treaties as a matter of international law. De Jong insisted that the argument that coercion is grounded in a lack of consent is no longer tenable given the content of Article 52 of the Vienna Convention and its subsequent interpretation.[43] Accordingly, De Jong suggested that the scope for

[38] De Jong (n 2) 220.

[39] ibid, 221.

[40] H Lauterpacht, *Private Law Sources and Analogies of International Law* (London, Longman, 1927) 167 cited in De Jong (n 2) 222.

[41] ibid, 165, quoted in De Jong (n 2) 223.

[42] Regarding Lauterpacht's conception of international law, see P Capps, *Human Dignity and the Foundations of International Law* (Oxford, Hart Publishing, 2009) 210–12; P Capps, 'Lauterpacht's Method' (2011) 82 *British Yearbook of International Law* 248; and M Koskenniemi, 'The Function of Law in the International Community' (2008) 79 *British Yearbook of International Law* 353.

[43] De Jong (n 2) 247.

private law analogies in this area has lapsed because States have consciously sought to regulate the parameters of coercion as a matter of international law.[44] However, it is possible to argue that the *Aminoil* case offers a more optimistic reading of the doctrine of coercion as a matter of international law. This authority suggests that the historical connection between the general principles of law found in municipal legal systems and international law in this area has not been lost entirely and that a broader doctrine of coercion, one that focuses on the absence of consent rather than on the means by which consent has been procured, already exists. Nevertheless, it is apparent that such a conception of coercion has not achieved the status of customary international law. This conclusion necessitates an assessment of whether the doctrine of coercion has attained the status of a general principle of law pursuant to Article 38(1)(c) of the ICJ Statute, which recognises that the general principles of law found in municipal legal systems are a source of international law.

In 1992, in the context of an assessment of the doctrine of unequal treaties in international law, Caflisch undertook a short survey regarding whether a general principle of unequal transactions had developed in the field of contract law in municipal legal systems.[45] After a brief comparative analysis of the approach adopted in several municipal jurisdictions, he concluded that no such general principle had evolved in the surveyed legal systems. Consequently, he concluded that no doctrine of 'unequal transactions' could be transposed into international law via Article 38(1)(c).[46] Caflisch's conclusion may be correct regarding the non-existence of a shared principle of unequal transactions in municipal legal systems. However, his willingness to equate the notion of unequal transactions with the doctrine of coercion is open to question. The notion of unequal transactions, as discussed by Caflisch, constitutes a broad set of circumstantial claims, which are rooted in the existence of an overwhelming imbalance in the bargaining positions of the parties to a contract, or in some kind of unconscionable behaviour by one party at the expense of another.[47] In sharp contrast, the doctrine of coercion is an intention-based legal principle, which is a recognised in numerous municipal legal systems. Moreover, certain municipal legal systems have recognised that duress is not restricted to the use of actual or threatened violence for the purpose of procuring a person's consent to enter into a contract.[48] Against this background, it is suggested that the question is not *whether* a doctrine of coercion, which encompasses improper forms of pressure, beyond instances of the threat or use of violence, is a general principle of law in municipal legal systems; rather, the question is *when* was this general principle established in municipal legal systems? It appears that such a broad

---

[44] ibid, 224.
[45] Caflisch (n 19) 57–59.
[46] ibid, 59.
[47] ibid, 59.
[48] For the English law position, see eg E Peel, *Treitel on The Law of Contract* (London, Sweet & Maxwell, 2007) 440.

conception of duress did not become widely established in municipal legal systems until the 1980s or the early-1990s.[49] Accordingly, it is difficult to argue that such a broad conception of duress existed as a general principle of law in municipal legal systems during the period in which the 1965 Lancaster House Agreement was concluded.[50] The recognition of such developments in municipal legal systems might also cast doubt on the relevance of the 1982 decision in the *Aminoil* case to any assessment of the validity of the 1965 Agreement as a matter of international law. Nevertheless, it should be acknowledged that is often difficult to calibrate the temporal dimension of doctrinal developments within legal systems in the absence of clear markers of normative development. Consequently, it is suggested that this provisional conclusion is not necessarily dispositive,[51] especially given the fact that the casual relationship between coercion and consent in relation to the conclusion of international agreements has an ancient pedigree in international law.

The recognition that a broad notion of coercion exists in international law is confronted by at least two further challenges: (i) the relativity of free will; and (ii) the need for cogent evidential requirements in order to establish actionable instances of coercion. Lauterpacht fully appreciated the problem of establishing freely given consent for the purpose of determining the legal validity of an agreement. Although he recognised that freedom of consent is 'the very essence of the notion of contract', he understood that free will is always relative as individuals are often compelled to enter into contracts as a result of 'inescapable economic or other considerations'.[52] Accordingly, he was of the opinion that even municipal legal systems 'cannot attach decisive importance to this kind of compulsion'.[53] However, Lauterpacht acknowledged that at least municipal legal systems protect an individual's free will from the consequence of threats of physical compulsion in contrast to the approach maintained by international law, at the time he was writing, when the threat or use of force to secure consent was still considered to be lawful.[54] This comparison demonstrates the challenge presented by gradations of pressure in the context of the formation of agreements for any legal system. Arguably, this problem is particularly significant for international law as *Realpolitik* considerations influence the decisions of States regarding the conclusion of treaties and national interests in general. Accordingly, it should be acknowledged that a freestanding doctrine of coercion in international law would have to cope with political considerations that would

---

[49] ibid, 440–47.

[50] This conclusion is in keeping with the established principle of inter-temporal law in international law, which holds that actions carried out in one period cannot be judged by the legal standards of another. See the *Island of Palmas* case (1928) 2 RIAA 829, 845. See also TO Elias, 'The Doctrine of Intertemporal Law' (1980) 74 *American Journal of International Law* 285.

[51] In contrast, in the *Island of Palmas* case (n 50), the temporal gap extended to a few centuries. See J Castellino and S Allen, *Title to Territory in International Law: A Temporal Analysis* (Aldershot, Ashgate, 2003).

[52] Lauterpacht, *Hersch Lauterpacht, International Law* (n 3) 352.

[53] ibid, 353.

[54] ibid, 352–53.

not be tolerated within municipal legal systems and this is an inevitable consequence of the horizontal structure of authority in the international legal system. Nevertheless, it should be recognised that political considerations are not materially different from economic considerations in relation to the use of coercion as a means of concluding an agreement – it is the use of coercive pressure which has the effect of vitiating one party's consent and not the lever used to procure consent that is important in such situations.

As the arbitration panel acknowledged in the *Dubai-Sharjah Border Arbitration* case, the fact that a treaty provision does not offend Article 52 of the Vienna Convention does not mean that some form of pressure has not been applied by a stronger party to induce a weaker party to enter into a treaty. In that case, the question was whether the rulers of the protected States of Dubai and Sharjah had been coerced into giving their consent to agreements which authorised the agent of the protecting State, the UK, to determine the boundaries between them. In its award, the panel observed: 'Every kind of international negotiation is subject to influences of this kind. Mere influences and pressures cannot be equated with the concept of coercion as it is known in international law'.[55] This observation supports the concern expressed by the representative of the Canadian government at the Vienna Conference, who stated that the existence of perfect equality between the parties to any treaty is imaginary and that if international law were to embrace such a relativistic approach to assessing the validity of any given treaty then the integrity of the law of treaties would be fundamentally compromised as a result.[56]

Against this background, how could a broad doctrine of coercion, one that encompasses economic and political forms of improper pressure, become established as part of the jurisprudence of modern international law? Despite the concerns expressed by the members of the International Law Commission in the 1960s; the representatives of developed States in the context of the Vienna Conference in 1968/69; and by international tribunals in the 1970s and 1980s, it is apparent that the barriers to the recognition of a broad conception of coercion in international law are largely evidential in nature. Consequently, obstacles to the task of establishing whether a given international agreement has been concluded as a result of coercion may be overcome if compelling evidence of the use of coercion can be produced. Moreover, it is clear that municipal legal systems have now developed sophisticated doctrines designed to regulate instances of coercion and duress in the field of contract law. Accordingly, the fears expressed by the above-mentioned constituencies have been shown to be largely unfounded and the argument that only instances of the threat or use of force for the purpose of procuring the conclusion of the treaty could be proved but that other forms of improper pressure could not be established, is not sustainable, in principle.

---

[55] *Dubai-Sharjah Border Arbitration* case (n 26) 571.
[56] See Murphy (n 9) 58–59.

Nevertheless, international tribunals have set a very high evidential standard for the purpose of proving an allegation of coercion as a matter of international law. In the *Dubai-Sharjah Border Arbitration* case, the panel observed that: 'it is manifestly clear that any allegation of duress, of whatever kind, which is alleged to vitiate consent must be the subject of very precise proof'.[57] Moreover, in the *Fisheries Jurisdiction* case, in the response to an unsubstantiated claim of duress, the ICJ noted that:

> It is equally clear that a court cannot consider an accusation of this serious nature on the basis of a vague general charge unfortified by evidence in its support. The history of the negotiations, which led up to the 1961 Exchange of Notes reveals that these instruments were freely negotiated by the interested parties on the basis of perfect equality and freedom of decision on both sides. No fact has been brought to the attention of the Court from any quarter suggesting the slightest doubt on the matter.[58]

However, in his separate Opinion in the *Fisheries Jurisdiction* case, Judge Padilla Nervo was more realistic when he observed that:

> there are moral and political pressures which cannot be proved by the so-called documentary evidence, but which are in fact indisputably real and which have, in history, given rise to treaties and conventions claimed to be freely concluded and subjected to the principle of *pacta sunt servanda*.[59]

A fundamental challenge with regard to establishing the use of coercion in relation to treaties concerns the way in which improper pressure manifests itself.[60] Two distinct approaches have been identified in this respect. One approach is to focus on the behaviour of the parties during the process of negotiating a treaty. In this respect, what matters is the way in which the treaty was concluded. If no evidence of duress during the negotiating process can be produced then the treaty has not been concluded by as a result of the use of coercion.[61] However, an alternative approach concentrates not on the conduct of the parties during the process of concluding a treaty but instead it looks at the substantive terms of the agreement to determine whether coercion has been used to procure the consent of the weaker party. This alternative conception equates coercion with the conclusion of unequal bargains.[62] It endorses the view that no reasonable party would freely consent to an agreement that would be harmful to its own interests. This approach assumes that a reasonable party would not enter into

---

[57] *Dubai-Sharjah Border Arbitration* case (n 26) 569.

[58] *Fisheries Jurisdiction* case *(Jurisdiction) (UK/Iceland)* (1973) ICJ Rep 14 [24].

[59] ibid, Dissenting Opinion of Judge Padilla-Nervo, 47.

[60] See generally De Jong (n 2) 234–35; Caflisch (n 19) 70–71, and Villiger (n 18) 646–47.

[61] Villiger draws a strange distinction between what happens during the process of negotiating a treaty and the process of concluding a treaty. He suggests that coercion is only relevant in situations when a treaty or agreement is being concluded rather than negotiated, at 645 [10–11]. This distinction is not recognised by de Jong and it is assumed that the distinction made by Villiger between concluding and negotiating is a distinction without a difference.

[62] Caflisch (n 19) 70.

such an agreement unless it had been coerced into the bargain.[63] It has been suggested that, in practice, the two opposing approaches tend to interact with one another: the use of coercion to procure the consent of a weaker party is likely to be revealed by the agreement's substantive provisions.[64] The rationale for this view appears to be grounded in the assumption that coercion would be unnecessary in situations where a party would have freely accepted the terms of an agreement anyway. However, it is clear from this combined approach that there must be cogent evidence of the use of improper pressure during the process of concluding an agreement – coercion will not be presumed by studying the terms of the agreement alone. Accordingly, viewed from one perspective, the combined approach adds very little to the first approach sketched out above.

The issue of whether coercion could only be established by reference to the behaviour of the parties during the process of concluding an agreement, or by an examination of the substantive terms of the agreement, was discussed in relation to the drafting of what became Article 52 of the Vienna Convention on the Law of Treaties both within the International Law Commission and, subsequently, during the Vienna Conference.[65] In general, representatives of the developed States argued in favour of limiting the doctrine of coercion to instances where force was used or threatened during the process of concluding an agreement whereas developing/socialist States favoured the substantive approach which focused on the inequality of the result. However, it is clear that the former approach ultimately prevailed. Article 52 provides that 'a treaty is void if its conclusion has been procured by the threat or use of force'. This interpretation was subsequently confirmed by the ICJ in the *Fisheries Jurisdiction* case, where it noted that:

> There can be little doubt, as is implied in the Charter of the United Nations and recognized in Article 52 of the Vienna Convention on the Law of Treaties, that under contemporary international law an agreement concluded under the threat or use of force is void.[66]

Consequently, it appears that not only did customary international law and treaty law restrict the doctrine of coercion to situations where the threat or use of force was used to procure the consent of a party to enter into a treaty, a claim of coercion could only be substantiated by the production of cogent evidence that the weaker party had been subjected to such a form of duress during the process of negotiating the treaty in question rather than by reference to a circumstantial assessment of the situation combined with an examination of the substantive terms of the resultant agreement. On this reading of the available material, it would seem that it would be very hard to plead coercion successfully

---

[63] ibid.

[64] See De Jong (n 2) 234.

[65] See Detter (n 2). See also *International Law Commission Yearbook* 1966, vol II, 246–47 and Caflisch (n 19) 71.

[66] *Fisheries Jurisdiction* case (n 58) [24].

in situations where force was not used or threatened to bring about the act of concluding a treaty. The extent to which this is a true and fair representation of modern international law will be considered below. However, first it is necessary to examine the treaty-making capacity of colonial entities as a matter of international law.

IV. INTERNATIONAL LEGAL PERSONALITY, TREATY-MAKING CAPACITY AND THE 1965 LANCASTER HOUSE AGREEMENT

A. International Legal Personality and Treaty-Making Authority in the Colonial Context

Traditional international law adopted the view that the relationship between a metropolitan State and its colonies was governed by the municipal legal order of the responsible State because it fell within the sphere of that State's domestic jurisdiction.[67] From this standpoint, it followed that the applicable law relating to a given colony was determined by the constitutional arrangements made for it by the municipal legislative mechanisms of the responsible State.[68] And, as a result, any such arrangements were beyond the scope of international law.[69]

Nevertheless, in the ground-breaking *Reparations Case* (1949),[70] the ICJ recognised that international legal personality is not restricted to States alone. Specifically, it observed that: 'The subjects of law in any legal system are not necessarily identical in their nature or in the extent of their rights, and their nature depends upon the needs of the community'.[71] Consequently, it follows that, if an entity possesses rights and/or obligations as a matter of international law, it may be capable of possessing international legal personality, at least for certain purposes.[72] As noted above, it has often been claimed that colonial entities did not possess international legal personality and that they lacked the capacity to enter into treaties at the level of international law.[73] But while this general position may have been correct for many colonial entities throughout

---

[67] The evolution of international jurisdiction in this area is considered in ch 5. Particular markers include: the *Nationality Decrees in Tunis and Morocco* case (1923) PCIJ Series B, No 4; and the UN Charter, Art 2(7) and its subsequent interpretation. See G Nolte in B Simma (ed), *The Charter of the United Nations: A Commentary*, vol I, 3rd edn (Oxford, Oxford University Press, 2012) 290–93.

[68] However, it should be noted that such an approach was only true in respect of non-self-governing territories pursuant to c XI of the Charter and not trust territories under cc XII and XIII of the Charter. See ch 5.

[69] See ch 5.

[70] *Advisory Opinion concerning Reparations for Injuries Suffered in the Service of the United Nations* (1949) ICJ Rep 174.

[71] ibid, 178.

[72] In the *Reparations* case, ibid, the ICJ endorsed the view that a subject of the law is an entity capable of possessing international rights and duties and of having the capacity to maintain its rights by bringing international claims.

[73] See A Aust, *Handbook of International Law*, 2nd edn (Cambridge, Cambridge University Press, 2010) 30.

much of the colonial era, it was not necessarily true in all cases. There are numerous examples of colonial entities being recognised as having a degree of international legal personality for certain limited purposes.[74] In principle, there is no reason why a colonial entity could not have had international legal personality in order to safeguard its international legal rights and/or obligations. This argument was strengthened by the initiatives of the League of Nations in respect of the mandates system and, subsequently, by the United Nations in relation to trust territories.[75] These were special regimes devised to address the challenge of what should be done with the colonial territories belonging to the Axis powers at the end of the First and Second World Wars. However, once the international legal system was prepared to acknowledge that colonial territories could have a separate and distinct status as a matter of international law – however uncertain that status actually was in theory and in practice – such arrangements brought into sharp relief the wider question of the international legal status of colonial territories in general. Chapter XI of the UN Charter established a modest framework for the international regulation of all colonial territories.[76] Chapter XI did not explicitly address the issue of whether non-self-governing territories had a separate and distinct status as a matter of international law. However, subsequent developments during the 1960s and 1970s – including the 1960 Colonial Declaration;[77] the 1966 International Covenants on Human Rights;[78] and the 1970 Declaration on Friendly Relations – all acknowledged that colonial peoples possessed a degree of international legal personality for certain purposes.[79] In the circumstances, the question of whether the elected representatives of the Mauritian colonial government possessed the requisite degree of international legal personality in order to conclude the 1965 Lancaster House Agreement must be considered.

[74] See OJ Lissitzyn, 'Territorial Entities other than independent States in the Law of Treaties' (1968) 125 *Recueil des cours* 1–91, 71. Good examples include India and the Philippines during the period when they were colonial territories.

[75] See the 1919 Covenant of the League of Nations, Art 22.

[76] This framework is considered in detail in ch 5.

[77] Declaration on the Granting of Independence to Colonial Countries and Peoples, UNGA Res 1514(XV), 14 December 1960.

[78] International Covenant on Civil and Political Rights 1966, 999 UNTS 171 (ICCPR); and International Covenant on Economic, Social and Cultural Rights 1966, 993 UNTS 3 (ICESCR). Joint Art 1(3) provides:

The State Parties to the present Covenant, including those having responsibility for the administration of Non-Self-Governing and Trust Territories, shall promote the realization of the right of self-determination, and shall respect that right, in conformity with the provisions of the Charter of the United Nations.

[79] See the Declaration on the Principles of International Law concerning Friendly Relations and Co-operation Among States in Accordance with the Charter of the United Nations, UNGA Res 2625(XXV), 24 October 1970. It provides, inter alia, that:

The territory of a colony or other non-self-governing territory has, under the Charter, a status separate and distinct from the territory of the State administering it; and such separate and distinct status under the Charter shall exist until the people of the colony or non-self-governing territory have exercised their right of self-determination in accordance with the Charter, and particularly its purposes and principles.

As this section addresses both the concept of international legal personality and the treaty-making capacity of colonial entities, the meaning and scope of the term 'treaty' must also be established in this context. Article 2(1)(a) of the Vienna Convention on the Law of Treaties 1969 provides that:

> 'treaty' means an: 'international agreement concluded between States in written form and governed by international law, whether embodied in a single instrument or in two or more related instruments and whatever its particular designation'.

Writing in 1968, Lissitzyn advances a broader conception of the notion of a 'treaty'. He suggested that it encompassed 'any agreement governed or which may be governed by public international law, regardless of form'.[80] It is clear that agreements concluded between States and territorial entities can also be classified as treaties as a matter of customary international law. Moreover, Lissitzyn suggested that, in practice, certain colonial entities may have acquired treaty-making capacities without any formal recognition that particular colonial entities possessed any such authority on the part of the responsible colonial power.[81] Nevertheless, it is apparent that the acquisition of such competencies remained exceptional during the colonial era. As a result, international agreements concluded between colonial entities and third States were generally regarded as being valid as a matter of international law, only if it was apparent that the parties intended such agreements to have the status of international treaties.[82] This approach would appear to have limited resonance in relation to the Lancaster House Agreement, since it was made by an administering State and a non-self-governing territory for which it was responsible. However, whether the elected representatives of the Mauritian colonial government had the capacity to conclude the 1965 Lancaster House Agreement will be explored in the next sub-section.

B. International Legal Personality and Treaty-Making Authority in the Mauritian Context

As a matter of UK constitutional law, the historical position was that a British colony did not possess international legal personality.[83] However, as the twentieth century progressed, the UK government began to draw a distinction between the British 'Dominions' and British 'colonial territories' in this respect. It acknowledged that the Dominions had possessed a substantial degree of legal personality for the purposes of international law for a considerable period of

---

[80] See Lissitzyn, 'Territorial Entities other than independent States in the Law of Treaties' (n 74) 12.

[81] ibid, 71.

[82] ibid, 83.

[83] While the term 'Overseas Territory' is now the preferred term, the British Overseas Territories Act 2002 did not expunge the term 'colony' and it is defined in sch 1 of the Interpretation Act 1978. See I Hendry and S Dickson, *British Overseas Territories Law* (Oxford, Hart Publishing, 2011) 3–5.

time before they were granted independence.[84] In contrast, British colonial territories did not typically enjoy responsible government before they acceded to independence; consequently, in the UK government's opinion, they did not possess a measure of international legal personality.[85]

The colony of Mauritius did not possess a distinct legal personality for the purposes of international law from the perspective of British constitutional law. The applicable constitutional arrangements were established by the Mauritius (Constitution) Order 1964[86] and the Mauritius Royal Instructions 1964.[87] Under these arrangements, the British Governor of Mauritius retained responsibility for its external affairs, defence and internal security. The Mauritian people only possessed a limited form of internal self-government through their democratically elected political representatives.[88] Consequently, the elected representatives of the Mauritian colonial government – the members of the Council of Ministers who formed the Mauritian delegation at the 1965 Constitutional Conference and who concluded the 1965 Lancaster House Agreement with the British government – did not have the authority to enter into international agreements according to British constitutional law. Further, in 1966, the UK government confirmed that it retained the authority to enter into international agreements on behalf of its colonies until they acceded to independence in a meeting of the Special Committee on Decolonisation ('C24'), which was directly concerned with the circumstances of the detachment of the Chagos Islands from Mauritius.[89]

Against this background, the general argument that, in the lead up to independence, a colony possesses a degree international legal personality, which was opposable against the responsible State, appears to be untenable as such a status would be antithetical to the municipal legal order created for that colony by the responsible State.[90] In the British context, this standpoint is supported by the constitutional doctrine that the UK and its colonies combine together to form the Crown's 'undivided realm'.[91] This doctrine empowers the UK government to

---

[84] See DP O'Connell, 'Independence and Succession to Treaties' (1962) 38 *British Yearbook of International Law* 84, 104. In the UK government's view, this necessitated the making of devolution agreements with such territories in advance of independence. See also M Craven, *The Decolonization of International Law: State Succession and the Law of Treaties* (Oxford, Oxford University Press, 2007) ch 2.

[85] See O'Connell, 'Independence and Succession to Treaties' (n 84) 104.

[86] See S De Smith, 'Mauritius: Constitutionalism in a Plural Society' (1968) 31 *Modern Law Review* 601, 1163.

[87] Ibid, 1206.

[88] Ibid, 601. For a brief overview of the constitutional arrangements in place for Mauritius during the mid-1960s, see K Roberts-Wray in *Commonwealth and Colonial Law* (London, Stevens & Sons, 1966) 727–30. See also 'Report of the Mauritian Constitutional Conference – September 1965 – Sessional Paper No 6 of 1965'.

[89] Special Committee on the Situation with Regard to the Implementation of the Declaration on the Granting of Independence to Colonial Countries and Peoples (known as 'C24'), A/6300/Rev 1, 684 [168–69] and the report [687].

[90] In the context of devolution agreements, this viewpoint is strengthened by doubts expressed about their legal significance. See O'Connell (n 84) 118.

[91] See ch 1 for a discussion of this doctrine of British constitutional law.

legislate in the overall interests of that realm even if those general interests may be detrimental to the interests of a particular colony. Accordingly, this doctrine could have been employed to justify the UK government's decision to legislate, by Order in Council, to detach the Chagos Islands from the colony of Mauritius. Specifically, the UK government could have argued that the defence considerations, which prompted the decision to establish a US military facility on the island of Diego Garcia, were in the overall interests of the undivided realm of the UK and its colonies.

As discussed in the last chapter, a popular view, which was expressed in different departments of the UK government during the period when the prospect of detaching the Chagos Islands from Mauritius was being mooted was that, as a matter of UK law, the Chagos Islands could be lawfully detached, via Order in Council, without the agreement of the elected representatives of the Mauritian colonial government. This position was articulated by the Foreign Office prior to the Mauritian Constitutional Conference in September 1965. The Colonial Secretary, Anthony Greenwood, informed the Mauritian delegation of this position in his initial discussion about the detachment of the Chagos Islands on 20 September 1965. It was also expressed by the British Prime Minister in his meeting with the Mauritian Premier on the morning of 23 September 1965. Further, the Colonial Secretary reminded the leaders of the three Mauritian political parties – the Mauritian Labour Party, Independence Forward Bloc and the Muslim Committee of Action – of this position during their meeting on the afternoon of 23 September 1965, when the terms of the Lancaster House Agreement were negotiated.[92]

Branley, an official in the British Colonial Office, subsequently defended the legality of a unilateral strategy regarding the detachment of the Chagos Islands from Mauritius. In official correspondence, he stated that the history of British colonial administration in Africa had demonstrated that numerous small island territories had been detached from larger colonies only to be reattached to other colonial units for the sake of administrative convenience. In the context of the Indian Ocean, Branley cited the examples of the islands of Aldabra and Providence, which had been detached from the colony of Mauritius in 1908, only to be reattached to the colony of the Seychelles; and in 1921, the same thing happened to the islands of Coetivy and Farquhar.[93]

According to the traditional approach adopted by British constitutional law, international law would only become relevant once a colony had been granted its independence and until such a moment international law had no application to the relations between a metropolitan State and its colonies. However, the British constitutional law doctrine of the Crown's undivided realm and the UK government's view that it possessed the constitutional authority to dismember

---

[92] See ch 3.

[93] PRO FCO 34/482, Branley to Jerrom, 20 December 1968 and J Chan-Low, 'The Making of the Chagos Affair: Myths and Reality' in S Evers and M Kooy (eds), *Eviction from the Chagos Islands: Displacement and Struggle for Identity Against Two World Powers* (Leiden, Brill, 2011) 72.

its colonial territories by Order in Council unilaterally both ignored the wider international shift in favour of decolonisation that had occurred by the early 1960s. In this respect, Branley overlooked the temporal aspect of the comparison between the examples of territorial readjustment that he cites from the early part of the twentieth century and the 1965 detachment of the Chagos Islands from the colony of Mauritius in order to create the BIOT. The examples given by Branley occurred at the zenith of the British Empire whereas the excision of the Chagos Islands from Mauritius happened at the height of the period of decolonisation. It is clear that Branley, who was writing in 1968, attached no significance to the international legal obligations imposed on administering States with regard to their non-self-governing territories by Chapter XI of the UN Charter; the institutional initiatives of the UN General Assembly concerning the processes of decolonisation; or the claim that the right of colonial self-determination had emerged with the adoption of the 1960 Colonial Declaration.[94]

The general position regarding the international legal personality and treaty-making capacities of colonial entities discussed in the previous sub-section does resolve the specific issue of whether the 1965 Lancaster House Agreement constitutes a treaty for the purposes of international law. First, it should be noted that the 1965 Agreement was concluded before the International Law Commission finalised its 1966 draft Convention on the Law of Treaties and thus before the conclusion of the Vienna Convention on the Law of Treaties. Accordingly, the Vienna Convention is only significant for the purposes of the present enquiry to the extent that it codified pre-existing customary international law regarding the conclusion of treaties. Secondly, the terms of the 1965 Agreement were contained in the official minutes of a meeting held on 23 September 1965 between the British Colonial Secretary and the elected representatives of the Mauritian colonial government. These minutes were subsequently authenticated by the Mauritian delegates on 6 October 1965 and formally approved by the Mauritian Council of Ministers on 5 November 1965.[95]

In the circumstances, a pertinent question, in the light of the provisions of Article 2(1)(a) of the Vienna Convention, quoted above, is whether the authenticated and approved minutes of an inter-governmental meeting constitute a treaty for the purposes of international law? In the *Maritime Delimitation and Territorial Questions* case *(Qatar/Bahrain) (Jurisdiction)*, the ICJ had to decide whether the signed minutes of a meeting between the Foreign Ministers of Qatar and Bahrain constituted a treaty for the purpose of providing the Court with jurisdiction over the dispute.[96] The ICJ held that the minutes were: 'not a

---

[94] This controversial issue is addressed in the next chapter.

[95] See the '1983 Excision Report', Mauritian Legislative Assembly, 'Report of the Select Committee on the Excision of the Chagos Archipelago (No 2 of 1983) (Port Louis, Mauritian Legislative Assembly 1983) app L, 58.

[96] *Maritime Delimitation and Territorial Questions* case *(Qatar/Bahrain) (Jurisdiction)* (1994) ICJ Rep 112.

simple record of a meeting . . . They enumerate the commitments to which the Parties had consented. They thus create rights and obligations in international law for the Parties. They constitute an international agreement'.[97] This decision provides powerful authority for the proposition that the form of the Lancaster House Agreement does not prevent it from being classified as a treaty as a matter of international law.

A fundamental difficulty in relation to the task of establishing both (i) whether the elected representatives of the Mauritian colonial government possessed international legal personality for the purpose of concluding the 1965 Lancaster House Agreement; and (ii) whether that Agreement could be considered to be a treaty as a matter of international law, stems from the fact that it was concluded between an administering State and one of its non-self-governing territories. This kind of agreement is very different from an agreement concluded between a colonial entity and a third State, as discussed above. The *Dubai-Sharjah Border Arbitration* case,[98] which centred on disputed boundary agreements concluded between the rulers of Dubai and Sharjah and the representative of the UK government in 1956 and 1957, would seem to be a material precedent regarding the issue of the status of agreements concluded between a colonial power and non-European political entity during the UN era. However, it is important to note that Dubai and Sharjah were protected States rather than colonies.[99] Consequently, they retained the capacity not only to make treaties on their own behalf with third States but also with the protecting State, the UK.[100] Accordingly, the boundary agreements in dispute in that case did not derive their legal validity from the UK's municipal legal order (ie British colonial law); instead, they had the status of international treaties; therefore, international law constituted the applicable legal order for the purpose of determining the nature and effects of those agreements. As a result, a distinction can be drawn between the status of the agreements which formed the basis of the *Dubai-Sharjah Border Arbitration* case and the status of the 1965 Lancaster House Agreement. As discussed above, colonial entities may possess a degree of international legal personality under certain conditions and they may have acquired the capacity to enter into treaties with third States. However, an agreement between an administering State and a non-self-governing territory is concluded, prima facie, within the municipal legal order of the administering State. Consequently, it is hard to resist the conclusion that, as the 1965 Agreement was concluded within the UK's municipal legal order, its legal validity should be determined exclusively by reference to the applicable municipal law – British colonial law – and that international law is irrelevant to any such assessment.

---

[97] ibid, [25].

[98] *Dubai-Sharjah Border Arbitration* case (n 26).

[99] In 1892, the UK entered into a series of exclusive agreements with the rulers of the Trucial States. However, the UK government never sought to interfere in the domestic affairs of the Trucial States. See the *Dubai-Sharjah Arbitration* award (n 26) 561–62.

[100] See Lissitzyn (n 74) 53–54.

The problem with viewing agreements between an administering State and a non-self-governing territory as arrangements falling exclusively within the municipal legal order of the responsible State is that it follows from this standpoint that the legal validity of any such agreement must lapse once that non-self-governing territory becomes an independent State. However, such a conclusion is deeply problematic in relation to the 1965 Lancaster House Agreement. It was clearly the intention of the UK government and the elected representatives of the Mauritian colonial government that the Lancaster House Agreement would be legally binding on Mauritius once it had acceded to independence.[101] Accordingly, the 1965 Agreement was concluded on basis that it would have ongoing legal effects as a matter of international law.

Moreover, as the previous chapter showed, the Lancaster House Agreement sanctioned the dismemberment of the Mauritian colonial unit on the eve of independence and the Chagos Islands were detached from Mauritius as a condition of Mauritian independence. The UK had identified Mauritius as a non-self-governing territory pursuant to Chapter XI of the UN Charter as far back as 1946 and, as the responsible administering State the UK owed a range of obligations to the Mauritian people as a matter of international law, which included the duty to promote full self-government for the island's inhabitants. Accordingly, the conditions in non-self-governing territories and the fate of the inhabitants of such territories had become a matter of international regulation.[102] Further, the 1960 Colonial Declaration proclaimed that all colonial peoples were the beneficiaries of the right to self-determination as a matter of international law.[103] Regarding the validity of the substantive provisions of the Lancaster House Agreement, it is important to note that paragraph 6 of the Colonial Declaration stated that: 'Any attempt aimed at the partial or total disruption of the national unity and the territorial integrity of a country is incompatible with the purposes and principles of the Charter of the United Nations'. This paragraph has been interpreted as constituting a prohibition on the dismemberment of colonial territories before they have had the chance to exercise their right to self-determination through the act of gaining their independence. As a result, it is arguable that the Lancaster House Agreement violated the spirit of Chapter XI of the Charter and the right of colonial self-determination.[104]

---

[101] Leaving aside the argument that the consent of the elected representatives of the Mauritian government was procured by coercion and the Lancaster House Agreement was invalid as a result.

[102] However imperfectly rendered by the framework established by the UN Charter actually was. This issue is addressed in detail in the next chapter.

[103] The Declaration on the Granting of Independence to Colonial Countries and Peoples, UNGA Res 1514(XV), 14 December 1960 ('Colonial Declaration') provides, inter alia that:

1. The subjection of peoples to alien subjugation, domination and exploitation constitutes a denial of fundamental human rights, is contrary to the Charter of the United Nations and is an impediment to the promotion of world peace and co-operation.

2. All people have the right to self-determination; by virtue of that right they freely determine their political status and freely pursue their economic, social and cultural development.

[104] This issue will be examined in the next chapter.

This was the conclusion that was reached by the UN General Assembly in December 1965.[105] The status of the right of colonial self-determination as a matter of international law in 1965 will be scrutinised in the next chapter. However, in any event, it is important to acknowledge that, both the intentions of the parties and the substantive provisions of the Lancaster House Agreement indicate that the legal validity of the 1965 Agreement cannot be determined by reference to the UK's municipal legal order alone.[106]

As noted above, certain officials in the UK government were unwilling to countenance the legal developments which had occurred in the colonial context as a result of the advent of the UN Charter and the initiatives which had been undertaken by the General Assembly in the 1950s and 1960s. Nevertheless, during the period when the creation of the BIOT was being contemplated, other officials in the UK government were more attuned to claims concerning the right to colonial self-determination within the General Assembly and the mounting international pressure to bring colonialism to a speedy end. Consequently, senior figures in the Colonial Office, the Foreign Office and in the UN Mission appreciated the ramifications of such developments for the detachment of Chagos Islands from Mauritius and they understood that the agreement of the elected representatives of the Mauritian government was necessary in order to avoid close scrutiny of the detachment by the UN monitoring bodies, especially the General Assembly's Special Committee on the Situation with Regard to the Implementation of the Declaration on the Granting of Independence to Colonial Countries and Peoples (known as 'C24'), and the Fourth Committee, which was charged with the task of overseeing the process of decolonisation. As noted in the last chapter, these concerns were apparent from the Colonial Secretary's note to the UK Prime Minister in advance of his meeting with the Mauritian Premier on 20 September 1965:

> I hope that we shall be as generous as possible and I am sure that we should not seem to be trading Independence for detachment of the Islands. That would put us in a bad light at home and abroad and would sour our relations with the new state. And it would not accord well with the line you and I have taken about the Aden base (which has been well received even in the Committee of 24). Agreement is therefore desirable[107]

Further, some officials were concerned about the weaknesses in the UK government's claim to the Chagos Islands, as seen from the perspective of the international community of States. For them, the agreement of the elected representatives of the Mauritian government was particularly significant because they thought that it would help to prevent the British sovereignty claim over the Chagos Islands from being challenged in the UN General Assembly.

---

[105] See UNGA Res 2066(XX), 16 December 1965 on the Question of Mauritius. This resolution is analysed in ch 6.
[106] See also T Grant, 'Who Can Make Treaties? Other Subjects of International Law' in D Hollis (ed), *The Oxford Guide to Treaties* (Oxford, Oxford University Press, 2013) 125, 139–40.
[107] PRO PREM 13/3320.

They reasoned that, if the elected representatives of the Mauritian government had consented to such a transaction, other States would have no grounds upon which to challenge the legality of the arrangement, particularly since the Mauritian government had received compensation for the loss of sovereignty over the Chagos Islands.

It transpired that the Lancaster House Agreement did not prevent international criticism of the transaction. In the General Assembly's Fourth Committee on 16 November 1965, Tanzania observed that the creation of the BIOT:

> was intended to permit the installation of military and naval bases by the Governments of the United Kingdom and the United States. The joint United Kingdom-United States project was aimed at reversing the course of history. It was contrary not only to resolution 1514(XV), but also to other resolutions adopted by different United Nations organs concerning specific colonial problems and the application of the principle of self-determination, which must be regarded as a general principle of international law. That principle would be meaningless if it could be circumvented and if, by the payment of compensation to the majority of the inhabitants of a colony, a Colonial Power could retain in perpetuity a part of the territory of that colony inhabited by a minority. The right of colonial peoples to self-determination could never be subject to financial dealings, which were particularly reprehensible when their purpose was the establishment of foreign bases in a colonial Territory.[108]

Despite such public criticism, the official record reveals that officials in the UK government were unperturbed:

> given the lack of any publicly aired Mauritian resentment against the continued detachment of these islands, the tacit agreement of an independent Mauritius to the existence of BIOT should dispose of the argument of a dependency with an administering power is no agreement at all.[109]

Evidently, the British strategy worked well, at least in the short term.

V. COERCION IN THE CONCLUSION OF TREATIES AND COLONIAL SELF-DETERMINATION

As discussed earlier in this chapter, international tribunals have consistently maintained that a high evidential threshold is required in support of a claim of coercion and that the doctrine of coercion is limited to the threat or use of force in connection with the conclusion of a treaty, both as a matter of treaty law and in customary international law. Nonetheless, the chapter also explored the extent to which international law recognises a conception of coercion which encompasses political and economic forms of coercion. In particular, it

---

[108] A/C 4/SR 1557, 229, and 230 [49–50].
[109] PRO FCO 58/353, No 61, JDB Shaw to JH Lambert, 12 February 1969; JH Lambert to JDB Shaw, 21 February 1969. See also MM Ticu, *Chagos: Where International Law Stops* (Utrecht, Utrecht University, 2012) (on file with the author) 45.

considered whether such a broad doctrine of coercion constitutes a general principle of law within the meaning of Article 38(1)(c) of the ICJ Statute, which enumerates the sources of international law. It concluded that it was unlikely that such a general principle of law was established in municipal legal systems when the 1965 Lancaster House Agreement was negotiated. However, even if such a principle of law had not been established in municipal legal systems at the relevant time, this conclusion does not exhaust the resonance of the doctrine of coercion for determining the validity of the 1965 Agreement at the level of international law.

A different approach to the question of whether the 1965 Agreement was the product of coercion requires an assessment of its substantive provisions in order to assess whether the Lancaster House Agreement amounted to a violation of the entitlement to colonial self-determination as a matter of international law.[110] In particular, paragraph 5 of the 1960 Colonial Declaration provided that:

> Immediate steps shall be taken, in Trust and Non-Self-Governing Territories . . . to transfer all powers to the peoples of those territories, without any conditions or reservations, in accordance with their freely expressed will and desire, without any distinction as to race, creed or colour, in order to enable them to enjoy complete independence or freedom.

As discussed in the previous chapter, the available evidence suggests that the 1965 Lancaster House Agreement was concluded on the understanding that the detachment of the Chagos Islands was the price to be paid for Mauritian independence. During the negotiations, representatives of the UK government made it clear that, under British colonial law, the Chagos Islands could lawfully be excised from the colony of Mauritius unilaterally via Order in Council, if the UK government so desired. It is apparent from official record that the motive for bringing the existence of such powers to the attention of the elected representatives of Mauritius was to impress upon them the fact that they really had very little choice regarding the decision to dismember the Mauritian colonial unit.

The strategy of procuring the consent of a non-European entity to conclude an agreement so that it can be used against third parties manifests certain parallels with the approach adopted by the European colonial powers regarding their policies of territorial acquisition during the nineteenth century.[111] During this period, the colonial powers were anxious to conclude treaties of cession with non-European political entities in Africa, Asia and the 'New World' in order to prevent other colonial powers from making similar claims to such territories. This approach of promoting the significance of such agreements for third parties was typically accompanied by sustained efforts to undermine the significance of such agreements for the non-European party.[112] Moreover, the legal

---

[110] It should be noted, at this stage, that the status of the right to colonial self-determination was controversial during the 1960s. This issue will be explored in ch 5.

[111] See generally Castellino and Allen, *Title to Territory in International Law* (n 51).

[112] See also the following US cases by Chief Justice Marshall: *Johnson v M'Intosh*, 21 US (8 Wheat) 543 (1823); *Cherokee Nation v Georgia*, 30 US (5 Pet) 1 (1831), 31 US (6 Pet) 515 (1832) and

significance of these agreements was denied at the level of international law. This was clear from Judge Huber's seminal analysis of the international law governing title to territory in *The Island of Palmas* case:

> As regards contracts between a state or a company such as the Dutch East India Company and native princes or chiefs of peoples not recognized as members of the community of nations, they are not, in the international law sense, treaties or conventions capable of creating rights and obligations such as may, in international law, arise out of treaties. But, on the other hand, contracts of this nature are not wholly void of indirect effects on situations governed by international law; if they do not constitute titles in international law, they are nonetheless facts of which that law must in certain circumstances take account[113]

In the context of the detachment of the Chagos Islands from the Mauritian colonial unit, the UK government sought to acquire the consent of the elected representatives of Mauritius so that an agreement could presented to the international community of States in the UN General Assembly, without the agreement having any direct legal significance for the Mauritian people since the Chagos Islands could have been detached unilaterally by Order in Council, in any event. The UK government hoped that the 1965 Agreement would deflect criticism of its actions which, prima facie, violated the international legal obligations that the UK owed to this non-self-governing territory. However, as discussed above, the Lancaster House Agreement did not prevent international criticism of the transaction from the international community of States.

It can be argued that the asymmetrical power relations between the UK and Mauritius had a profound effect not only on the substance of the 1965 Lancaster House Agreement but also on the way it was concluded. The fact that this agreement was concluded between an administering State and a non-self-governing territory for which it was responsible as a matter of international law cannot be ignored. This is a very different kind of bargain to an agreement concluded between sovereign States on the basis of equality, freedom of choice and consent. It is conceivable that an agreement between an administering State and a non-self-governing territory could be concluded as a result of the application of improper pressure, especially where that agreement amounts to a significant benefit to the administering State while being materially disadvantageous to the colony in question. Officials in the UK government fully appreciated the weaknesses inherent in such agreements, at least during an era of widespread decolonisation. However, the UK government's strategy was founded on the expectation that the government of the newly independent State of Mauritius would not do anything to jeopardise the transaction at the international level.[114]

The pressure applied by the UK government in order to procure the consent of the elected representatives of the Mauritian colonial government might not

---

see SJ Anaya, *Indigenous Peoples in International Law*, 2nd edn (New York, Oxford University Press, 2004) 23–24.

[113] *Island of Palmas* case (n 50) 838.

[114] The standpoint was apparent from official correspondence quoted above (n 109).

be of the kind that would have invalidated the 1965 Lancaster House Agreement when judged by reference to the principle of customary international law which was codified in Article 52 of the Vienna Convention as the UK government did not procure consent by recourse to the threat or use of force. However, this is not to deny that the pressure used for this purpose was not improper and substantial in its effects. It is suggested that the very nature of the relationship between an administering State and a non-self-governing territory creates conditions which are inherently favourable to the administering State when agreements are being concluded between them. Accordingly, the causal relationship between the coercion used and the consent procured should be readily presumed in such cases. Such a presumption would be significant in the context of the 1965 Lancaster House Agreement. It is clear that, in relation to the detachment of the Chagos Islands, the elected representatives of the Mauritian government had no meaningful choice but to give their consent to the course of action proposed by the UK government given the threat that the Chagos Islands would be unilaterally excised from the colony of Mauritius, if they resisted.

The argument that the elected representatives of the Mauritian colonial government had a sufficient degree of international legal personality to negotiate and conclude the 1965 Lancaster House Agreement is credible. The inhabitants of this non-self-governing territory had a separate and distinct status from the State which administered them as a consequence of the obligations enumerated in Chapter XI of the UN Charter.[115] However, the argument that the resultant 1965 Agreement was invalid because the consent of the Mauritian ministers had been procured by the use of coercion as a matter of international law is less convincing given that – in the contemporaneous customary international law – the doctrine of coercion was restricted to instances where force had been threatened, or used to bring about the conclusion of a treaty. A plausible argument may be that the Lancaster House Agreement was, in fact, concluded as a result of the use of coercive pressure and that a presumption of duress should arise in cases where agreements are concluded between an administering State and a non-self-governing territory. However, there is no evidence to suggest that this argument would have been supported by the international law in force at the time the Lancaster House Agreement was concluded. Accordingly, it would appear that the question of whether the 1965 Agreement was invalid as a matter of international law turns on whether its substantive provisions amounted to a violation of the Mauritian people's right to self-determination. This issue will be explored in the next two chapters of this book.

VI. CONCLUSION

This chapter examined a number of interpretations of the status and legal validity of the 1965 Lancaster House Agreement. One interpretation would be

---

[115] These developments in international law will be analysed in the next two chapters.

dependent on the view that, in the context of the conclusion of treaties, the doctrine of coercion is restricted to situations where force is threatened, or used, to procure the consent required to conclude a treaty as a matter of international law. It is clear that the UK did not use any form of military aggression as a means of securing the consent of the elected representatives of the Mauritian colonial government to enter into the 1965 Agreement. Consequently, this reading would suggest that the 1965 Agreement constitutes a valid treaty as a matter of international law. An alternative interpretation would suggest that the 1965 Agreement is not a treaty at all; instead, it is the product of the UK's municipal legal order and, as a result, it has no significance for international law whatsoever. To this end, it could be argued that the elected representatives of the Mauritian colonial government did not possess international legal personality for the purpose of negotiating the Lancaster House Agreement as, in accordance with UK constitutional law (colonial law), the colony of Mauritius was not recognised as having international legal personality nor any independent capacity to make treaties on its own behalf.

However, neither of the above readings of the legal status and validity of the 1965 Lancaster House Agreement is convincing. First, the narrowness of the doctrine of coercion in customary international law in relation to the conclusion of treaties is open to question at the level of principle. If customary international law has long insisted that treaties must be concluded as a result of freely given consent, and it recognises that treaties may be declared invalid in situations where a causal link exists between the use of coercive pressure and the vitiated consent, it should be immaterial whether the duress takes the form of military aggression or political/economic pressure, as long as the use of improper pressure can be substantiated. Support for this proposition can be found in the provisions of the 1969 UN Declaration on the Prohibition of Military, Political or Economic Coercion in the Conclusion of Treaties and in the 1982 award in the *Aminoil* case. Moreover, a broader conception of coercion has evolved in numerous municipal legal systems, which encompasses economic duress and it is arguable that such an interpretation of the doctrine of coercion has now become a general principle of law for the purpose of Article 38(1)(c) of the ICJ Statute. Nevertheless, it should be acknowledged that it is unlikely that such a general principle of law was established by the time that the 1965 Lancaster House Agreement was concluded. Accordingly, it would be difficult to claim that international law conclusively recognised an expansive interpretation of the doctrine of coercion – one that extended beyond proven instances of the threat or use of military force during the conclusion of an international agreement – at the critical date. Nevertheless, the normative ambiguity discussed above indicates that the customary international law position is not invulnerable to challenge and the special circumstances surrounding the 1965 Lancaster House Agreement must be taken into account in an assessment of its validity as a matter of international law. The fact that the 1965 Agreement was concluded between the elected representatives of a non-self-governing territory and the government of the responsible administering State during the period of widespread decolonisation in accordance with the provisions of the UN Charter and the sustained initiatives of the UN General Assembly – including the 1960 Colonial Declaration which proclaimed the existence of the right to self-determination in international law – cannot be ignored. Moreover, the significance of the international law relating to decolonisation is heightened by the fact that the terms of the Lancaster House Agreement provided for the dismemberment of the colony of Mauritius in the lead up to its accession to independence and that the available evidence strongly suggests that it was a condition of Mauritian statehood.

The final part of the chapter acknowledged that, if the 1965 Lancaster House Agreement was the product of the UK's municipal legal order, it would be difficult to question the legal validity of the 1965 Agreement according to the rules and principles of international law. However, the chapter argued that the validity of the Lancaster House Agreement could not be determined exclusively by reference to the provisions of UK municipal law; instead it suggested that the 1965 Agreement was a significant instrument for the purposes of the international legal order. This argument presupposes that the elected representatives of the Mauritian colonial government possessed a degree of international legal personality for the purpose of concluding the Lancaster House Agreement and it draws on Mauritius's status as a non-self-governing territory and on the evolution of the right of colonial self-determination during the period in question. The next two chapters consider the ramifications of this claimed entitlement for the validity of the 1965 Agreement in greater detail and for Mauritius's claim of sovereignty over the Chagos Islands in general.

5

Detaching the Chagos Islands from Mauritius: The Status of Colonial Self-determination in International Law during the mid-1960s

I. INTRODUCTION

T HIS CHAPTER SEEKS to establish the normative significance of the right of self-determination during the period in which the 1965 Lancaster House Agreement and the 1965 BIOT Order in Council effected the detachment of the Chagos Islands from the colony of Mauritius. It follows that, if the right of colonial self-determination had achieved the status of binding international law by 1965, the dismemberment of Mauritius before it had acceded to independence would have amounted to a prima facie violation of this entitlement. It is often assumed that all colonial peoples acquired the right to self-determination as a result of the adoption, by the UN General Assembly, of the Declaration on the Granting of Independence to Colonial Countries in 1960 (the 'Colonial Declaration').[1] It is incontrovertible that the right of colonial self-determination acquired the status of customary international law (CIL) at some point during the wider process of 'Third World' decolonisation. However, given the temporal dimension of the enquiry being undertaken in this book, the key questions for the present purpose are when, and how, did the right of colonial self-determination achieve its international legal character. If the right of colonial self-determination acquired its binding character as a matter of international law – vis-a-vis the UK – after the Chagos Islands were detached from Mauritius then, in principle, it would be hard to establish that such an event amounted to a violation of the right to self-determination in the Mauritian context. While attitudes towards colonialism were starting to change during the early part of the twentieth century, colonialism was not considered to be unlawful according to the text of the UN Charter.

---

[1] UNGA Res 1514(XV), 14 December 1960. eg this assumption was made by the drafters of the Mauritian Legislative Assembly, 'Report of the Select Committee on the Excision of the Chagos Archipelago (No 2 of 1983)' (Port Louis, Mauritius Legislative Assembly, 1983) ('the Excision Report') 37.

As it turned out, the colonial powers were on the wrong side of history but, while the international community of States turned sharply against colonialism during the 1960s, such a dramatic turn of events was not necessarily foreseeable in the 1950s. Against this background, this chapter engages in a temporal assessment of the evolution of the right to self-determination in the colonial context in an effort to establish whether it can be said, with a reasonable degree of certainty, that the right of colonial self-determination had acquired binding force as a matter of international law by the time the Chagos Islands were detached from Mauritius.

II. LEGAL RULES, LEGAL PRINCIPLES AND LEGAL RIGHTS

International lawyers are prone to using the concepts of legal rules, legal principles and legal rights interchangeably. For instance, Shaw views international law as a body of legal rules applicable to States;[2] however, he also sees it as a system based on a set of core legal principles. In this respect, Shaw believes self-determination to be a key principle of international law but also that it possesses the quality of a legal right in certain situations.[3] Other international lawyers have suggested that self-determination is not only a legal principle but a legal rule and a legal right as well.[4] Initially, self-determination was widely considered to be an organising political principle of international society.[5] However, during the early-twentieth century, it slowly began to acquire legal resonance, albeit only in exceptional conditions.[6] It was subsequently endorsed as a broad legal principle in the UN Charter.[7] Further, during the late-1950s, the UN General Assembly, controversially, began to refer to it as a right in a series of General Assembly resolutions.[8] Finally, in 1960, the entitlement to colonial self-determination was proclaimed in the Colonial Declaration.[9] This claim was reinforced in the 1970 Declaration on Friendly Relations, a development which confirmed that the right of colonial self-determination had acquired the character of CIL.[10]

---

[2] See MN Shaw, *International Law,* 6th edn (Cambridge, Cambridge University Press, 2008) 1–2.

[3] ibid, 252. See also 251–57.

[4] See K Knop, *Diversity and Self-determination in International Law* (Cambridge, Cambridge University Press, 2002) 30–33.

[5] For a brief overview, see M Koskenniemi, 'National Self-determination Today: Problems of Legal Theory and Practice' (1994) 43 *International and Comparative Law Quarterly* 241.

[6] As eg in cases of State dissolution; see the 1920 *Aaland Islands* case (1920) *League of Nations Official Journal*, Special supp No 3, 3 (International Committee of Jurists); and Report to the League of Nations Council B7 21/68/106 (1921) (Commission of Rapporteurs). See below.

[7] See UN Charter, Arts 1(2) and 55, discussed below.

[8] See below.

[9] UNGA Res 1514(XV), 14 December 1960 ('Colonial Declaration'). See below.

[10] United Nations Declaration on the Principles of International Law concerning Friendly Relations and Co-operation Among States in Accordance with the Charter of the United Nations, UNGA Res 2625(XXV)(1970), 24 October 1970. See below.

In the 1971 *Namibia Advisory Opinion*, the ICJ affirmed the customary character of self-determination in colonial situations.[11] However, in this context, it referred to self-determination as a principle of CIL.[12] In contrast, in the 1975 *Western Sahara Advisory Opinion*, the ICJ was willing to adopt the language of rights in relation to the norm of self-determination.[13] Nevertheless, the ICJ also referred to self-determination as a principle of international law which could be defined as 'as the need to pay regard to the freely expressed will of peoples'.[14] After approving of the stance adopted in the *Namibia* case,[15] the Court observed that:

> The *principle of self-determination as a right of peoples*, and its application for the purpose of bringing all colonial situations to a speedy end, were enunciated in the Declaration on the Granting of Independence to Colonial Countries and Peoples, General Assembly resolution 1514 (XV).[16]

In the light of the ICJ's jurisprudence, which appears to view self-determination as both a principle and a right and the apparent reluctance of leading international lawyers to distinguish between legal rules and principles how can we differentiate between 'rules', 'principles' and 'rights' at the level of international law?

Legal philosophers have taken great care to differentiate between legal rules, principles and rights. For instance, in the Anglo-American positivist tradition, Hart claimed that a legal system is constituted by a body of legal rules.[17] It has been suggested that rules manifest a definite and imperative quality – they demand compliance within the established sphere of their application.[18] Hart's approach was premised on the view that the meaning of a legal rule is clear in relation to a range of core situations and, in such cases, the subjects of the rule are certain.[19] Nevertheless, Hart understood that legal rules cannot possibly cater for all situations.[20] It is inevitable that gaps in the law will emerge where

[11] *Namibia Advisory Opinion* (1971) ICJ Rep 16.
[12] The ICJ observed that 'the subsequent development of international law in regard to non-self-governing territories, as enshrined in the Charter of the United Nations, made the principle of self-determination applicable to all of them'; ibid, [52].
[13] See the *Western Sahara Advisory Opinion* (1975) ICJ Rep 12 [55], [57], [61] and [70–71]. The ICJ was clearly prompted by certain General Assembly resolutions in this regard – including UNGA Res 1514(XV)(1960), UNGA Res 1541(XV)(1960), UNGA Res 2625(XXV)(1970), and specifically in the context of Western Sahara, UNGA Res 3292 (XXIX)(1974).
[14] ibid, [59].
[15] ibid, [54].
[16] ibid, [55]. Emphasis added.
[17] See H Hart, *The Concept of Law*, 2nd revised edn (Oxford, Oxford University Press, 1994) ch 5.
[18] This is Dworkin's interpretation of Hart's position. See R Dworkin, *Taking Rights Seriously* (London, Duckworth, 1977) 22–28.
[19] See Hart, *The Concept of Law* (n 17) 126.
[20] There will always be cases in which their application is rendered uncertain either because the particular case in question was unforeseen at the time the rule was forged; or the rule's objective is relatively indeterminate; or because of linguistic difficulties which hamper the rule's application; ibid, 128.

rules run out.[21] Hart believed that judges possess considerable residual discretion to determine the content of the law in such situations.[22] In contrast, other theorists, most notably Dworkin, have argued that a legal system cannot be reduced to a body of legal rules;[23] it is also made up of legal principles. Legal principles are abstract in nature, they do not have a decisive effect but instead they have 'weight'.[24] Principles are particularly useful in situations where no legal rules exist, or their application remains uncertain. Non-conclusive principles may be taken into consideration by judges in the context of a legal dispute and they may influence the outcome of a given case. According to Dworkin, because legal rules apply in an 'all or nothing' fashion it follows that distinct rules do not conflict with one another.[25] Raz takes issue with Dworkin.[26] He argues that rules and principles are much closer than Dworkin is prepared to acknowledge.[27] In particular, Raz contends that the relationship between rules and principles is much more complicated than Dworkin's account suggests and that it is difficult to differentiate clearly between these two concepts in many cases.[28] Nonetheless, Raz identifies a number of important differences between rules and principles. He observes that rules are specific normative acts whereas principles are highly unspecific in nature. Accordingly, Raz suggests that the content of any given principle is justified by reference to a wide range of factors while the content of a particular rule is informed by a narrower range of considerations. Consequently, he claims that legal principles can be used to justify legal rules but that the reverse is not true.[29] Secondly, Raz argues the unspecified nature of principles means that principles are often expressed in ways that leave their subjects unclear and further elaboration is typically required if the subjects of non-conclusive principles are to be established.[30] In other words, he indicates that legal principles are ambiguous both in terms of the normative obligations that they generate and with regard to their addressees.

This debate has significantly informed Anglo-American approaches to the nature and effect of rules and principles at the level of international law and, according to Knop, this is apparent from the work of Crawford and Schachter.[31] In addition, it is clear that international lawyers from the continen-

---

[21] ibid, 128.

[22] ibid, 129–30.

[23] See Dworkin, *Taking Rights Seriously* (n 18) 22.

[24] ibid, 22–28.

[25] ibid, 22–28

[26] J Raz, 'Legal Principles and the Limits of Law' (1971–72) 81 *Yale Law Journal* 823. Raz focuses on the arguments advanced by R Dworkin in 'The Model of Rules' (1967) 35 *University of Chicago Law Review* 14, which is reproduced in *Taking Rights Seriously*, ibid.

[27] See Hart (n 17) 'Postscript', 263–68.

[28] Raz, 'Legal Principles and the Limits of Law' (n 26) 828–36.

[29] ibid, 838–39.

[30] ibid, 836.

[31] See Knop, *Diversity and Self-determination in International Law* (n 4) 30–38. For this purpose, Knop places particular reliance on J Crawford, Book Review of A Cassese, *Self-Determination of Peoples: A Legal Reappraisal* (Cambridge, Cambridge University Press, 1995) (1996) 90 *American Journal of International Law* 331; J Crawford, *The Creation of States In International Law*, 1st edn

tal tradition, such as Cassese, have adopted a comparable approach.[32] Crawford approves of Cassese's conclusion that self-determination can be pared down to a single overarching legal principle and a number of specific legal rules.[33] However, in his own analysis of the character of self-determination, Crawford prefers to conceptualise self-determination as a principle of international law and also as a legal right, in certain prescribed situations.[34] In his view, self-determination only acquires the character of an international legal right in cases where its subjects are certain (ie where the unit for the purpose of the exercise of the right can be established). Further, it appears that, for Crawford, legal rights can be equated with legal principles and therefore, there is no need to rely upon more specific forms of normative obligation – legal rules – for the purpose of recognising and implementing international legal rights.

As noted above, according to Crawford, the right of self-determination arises in situations where the subjects of the right are known whereas the principle of self-determination is normatively significant in cases where its subjects are not clearly ascertainable.[35] Knop suggests that Schachter's conception of self-determination has also been heavily influenced by Hart's work.[36] She suggests that he adopted Hart's recognition that a norm may have a definite meaning in a series of core cases but that the norm becomes increasingly indeterminate beyond such situations.[37] However, the key difference between Hart and Schachter is that Hart pioneered his concept of law in relation to legal rules whereas Schachter applied Hart's core/penumbra divide in relation to legal principles. Thus, while both Crawford's and Schachter's understanding of the conceptual basis of normative obligation at the international level is conditioned by Hart's treatment of the concept of law, they both discount the main focus of Hart's analysis – legal rules. What is the justification for this apparent misapplication of a cardinal component of Hart's groundbreaking approach to the concept of law? The focus on principles might be justified by reference to the nature of normative obligations at the international level. Principles are especially important in international law because the international legal system typically operates at a more abstract level than national legal systems. The social, economic, political and cultural conditions which exist within individual States are very different and it is often difficult to develop international law – either by way of treaty or CIL – that manifests the level of specificity required

(Oxford, Oxford University Press, 1977); and O Schachter, 'The Relation of Law, Politics and Action in the United Nations' (1963) 109 *Hague Recueil* 169–256.

[32] See A Cassese, *Self-Determination of Peoples: A Legal Reappraisal* (Cambridge, Cambridge University Press, 1995) 126–33. And see below.

[33] See Crawford's Book Review (n 31) 331.

[34] See J Crawford, *The Creation of States in International Law*, 2nd edn (Oxford, Oxford University Press, 2006) 127.

[35] ibid, 126. This would appear to be consistent with Raz's view that the subjects of legal principles are indeterminate and that further work needs to be done to identify them. However, as noted above, Raz did not see this feature to be the pivotal distinction between legal rules and principles.

[36] Knop (n 4) 36.

[37] ibid, 36.

for international legal norms to satisfy the definite application associated with legal rules. Further, in many areas, international legal norms require the development of corresponding national laws in order to achieve the level of specificity required for them to be rendered effective in concrete settings.[38] Consequently, international legal norms often assume a degree of latitude in their application in recognition of the importance of contextual factors. It could be argued that international legal rights and obligations are relatively indeterminate and the principle of self-determination may be viewed as a case in point. But why does this matter? It matters because, if principles are viewed as being the driving force of international law then the basic normative components of the international legal systems are indeterminate from the outset. If core cases are characterised by reference to non-conclusive principles then they are relatively indeterminate whereas the cases where there is a penumbra of doubt – to use Hart's language – are at risk of being wholly incoherent.[39]

Strangely, Cassese's approach is more consistent with the Anglo-American positivist tradition than the approach adopted by Crawford or Schachter. Cassese claims that self-determination constitutes a rule of international law in colonial situations and he offers three arguments in support of his claim.[40] First, Cassese argues that the rule's subjects are clear – it is applicable in respect of colonial peoples (ie the inhabitants of non-self-governing territories and trust territories pursuant to Chapters XI and XII of the UN Charter, respectively).[41] Secondly, he contends that the means by which this rule can be applied are established – via referenda and plebiscites. Finally, Cassese argues that the aim of the rule is also clear – the achievement of decolonisation through a range of options which include independence and integration or association with another State.[42] Applying Crawford's standpoint – adjusted to apply to legal rules – the rule of self-determination in international law gives rise to the recognition of an international legal right in circumstances where the rule's applicability can be established.[43] Moreover, as the correlative of a right is a duty, where a given colo-

---

[38] It should be noted that this generalisation may be more significant in relation to certain areas of international law than others – international human rights law may be considered to be an example par excellence.

[39] This would seem to justify Koskenniemi's view that self-determination can mean anything the interpreter wishes it to mean. See M Koskenniemi, 'What is International Law For?' in MD Evans (ed), *International Law*, 3rd edn (Oxford, Oxford University Press, 2010) 32. For a different perspective, see Knop (n 4) 29–49.

[40] See Cassese, *Self-Determination of Peoples* (n 32) 129.

[41] In accordance with the provisions of the Colonial Declaration (UNGA Res 1514(XV)(1960) and the Declaration on Friendly Relations (UNGA Res 2625(XXV)(1970). See below. These provisions also extend to the inhabitants of mandated territories, pursuant to the 1919 Covenant of the League of Nations, Art 22.

[42] See Cassese (n 32) 129 (drawing on the provisions of UNGA Res 1541(XV)(1960) and UNGA Res 2625(XXV)(1970)). See below.

[43] Hohfeld's scheme shows that the existence of a legal rule does not necessarily correspond to the existence of a right. However, self-determination is best understood as a right rather than as a privilege, power or immunity, in situations where the existence of such a rule can be established. See W Hohfeld, 'Fundamental Legal Conceptions as Applied in Judicial Reasoning' (1913) 23 *Yale Law Journal* 16 and (1917) 26 *Yale Law Journal* 710.

nial people seek to exercise their right to self-determination, the responsible administering State is under a corresponding obligation to facilitate its exercise.

Nevertheless, it is important to remember that the above-mentioned rule of self-determination emerged gradually through a series of incremental steps. The UN Charter endorsed self-determination as a highly unspecific principle in Article 1(2). It only acquired the character of a rule of international law in colonial situations – and a right for colonial peoples – through a series of General Assembly resolutions that built on the unpromising foundations of Chapter XI of the UN Charter.[44] The process by which the principle was transformed into a right was accelerated by the adoption of the Colonial Declaration in 1960,[45] and it culminated in the 1970 Declaration on Friendly Relations, which confirmed the status of this rule and entitlement as a matter of CIL.[46]

Cassese maintained that the principle of self-determination – articulated as the need for governments to 'pay regard to the freely expressed will of peoples' – possesses a degree of residual authority which enables it to legitimise self-governing institutional arrangements that are in keeping with its normative essence.[47] Consequently, the principle has remained normatively significant beyond the sphere of the rule's application and it has proved the underpinnings for the way that self-determination has evolved outside of the colonial context.[48] Cassese claims that the principle acts as a basic standard of interpretation in situations where customary rules are ambiguous.[49] Another function of the principle, in Cassese's view, relates to the method of exercising the right of self-determination – the procedures through which the free and genuine expression of the will of the people can be channelled.[50]

III. THE RISE OF THE PRINCIPLE OF SELF-DETERMINATION AND INTERNATIONAL LAW

Throughout the nineteenth century, the political principle of self-determination was associated with the genesis of the nation-State.[51] During this period, the State was considered to be the political manifestation of its constituent 'nation'. In theory, this enabled a 'nation' to create its institutional form – it ensured that the political unit and its corresponding 'nation' remained congruent.[52] From

---

[44] These early resolutions are discussed below.
[45] UNGA Res 1514(XV)(1960); see below.
[46] UNGA Res 2625(XXV)(1970); see below.
[47] See Cassese (n 32) 128–33.
[48] However, this development has also been facilitated by the creation of further legal rules concerning self-determination by treaty law.
[49] Cassese (n 32) 132.
[50] ibid, 131–32.
[51] See MC Lâm, *At the Edge of the State: Indigenous Peoples and Self-Determination* (New York, Transnational Publishers, 2000).
[52] E Gellner, *Nations and Nationalism* (Oxford, Blackwell, 1990) 1; see also A Smith, *Ethnic Origins of Nations* (Oxford, Blackwell, 1986); E Hobsbawm, *Nations and Nationalism Since 1780:*

this perspective, the principle of self-determination was viewed as the expression of the achievement of the condition of statehood and a nation that had attained statehood was entitled to determine its own political destiny. However, in practice, the nationalist cause gained little succour from the inter-State system and the claim that such a radical interpretation of the principle of self-determination informed the organisation of the inter-State system was imaginary.[53] Nonetheless, at a political level, this romantic conception of self-determination had a tremendous impact on the struggles within established States and it contributed not only to the forging of new States from the ancient regime but also the casting off the shackles of Empire.

The link between national identity and self-determination was apparent in President Wilson's efforts, during the 1919 Versailles Settlement, to enable oppressed ethnic nationalities to govern themselves as a way of promoting international peace and security.[54] The core component of Wilson's conception of self-determination was that the doctrine amounted to a manifestation of popular sovereignty – all peoples should have the right to choose their own governments through processes which could establish their will.[55] The Wilsonian conception of self-determination and the interpretation of self-determination favoured in the *Aalands Islands* case, which was decided under the auspices of the League of Nations,[56] showed that the principle of self-determination could be rendered accessible to sub-State societal groups during the first decades of the twentieth century. However, these isolated instances of self-determination did little to change the general understanding of the nature and scope of self-determination during this period. Although the Wilsonian conception of self-determination became an important political slogan in the aftermath of the First World War it did not find its way into the final text of the 1919 Covenant of the League of Nations.[57] Moreover, in the *Aaland Islands* case, both the International Commission of Jurists and the Commission of Rapporteurs confirmed that self-determination was a political principle, which was not part of international law.[58] Consequently, prior to the founding of the United Nations, self-determination was still widely regarded as a political tenet even though

Programme, Myth, Reality, 2nd edn (Cambridge, Cambridge University Press, 1992); K Deutsch and W Foltz, *Nation Building* (New York, Atherton Press, 1963); and N Berman, 'But the Alternative is Despair' (1993) 106 *Harvard Law Review* 1792.

[53] See Koskenniemi, 'National Self-determination Today' (n 5). See also H Hannum, 'Rethinking Self-determination' (1993) 34 *Virginia Journal of International Law* 1.

[54] This approach was based on three interrelated factors: first, identifiable peoples were to be accorded independent Statehood; second, disputes concerning the status of particular areas were to be resolved by reference to plebiscites; and third, where minority ethnic nationalities were too small to be granted statehood they would be protected through protective treaty regimes supervised by the League of Nations; see J Castellino, *International Law and Self-Determination* (The Hague, Martinus Nijhoff, 2000) 15.

[55] See Cassese (n 32) 19.

[56] *Aaland Islands* case (n 6), and Report to the League of Nations Council B721/68/106 (1921) (Commission of Rapporteurs).

[57] See Cassese (n 32) 22.

[58] ibid, 30.

there were signs that its legal character was in the process of emerging during the lifetime of the League.

IV. THE PRINCIPLE OF SELF-DETERMINATION IN THE UN CHARTER

Article 1(2) of the UN Charter provides that the purposes of the United Nations include: 'to develop friendly relations among nations based on respect for the principle of equal rights and self-determination of peoples'. However, the drafting of this provision was controversial. States which participated in the 1945 San Francisco UN Conference on International Organisation, at which the UN Charter was finalised, were anxious to ensure that the principle could not be invoked as a justification for secession or as a means for the inhabitants of non-self-governing territories to achieve independence.[59] Accordingly, in 1945, the principle of self-determination simply proclaimed States should grant self-government as far as possible to the peoples within their jurisdiction.[60]

At the end of the Second World War, the Allies had to decide what to do with the colonial territories belonging to the Axis powers. In the UN Charter, they resolved to place these territories under international supervision by extending the mandate system, which had been created via Article 22 of the Covenant of the League of Nations. These colonial territories were classified as 'trust territories' and a system providing for the international supervision of trust territories was established in Chapters XII and XIII of the UN Charter to ensure that progressive steps were taken so that the inhabitants of each territory could be readied for independence or self-government. Although the responsibility for each particular trust territory was assigned to an administering authority, technically, the responsible State did not exercise sovereign authority over such territories; rather, sovereignty remained in abeyance until independence (or self-government) was achieved.[61] However, the recognition of the general case for granting independence to the inhabitants of trust territories and the institutional measures that were put in place to monitor developments in such territories drew attention to the wider question of the status of those colonial territories which belonged to the Allies. While the colonial powers resisted the idea of decolonisation; socialist States were ideologically committed to the eradication of colonialism;[62] the USA was uncomfortable about the prospect of perpetuating colonialism; and the 1945 San Francisco Conference included representatives from many 'Third World' States which maintained a resolute anti-colonial outlook. In the light of such international pressure and given the

---

[59] T Musgrave, *Self-determination and National Minorities* (Oxford, Oxford University Press, 1994) 63–64. The concept of non-self-governing territories was created and regulated in c XI of the UN Charter; see below.
[60] See Cassese (n 32) 42.
[61] See *Advisory Opinion Concerning the International Status of South West Africa* (1950) ICJ Rep 128, 150 (Separate Opinion of Judge McNair).
[62] See Cassese (n 32) 14–18.

declared purposes and principles of the United Nations, the case for some form of international regulation of all colonial territories was irresistible.[63] In the UN Charter the international community of States had committed itself to the promotion of human rights and to the principles of equal rights and self-determination. As a result, in principle, situations where self-government had not yet been achieved could not be ignored.[64]

V. CHAPTER XI AND CHAPTER XII OF THE UN CHARTER

Chapter XI of the UN Charter created the category of non-self-governing territories and it declared that States which administered such territories owed their inhabitants a number of international legal obligations. Specifically, Article 73 provided that:

> Members of the United Nations which have or assume responsibilities for the admin-istration of territories whose peoples have not yet attained a full measure of self-government recognize the principle that the interests of the inhabitants of these terri-tories are paramount, and accept as a sacred trust the obligation to promote to the utmost, within the system of international peace and security established by the pre-sent Charter, the well-being of the inhabitants of these territories, and to this end:
>
> (a) to ensure, with due respect for the culture of the peoples concerned, their politi-cal, economic, social and educational advancement, their just treatment, and their protection against abuses;
>
> (b) to develop self-government, to take due account of the political aspirations of the peoples, and to assist them in the progressive development of their free political institutions, according to the particular circumstances of each territory and its peoples and their varying stages of advancement; . . .
>
> (e) to transmit regularly to the Secretary-General for information purposes, subject to such limitations as security and constitutional considerations may require, sta-tistical and other information of a technical nature relation to the economic, social, and educational conditions in the territories for which they are respectively responsible

The above-mentioned obligations were rather modest in nature, particularly when compared with the obligations established in Chapters XII and XIII in respect of trust territories. In particular, Article 76 of the UN Charter provided that:

> The basic objectives of the trusteeship system, in accordance with the Purposes of the United Nations laid down in Article 1 of the present Charter, shall be:
>
> (a) to further international peace and security;
>
> (b) to promote the political, economic, social, and educational advancement of the inhabitants of the trust territories, and their progressive development towards

---

[63] See the UN Charter, Arts 1 and 2.
[64] See the UN Charter, Art 1(2); and RY Jennings and A Watts, *Oppenheim's International Law,* vol 1, 9th edn (London, Longman, 1992) 282.

self-government or independence as may be appropriate to the particular circumstances of each territory and its peoples and the freely expressed wishes of the peoples concerned, and as may be provided by the terms of each trusteeship agreement;

(c) to encourage respect for human rights and for fundamental freedoms for all without distinction as to race, sex, language, or religion, and to encourage recognition of the interdependence of the peoples of the world; and

(d) to ensure equal treatment in social, economic, and commercial matters for all Members of the United Nations and their nationals, and also equal treatment for the latter in the administration of justice

Article 76(b) ensured that the inhabitants of trust territories could look forward to independence or self-government in due course and, to this end, it provided that the responsible administering authority had to take into account their freely expressed wishes. Moreover, under Articles 83 and 85, trust territories were monitored by the General Assembly and Security Council and the governance of each trust territory was supervised by the Trustee Council to ensure that administering authorities were complying with the terms of the trust agreement in question.

In contrast, the provisions of Chapter XI were much less robust. Article 73 embraced the concept of the 'sacred trust' that had been proclaimed in Article 22 of the Covenant of the League of Nations.[65] Moreover, it recognised that the 'interests' of the inhabitants of each non-self-governing territory were paramount and, in Article 73(b), it aimed to develop self-government for such 'peoples'. However, administering States were only required 'to take due account of the political aspirations of the peoples' for this purpose; they were not under an obligation to give effect to the freely expressed will of the inhabitants of such territories.[66] Moreover, in Article 73, the emphasis was on guaranteeing just treatment and protecting the inhabitants of non-self-governing territories from 'abuses' rather than on the protection and promotion of human rights and fundamental freedoms.[67] In addition, Chapter XI identified that the Charter objective in issue was the progressive achievement of self-government for the inhabitants of non-self-governing territories whereas the aim in respect of trust territories was the realisation of 'independence' or 'self-government' for the people concerned – an outcome that would be determined by the declared wishes of the inhabitants of the territory in question. Finally, and perhaps most

---

[65] See *Advisory Opinion Concerning the International Status of South West Africa* (n 61). The 1919 Covenant of the League of Nations, Art 22(1) provides:

To those colonies and territories which as a consequence of the late war have ceased to be under the sovereignty of the State which formerly governed them and which are inhabited by peoples not yet able to stand by themselves under the strenuous conditions of the modern world, there should be applied the principle that the well-being and development of such peoples form a sacred trust of civilisation and that securities for the performance of this trust should be embodied in this Covenant.

[66] See Art 76(b) in respect of trust territories.
[67] See Art 76(b) in respect of trust territories.

significantly, Chapter XI did not establish any institutional machinery to monitor developments in non-self-governing territories in contrast to the extensive measures put in place to supervise developments occurring in trust territories.

Nevertheless, Article 73(e) did create a narrow range of legal obligations for administering States in respect of non-self-governing territories. Under this provision, they were required to furnish the UN Secretary-General with a range of technical and statistical information relating to the economic, social and educational conditions prevailing in each non-self-governing territory for which they were responsible. However, this duty to transmit information did not extend to a requirement to provide data regarding the political conditions in particular territories or to report on any progressive steps taken by the administering State to deliver self-government for the people concerned. Moreover, it is notable that this limited range of information was further qualified by reference to constitutional or security considerations. But while Article 73 was drafted in rather modest and ambiguous terms it did establish normative standards and its provisions cannot be viewed as being hortatory, even though it was programmatic in character. Accordingly, along with Chapters XII and XIII, Chapter XI signalled a major breakthrough as, together, they brought the status of colonial territories decisively into the sphere of international law.

But while the drafters of the UN Charter devised the concept of non-self-governing territories to characterise those dependent territories belonging to the remaining colonial powers, Article 73 did not attempt to define this concept nor did it classify any dependent territories as non-self-governing territories for the purposes of implementing the responsibilities expressed in Chapter XI. This lack of definition suggests that the drafters favoured a voluntary approach to the identification of particular non-self-governing territories by the administering State concerned. Moreover, the absence of any meaningful regulation of the conditions and developments in non-self-governing territories – save for the limited reporting requirements contained in Article 73(e) – were indicative of a light touch approach to the international regulation of such colonial territories. The limited approach can be explained by reference to the established principle of exclusive jurisdiction in relation to domestic affairs, which was reinforced in Article 2(7) of the UN Charter. It provided that:

> Nothing contained in the present Charter shall authorize the United Nations to intervene in matters which are essentially within the domestic jurisdiction of any State or shall require the Members to submit such matters to settlement under the present Charter

As far as the colonial powers were concerned, even though the status of all colonial territories had become a matter of international concern pursuant to the provisions of the UN Charter, developments within colonial territories remained within the exclusive preserve of the responsible administering State. This position was supported by a careful reading of Chapters XI, XII and XIII of the

Charter.[68] The colonial powers argued that while they were prepared to promote self-government for the inhabitants of non-self-governing territories, Article 73 did not confer any legal rights on the peoples concerned. Moreover, in their view, the aim of self-government would be satisfied by the development of a sufficient degree of representative government within the colonial framework established by the responsible administering State.[69] This limited conception of self-government was consistent with the common position adopted during the process of drafting the Charter. During the drafting of Chapter XI, the representative of the Soviet Union proposed that the formula of 'self-government *or* independence', which the drafters agreed should be the aim in respect of trust territories, should be extended to apply to non-self-governing territories as well. However, this proposal was firmly rejected by the colonial powers and it was subsequently withdrawn.[70]

Chapter XII made it clear that decolonisation was the object of the international regulation of trust territories. However, the same could not be said of Chapter XI in relation to non-self-governing territories. It was for the responsible State to decide whether to identify a colonial territory as a non-self-governing territory. Further, it is clear that, according to the text of the Charter, administering States were under no duty to bring colonialism to an end. As noted above, no international supervisory machinery was established to monitor conditions in non-self-governing territories, save for the highly circumscribed reporting requirements contained in Article 73(e). Finally, unlike the position in relation to trust territories where sovereignty remained in abeyance during the period of dependency, administering States exercised sovereign authority over their non-self-governing territories.[71] Taking the above factors together, in 1945, it was evident that international law had not adopted the standpoint that colonialism was unlawful per se.[72] Accordingly, the exclusive jurisdiction argument advanced by the colonial powers during this period was still a credible interpretation of the contemporaneous applicable international law.

---

[68] 'It was realised then [in 1945], and it remains true now, that in many non-self-governing territories sovereignty or jurisdiction vests in the administrating states; and nothing was written into the Charter to change this fundamental fact. On the other hand, there are other non-self-governing territories – trust territories – where supervision lies in the hands of the United Nations: and in such territories the United Nations can and should hold the administering power to strict accountability. Charter deals with the former; Chapters XII and XIII with the latter . . . Chapters XII and XIII materially alter the status of non-self-governing territories coming within their scope. Chapter XI does not. No effort should be made to blur this distinction'. (USA representative, GAOR 4th committee, 37th meeting, 6 October 1947, 42–43), quoted in Crawford, *The Creation of States in International Law* (n 34) 613.

[69] U Fastenrath in B Simma (ed), *The Charter of the United Nations: A Commentary*, vol II, 3rd edn (Oxford, Oxford University Press, 2002) 1829–39.

[70] Jennings and Watts, *Oppenheim's International Law* (n 64) 282 and see Musgrave, *Self-determination and National Minorities* (n 59) 65–66.

[71] This was confirmed by the ICJ in the 1975 *Western Sahara* case (n 13) [43].

[72] See Jennings and Watts (n 64) 282.

Nevertheless, the acceptance of this argument would amount to a denial of the standpoint that colonialism was a legitimate subject of international concern. The terms of Chapter XI were the product of a difficult compromise. The colonial powers were not ready to accept the end of colonialism and the international law – which they had largely created – did not then reflect the illegitimacy of colonialism. But while the historical inevitability of decolonisation may not have been obvious to all States at the end of the Second World War the international regulation of mandated and trust territories meant that the colonial powers had to give some ground. These developments prompt a number of questions including: to what extent did this paradigm shift open up the governance of colonial territories to international regulation and, more specifically, what space did this create for the emergence of a nascent international law of decolonisation? The lack of parity between the international regulation of trust territories and non-self-governing territories, both in terms of the obligations imposed on administering States and the level of international supervision exercised in relation to the two kinds of colonial territories clearly concerned the UN General Assembly. The lack of a principled basis for this differentiation, in the eyes of many UN member States, was significant. As a result, the General Assembly, which had quickly acquired an in-built 'Third World' majority, recognised the need for concerted action in order to establish an international regime dedicated to the implementation of the responsibilities articulated in Chapter XI of the Charter and the progressive achievement of decolonisation in both non-self-governing territories and trust territories alike.

VI. HOLISTIC INTERPRETATIONS OF THE CHARTER: ARTICLE 1 AND CHAPTERS XI AND XII

A. Self-determination and the Drafting of the UN Charter

During the 1945 San Francisco Conference on International Organisation, the Soviet Union proposed that the principle of self-determination be included in the Charter.[73] This proposal was accepted and Article 1(2) of the Charter identified the aim of developing friendly relations between nations, based on respect for the principles of equal rights and the self-determination of peoples, as one of the purposes of the United Nations. Nevertheless, the drafters of the Charter struggled to reach agreement on the principle's meaning. A consensus was reached on what self-determination did not mean – it did not imply a right to secession for part of the population of a sovereign State nor did it entitle *all* colonial peoples to achieve independence.[74] The conception of self-determination, which was impliedly endorsed by the representatives of participating States, was that self-

---

[73] Cassese (n 32) 38.
[74] ibid, 43.

determination encompassed the idea that the population of a sovereign State should be recognised as having the entitlement to govern themselves.[75] This standpoint was consistent with the classical interpretation of the principle of self-determination.[76] Accordingly, at this stage, the principle of self-determination was equated with the notion of self-government. Some commentators have suggested that, irrespective of the heavily qualified interpretation of the principle of self-determination favoured by the drafters of the UN Charter, the inclusion of the principle in the Charter signalled the emergence of self-determination as a normative principle.[77] However, although it is apparent that the UN Charter provided the foundations for the transposition of self-determination from a political concept into a principle of international law, this development was not obvious from the text of the Charter and such an interpretation is not supported by the *travaux* either.

B. Self-determination and the Concept of 'People-hood'

As discussed above, there was considerable uncertainty regarding the status and scope of the principle of self-determination at the moment when the United Nations was founded. During this period, the unit by which the principle was rendered sensible was relatively unproblematic – in general, self-determination was a principle that applied only to States.[78] It has been claimed that the notion of 'people-hood', which was subsequently recognised as the basic unit for the purpose of the exercise of the right to self-determination during the process of decolonisation,[79] was applicable to the inhabitants of non-self-governing territories by virtue of the UN Charter. Consequently, it has been argued that the drafters of the Charter did not intend to restrict the principle of self-determination to States alone.[80] This argument presupposes that the principle of self-determination and the concept of 'people-hood' have always been inextricably linked. However, in order to ascertain the meaning of 'people-hood' in relation to the Charter, it is useful to recall that Article 4(1) provides that UN

---

[75] ibid.

[76] While there was some support for the view that the principle of self-determination could be exercised by a free and genuine expression of the will of the people concerned it was unclear how such a principle could be implemented in States that did not conform to the democratic standards of government favoured by Western States; Musgrave (n 59) 64. Cassese (n 32) 41 indicated that many of the States which participated in the drafting of the UN Charter had authoritarian systems of government and consequently the Wilsonian conception of self-determination had limited appeal in this context.

[77] Cassese (n 32) 43.

[78] See H Kelsen, *The Law of the United Nations* (1951) 52, discussed in Musgrave (n 59) 149.

[79] Para 2 of the Colonial Declaration, UNGA Res 1514(XV), 14 December 1960, provides: 'All peoples have the right to self-determination; by virtue of that right they freely determine their political status and freely pursue their economic, social and cultural development'.

[80] See Musgrave (n 59) 149.

membership is restricted to States.[81] On one reading of the Charter, it would appear that only those 'peoples' which had attained statehood could be considered to be nations eligible to join the United Nations and only States are entitled to have their equal rights and their political choices respected. In this regard, the UN Charter seems to confirm the classical conception of the principle of self-determination with its strong association with the genesis of the nation-State. From this perspective, self-determination was viewed as a consequence of the achievement of the condition of statehood – a nation that had attained statehood was entitled to determine its own political destiny.

The argument that the notion of 'people-hood' and the principle of self-determination were not closely associated with one another – at least before the 1960s – is supported by a careful examination of the UN Charter and by the general conception of self-determination which existed prior to the advent of the United Nations. The notion of 'people-hood' is used in different parts of the UN Charter. It is mentioned in Article 1(2) in the context of the purposes of the United Nations.[82] It is also used in Article 73 and Article 76 to describe the inhabitants of non-self-governing territories and trust territories, respectively. The *travaux* reveals that, during the drafting of Chapter XI, no clear distinction was drawn between the terms 'peoples' and 'inhabitants' – they were used interchangeably to describe the populations of non-self-governing territories.[83] Accordingly, it is evident that the concept of 'people-hood' was not intended to be restricted to the inhabitants of independent States (ie populations that had already achieved 'self-government' or 'self-determination'). Instead, a 'people' could be the inhabitants of an independent State or the inhabitants of a dependent territory; the concept was apt to describe societal groups in general.

At the time the UN was founded, the concept of people-hood had not yet achieved an overt association with the principle of self-determination. This connection only evolved gradually from the 1960s onwards, via the terms of the 1960 Colonial Declaration,[84] and the provisions of Joint Article 1 of the International Covenants on Human Rights.[85] This subsequent association has led some contemporary scholars to overstate the historical connection between, on the one hand, Articles 1 and 55, concerning the principle of self-determination, and Articles 73 and 76, regarding the achievement of self-government for the inhabit-

---

[81] UN Charter, Art 4(1) provides that 'Membership in the United Nations is open to all other peace-loving states which accept the obligations contained in the present Charter and, in the judgment of the Organization, are able and willing to carry out these obligations'.

[82] This provision is echoed in Art 55 in relation to the c IX provisions regarding international economic and social co-operation.

[83] Musgrave (n 59) 154–55.

[84] See The Colonial Declaration (UNGA Res 1514(XV)(1960), para 2 (n 79).

[85] The International Covenants, Joint Art 1(1) provides that 'All peoples have the right of self-determination. By virtue of that right they freely determine their political status and freely pursue their economic, social and cultural development'. International Covenant on Civil and Political Rights (1966) 999 UNTS 171; and International Covenant on Economic, Social and Cultural Rights (1966) 993 UNTS 3.

ants of dependent territories, on the other.[86] For example, Fastenrath suggests that the use of the term 'peoples' in these provisions shows that the principle of self-determination was applicable to the populations of independent States and dependent territories alike. In his view, the fact that this nexus was not appreciated by the representatives of those States which participated in the 1945 San Francisco Conference can be attributed to a doctrinal misunderstanding.[87] However, the *travaux* reveals that the absence of a connection between the notion of 'people-hood' and self-determination was not the result of a mistake. The drafters of the Charter made a conscious decision to withhold the principle of self-determination from colonial populations for fear that it would license widespread demands for independence.[88] Thus while, in 1945, the principle of self-determination amounted to no more than an entitlement to self-government, the international community of States understood that the principle was restricted to those nations which had already attained statehood – it was only applicable to those nations whose right to self-government had manifested itself externally via their accession to statehood. In contrast, internal self-government was a condition that was attainable by a wider range of communities, including the inhabitants of dependent territories. They were clearly distinguishable from the inhabitants of independent States and while the notion of self-government was potentially applicable to both types of communities, according to the text and *travaux* of the UN Charter, the principle of self-determination was only relevant to the latter.

It is clear that the concept of 'people-hood' was used as an interchangeable term for a wide range of societal groups rather than as the basic unit for the purpose of the exercise of the right of self-determination during the period when the UN Charter was being drafted. The inhabitants of non-self-governing territories were not entitled to independence as the outcome of a series of progressive measures.[89] Chapter XI may have been formulated in vague terms but it clearly did not contemplate the achievement of self-determination (ie an external form of self-government) for the populations concerned. In the context of dependent territories, the colonial powers viewed self-government as a condition that fell short of independence and thus short of the pre-condition for the achievement of self-determination. As a result, it was believed that representative institutions could be established so that colonial populations could exercise a degree of internal territorialised autonomy akin to some form of devolved government without the need for decolonisation.[90]

---

[86] See Musgrave (n 59) ch 7 and Fastenrath, *The Charter of the United Nations* (n 69).
[87] Fastenrath (n 69) 1831.
[88] See Cassese (n 32) 42.
[89] In contrast to the inhabitants of trust territories according to Art 76(b), quoted above.
[90] Fastenrath (n 69) 1835.

VII. THE GENERAL ASSEMBLY: CHAPTER XI AND THE PROGRESSIVE
DEVELOPMENT OF THE RIGHT TO SELF-DETERMINATION

In the aftermath of the Second World War, the colonial powers refused to accept that the end of Empire was in sight. This position goes a long way to explaining the strategies which they adopted to resist the incremental steps taken by the General Assembly to bring about decolonisation. During this period, they maintained that the circumstances and governance of colonial territories was a matter which fell within the domestic jurisdiction of the responsible colonial power pursuant to a well-established CIL principle, which was reaffirmed in Article 2(7) of the UN Charter.[91] However, the Charter's differentiation between the international regulation of trust territories and non-self-governing territories lacked any discernible basis in principle and this anomalous situation deeply impressed the UN membership, which even at that time included a considerable number of post-colonial States and socialist States that were ideologically committed to the eradication of colonialism. Moreover, at a normative level, the precise meaning and scope of the principles of self-government and self-determination were under-developed in the international law of the time, especially in the colonial context. Nonetheless, the terms of Chapter XI rendered the conditions in non-self-governing territories amenable to scrutiny by the General Assembly, pursuant to Article 10 of the UN Charter.[92] Against this background, the General Assembly recognised the need for concerted action to establish an international regime for the implementation of the responsibilities articulated in Article 73 of the Charter with a view to the progressive achievement of self-government for the inhabitants of non-self-governing territories and trust territories alike.[93]

As noted above, Article 73(e) of the UN Charter required administering States to transmit certain information concerning those non-self-governing territories, for which they were responsible, to the UN Secretary-General. In resolution 9(I)(1946), the General Assembly requested that the Secretary-General include a summary of the information provided by administering States in relation to their non-self-governing territories in the Secretary-General's annual report so that the General Assembly could review this information on an annual basis. In 1946, a number of colonial powers – Australia, Belgium, Denmark, France, Netherlands, New Zealand, UK and USA – notified the

---

[91] The scope of the concept of domestic jurisdiction is considered below.

[92] The UN Charter, Art 10 provides: 'The General Assembly may discuss any questions or any matters within the scope of the present Charter or relating to the powers and functions of any organs provided for in the present Charter, and . . . may make recommendations to the Members of the United Nations or to the Security Council or to both on any such questions or matters'; see G Nolte in B Simma (ed), *The Charter of the United Nations: A Commentary*, vol I, 3rd edn (Oxford, Oxford University Press, 2012) 295–96.

[93] Art 76(b) also acknowledged that independence was also an outcome which was available to the inhabitants of trust territories.

Secretary-General that they were prepared to transmit the information required by Article 73(e) in relating to their non-self-governing territories. As a result, General Assembly resolution 66(I)(1946) listed 74 territories which had been identified as non-self-governing territories by the responsible administering States. In addition, this resolution established a timetable for the transmission of such information and it created an Ad Hoc Committee to consider this information ahead of the General Assembly's annual sessions.

The General Assembly gradually began to assert itself as the lead agency regarding the international supervision of non-self-governing territories. In 1949, the Ad Hoc Committee, created by resolution 66(I)(1946), was replaced by a Special Committee on Information on Non-Self-Governing Territories.[94] This was part of a wider initiative to establish an effective institutional framework to monitor conditions in non-self-governing territories. During this period, the General Assembly claimed an entitlement: 'to express its opinion on the principles which have guided or which may in the future guide the Members concerned in enumerating the territories for which the obligation exists to transmit information under Article 73(e) of the Charter'.[95] In order to provide such guidance, the General Assembly established another Ad Hoc Committee, which was given the task of identifying the factors by which self-government could be achieved.[96] It was during this process that the General Assembly began to associate the notion of self-government with the principle of self-determination. This instance of normative development was also informed by the work then being undertaken by the Commission on Human Rights in connection with the drafting of the International Covenants on Human Rights.[97] An amended version of a draft resolution on self-determination, which had been developed by the Commission, was endorsed by the General Assembly in resolution 637(VII) (1952). Specifically, it provided, inter alia, that:

> The State Members of the United Nations shall recognize and promote the realization of the right of self-determination of the peoples of Non-Self-Governing and trust territories that are under their administration and shall facilitate the exercise of this right by the peoples of such territories according to the principles and spirit of the Charter of the United Nations in regard to each territory and to the freely expressed wishes of the peoples concerned, the wishes of the people being ascertained through plebiscites or other recognized democratic means

Objections from a number of States were made during the process of drafting this resolution. In particular, it was claimed that, as the resolution addressed the matter of the internal political structures of the States, it contravened the

---

[94] UNGA Res 569(IV)(1949).

[95] UNGA Res 334(IV)(1949).

[96] This Ad Hoc Committee on Factors was established: 'to examine the factors which should be taken into account in deciding whether any territory is or is not a territory whose people have not yet attained a full measure of self-government'. The Committee's recommendations were included in UNGA Res 567(VI)(1951); UNGA Res 648(VII)(1952) and UNGA Res 742(VIII)(1953). See below.

[97] UNGA Res 545(VI)(1951).

provisions of Article 2(7) of the UN Charter. Protests were also made regarding the attempt to reformulate self-determination as a legal right given that the UN Charter only referred to the principle of self-determination in Articles 1(2) and 55. However, resolution 637 was adopted by 40 votes to 14 with 6 abstentions. Higgins, writing in 1963, claimed that the General Assembly's adoption of this resolution demonstrated that the domestic jurisdiction argument could not prevent the right of self-determination from being applicable to dependent territories or from international scrutiny of developments within such territories.[98] But while resolution 637 provided cogent evidence of a shift in favour of the normative significance of self-determination the voting record was hardly decisive. Nevertheless, in resolution 1188(XIV)(1959), the General Assembly reinforced the view that the principle of self-determination had acquired the character of an international legal entitlement on the basis that the persistent disregard for this 'right' weakens the basis of friendly relations between nations.[99]

Despite these developments, there is evidence in support of the view that self-determination did not become normatively significant until the 1960s.[100] For instance, in 1955, the General Assembly's Third Committee was engaged in the task of drafting the International Covenants on Human Rights. In the context of the Committee's work in drafting the provisions concerning self-determination the UK government contended that 'Self-determination is a political principle of very great importance, whose application in practice involves political issues and may have to be subordinated to equally important principles such as the maintenance of peace'.[101] There was widespread opposition during this period, from both the established colonial powers and from post-colonial States, to the inclusion of a general right of self-determination in the International Covenants.[102] This opposition reflected shared concerns regarding secessionist interpretations of self-determination which were particularly prevalent during this period. Nevertheless, the final version of draft Article 1 of the International Covenants, concerning the right of self-determination, was adopted in by the General Assembly's Third Committee in 1955 with a voting record of 32-12-13.[103] While this outcome provides further proof that the right of self-determination was attracting the support of the international community of States, the

---

[98] R Higgins, *The Development of International Law Through the Political Organs of the United Nations* (London, Oxford University Press, 1963) 92. Higgins argued that self-determination constituted an area of legitimate international concern because of its relationship with the maintenance of international peace and security. In her opinion, 'people seeking independence from those unwilling to grant it . . . are likely to disturb the peace', at 93.

[99] Nolte observes that the adoption of this resolution represented a decisive moment in the evolution of the jurisprudence of self-determination. See Nolte, *The Charter of the United Nations* (n 92) 300.

[100] With the adoption of the Colonial Declaration (UNGA Res 1514(XV)(1960) and the finalising of the International Covenants on Human Rights (1966).

[101] A/2910/Add 1.

[102] See Cassese (n 32) 48–52.

[103] GAOR 10th session, Third Committee, 676th meeting [27].

level of support apparent for this development at this point in time was far from overwhelming; it was clearly not sufficient to underpin a claim that the right of self-determination had achieved normative significance beyond the context of the drafting of the Covenants. Further, the ongoing controversy surrounding the meaning of self-determination during the drafting process supports the view that self-determination did not acquire a nascent legal character before 1966, when the International Covenants were finalised.[104]

A. The General Assembly and the Supervision of Non-Self-Governing Territories

Article 73(e) of the UN Charter required administering States to transmit statistical information relating to the economic, social and educational conditions prevailing in their non-self-governing territories. This information was further qualified by security and constitutional considerations. However, the General Assembly soon began to request that administering States provide a wider range of information than that which was required by this provision. To this end, the Ad Hoc Committee on Information encouraged administering States to provide information relating to the political conditions subsisting in their non-self-governing territories on a voluntary basis.[105] However, Belgium, France and the UK initially refused to provide such additional information in their annual reports. The General Assembly repeated its request for such information in subsequent resolutions. In resolution 637(VII)(1952), the General Assembly recommended that administering States should provide information in respect of each of their non-self-governing territories: 'regarding their political progress and the measures taken to develop their capacity for self-determination and to satisfy their political aspirations and to promote the progressive development of their free political institutions'. From 1962 onwards the Special Committee on Information regularly examined information regarding the political and constitutional developments in non-self-governing territories.[106] This incremental shift in favour of the supply of political information demonstrated the value of sustained institutional pressure applied by the General Assembly in relation to non-self-governing territories: administering States were cajoled into providing

---

[104] The ICESCR and the ICCPR were adopted by the General Assembly in UNGA Res 2200 (XXI)(1966) on 16 December 1966. It is arguable that, as a matter of treaty law, the right of self-determination did not attain full normative significance until the Covenants entered into force. The ICESCR entered into force on 3 January 1976 and the ICCPR on 23 March 1976.

[105] This position was first endorsed by the General Assembly in UNGA Res 144(II)(1947). In UNGA Res 848(IX)(1954), the Assembly reiterated the need for the transmission of political information stating that the objectives contained in Art 73 'relate to the political as well as the economic, social and educational advancement of the peoples concerned'. In UNGA Res 1468(XIV)(1959), the Assembly urged administering States to provide political information given the: 'inextricable relationship between developments in political and functional fields'.

[106] This practice was continued by C24 when it assumed the responsibilities of the Special Committee on Information in 1963.

such information even though they insisted that they were under no legal obligation to provide it.[107]

VIII. NON-SELF-GOVERNING TERRITORIES

Chapter XI of the UN Charter does not define the concept of non-self-governing territories. Initially, the General Assembly accepted the argument, advanced by administering States, that the identification of non-self-governing territories was a matter for the responsible States rather than the General Assembly. On this understanding, a number of colonial powers chose to identify their colonies as non-self-governing territories for the purposes set out in Article 73.[108] However, while some administering States complied with the provisions of Chapter XI reluctantly, others refused.[109] In general, the colonial powers maintained the view that conditions within their dependent territories fell within their domestic jurisdiction and that the General Assembly's authority to monitor development within non-self-governing territories was heavily circumscribed. The General Assembly's increasingly assertive approach to the promotion of the international surveillance of non-self-governing territories, and its attempts to develop the notion of self-government in the colonial context, led to the adoption of a series of defensive strategies on the part of administering States that had their origins in the domestic jurisdiction argument.[110]

A. The Scope of the Concept of Domestic Jurisdiction

The colonial powers objected to the General Assembly's increasingly assertive role in relation to the monitoring of non-self-governing territories on the ground that such action amounted to an intervention into the domestic jurisdiction of the State in question thereby compromising the principle expressed in Article 2(7) of the UN Charter.[111] From their perspective, the modest terms of Chapter XI did not render colonial territories susceptible to the scrutiny of the General Assembly. Moreover, while Article 73(e) did create an international legal obligation, which required that administering States transmit certain kinds of information relating to their non-self-governing territories to the Secretary-General,

---

[107] The UK provided such information from 1961 onwards but the government made it clear that the information was provided on a voluntary basis and not as a result of the existence of a binding international legal obligation. See Jennings and Watts (n 64) 291–92. For a short history of the UK government's relations with C24, see I Hendry and S Dickson, *British Overseas Territories Law* (Oxford, Hart Publishing, 2011) 247–50.

[108] As discussed above.

[109] Spain and Portugal refused to identify their colonial territories as non-self-governing territories on joining the United Nations in 1955.

[110] The most notorious of these defensive strategies being the Belgian Thesis, discussed below.

[111] The significance of the domain reserve as an organising principle of the UN was recognised at the San Francisco Conference on International Organisation 1945; see Nolte (n 92) 290–93.

it did not license the General Assembly to construct institutional apparatus for the purpose of monitoring developments in such territories.

It was in this context that the 'Belgian Thesis' was advanced.[112] It asserted that Chapter XI was concerned with non-self-governing territories rather than colonialism per se. As a result, the Belgian government argued that the question of self-government should be addressed to the constituent peoples of *all* States not only those peoples subject to colonialism. It followed that, if distinct 'peoples' within independent States were denied effective self-government, they should be granted the right of self-determination. Given Belgium's oppressive activities in the Congo, this argument was widely regarded as a cynical strategy designed to limit the scope of the notion of self-government by frightening independent States into refusing to condone its colonial application.[113] But while the Belgian Thesis was rejected by the UN membership it contributed to the arguments about the scope of administering States' domestic jurisdiction which had the effect of restricting the ability of the Special Committee on Information to investigate conditions in particular non-self-governing territories. Consequently, during this period, it limited itself to issuing general recommendations to administering States, which significantly undermined the value of the Committee's work, in practice.[114]

However, defensive claims that political conditions prevailing in non-self-governing territories, and that the progressive achievement of self-government for the inhabitants of such territories fell within the exclusive preserve of the responsible State proved to be unsustainable in the light of the general commitments contained in Chapter XI and, over time, the resistance of the colonial powers weakened in the face of the progressive work undertaken by the General Assembly in this field.[115] Moreover, the defensive arguments advanced by the colonial powers did not accord with the well-established general position adopted by international law regarding the scope of the concept of domestic jurisdiction. Although the PCIJ observed in the *Nationality Decrees in Tunis and Morocco* case that matters which fall within a State's domestic jurisdiction are matters that are not regulated by international law, it also noted that 'The question whether a certain matter is or is not solely within the jurisdiction of a State is essentially a relative question; it depends upon the development of international relations'.[116] In this case, the PCIJ was engaged in the task of interpreting the nature and scope of Article 15(8) of the Covenant of the League of

---

[112] This was the argument advanced at the General Assembly's Fourth Committee by the Belgian government in 1952. For an overview see Crawford (n 34) 607; N Berman, 'Sovereignty in Abeyance: Self-determination and International Law' (1988–89) 7 *Wisconsin International Law Journal* 51, 89–90; and JL Kunz, 'Chapter XI of the United Nations Charter in Action' (1954) 48 *American Journal of International Law* 103

[113] See CJ Iorns, 'Indigenous Peoples and Self-determination: Challenging State Sovereignty' (1992) 24 *Case Western Reserve Journal of International Law* 199, 251–56.

[114] See UNGA Res 847(IX) 22 November 1954.

[115] See UNGA Res 334 (IV)(1949) and UNGA Res 1467(XIV)(1959).

[116] *Nationality Decrees in Tunis and Morocco* case (1923) PCIJ Series B, No 4.

Nations, which expressly recognised that whether a matter fell within the domestic jurisdiction of a State, or not, was to be determined by international law. But while the UN Charter contained no analogous provision for the purpose of identifying the scope of the concept of domestic jurisdiction, it was widely accepted that its drafters did not intend to alter the approach adopted by the PCIJ in the *Nationality Decrees* case.[117]

As a consequence of the presumption in favour of international jurisdiction,[118] the General Assembly's actions concerning the international surveillance of non-self-governing territories and the normative evolution of the relationship between self-government and self-determination in the colonial context must be seen as legitimate developments even though they had the effect of reducing the scope of the notion of domestic jurisdiction considerably. This conclusion was justified by the fact that Chapter XI brought non-self-governing territories within the scope of international jurisdiction. Further, it has been claimed that the fact that a given field has been regulated by international law in general terms is a sufficient basis for generating a corresponding diminution in the domestic jurisdiction of those States affected by the development in question.[119] Accordingly, the argument that the obligations enumerated in Article 73 are modest, programmatic and ambiguous, or that Article 73(e) did not expressly authorise the General Assembly to monitor developments in non-self-governing territories do not weaken the case for international supervision of such territories. Through the UN Charter, the international community of States has chosen to regulate non-self-governing territories by reference to international law. Consequently, such territories have become an area of international concern and the General Assembly acquired a legitimate interest in the realisation of the objectives set out in Chapter XI pursuant to the operation of Article 10 of the UN Charter, as a result.[120]

Nonetheless, it should be acknowledged that the General Assembly's institutional initiatives in relation to non-self-governing territories could only be considered to be legitimate if it could be established that it was acting within the scope of its competency. Higgins, writing in 1963, indicated that the authority to resolve disputes concerning the correct interpretation of the provisions of the UN Charter rests with the organ which is responsible for the application of the disputed provisions.[121] Further, Higgins noted that the organs of the UN consider themselves to be entitled to determine the scope of their own sphere of competence and this standpoint has not been subsequently challenged by the

---

[117] See Higgins, *The Development of International Law Through the Political Organs of the United Nations* (n 98) 65–67; L Goodrich et al, *Charter of the United Nations: Commentary and Documents*, 3rd edn (New York, Columbia University Press, 1969) 60–66; and Nolte (n 92) 290–93. This was confirmed by the ICJ in its *Advisory Opinion on the Interpretation of the Peace Treaties with Bulgaria, Hungary and Romania* (1950) ICJ Rep 65.

[118] See Higgins (n 98) 76–77.

[119] See Nolte (n 92) 291.

[120] See Art 10 (n 92).

[121] Higgins (n 98) 72–73.

ICJ.[122] As such, it is up to the organ charged with a particular responsibility to determine whether or not a given matter is suitable for international jurisdiction. The difficulty with this position in the present context is that the General Assembly was not expressly charged with the task of supervising developments in non-self-governing territories nor was it given the responsibility of bringing about decolonisation by the Charter. Accordingly, if the General Assembly was the sole judge of the scope of its own competence to intervene in the governance of colonial territories then its authority in relation to such matters would remain open to challenge by disgruntled colonial powers. Seen from this perspective, the view that the General Assembly had exceeded the powers granted to it by the UN Charter in this respect was a, prima facie, credible position.

B. The Concept of Non-Self-Governing Territories

The General Assembly's efforts to monitor developments in non-self-governing territories were also hampered by conceptual problems. Not only did the lack of a reliable definition of the concept of non-self-governing territories hinder the implementation of the reporting obligations contained in Chapter XI significantly, it also undermined the General Assembly's efforts to construct an institutional framework for the international supervision of such territories. Consequently, the General Assembly began to focus on the task of identifying the factors that could be used to determine whether a non-self-governing territory had achieved a full measure of self-government.[123] But rather than attempt to define the abstract concept of a non-self-governing territory, the General Assembly concentrated on the ways in which such territories could achieve a full measure of self-government. For instance, paragraph 6 of resolution 742(VIII) (1953) proclaimed that 'the manner in which Territories referred to in Chapter XI of the Charter can become fully self-governing is primarily through the attainment of independence'. This resolution also acknowledged, in paragraph 5, that self-government could be achieved by the formation of an association with the administering State or integration with another State, if that decision was the outcome of the freely expressed will of the people concerned. An extensive list of factors, which were deemed to be indicative of whether the outcome of full self-government had been attained, was annexed to the resolution. However, as Fastenrath observed, the General Assembly's preferred outcome was clearly independence and the options of association and integration were heavily qualified so as to ensure that any process conducted in the name of delivering self-government was a genuine exercise which would be demonstrably

---

[122] ibid, 72–73.
[123] This work was undertaken by the Ad Hoc Committee on Factors (Non-Self-Governing Territories) and it led to the adoption of UNGA Res 567(VI)(1951) and UNGA Res 648(VII)(1952) culminating in UNGA Res 742(VIII)(1953).

the freely expressed will of the inhabitants of the non-self-governing territory in question.[124]

There were a number of problems with this attempt to articulate the scope of self-government in the context of dependent territories. First, General Assembly resolution 742(VIII)(1953) presupposed that the concept of a non-self-governing territory was already clear. Chapter XI did not list the territories to which it applies nor did it enumerate the core components of the concept of a non-self-governing territory.[125] However, resolution 742 ignored the definitional problem. As noted above, paragraph 6 provided: 'the manner in which Territories referred to in Chapter XI of the Charter can become fully self-governing'. Resolution 742 concentrated almost exclusively on measuring the achievement of full self-government in non-self-governing territories. However, because it merely assumed that all colonial territories that were not trust territories were, by default, non-self-governing territories, it overlooked the complexities inherent in the notion of self-government in dependent territories.[126] Accordingly, the General Assembly's failure to ensure that the concept of a non-self-governing territory was defined before the issue of the achievement of self-government was addressed did the cause of the realisation of self-government in the colonial context little service.[127] Secondly, the preferred outcome of independence had no basis in Chapter XI of the Charter. As discussed above, administering States remained committed to the domestic jurisdiction argument during this period, and the idea that self-government could be attained within a colonial framework (ie without accession to independence) remained credible. Consequently, in 1953, it would have been plausible to have taken the view that resolution 742 was ultra vires the UN Charter. Finally, given that the concept of non-self-governing territories was politically contentious at this time, it was important to ensure that any effort to promote a workable notion of self-government was both clear and simple so that administering States would be in no doubt as to how self-government could be achieved and measured. Although the list of factors which were appended to resolution 742 represented a genuine effort to measure the attainment of self-government in the colonial context, the highly abstract nature of this attempt at formulation and the sheer complexity of the exercise combined to render this endeavour unsuccessful.

IX. THE COLONIAL DECLARATION

While the General Assembly took decisive action regarding the elaboration of the concept of self-government in relation to non-self-governing territories in a

[124] Fastenrath (n 69) 1834–35.
[125] It does not define the concept of a metropolitan State either; Crawford (n 34) 606.
[126] Some of these complexities were exploited by Belgium when it advanced the Belgian Thesis. See below.
[127] This mistake was subsequently corrected in 1960 by UNGA Res 1541(XV)(1960); see below.

series of initiatives throughout the 1950s, the real breakthrough came with the adoption of the Declaration on the Granting of Independence to Colonial Countries and Peoples ('Colonial Declaration') on 14 December 1960.[128] It proclaimed that all colonial peoples possessed the right to self-determination and it elaborated the content of this right in seven substantive paragraphs:

1. The subjection of peoples to alien subjugation, domination and exploitation constitutes a denial of fundamental human rights, is contrary to the Charter of the United Nations and is an impediment to the promotion of world peace and co-operation.

2. All peoples have the right to self-determination; by virtue of that right they freely determine their political status and freely pursue their economic, social and cultural development.

3. Inadequacy of political, economic, social or educational preparedness should never serve as a pretext for delaying independence.

4. All armed action or repressive measures of all kinds directed against dependent people shall cease in order to enable them to exercise peacefully and freely their right to complete independence; and the integrity of their national territory shall be respected.

5. Immediate steps shall be taken, in Trust and Non-Self-Governing Territories . . . to transfer all powers to the peoples of those territories, without any conditions or reservations, in accordance with their freely expressed will and desire, without any distinction as to race, creed or colour, in order to enable them to enjoy complete independence or freedom.

6. Any attempt aimed at the partial or total disruption of the national unity and the territorial integrity of a country is incompatible with the purposes and principles of the Charter of the United Nations.

7. All States shall observe faithfully and strictly the provisions of the Charter of the United Nations, the Universal Declaration of Human Rights and the present Declaration on the basis of equality, non-interference in the internal affairs of all States, and respect for the sovereign rights of all peoples and their territorial integrity.

The Colonial Declaration had major political and legal implications for all colonial populations and administering States. For the present purpose of considering the relationship between the Colonial Declaration and the notion of self-government, as identified in Chapters XI and XII of the UN Charter, the Declaration reinterpreted the objective of securing self-government for the inhabitants of non-self-governing territories, as per Article 73(b), and as an option available to the inhabitants of trust territories, via Article 76(b), as an international legal entitlement to self-determination which belonged to all colonial peoples. Moreover, it strongly associated the exercise of this right with the achievement of independence – the genesis of a new post-colonial State.

---

[128] UNGA Res 1514(XV), 14 December 1960. It was adopted by 89 votes and no votes against (with 9 abstentions).

X. GENERAL ASSEMBLY RESOLUTION 1541(XV)(1960)

On the day after the General Assembly adopted the Colonial Declaration it adopted resolution 1541, which revisited the concept of a non-self-governing territory for the purpose of bringing about decolonisation.[129] In contrast to previous initiatives, which saw the General Assembly focus on the notion of self-government, on this occasion, it sought to define the concept of a non-self-governing territory by reference to its essential features before going on to identify the modalities by which self-government could be achieved: independence, integration with an independent State or association with an established State. To this end, the annex to resolution 1541(XV) provided, inter alia, that:

Principle I

The authors of the Charter of the United Nations had in mind that Chapter XI should be applicable to territories which were then known to be of the colonial type. An obligation exists to transmit information under Article 73e of the Charter in respect of such territories whose peoples have not yet attained a full measure of self-government.

Principle II

Chapter XI of the Charter embodies the concept of Non-Self-Governing Territories in a dynamic state of evolution and progress towards a 'full measure of self-government'. As soon as a territory and its peoples attain a full measure of self-government, the obligation ceases. Until this comes about, the obligation to transmit information under Article 73 e continues.

Principle III

The obligation to transmit information under Article 73 e of the Charter constitutes an international obligation and should be carried out with due regard to the fulfilment of international law.

Principle IV

Prima face there is an obligation to transmit information in respect of a territory which is geographically separate and is distinct ethnically and/or culturally from the country administering it.

Principle V

Once it has been established that such a prima facie case of geographical and ethnical or cultural distinctness of a territory exists, other elements may then be brought into consideration. These additional elements may be, inter alia, of an administrative, political, juridical, economic or historical nature. If they affect the relationship between the metropolitan State and the territory concerned in a manner which arbitrarily places the latter in a position or status of subordination, they support the presumption that there is an obligation to transmit information under Article 73 e of the Charter.

---

[129] 'Principles which should guide Members in deciding whether or not an obligation exists to transmit the information called for under Article 73(e) of the Charter', UNGA Res 1541(XV), 15 December 1960.

Principle VI

A Non-Self-Governing Territory can be said to have reached a full measure of self-government by:

(a) Emergence as a sovereign independent State;
(b) Free association with an independent State; or
(c) Integration with an independent State.

The General Assembly clearly intended principles 2 and 3 to work together to ensure that an administering State's obligations to any given non-self-governing territory would endure until the territory achieved full self-government. Consequently, it was accepted that an administering State was entitled to exercise sovereign authority over a non-self-governing territory while it continued to bear international responsibility for such a territory. Accordingly, it was assumed that sovereignty was temporally restricted – an administering State could only exercise such authority until the territory achieved a full measure of self-government.[130] Principle 3 confirmed that an administering State remained under an international legal obligation to transmit information concerning such a territory until such a time as self-government is achieved.[131]

Principle 4 defined a non-self-governing territory for the purposes of deciding which colonial populations were entitled to exercise self-government as one that was geographically separate, and ethnically/culturally distinct from the metropolitan State administering it. This provision could be criticised for promoting the notion that colonialism was exclusively an overseas phenomenon ('salt-water colonialism'). Nevertheless, it helped to undermine the objections that underpinned the controversial Belgian Thesis. Moreover, by identifying the various institutional and historical factors that could create and/or sustain a relationship between the administering State and the population of a colonial territory based on domination and subordination, principle 5 ensured that resolution 1541 avoided the charge that non-self-governing territories were purely a product of geography and ethnic diversity. Principle 6 acknowledged that full self-government could be achieved by either accession to independent statehood, integration or free association with an independent State.[132] Consequently, resolution 1541 produced a succinct and comprehensive definition of the concept of a non-self-governing territory and of the ways in which self-government could be realised by the inhabitants of such territories.[133]

In part, the General Assembly's approach was prompted by the refusal of Spain and Portugal, who joined the UN in 1955, to identify their colonies as non-self-governing territories and thus to commence their reporting obligations under Article 73(e) of the Charter. As a result, in resolution 1542, the General Assembly took the exceptional step of identifying Portugal's dependent

---

[130] Crawford (n 34) 613–15. See also Cassese (n 32) 187.
[131] Principle II, UNGA Res 1541(XV)(1960).
[132] On the issue of association, see Crawford (n 34) 625–33. The option of association and integration were elaborated in principles 7, 8 and 9 of UNGA Res 1541.
[133] UNGA Res 1541(XV)(1960) voting record: 69 voted in favour, 2 voted against and 21 abstained.

territories as non-self-governing territories unilaterally.[134] This development showed the General Assembly's growing confidence regarding its role in the international supervision of non-self-governing territories and it demonstrated that what had started as a voluntary process, with resolution 66(I)(1946), had acquired a compulsory dimension, albeit in exceptional circumstances. More generally, the General Assembly began to assert itself concerning decisions about whether self-government had been attained in general. To this end, it started to claim that it had at least joint authority along with the responsible administering State regarding determinations about the achievement of self-government in concrete cases.[135]

In 1961, the Special Committee on the Situation with Regard to the Implementation of the Declaration on the Granting of Independence to Colonial Countries and Peoples, which became widely known as 'C24', was created by the General Assembly.[136] The new Special Committee was charged with the task of overseeing the implementation of the Colonial Declaration. It soon replaced the Special Committee on Information from Non-Self-Governing Territories and it assumed the responsibility for reviewing the reports on non-self-governing territories submitted by administering States pursuant to Article 73(e). It also acquired the power to organise visiting missions to non-self-governing territories and to receive information and petitions from individuals or groups in such territories. Further, it was given the capacity to adopt resolutions for consideration by the General Assembly's Fourth Committee, and ultimately the General Assembly itself. Consequently, by the early-1960s, a sophisticated legal and institutional regime had evolved which facilitated the realisation of the right to self-determination in non-self-governing territories. Accordingly, by this time, the institutional initiatives fostered by the General Assembly meant that there was little difference, in practice, between the level of supervision exercised by C24 over non-self-governing territories and that conducted by the Trustee Council in respect of trust territories.[137] Therefore, by the early 1960s, the General Assembly had mustered the institutional structures to monitor developments in non-self-governing territories from a very unpromising reporting obligation included in Article 73(e) of the Charter. However, the

---

[134] Spain had relented by this time and it had given an undertaking to comply with the requirements declared in c XI. See UNGA Res 1542(XV)(1960). Neither Portugal nor France differentiated between their colonial territories and their metropolitan areas. In principle, French and Portuguese Overseas Territories were as much part of France or Portugal, respectively, as their European territories. This standpoint made it particularly difficult for France and Portugal to accept the concept of non-self-governing territories as it had been developed by the General Assembly in UNGA Res 742(VIII)(1953) and, more clearly, in UNGA Res 1541(XV)(1960).

[135] Crawford suggests that the question of whether full self-government has been has been attained was to be determined by the administering State in conjunction with the General Assembly 'either specifically or by some such unequivocal act as admission to United Nations membership'; Crawford (n 34) 622–33.

[136] C24 was established by UNGA Res 1654(XVI), 27 November 1961.

[137] The Colonial Declaration was drafted in such a way that it was to be applicable to both kinds of dependent territories.

success of the General Assembly's institutional initiatives in this context stemmed largely from its ability to harness the Charter's general provisions on self-determination and human rights as well as the specific regime devised in respect of trust territories and as a result of the interpretation of these provisions in a manner that reflected wider political developments which had occurred during the post-Charter era.

The tide of history turned sharply against colonialism during the 1960s. By 1970, with the adoption of the Declaration on Friendly Relations,[138] the right of colonial self-determination had become firmly established as a CIL principle and it was accepted as such by those States that administered non-self-governing territories.[139] The ICJ subsequently confirmed the customary status of the principle and right of self-determination in its 1971 *Namibia Advisory Opinion* and 1975 *Western Sahara Advisory Opinion*. The right of self-determination was subsequently reinforced, as a matter of treaty law, by the entry into force of the International Covenants on Human Rights in 1976. Joint Article 1 provided that:

(1) All peoples have the right of self-determination. By virtue of that right they freely determine their political status and freely pursue their economic, social and cultural development.

(2) All peoples may, for their own ends, freely dispose of their natural wealth and resources without prejudice to any obligations arising out of international economic co-operation, based upon the principle of mutual benefit, and international law. In no case may a people be deprived of its own means of subsistence.

(3) The State Parties to the present Covenant, including those having responsibility for the administration of Non-Self-Governing and Trust Territories, shall promote the realization of the right of self-determination, and shall respect that right, in conformity with the provisions of the Charter of the United Nations.[140]

By the 1970s, the international law governing decolonisation had been clearly established. It meant that, by this time, Franck and Hoffman could safely characterise decolonisation as 'an irresistible tide of historical inevitability'.[141] However, it should be recalled that, during the 1950s, the outcome of the contests fought in the General Assembly between the colonial powers and those States who were committed to the eradication of colonialism was far from certain. Further, even when political victory was assured with the adoption of the Colonial Declaration in 1960, the general standpoint of international law regarding political initiatives remained contentious, as demonstrated by the tensions apparent within the ICJ's decision in the *South West Africa* cases *(Second Phase)*.[142]

---

[138] UNGA Res 2625(XXV)(1970).

[139] See below.

[140] International Covenant on Civil and Political Rights 1966, 999 UNTS 171 (ICCPR); and International Covenant on Economic, Social and Cultural Rights 1966, 993 UNTS 3 (ICESCR).

[141] See TM Franck and P Hoffman, 'The Right of Self-Determination in Very Small Places' (1975–76) 8 *New York University Journal of International Law and Politics* 331.

[142] *South West Africa* cases *(Ethiopia v South Africa and Liberia v South Africa) (Second Phase)* (1966) ICJ Rep 6 discussed in parts XIV and XV below..

Against this background, and in the light of the temporal enquiry being pursued in this book, it is vital to determine the extent to which the right of colonial self-determination evolved during the late-1950s and early-1960s and to establish the status and basis of this entitlement as a matter of international law during the mid-1960s when the Chagos Islands were excised from the colony of Mauritius. Further, it is crucial to decide the weight that should be attached to the actions and resolutions of the General Assembly in the colonial context and the legal effects of such institutional activity – did they derive their authority directly from the relevant provisions of the UN Charter and thus constitute authoritative instances of treaty interpretation or did they prompt the emergence of binding CIL in this area?

Virtually all international lawyers would accept that the right of colonial self-determination had acquired CIL status by the time of the Declaration on Friendly Relations in 1970 and, in treaty law, by virtue of the entry into force of the International Covenants in 1976. However, some commentators have argued that the right to colonial self-determination derived its legal authority directly from the UN Charter and that the right emerged as a result of the adoption of a series of General Assembly resolutions during the 1950s, which culminated in the adoption of the Colonial Declaration in 1960.[143] This approach has the advantage of attributing presumptive legal validity to sustained activity by the General Assembly in specific situations, or with regard to particular matters. Other international lawyers argue that the right of colonial self-determination acquired its legal character via the emergence of CIL, which crystallised as a result of the concerted action taken by the General Assembly.[144] Further, a number of international lawyers have suggested that both treaty law – through the provisions of the Charter and the drafting of the International Covenants – and CIL worked together concerning the development of the right to colonial self-determination during the 1960s.[145] However, other international lawyers have challenged these arguments claiming that the legal character of the right of colonial self-determination was not established conclusively as a matter of CIL until the adoption of the Declaration on Friendly Relations in 1970.[146] As noted at the outset of this chapter, the claim that the detachment of the Chagos Islands from the colony of Mauritius – pursuant to the 1965 Lancaster House Agreement and the 1965 BIOT Order in Council – constituted a violation of the Mauritian people's right to self-determination, presupposes that this right was established as a matter of international law in 1965. Consequently, in order to facilitate the enquiry being undertaken in this book, it is necessary to establish,

---

[143] See Higgins (n 98); and MN Shaw, *Title to Territory in Africa: International Legal Issues* (Oxford, Clarendon Press, 1986), discussed below

[144] Crawford (n 34) and Cassese (n 32), discussed below.

[145] Crawford (n 34); Cassese (n 32), and Shaw, *Title to Territory in Africa* (n 143), discussed below.

[146] See R Emerson, 'Self-determination' (1971) 65 *American Journal of International Law* 459; Jennings and Watts (n 64); and Hendry and Dickson, *British Overseas Territories Law* (n 108), discussed below.

as far as possible, the precise moment at which the colonial manifestation of the right to self-determination acquired its international legal character and how this status was achieved. With this aim in mind, this chapter will first consider whether the right of colonial self-determination acquired this character as a result of the progressive interpretation of the provisions of the UN Charter, and thus its development can be attributed to advances in treaty law; secondly, it will explore whether the normative significance of the right of colonial self-determination acquired the status of generally binding CIL.

XI. CHARTER-BASED ARGUMENTS

Jennings and Watts, the editors of the ninth edition of *Oppenheim's International Law*, observed that the maintenance of colonial territories was not inconsistent with the text of the Charter.[147] Further, in the *Western Sahara* case, the ICJ acknowledged that Chapter XI of the Charter did not undermine the sovereign authority possessed by administering States in respect of their non-self-governing territories.[148] Accordingly, while it is clear that the commitments contained in Chapter XI were of a legal character, they were programmatic in nature and the text of Article 73 did not create direct entitlements for the inhabitants of non-self-governing territories. In this vein, Fastenrath acknowledges that Chapter XI of the UN Charter provided an initial framework for the pursuit of the goal of decolonisation by the General Assembly even though it significantly strengthened the commitments declared in Article 73 during the 1950s.[149] However, he suggested that the Charter framework was superseded by the Colonial Declaration, with its emphasis on the right of colonial self-determination; the object of independence; and the institutional initiatives that were implemented as a result of its adoption.[150] By implication, Fastenrath suggests that the Colonial Declaration's legal authority must be located elsewhere – in CIL.

Jennings and Watts acknowledged that the issue of the satisfactory implementation of the responsibilities articulated in Chapter XI of the UN Charter was undoubtedly an area of international concern, which justified the General Assembly's attention.[151] Consequently, they accepted that the General Assembly's concerted efforts to establish a supervisory framework to ensure that administering States were complying with the objectives expressed in Chapter XI was a legitimate endeavour, especially given that Article 73 did not

---

[147] See Jennings and Watts (n 64) 282. It should be noted that the ICJ has favoured a literal construction of the UN Charter on many occasions; see the *Admissions* case (1950) ICJ Rep 4. It reinforced this approach in the *Territorial Dispute (Libya/Chad)* case (1994) ICJ Rep 6, when it observed that 'Interpretation must be based above all upon the text of a treaty', at [41].

[148] This was confirmed in *Western Sahara* case (n 13) [43].

[149] Fastenrath (n 69) 1839.

[150] ibid.

[151] Jennings and Watts (n 64) 291.

create the institutional machinery required for international oversight of developments in non-self-governing territories.[152] However, Jennings and Watts expressed their concerns about the extent to which the General Assembly sought to regulate matters which, in their view, were essentially within the domestic jurisdiction of the administering States concerned. In particular, they suggest that the Charter did not authorise the General Assembly to expand the kinds of information that administering States were required to transmit pursuant to Article 73(e) to include information on political and constitutional conditions in non-self-governing territories; nor did it have the authority to develop the notion of self-government in relation to such territories or to equate self-government with the principle of self-determination (or self-determination with independence); neither did the Charter justify the General Assembly's demands, in the Colonial Declaration, for the immediate termination of all colonial situations irrespective of the readiness of the peoples concerned to assume obligations associated with the exercise of sovereign authority.[153] As a result, Jennings and Watts concluded that the actions of the General Assembly in relation to non-self-governing territories have: 'erod[ed] the significance of Article 2(7) of the Charter in this context virtually to the point of disappearance'.[154]

In sharp contrast, Crawford, Higgins and Shaw have all argued that the concerted action of the General Assembly in this area rendered the international regulation of non-self-governing territories legitimate and that the contours of the domestic jurisdiction of administering States in relation to their colonial territories were fundamentally altered as a result. Crawford claims that the Colonial Declaration has achieved a quasi-constitutional status in international law, which is comparable to the Universal Declaration of Human Rights and the Charter itself.[155] He believes that the normative foundations of the Colonial Declaration are to be found in the Charter.[156] Crawford harnesses the ICJ's decision in the *Expenses Advisory Opinion* in support of the proposition that a strong presumption exists in favour of the legal validity of concerted General Assembly action within a given area.[157] Moreover, he alludes to the fact that, in the 1971 *Namibia Advisory Opinion*, the ICJ acknowledged that the institutional initiatives of the General Assembly in the colonial context – with specific reference to the Colonial Declaration – have facilitated the development of the principle of self-determination, which was rendered applicable to all non-self-governing territories as a result.[158] Further, in both the *Namibia* case and the 1975 *Western Sahara* case, the ICJ recognised the vital role played by the General Assembly in establishing the law of decolonisation. Crawford invokes the *Namibia* case to show that the central concepts expressed in Article 22 of the 1919 Covenant of

---

[152] ibid.
[153] ibid, 294.
[154] ibid.
[155] This claim was made in para 7 of the Colonial Declaration.
[156] See Crawford (n 34) 604.
[157] See the *Expenses Advisory Opinion* (1962) ICJ Rep 151, 168.
[158] Crawford (n 34) 604–05. See *Namibia* case (n 11) [52–53].

the League of Nations, including the concept of the sacred trust, were intended to be evolutionary rather than static in nature.[159] He suggests that the same reasoning could be used to explain the nature of the responsibilities declared in Chapter XI of the Charter in respect of non-self-governing territories.[160] Accordingly, seen from this perspective, the emergence of the right of colonial self-determination may be attributed to the purposive interpretation of the successive constitutional treaties of the international community of States.

Higgins, writing in 1963, claimed that the trend towards the recognition of self-determination as a legal right belonging to colonial peoples was sharply accelerated by the adoption of the Colonial Declaration in 1960.[161] She alluded to the fact that no member State voted against the Declaration and that the number of abstentions was very low in support of this contention. Accordingly, she asserted that 'The resolution must be taken to represent the wishes and beliefs of the full membership of the United Nations'.[162] Higgins did not make the claim that General Assembly resolution 1514(XV)(1960) possessed legal authority per se; rather, she argued that the Colonial Declaration, combined with the UN practice that had already evolved through a series of General Assembly resolutions, provided cogent proof that a legal right to self-determination had emerged.[163] In support of this conclusion, Higgins also relied upon the adoption of the draft version of joint Article 1 of the International Covenants by the General Assembly's Third Committee in 1955.[164] She argued that such a development demonstrated the normative significance of the right to self-determination, despite the fact that the Covenants had not been adopted by the General Assembly or opened for ratification, at the time she was writing.

Writing in 1986, Shaw, like Higgins before him, situated the development of the right of self-determination in a series of incremental general initiatives pursued by the General Assembly from the early 1950s onwards, which were reinforced by the application of the right in specific situations.[165] Shaw accepted that the principle of self-determination crystallised into CIL during the process of decolonisation.[166] Nonetheless, he preferred to adopt the view that the right of self-determination finds its normative foundation in the UN Charter and that the series of General Assembly resolutions, which culminated in the adoption of the Colonial Declaration, constitute authoritative interpretations of the Charter.[167] For Shaw, this approach was desirable because, in his view:

[159] *Namibia* case (n 11).
[160] ibid.
[161] Higgins (n 98) 100.
[162] ibid, 101.
[163] ibid, 104.
[164] See discussion in text accompanying n 103.
[165] As evidenced by a series of General Assembly resolutions including UNGA Res 545(VI)(1951), UNGA Res 637(VII)(1952), UNGA Res 1188(XIV)(1959), UNGA Res 1514(XV)(1960), UNGA Res 2200(XXI)(1966) and UNGA Res 2625(XXV)(1970).
[166] Shaw (n 143) 89, quoted part of a passage from Judge Dillard's Separate Opinion in the 1975 *Western Sahara* case (n 13) 121, as discussed below.
[167] Shaw (n 143) 73–76.

A norm created as a result of Charter interpretation, it should be noted, will bind all members of the United Nations, while a customary rule will bind all States save those objecting *ab initio*. Thus, the former method would appear to be more advantageous, particularly as regards, for example, South Africa. Indeed the fact that self-determination applies virtually exclusively within the colonial sphere (although with some potential for development) is a further argument favouring the Charter interpretation approach, since the distinction between colonies and metropolitan territories is one made by the Charter.[168]

Shaw accepted that in order for General Assembly resolutions to have the capacity to constitute authoritative interpretations of the Charter, which were then binding upon member States they: (i) must be drafted in a way that evinces normative intention; and (ii) must attract the overwhelming support of the UN membership.[169] He acknowledged that it is difficult to establish, in abstract terms, how much activity and support is required to produce a binding interpretation of the provisions of the UN Charter on any given issue as much depends on the circumstances of the particular situation and the extent to which other legal principles and political considerations inform the General Assembly resolution/s in question.[170] However, he suggested that, if a considerable number of resolutions have been adopted addressing a specific issue, or situation, and the two requirements set out above are satisfied then such institutional activity may give rise to a presumption that an authoritative interpretation of the Charter has been rendered by the General Assembly.[171]

Shaw did not claim that General Assembly resolutions create international law per se. The UN Charter did not confer upon the General Assembly the power to issue authoritative interpretations of the provisions of the Charter and it is clear from the *travaux* that a conscious decision was made by the drafters of the Charter not to grant the General Assembly such a power.[172] Nevertheless, Shaw cautioned against static approaches to treaty interpretation.[173] He identified the need to be able to harmonise the Charter with those progressive practices which have been embraced overwhelmingly by the membership of the UN since it was established.[174] Moreover, it is an axiom of modern international law that the interpretation of a treaty can be informed by subsequent practices adopted by the parties.[175] Viewed from this perspective, the concerted actions of

---

[168] ibid, 90.

[169] ibid, 73–74.

[170] ibid, 74.

[171] ibid, 75.

[172] See J Castañeda, *Legal Effects of United Nations Resolutions* (New York, Columbia University Press, 1969) 122.

[173] Shaw (n 143) 86.

[174] ibid, 82.

[175] This was confirmed in the Vienna Convention on the Law of Treaties 1969. Art 31(3) provides that, for the purpose of interpreting a treaty, a court may have regard to:

(a) any subsequent agreement between the parties regarding the interpretation of the treaty or the application of its provisions;

member States, acting in the crucible of the General Assembly, can be seen as having the general authority to produce valid interpretations of the Charter, which, as a result, acquire binding effect as a matter of treaty law.

Against this background, Shaw pointed out that a number of States considered resolution 1514(XV)(1960) to constitute an authoritative interpretation of the Charter during the process of its adoption.[176] However, he identified a number of textual inconsistencies which exist between the Colonial Declaration and the relevant provisions of the UN Charter. For instance, paragraph 1 of the Colonial Declaration provides that 'The subjection of peoples to alien subjugation, domination and exploitation constitutes a denial of fundamental human rights, is contrary to the Charter of the United Nations and is an impediment to the promotion of world peace and co-operation'. Shaw noted that both Chapter XI, in respect of non-self-governing territories, and Chapter XII, in respect of trust territories, recognise the existence of relationships of dependence and subordination between colonial territories and their administering States. Accordingly, rather than adopting the position that colonialism constituted a denial of fundamental human rights, the UN Charter accepted and thus legitimises colonialism, albeit on a qualified basis.[177] Further, while paragraph 3 of the Colonial Declaration claimed that the inadequacy of conditions within a colonial territory shall not be used as a pretext for delaying independence, Shaw observed that both Article 73(b) and Article 76(b) recognise the existence of an obligation on the part of administering States to assist in the progressive development and advancement of the inhabitants of dependent territories.[178] Consequently, the UN Charter conceived of the achievement of self-government in the colonial context as the outcome of an incremental process. Moreover, Shaw noted that the references in paragraphs 3, 4 and 5 of the Colonial Declaration to the realisation of the right of self-determination by the achievement of independence are inconsistent with the provisions of other General Assembly resolutions;[179] and the goal of independence is not acknowledged in the Charter, at least not for non-self-governing peoples. Further, Shaw accepted that the reference, in paragraph 5, to the need to take 'immediate steps' to transfer all powers to the peoples of non-self-governing territories and trust

---

(b) any subsequent practice in the application of the treaty which establishes the agreement of the parties regarding its interpretation;

(c) any relevant rules of international law applicable in the relations between the parties.

The Vienna Convention's recognition of the influence of subsequent agreements and practice on treaty interpretation demonstrates the evolutionary nature of international law. Art 31 reinforces the idea that specific developments should be interpreted in ways that are consistent with the background rules of international law.

[176] These States included Liberia, Madagascar, Peru, Tunisia and Yugoslavia, identified by Shaw (n 143) 77.

[177] ibid.

[178] ibid, 77–78.

[179] ibid, 79. These resolutions include UNGA Res 1541(XV)(1960) and UNGA Res 2625(XXV) (1970).

territories was not an obligation that was recognised in the Charter.[180] Finally, he appreciated the fact that the decision to amalgamate non-self-governing territories and trust territories for the purpose of identifying the rights and obligations proclaimed in the Colonial Declaration could be seen as a weakness in the argument that resolution 1514 represented an authoritative interpretation of the UN Charter.[181]

However, Shaw was not prepared to accept that these inconsistencies meant that the provisions of the Colonial Declaration amounted to a series of policy recommendations rather than a collection of valid interpretations of the Charter. He adopted the view that certain parts of the Colonial Declaration are suggestive rather than indicative of legal obligation. He argued that the focus on independence in the Colonial Declaration may not have been legally binding given the different approaches adopted in other General Assembly resolutions.[182] Further, he appreciated that both the reference, in the preamble, to 'the need to bring colonialism to a speedy end' and the need to take 'immediate steps' to transfer all powers to the inhabitants of non-self-governing territories and trust territories in paragraph 5 of the Declaration are hortatory in character.[183] However, Shaw was adamant that parts of the Colonial Declaration represented authoritative interpretations of the UN Charter which were legally binding on member States as certain provisions satisfied the requirements identified above.[184] He did not identify which particular provisions of the Colonial Declaration attained this status as a matter of treaty law but it would appear that the core provision, contained in paragraph 2 – that colonial peoples possess the right of self-determination – would satisfy the conditions enumerated by Shaw and also the obligation not to dismember colonial units prior to the exercise of the right to self-determination, as expressed in paragraph 6.[185]

The treaty interpretation route to legal validity is understandably attractive as it entails that there would be no need to establish the onerous prerequisites for the emergence of CIL. Initially the General Assembly claimed that its competence to address situations arising in non-self-governing territories was derived from Chapter XI of the UN Charter.[186] However, with the adoption of the Colonial Declaration, the General Assembly, and its Committees, began to refer to the Colonial Declaration as the source of its authority to act in relation to non-self-governing territories. Shaw also observed that this development marked the beginnings of a more robust approach towards the project of decolonisation on the part of the General Assembly.[187]

---

[180] ibid, 78.
[181] ibid.
[182] ibid, 78–79. See UNGA Res 1541(XV)(1960) and UNGA Res 2625(XXV)(1970).
[183] ibid, 79.
[184] ibid.
[185] This is apparent from Shaw's discussion of the significance of para 6, ibid, 181–82 and 187–89.
[186] ibid 84.
[187] ibid, 76 and 80.

The General Assembly's efforts, via a series of resolutions, to extend the scope of the reporting obligation, contained in Article 73(e), to include information concerning the political conditions prevailing in non-self-governing territories represents an example of the kind of subsequent practice that could amount to an authoritative interpretation of the Charter.[188] However, from 1961 onwards, the General Assembly began to declare that the authority for the adoption of specific resolutions relating to decolonisation was derived from the right of self-determination, as proclaimed in the Colonial Declaration, rather than from Chapter XI of the UN Charter. This new practice suggests that the General Assembly was no longer of the view that the authority for its work in the colonial context was grounded in specific provisions of the Charter. Consequently, in relation to the process of decolonisation, it seems as though the General Assembly was engaged in the act of furthering the fundamental purposes and principles of the Charter.[189] If the legal authority underpinning the Colonial Declaration was to be found in the UN Charter, on the ground that the Declaration constitutes an authoritative interpretation of that treaty, any resolution concerned with the conditions in non-self-governing territories (or trust territories) should identify the corresponding provisions of the Charter – Chapter XI or Chapter XII – as the basis for its authority. However, viewed from this standpoint Shaw's argument appears somewhat strained. For example, resolution 1654(XVI)(1961), which established C24, referred to the right of self-determination as expressed in the Colonial Declaration, as the source of its authority rather the corresponding provisions of the Charter. According to the logic of Shaw's argument, resolution 1654 represents an instance of the interpretation of an interpretation of the Charter – the Colonial Declaration itself being an instance of treaty interpretation. Clearly, the practice of the General Assembly in its own resolutions shows that the veracity of the treaty interpretation argument regarding the legal authority of the Colonial Declaration is open to question.[190]

Further, Shaw's analysis regarding the Colonial Declaration's legal authority was frustrated by his own admission that, while the ICJ subsequently condoned the principle of self-determination in the colonial context, it did not specifically identify the juridical basis for this instance of normative development.[191] In particular, Shaw noted that, in the 1971 *Namibia* case, the ICJ recognised the developments which had rendered the principle of self-determination applicable to all non-self-governing territories. But while the Court referred to Article 73 of the Charter and CIL in this context, it did not elaborate on the juridical basis of

---

[188] eg both UNGA Res 742(VIII)(1953) and UNGA Res 1541(XV)(1960) locate their authority in c XI of the Charter.

[189] This shift can be illustrated by examining the adoption of UNGA Res 1654(XVI)(1961), which established C24. This new practice was also apparent in the subsequent work of C24 concerning the implementation of the Colonial Declaration. Shaw also acknowledged this shift (n 143) 84.

[190] Shaw also considers whether the right to colonial self-determination derived its legal character from CIL; ibid, 86–89. However, he expressly preferred the treaty interpretation argument, at 89.

[191] ibid, 89–90.

the principle of self-determination. Further, as Shaw pointed out, in the 1975 *Western Sahara* case, the ICJ identified the Colonial Declaration as an 'important stage' in the development of the principle of self-determination regarding non-self-governing territories and that, in general terms, it provided 'the basis for the process of decolonization'. However, as Shaw observed, in that case, the ICJ failed to discuss the precise normative foundations of this profound development.[192] One conclusion might be that the judges in this case were uncertain as to the juridical basis of the evolution of the right to self-determination in international law given the difficulty in distinguishing between instances of Charter interpretation and situations where CIL may have emerged. However, the better view would seem to be that the ICJ's broad reference to CIL in relation to its discussion of the Colonial Declaration is dispositive – the origins of its normative significance are to be found in CIL.

XII. THE FORMATION OF GENERAL CUSTOMARY INTERNATIONAL LAW

It is has also been argued that the right of self-determination acquired the character of CIL as a result of a series of General Assembly resolutions. However, it is necessary to establish the general prerequisites concerning the formation of CIL before the integrity of this specific claim can be tested. Article 38(1)(b) of the ICJ Statute recognised that 'international custom, as evidence of a general practice accepted as law' is a source of international law. Customary law is particularly well-suited to the structure of the international legal system. It enables international law to evolve informally by direct reference to the conduct of States and it reflects the needs and practice of States at any given time. According to section 102 of the American Law Institute's Third Restatement of Foreign Law, CIL 'results from a general and consistent practice of States followed by them from a sense of legal obligation'.[193]

A. State Practice

In the *North Sea Continental Shelf* cases, the ICJ observed that:

> State practice, including that of States whose interests are specially affected, should have been both extensive and virtually uniform in the sense of the provision invoked;

---

[192] ibid, 90, noted that in the 1975 *Western Sahara* case (n 13), Judge Dillard in his Separate Opinion, at 121, did not offer any analysis regarding the way in which self-determination emerged as a right in international law despite the fact that he referred to numerous General Assembly resolutions in support of his conclusion that it is such a right.

[193] American Law Institute, *Third Restatement of Foreign Law* (St Paul, American Law Institute, 1987).

and should moreover have occurred in such a way as to show a general recognition that a rule of law or legal obligation is involved.[194]

This high threshold – that State practice must be both extensive and virtually uniform in support of the emergence of a new CIL – was reappraised in the *Nicaragua* case, where the ICJ observed that:

> It is not to be expected that in the practice of States the application of the rules in question should have been perfect, in the sense that States should have refrained, with complete consistency, from the use of force or from intervention in each other's internal affairs. The Court does not consider that, for a rule to be established as customary, the corresponding practice must be in absolutely rigorous conformity with the rule. In order to deduce the existence of customary rules, the Court deems it sufficient that the conduct of States should, in general, be consistent with such rules, and that instances of State conduct inconsistent with a given rule should generally have been treated as breaches of that rule, not as indications of the recognition of a new rule.[195]

The requirement that State practice must be extensive and representative of the interests of all those affected by the emergence of a new practice should not be interpreted as a requirement that individual States must give their consent before they are bound by a new CIL principle.[196] Although the consent of a sufficient number of interested States is required for the formation of CIL rule, the authoritative 'Statement of Principles Applicable to the Formation of General Customary International Law', which was produced by the International Law Association in 2000, did not condone the view that CIL is a form of tacit treaty law.[197]

The ICJ acknowledged, in the *North Sea Continental Shelf* cases, that certain States may be 'specially affected' by the formation of a CIL principle in a particular field. Consequently, the views of such States may have additional weight as to whether the new practice or claim may prompt the emergence of a new CIL principle. The question of which States are deemed to be 'specially affected' by the emergence of a new practice will depend on the specific field in issue and the geographical context in which the question arises. However, it has been noted that, if the emergence of a new practice involves the interests of the major powers, they will typically be considered to be 'specially affected' and their actions and attitude towards the practice will be significant for the purpose of determining whether a new CIL principle has been established.[198] Accordingly, it follows that, if 'specially affected' States protest against a new practice, or if they refuse to endorse it, the new practice will not be considered to have led to

---

[194] *North Sea Continental Shelf* cases *(Federal Republic of Germany v Denmark and The Netherlands)* (1969) ICJ Rep 3, 43. This approach was consistent with previous ICJ decisions. See *Anglo-Norwegian Fisheries* case *(UK/Norway)* (1951) ICJ Rep 116.

[195] *Nicaragua* case *(Nicaragua/US) (Merits)* (1986) ICJ Rep 14, 98.

[196] See the International Law Association's 'Statement of Principles Applicable to the Formation of General Customary International Law' (2000).

[197] ibid, 24 (disregarding the exceptional application of the persistent objector principle).

[198] ibid, 17.

the creation of a new CIL rule, as the State practice in question would not be extensive and representative of all the interests that would be affected by a change in the customary position.[199]

B. Opinio Juris

CIL is not created by State practice alone. It is also necessary to show that States behave as though they are under a legal obligation to follow a particular practice. As the ICJ stated in *North Sea Continental Shelf* cases:

> Not only must the acts concerned amount to a settled practice, but they must also be such, or carried out in such a way, as to be evidence of a belief that this practice is rendered obligatory by the existence of a rule of law requiring it. The need for such a belief, i.e. the existence of a subjective element, is implicit in the very notion of *opinio juris sive necessitates*. The States concerned must therefore feel that they are conforming to what amount to a legal obligation.[200]

The *North Sea Continental Shelf* cases indicates that *opinio juris* is derived from the subjective views of States engaged in a particular practice. However, States rarely make their intentions explicit and their decisions are usually motivated by a mixture of legal and non-legal considerations. One approach to the problem of establishing the subjective views of States is to presume that, when a State adopts a particular practice, it is entitled to act in such a way as a matter of international law. This approach allows the requisite *opinio juris* to be satisfied unless evidence of a contrary intention can be shown. This approach was infamously adopted in the *Lotus* case, where the PCIJ observed that:

> The rules of law binding upon States . . . emanate from their own free will as expressed by the conventions or by the usages generally accepted as expressing principles of law and established in order to regulate the relations between these co-existing independent communities or with a view to the achievement of common aims.[201]

The '*Lotus* principle' was echoed by the ICJ in the *Nicaragua* case, where it noted that 'In international law there are no rules, other than such rules as may be accepted by the States concerned, by treaty or otherwise . . . and this principle is valid for all States without exception'.[202] Akehurst suggested that the standpoint that the actions of a State are presumed to be lawful unless they have been specifically prohibited by international law makes sense in relation to international legal claim-rights because: 'a claim that States are entitled to act in a particular way can be inferred from the fact that they do act in that way', as

---

[199] According to the ILA's 2000 report, 'one reason why it is impossible to put a precise figure on the extent of participation required is that the criterion is in a sense *qualitative* rather than *quantitative*. That is to say, it is not simply a question of how many States participate in the practice, but *which* States', ibid, 26.

[200] *North Sea Continental Shelf* cases (n 194) 44. *Opinio juris sive necessitatis* translates to the opinion that it is a necessary law.

[201] *SS Lotus* case *(France/Turkey)* (1927) PCIJ Rep Ser A No 10, 18.

[202] *Nicaragua* case (1986) (n 195) [269].

long as any affected States acquiesce in the light of such behaviour.[203] However, the freedom of action that underpins the *Lotus* principle warrants a different approach in relation to legal obligations. In this context, Akehurst argued that for a CIL rule which imposes a duty to arise, there must be cogent evidence that States consider themselves to be under an obligation to act, or refrain from acting, in a particular manner.[204] Consequently, it must be shown that an international legal obligation exists to that effect.

Many international lawyers would question whether the *Lotus* principle, with its emphasis on concrete State practice, should be the starting point for determining the existence of CIL rules in a given area. Some international lawyers believe that *opinio juris* is the most important element in the formation of CIL.[205] For them, State practice merely provides evidence that States are acting in response to an acknowledged legal obligation, which is binding upon them.[206] Promoting the importance of the *opinio juris* requirement and reducing the importance of State practice allows CIL rules to be created without much in the way of concrete State practice having been undertaken. Although, as noted above, it is often difficult to adduce evidence of the subjective intentions of a particular State, it may be possible to identify the shared intentions of a group of States by reference to international instruments produced by international organisations, such as in the UN General Assembly. General Assembly resolutions are not legally binding in themselves and they do not usually provide evidence of an intention, on the part of States, to create CIL rules. However, the provisions of a particular resolution may become normatively significant and this was acknowledged by the ICJ in the *Nuclear Weapons* case, when it noted that:

> The Court notes that General Assembly resolutions, even if they are not binding, may sometimes have normative value. They can, in certain circumstances, provide evidence important for establishing the existence of a rule or the emergence of an *opinio juris*. To establish whether this is true of a given General Assembly resolution, it is necessary to look at its content and the conditions of its adoption; it is also necessary to see whether an *opinio juris* exists as to its normative character. Or a series of resolutions may show the gradual evolution of the *opinio juris* required for the establishment of a new rule.[207]

The provisions of a given resolution may show that States consider themselves to be legally obligated to follow a certain practice, thus satisfying the *opinio juris* requirement for the formation of a CIL principle. This approach takes into

[203] M Akehurst, 'Custom as a Source of International Law' (1974–75) 47 *British Yearbook of International Law* 1, 38.

[204] ibid, 37–38.

[205] B Cheng, 'United Nations Resolutions on Outer Space: "Instant" International Customary Law?' (1965) 5 *Indian Journal of International Law* 23.

[206] Consequently, as Lowe observes: 'If rules derive their authority from the fact that States have consented to be bound by them, proof of that consent should be enough to establish that they are bound'; V Lowe, *International Law* (Oxford, Clarendon Press, 2007) 53.

[207] *Nuclear Weapons* case (1996) ICJ Rep 226 [70].

account the voting records of States in relation to particular General Assembly resolutions and it attaches weight to statements made by States in the context.

In the *Nicaragua* case, the ICJ decided that the provisions of the Declaration on the Principles of International Law concerning Friendly Relations and Co-operation Among States in Accordance with the Charter of the United Nations could satisfy the *opinio juris* required to support the existence of a CIL principle concerning the prohibition on the use of force in international law.[208] Clearly, the degree of evidence required to establish the requisite *opinio juris* will depend on the circumstances of a given case and the nature of the principle in question. It has been suggested that if the practice in question is of central importance to the international community then a Court may be satisfied by little in the way of evidence of *opinio juris*. However, if the practice is new or controversial then considerably more evidence of *opinio juris* may be required before it could be recognised as having acquired customary status.[209] This relativist approach appears to have been endorsed by the ICJ in the *Nicaragua* case when it acknowledged that the prohibition on the use of force was so important to the international legal system that the State practice in support of the existence of the customary status of such a principle was readily accepted by the ICJ by way of a very limited enquiry. It has been suggested that this outcome should be viewed as a reflection of the principle's systemic importance.[210] Nevertheless, the fact that CIL may be created through the adoption of a General Assembly resolution does not mean that the resolution itself becomes legally binding; rather, the content of the General Assembly resolutions in question, along with other relevant information gleaned from the circumstances surrounding its adoption, provide the context for establishing the *opinio juris* required to establish a CIL principle. According to an orthodox interpretation of the formation of CIL, if a putative principle suggested by the evidence of *opinio juris* is also supported by the practice of States, at that point, the principle may acquire CIL status.

In its *Statement*, the ILA suggested that, if a particular General Assembly resolution, which was drafted in normative language, made an assertion – either expressly or impliedly – that a CIL principle exists, a rebuttable presumption would be generated in favour of such a principle.[211] Moreover, the *Statement* claimed that, in highly exceptional situations, a General Assembly resolution could
create CIL by itself. However, in order for this to happen, the resolution would not only have to evince a clear intention that the General Assembly meant to establish a CIL principle, it would also need to secure the unanimous (or near

---

[208]   *Nicaragua* case *(Merits)* (n 195) [205].
[209]   See F Kirgis, 'Custom on a Sliding Scale' (1987) 81 *American Journal of International Law* 146.
[210]   See ILA report (n 196) 41 and Kirgis, 'Custom on a Sliding Scale' (n 209) 149.
[211]   Further, the ILA report indicated that such a resolution could not be invoked against States that voted against its adoption. However, it noted that the position for State that abstained from voting was not entirely clear; ibid, 58.

unanimous) support of the UN membership.[212] The *Statement* suggested that the justification for having a higher threshold than that usually required for the formation of general CIL arises from the fact that all member States would have the opportunity to register their position on the matter under consideration by virtue of their voting rights in the General Assembly.[213] Moreover, the *Statement* suggests that this approach would prevent the potential danger of the General Assembly becoming a general global legislature, which would clearly be contrary to the provisions of the UN Charter. Consequently, this approach means that the General Assembly could only have the capacity to create CIL directly where true consensus existed among the international community of States on a particular issue.[214]

Further, according to the ILA's *Statement*, two other consequences of this approach are that no corresponding State practice would be required in order for CIL to be created in keeping with the provision of the resolution in question.[215] First, this approach would seem to suggest that CIL could established by the presence of *opinio juris* alone. However, in order to reach this conclusion one would have to overlook the fact that, as is acknowledged elsewhere in the ILA's *Statement*, the act of voting in the General Assembly and statements made by States (and other actions undertaken in that context) may all be viewed as manifestations of State practice.[216] Consequently, both the traditional requirements for the formation of CIL can be satisfied in such exceptional circumstances. Secondly, it would follow from the above analysis that, in highly exceptional circumstances, CIL could be created instantly. While there is no fixed time requirement for the creation of a CIL principle, according to the orthodox view, a sufficient period of time must have passed in order to show that: (i) the principle has been accepted as law by a sufficient number of States; and (ii) there is a consistent pattern of support for the principle in the State practice. The passage of time is only relevant for the purpose of demonstrating that a particular CIL principle is established within the corpus of international law. If the legal status of a particular principle can be established quickly then this is merely a reflection of its widespread acceptance by the international community of States.[217] As the most important factor in the formation of CIL is whether the putative principle has been widely accepted by the international community of States, in principle, it is entirely conceivable that a CIL principle could be created instantly, if the conditions in support of such an outcome were satisfied.

---

[212] ibid, 63–64.
[213] ibid, 64.
[214] ibid.
[215] ibid.
[216] ibid, 60–61.
[217] As the ICJ stated in the *North Sea Continental Shelf* cases: 'Although the passage of only a short period of time is not necessarily, or of itself, a bar to the formation of a new rule of customary international law on the basis of what was originally a purely conventional rule, an indispensable requirement would be that within the period in question, short though it might be' (n 194) 43.

However, it is clear that very few General Assembly resolutions will satisfy the highly exceptional circumstances which would mean they could generate CIL of their own accord. For instance, the UN Declaration of Legal Principles Governing the Activities of States in the Exploration and Use of Outer Space,[218] which established the initial governing principles concerning Outer Space, was adopted without dissent. Moreover, State practice in this context was widely regarded to be supportive of the creation of a new CIL principle which prevented States from making sovereign claims to celestial bodies. However, the assertion that the 1963 UN Declaration on the Exploration and Use of Outer Space actually gave rise to a CIL principle that prohibited sovereign claims to celestial bodies is questionable. Cheng, who pioneered the concept of 'instant custom' in this context, ultimately reached the conclusion that the terms of the Declaration did not manifest enough widespread and representative agreement for the creation of an instant CIL principle on this issue.[219] In contrast, the 1970 Declaration on Friendly Relations,[220] which was adopted by consensus, is an example of a General Assembly resolution that is widely considered to have attained CIL status.[221]

XIII. SELF-DETERMINATION, THE COLONIAL DECLARATION AND CUSTOMARY INTERNATIONAL LAW

The status of the right of colonial self-determination as a matter of CIL was assured by the time the Declaration on Friendly Relations was adopted in 1970. However, the aim of this chapter is to determine how and when the right of self-determination acquired this legal character status given its importance to an assessment of whether the legal instruments used to excise the Chagos Islands from Mauritius – the 1965 Lancaster House Agreement and the 1965 BIOT Order in Council – constituted a violation of CIL.

The question of the customary status of the right of colonial self-determination, as proclaimed and elaborated in the Colonial Declaration, has been the subject of considerable scholarly attention since the 1960s. As discussed in the previous section, a traditional approach would hold that CIL crystallises through recognisable instances of concrete State practice being repeated by a number of States over a significant period of time. The idea that a long-standing practice, accepted as binding by a community, is commonly seen

---

[218] UNGA Res 1962(XVII)(1963).

[219] ILA report (n 196) 62. Moreover, the fact that a treaty, the 'Treaty on Principles Governing the Activities of States in the Exploration and Use of Outer Space' (1967) was concluded not long after the Declaration was adopted by the General Assembly in order to clarify the legal regime governing the use of Outer Space supports the view that States did not consider the Declaration to have created binding CIL rules in this area of international law.

[220] UNGA Res 2625(XXV)(1970).

[221] As discussed above, in the *Nicaragua* case (n 195), the ICJ decided that the resolution represented CIL regarding the prohibition on the use of force without referring to any State practice in support of its provisions.

as being inherent within the concept of custom, regardless of its particular setting and such a viewpoint is consistent with the terms of Article 38(1)(b) of the ICJ Statute.[222] As discussed above, support for the provisions of the Colonial Declaration can be gleaned from the UN Charter and from a number of General Assembly resolutions. But, although the UN Charter and General Assembly practice were part of the wider normative background to the Colonial Declaration, it is arguable they did not provide the normative foundations for the rights and obligations proclaimed in resolution 1514(XV)(1960), at least for the purposes of the creation of CIL.

As noted above, the Colonial Declaration was adopted by the General Assembly with an overwhelming majority and with no member States voting against the resolution. Further, although General Assembly resolutions are not legally binding instruments per se, they can prompt the development of CIL if they are intended to have normative significance and they attract the overwhelming support of member States. In assessing the legal status of the Colonial Declaration, it should be acknowledged that the language used in the Declaration is of a mandatory nature and, prima facie, it evinces a clear intention that its provisions were meant to have normative significance. However, as discussed above, the way in which States viewed the Colonial Declaration is an important factor as to whether its provisions could be considered to be representative of CIL. It is apparent that the clear majority of those States which voted in favour of resolution 1514 believed that they were establishing a normative framework for decolonisation and this was supported by statements made by States in the context of the Declaration's adoption.[223] Consequently, it could be argued that the provisions of the Declaration constitute manifestations of *opinio juris* in support of the customary status of the right of colonial self-determination. Further, the conduct of individual States – by voting in favour of the resolution, and by making concomitant statements that endorse its normative significance – could be interpreted as instances of State practice that support the view that the Declaration attained the status of CIL very quickly.

In the 1971 *Namibia Advisory Opinion*, the ICJ identified the Charter obligations expressed in Article 73 and the provisions of the Colonial Declaration as important markers in the development of international law, which, in its view, had the effect of rendering the principle of self-determination applicable to all non-self-governing territories.[224] However, in that case, the ICJ did not address the status of the rights and obligations contained in the Colonial Declaration directly – its focus was on interpreting the obligations imposed on South Africa in relation to the mandated territory of Namibia under Article 22 of the 1919 Covenant of the League of Nations. Nonetheless, it did observe that the task of interpreting the relevant provisions of the Covenant could not: 'remain unaffected by the subsequent development of international law, through the Charter

---

[222] See ILA report (n 196) 63.
[223] See Shaw (n 143) 77; and Cassese (n 32) 69–70.
[224] *Namibia* case (n 11) [52].

of the United Nations and by way of customary law'.[225] Given that Article 73 of the Charter and the Colonial Declaration were the only sources referred to in the Court's discussion of the development of international law in this field after the Covenant of the League of Nations was adopted, it appears to follow that the ICJ considered the central provisions of the Colonial Declaration – that all colonial peoples possess the right of self-determination – to be representative of CIL in this area.

Cassese, writing in 1995, suggested that the provisions of the Colonial Declaration quickly attained the status of CIL.[226] He claimed that, in adopting the Colonial Declaration, the UN membership took a collective stand against colonialism and the elements of CIL were satisfied by the way that States responded to the terms of the Declaration. In Cassese's view, the density of State practice which subsequently emerged meant that the rights and obligations proclaimed in resolution 1514 had acquired CIL status by the end of 1960,[227] which seems to suggest that the Colonial Declaration became representative of the CIL relating to self-determination in the colonial context almost instantly. Further, at the level of treaty law, Cassese argues that the adoption of draft Article 1 of the International Covenants by the General Assembly's Third Committee in 1955 had the effect of writing an entitlement to self-determination into Chapters XI and XII of the UN Charter.[228] As a result, in Cassese's opinion, the right of self-determination, in effect, replaced the references to 'self-government' in Articles 73 and 76 irrespective of the fact that the International Covenants were not finalised until 1966 when they were approved by the General Assembly and opened for ratification.

In contrast, writing in 1969, Castañeda suggested that the Colonial Declaration exhibited a significant level of political authority but, in his view, it fell short of creating international legal obligations in the colonial context.[229] In his opinion, General Assembly resolution 1514 did not impose legal obligations on the colonial powers to grant independence to all colonial peoples on an immediate and unconditional basis. However, while he thought the Declaration was programmatic in nature, he believed that it signalled the repudiation of colonialism, in at least two respects.[230] First, by rejecting the distinction between 'advanced' and 'backwards' peoples that underpinned the notion of the sacred trust, which had been established by Article 22 of the 1919 Covenant, in relation to the mandates system, and replicated in Article 73 of the Charter with regard to non-self-governing territories, the Colonial Declaration repudiated the notion of tutelage that characterised the way in which international law had sought to address colonial situations up until that point. Secondly, the Colonial

---

[225] ibid, [53]. The ICJ observed that 'These developments leave little doubt that the ultimate objective of the sacred trust was the self-determination and independence of the peoples concerned'.
[226] Cassese (n 32) 59.
[227] ibid, 58.
[228] ibid.
[229] Castañeda, *Legal Effects of United Nations Resolutions* (n 172) 175.
[230] ibid.

Declaration refused to accept that the inadequacy of conditions in colonial territories – the degree of preparedness of colonial peoples for self-government – should serve as a barrier to independence.[231] In adopting this standpoint, the Declaration sought to marginalise an argument that, given the considerable socio-economic and political disparities between metropolitan States and non-self-governing territories, would have otherwise jeopardised the prospect of decolonisation in many situations. Consequently, according to Castañeda, the Colonial Declaration was significant because it drew upon the post-Charter developments, which were largely initiated by the General Assembly, in order to proclaim the illegitimacy of colonialism and, as a result, it sought to establish the postulates for decolonisation.[232]

Knop also appreciates the paradigm shift that the Colonial Declaration represented. She observes that the notion of tutelage, which was embodied in the concept of the sacred trust, assumed that guardianship was supposedly warranted because colonial peoples were perceived as being 'backwards, but educable'.[233] International law's traditional approach to the situation of colonial peoples was perhaps best captured by Judge McNair's rendering of the concept of the sacred trust in his Separate Opinion in the *International Status of South West Africa Advisory Opinion*, where he observed that:

> Nearly every legal system possesses some institution whereby the property (and sometimes the persons) of those who are not *sui juris*, such as a minor or a lunatic, can be entrusted to some responsible person such as a trustee or *tuteur* or *curateur*. The Anglo-American trust serves this purpose, and another purpose even more closely akin to the Mandates System, namely, the vesting of property in trustees, and its management by them in order that the public or some class of the public may derive benefit or that some public purpose may be served. The trust has frequently been used to protect the weak and the dependent.[234]

As Knop explains, in opposition to the paternalism that underpinned the concept of the sacred trust contained in Article 22 of the Covenant of the League of Nations, in relation to the mandates system and in Article 73 of the UN Charter, in relation to non-self-governing territories, the Colonial Declaration amounted to a demand for equality on behalf of colonial peoples. It sought to harness the Charter's general provisions concerning the equality of all peoples and self-determination, contained in Article 1(2), in order to bring about decolonisation. Moreover, whereas the concept of the sacred trust anticipated that self-government would be achieved eventually it was widely thought that this outcome would involve a lengthy, incremental process by which colonial peoples

---

[231] See UNGA Res 1514(XV)(1960), para 3.
[232] Castañeda (n 172) 175.
[233] Knop (n 4) 195.
[234] *Advisory Opinion Concerning the International Status of South West Africa* (n 61) (Separate Opinion of Judge McNair) 149. However, this perspective has a much longer heritage; see A Anghie, *Imperialism, Sovereignty and the Making of International Law* (Cambridge, Cambridge University Press, 2004) 13–31; and SJ Anaya, *Indigenous Peoples in International Law*, 2nd edn (New York, Oxford University Press, 2004) 23–26.

would earn their sovereignty, in contrast the Colonial Declaration sought to accomplish colonial self-determination through a rights-based approach.[235] According to the terms of the Colonial Declaration, decolonisation was not conditional on the readiness of colonial peoples for independence (paragraph 3) nor was it subject to reservations or conditions (paragraph 5). Independence was not a something that was granted by the colonial powers; instead, it was a status that flowed from an entitlement that all peoples – including colonial peoples – possessed: the right to self-determination.[236]

In both the 1971 *Namibia* case and the 1975 *Western Sahara* case, the ICJ treated the Colonial Declaration as though it were representative of CIL without adducing evidence of concrete State practice in support of its provisions.[237] Consequently, in these cases, it seems as though the Court's interpretation of the Colonial Declaration is comparable to the way in which it subsequently harnessed the provisions of the 1970 Declaration on Friendly Relations in support of the existence of a CIL prohibition on the use of force in the *Nicaragua* case.[238] As noted above, in that case, resolution 2625 only satisfied the *opinio juris* requirement for the formation of the CIL principle in question; the widespread support that the resolution attracted from the international community of States and the importance of its substantive provisions concerning the prohibition on the use of force for the international legal system meant that there was no need to establish that it had been adopted in the concrete practice of States – it could be readily presumed.[239] But could such an approach be followed in relation to the Colonial Declaration? In answering this question, it is important to note that there are significant differences between the 1970 Declaration on Friendly Relations and the 1960 Colonial Declaration. First, the Declaration on Friendly Relations was adopted by consensus and so it satisfied the stringent requirements, identified in the ILA's 2000 *Statement*, for a General Assembly resolution, which purports to declare a CIL principle, to constitute irrebuttable proof of the existence such a principle.[240] Secondly, as discussed in the last section, in general, the views and practices of those States, which would be 'specially affected' by the formation of CIL in a particular area, are considered to be particularly significant in assessing a claim that a CIL principle has emerged (or changed). Consequently, for the purpose of assessing whether the right of colonial self-determination acquired CIL status by virtue of the adoption of the Colonial Declaration, it is important to acknowledge that the major colonial powers – the UK, France, Belgium, Spain, Portugal and the USA – abstained from voting on the adoption of resolution 1514. This fact led some international lawyers to suggest that the failure of those States which exercise sover-

---

[235] Knop (n 4) 200.
[236] See Fastenrath (n 69) 1836.
[237] This approach was also extended to UNGA Res 1541(XV)(1960) by the ICJ in 1975 *Western Sahara* case (n 13) [57].
[238] As discussed above.
[239] This position was advanced by Kirgis (n 209) 149 and endorsed in the ILA report (n 196) 42.
[240] See the ILA report (n 196) 62.

eignty over non-self-governing territories to vote in favour of the Colonial Declaration should be viewed as significant. Moreover, this interpretation supported the conclusion that the right of colonial self-determination was not established as a CIL principle as a result.[241] However, while the concept of 'specially affected' States and its effect in relation to the formation of CIL is firmly established in the ICJ's jurisprudence, this still leaves the question of which States could be considered to be 'specially affected' by the alleged emergence of the right of colonial self-determination as a matter of CIL as a result of the adoption of the Colonial Declaration. Should the views of administering States be given additional weight regarding the question of whether CIL recognised that all colonial peoples possessed the right to self-determination or should the view that all States were affected by colonialism have prevailed at this stage given that, by 1960, it was widely perceived to be a scourge on humanity and inconsistent with the fundamental principles declared in the UN Charter? Evidently, in such situations, the concept of 'specially affected' States had limited resonance. Nevertheless, the views of administering States must have had some significance concerning the claim that the right of self-determination had emerged in the colonial context.[242]

Judge Dillard in his Separate Opinion in the *Western Sahara* case set out the competing arguments regarding whether the right to colonial self-determination had acquired CIL status by virtue of the Colonial Declaration and the General Assembly resolutions that followed it. This passage is worth quoting in full:

> At one extreme is the contention that even if a particular resolution of the General Assembly is not binding, the cumulative impact of many resolutions when similar in content, voted for by overwhelming majorities and frequently repeated over a period of time may give rise to a general *opinio juris* and thus constitute a norm of customary international law. According to this view, this is the precise situation manifested by the long list of resolutions which, following in the wake of resolution 1514 (XV), have proclaimed the principle of self-determination to be an operative right in the decolonization of non-self-governing territories.
>
> At the opposite pole are those who, resisting generally the law-creating powers of the General Assembly, deny that the principle has developed into a "right" with corresponding obligations or that the practice of decolonization has been more than an example of a usage dictated by political expediency or convenience and one which, in addition, has been neither constant nor uniform.
>
> I need not dwell on the theoretical aspects of this broad problem which, as everyone knows, commands an immense literature. Suffice it to call attention to the fact that the present Opinion is forthright in proclaiming the existence of the "right" in so far as the present proceedings are concerned.[243]

---

[241] See Jennings and Watts (n 64) 295; Emerson, 'Self-determination' (n 146) 462; and R Rosenstock, 'The Declaration of Principles of International Law Concerning Friendly Relations: A Survey' (1971) 65 *American Journal of International Law* 713, 730.

[242] Emerson (n 146) 461.

[243] Judge Dillard's Separate Opinion in the 1975 *Western Sahara* case (n 13) 121. The progressive aspect of this formulation is reminiscent of the approached adopted by Judge Tanaka in the *South West Africa* cases (n 142), discussed below.

Judge Dillard was of the view that the right of colonial self-determination had acquired the status of CIL as a result of the concerted action undertaken by the General Assembly in a series of resolutions. However, it is important to appreciate that he identified the Colonial Declaration as the starting point of this transformative process rather than its culmination. Further, Judge Dillard reached his conclusion about the legal character of self-determination in 1975, long after the Declaration on Friendly Relations had been adopted.

Accordingly, it is difficult to reach the conclusion that the Colonial Declaration created an enforceable right to self-determination for all colonial peoples and that it imposed an immediate obligation on administering States to grant such a right. Moreover, it should be recognised that the persuasive idea that there is a sliding scale between *opinio juris* and State practice for the purpose of the formation of CIL was only advanced in the context of *Nicaragua* case in relation to the existence of a negative obligation – the prohibition on the use of force. In contrast, the argument that administering States were obligated to facilitate the right of self-determination for all colonial peoples by immediately granting independence to the inhabitants of all colonial territories would amount to the imposition of a positive obligation on administering States. According to the *Lotus* principle, those States, which would be subject to such an international legal obligation, should have endorsed the claim that such a CIL principle had emerged in order for such obligations to be binding upon them. Moreover, if the provisions of the Colonial Declaration did achieve CIL status almost instantly, as has been claimed, the perpetuation of colonialism would have amounted to a violation of international law from that moment onwards. That many colonial situations endured throughout the 1960s, and beyond, with relatively few instances being the subject of international litigation, indicates that most States did not adopt the view that colonialism per se amount to a violation of CIL during the period in question.

However, the traditional approach to the formation of CIL is vulnerable to challenge regarding the crystallisation of the right to colonial self-determination as a CIL principle, on its own terms. If, for the formation of CIL, the requisite State practice had to take concrete forms of action then clearly the massive wave of decolonisation that swept through African and Asia during the early part of the 1960s would support the view that the right of colonial self-determination had become a CIL principle, at least by the middle of the decade. Notwithstanding this argument, during the 1960s, certain international lawyers argued that even if it could be shown that State practice in support of such a CIL principle could be established, it was still necessary to show that the State practice was rooted in a sense that it was legally required – the *opinio juris* requirement. Writing in the late-1960s, Gross claimed that, in effecting decolonisation, the colonial powers had not acted out of a sense of legal obligation; rather, their decision to grant independence to specific colonial territories had been dictated by considerations of political expediency.[244] Moreover, it was argued that the policy of decolonisation was determined by a range of contextual factors and implemented according to a timetable determined by administering States rather than as a result of any rights claimed by the colonial peoples concerned.

The difficulty in establishing when the right of self-determination crystallised as a matter of CIL is exacerbated by the general problem of evaluating State behaviour in response to a new practice, or claim, that a CIL principle has emerged. States may not protest against a new practice or claim for a range of political reasons and so it is invariably hard to determine the importance of a failure to object and thus to reach the conclusion that inaction should be equated to acquiescence to the emergence of a new CIL principle, or a change in the customary position. This general problem is significant in relation to the process of decolonisation and claims made in General Assembly resolutions regarding the normative significance of self-determination in that context. While the colonial powers objected to the General Assembly's increasingly assertive approach in relations to colonial issues throughout the 1950s, by 1960, they had changed their tactics. During the 1960s, they largely adopted an approach which could be viewed as passive resistance. They did not vote against resolution 1514 or resolution 1541; instead, they decided not to participate in such exercises and they refused to recognise the normative significance of the resulting resolutions.[245] For instance, in relation to resolution 1541, the UK and France argued that the prescriptive approach to the modalities of self-government, expressed in principles VII to IX of the resolution, had no basis in either CIL or in the Charter.[246] Consequently, they maintained the view that the responsibilities they owed to the inhabitants of their non-self-governing territories were restricted to those obligations declared in Chapter XI of the Charter.[247]

It is significant that the Colonial Declaration is not even mentioned in the 1970 Declaration on Friendly Relations.[248] General Assembly resolution 2625(XXV)(1970) elaborated the fundamental principles contained in the UN Charter and it is widely considered to be representative of CIL concerning the areas of international law that it addressed. As noted previously, the adoption of the 1970 resolution was the moment when the colonial powers decisively

---

[244] See Emerson (n 146) 461, drawing on the work of Leo Gross; see L Gross, 'The Right to Self-determination in International Law' in M Kilson (ed), *New States in the Modern World* (Cambridge, Harvard University Press, 1975) 139.

[245] It should be noted that while a clear majority of Member States voted in favour of UNGA Res 1541, the resolution did not attract the level of support extended to the Colonial Declaration. 69 States voted in favour, 2 voted against and 21 abstained.

[246] For a discussion of the French position in the context of the dispute over the international status of the island of Mayotte in the Comoros Archipelago, see Musgrave (n 59) 185. For a discussion of the British position, see Hendry and Dickson (n 108) 251–52.

[247] However, in the *Western Sahara* case (n 13), the ICJ went to great lengths to emphasise the normative significance of UNGA Res 1541(XV)(1960) in relation to the process of decolonisation, at [57].

[248] UNGA Res 2625(XXV)(1970).

endorsed the right of colonial self-determination as a matter of CIL.[249] Rosenstock attributed the absence of any reference in resolution 2625 to the Colonial Declaration to the depth of feeling, on the part of the colonial powers, that resolution 1514 amounted to a set of political desiderata rather than the development of the relevant principles of international law, which had their origins in the UN Charter.[250]

The key provision of the 1970 Declaration on Friendly Relations concerning the right of self-determination is reminiscent of the way in which the right was formulated in both paragraph 2 of the Colonial Declaration and in joint Article 1 of the International Covenants. It provided that:

> By virtue of the principle of equal rights and self-determination of peoples enshrined in the Charter of the United Nations, all peoples have the right freely to determine, without external interference, their political status and to pursue their economic, social and cultural development, and every State has the duty to respect this right in accordance with the provisions of the Charter.

Rosenstock claimed that the process of drafting the Declaration on Friendly Relations marked the first occasion when the colonial powers were prepared to accept the normative significance of many of the principles of decolonisation which had been expressed in the Colonial Declaration.[251] The resolution proclaimed the need: 'To bring a speedy end to colonialism, having due regard to the freely expressed will of the peoples concerned'.[252] Further, it recognised that 'the subjection of peoples to alien subjugation, domination and exploitation constitutes a violation of the principle [of equal rights and self-determination], as well as a denial of fundamental human rights, and is contrary to the Charter'.[253] Moreover, resolution 2625 made a significant breakthrough when it expressly confirmed what was only implicit in resolution 1514:[254] colonial peoples have a separate and distinct status from the States that administered them for the purpose of the exercise of the right to self-determination.[255] Further,

---

[249] See Hendry and Dickson (n 108) 252.

[250] See Rosenstock, 'The Declaration of Principles of International Law Concerning Friendly Relations (n 241) 730–31.

[251] It should be noted that the drafting process began in 1964; ibid, 731.

[252] Although Rosenstock argues that the inclusion of this statement in the preamble suggests that UNGA Res 2625 had a programmatic dimension; ibid, 731.

[253] This provision should be compared with para 1 of the Colonial Declaration which provides that 'The subjection of peoples to alien subjugation, domination and exploitation constitutes a denial of fundamental human rights, is contrary to the Charter of the United Nations and is an impediment to the promotion of world peace and co-operation'.

[254] It should be noted this connection was also made in UNGA Res 1541(XV)(1960) in relation to the achievement of full self-government.

[255] It provides that:

> The territory of a colony or other non-self-governing territory has, under the Charter, a status separate and distinct from the territory of the State administering it; and such separate and distinct status under the Charter shall exist until the people of the colony or non-self-governing territory have exercised their right of self-determination in accordance with the Charter, and particularly its purposes and principles.

resolution 2625 addressed the question of the modalities of self-determination. In particular, it stated that:

> The establishment of a sovereign and independent State, the free association or integration with an independent State or the emergence into any other political status freely determined by a people constitute modes of implementing the right of self-determination by that people.

The Declaration on Friendly Relations signalled that the colonial powers were prepared to accept that the right of colonial self-determination had acquired the status of CIL and that the modalities of the exercise of this right included independence, association and integration. However, it represented a less prescriptive approach to decolonisation in key respects. First, in contrast to the Colonial Declaration, which tied the exercise of the right to self-determination to the achievement of independence, the Declaration on Friendly Relations acknowledged that independence is just one of a number of legitimate outcomes regarding the exercise of the right to self-determination by the people concerned.[256] Further, resolution 2625(XXV)(1970) recognised the existence of a fourth option – 'the emergence into any other political status freely determined by a people'. Certain colonial powers viewed the inclusion of this residual option as important because it recognised the validity of any *sui generis* constitutional arrangements made in respect of dependent territories that did not fit into the modalities condoned in resolution 1541(XV)(1960).[257]

This guided but less prescriptive approach to decolonisation proved to be acceptable to the colonial powers. Until the adoption of resolution 2625, the confirmed position of both the UK and France was that the governing principles of international law concerning the conduct of administering States in respect of their non-self-governing territories were contained in the UN Charter and not in resolution 1514 and resolution 1541. For instance, in relation to the dispute over the island of Mayotte in the Comoros Archipelago, France argued that paragraph 6 of the Colonial Declaration – that colonial units must not be partitioned prior to the exercise of the right to self-determination – was not an international legal obligation declared in the UN Charter whereas the need to have regard to the interests of the inhabitants of non-self-governing territories was an obligation expressed in Chapter XI of the Charter.[258]

---

[256] Musgrave (n 59) 185–86.

[257] For the British position, see Hendry and Dickson (n 108) 251–52. However, the extent to which such constitutional arrangements satisfy the requirements of decolonisation is debatable. In the context of the Pitcairn Islands, a British Overseas Territory, see S Allen, 'The Pitcairn Prosecutions and the Rule of Law' (2012) 75 *Modern Law Review* 1150.

[258] The dispute concerning the island of Mayotte is examined in the next chapter.

XIV. THE ICJ AND COLONIAL SELF-DETERMINATION:
FORMALISM VERSUS TELEOLOGY

There is sufficient evidence to support the view that the status of the right of colonial self-determination as a matter of CIL remained unresolved throughout the 1960s. Given the divergent views of interested States on this issue, it is worth considering the way in which the ICJ addressed the international law relating to decolonisation during the period under investigation. It is notable that tensions within the international judiciary regarding the precise relationship between international law and politics were becoming increasingly apparent during that time. The extent to which individual judges at the ICJ held different views about the nature and scope of this relationship was most clearly illustrated in the Court's judgment, and by the individual Opinions delivered in the *South West Africa* cases *(Second Phase)*.[259]

South West Africa was a German colony prior to the First World War. It was placed under a mandate in accordance with Article 22 of the 1919 Covenant of the League of Nations and South Africa was appointed as the administering authority for the territory. However, when the United Nations was founded, South Africa refused to conclude a trust agreement in respect of this territory, as required for the purposes of Chapter XII of the UN Charter. Consequently, in 1946, when the League of Nations was formally dissolved, South Africa claimed that the mandate had expired and it was free to annex South West Africa. The General Assembly requested an Advisory Opinion from the ICJ on the question of whether the mandate had elapsed. In its *Advisory Opinion on the International Status of South West Africa*, the ICJ decided that South Africa's responsibilities under the mandate had not elapsed, despite the dissolution of the League of Nations.[260] South Africa refused to accept this decision. In 1960, Ethiopia and Liberia – who were both members of the League – commenced twinned proceedings against South Africa to compel it to carry out its obligations in respect of the mandated territory. The applicants alleged that South Africa had breached its obligations to the inhabitants of South West Africa; the League itself; and to the membership by introducing a policy of racial discrimination into the territory. They argued that they had the necessary standing to institute legal proceedings against South Africa under Article 7 of the Mandate Agreement.[261] However, South Africa disputed whether this provision gave individual members the standing to challenge the conduct of an administering authority in relation to a mandated territory.

---

[259] *South West Africa* cases (n 142).

[260] *Advisory Opinion Concerning the International Status of South West Africa* (n 61).

[261] Art 7 of the Mandate Agreement provided that 'If any dispute whatever should arise between the Mandatory and another Member of the League of Nations relating to the interpretation or the application of the provisions of the Mandate, such dispute, if it cannot be settled by negotiation, shall be submitted to the Permanent Court of International Justice provided for by Article 14 of the Covenant of the League of Nations'.

In the *South West Africa* cases *(Preliminary Objections)*, the ICJ decided, by a narrow majority, that the applicants had the necessary standing to bring the proceedings against South Africa in respect of its conduct in South West Africa.[262] As a result, the cases moved to a second phase where the merits of the applicants' claims would be considered. However, in a volte face, in the *South West Africa* cases *(Second Phase)*, the ICJ decided that South Africa's obligations in respect of the mandated territory were owed to the League itself rather than to individual members. In effect, this decision meant that the applicants did not have the standing to bring their cases to the ICJ after all and the cases were dismissed.[263] However, this result was achieved by a 'statutory majority' of the Court.[264] The different outcomes in the 1962 cases and the 1966 cases can be explained by the fact that the Court, which reached the decisions in the *Second Phase*, had a different judicial composition from the one that decided the cases at the *Preliminary Objections* stage. [265]

Writing in 1967, Friedmann, examined the significance of the *Second Phase* decisions. He observed that, after the 1962 decisions, the parties, and all interested observers, were expecting the Court to engage in a thorough assessment of the status and scope of the principles of equal treatment and the prohibition on racial discrimination in international law and their application in the territory of South West Africa.[266] Friedmann suggested that the justification for the approach adopted by the majority of the Court in 1966 lay in wider concerns about the interrelationship between the spheres of international law and international politics. This prompted him to observe that 'It is to be feared that, in this case, the ICJ has dealt a devastating blow to the hope that it might be able to deal with explosive and delicate international issues'.[267] It turned out that Friedmann was right – the way that the ICJ addressed the *Second Phase* of the *South West Africa* cases did represent a pivotal moment in the history of the Court.[268] His fears were subsequently confirmed, as the decisions were viewed as the reason for a decline in the number of cases that were subsequently referred to the ICJ: States seemed to lose faith in the Court's ability to deal with international legal disputes, which often involve a complex mixture of legal and political issues.[269]

---

[262] *South West Africa* cases *(Ethiopia v South Africa and Liberia v South Africa) (Preliminary Objections)* (1962) ICJ Rep 319.

[263] The Court failed to acknowledge the general interest that States have in the maintenance of international law, a position that it reversed at the first opportunity. See the *Barcelona Traction* case *(Spain/Belgium)* (1970) ICJ Rep 3.

[264] 7-7. The President cast the deciding vote.

[265] See J Crawford, 'The General Assembly, the International Court and Self-determination' in V Lowe and M Fitzmaurice (eds), *Fifty Years of the International Court of Justice: Essays in Honour of Sir Robert Jennings* (Cambridge, Grotius Publications, 1996) 585, 587–88.

[266] WF Friedmann, 'The Jurisprudential Implications of the South-West Africa Case' (1967) 6 *Columbia Journal of Transnational Law* 1, 1.

[267] ibid, 16.

[268] Crawford, 'The General Assembly, the International Court and Self-determination' (n 265) 587.

[269] ibid, 587–88.

This was the moment when the ICJ was confronted with a difficult choice regarding the nature of its role as the juridical conscience of the international community and its relationship with the political organs of the United Nations. Crawford suggests that the judges who were sitting at the ICJ at the time of the *Second Phase* decisions could be divided into two broad camps.[270] The first group of judges, which constituted the majority in 1966, could be characterised by their commitment to formalism with its strict separation between law and morality/politics – with its strong association with Anglo-American positivism – and a voluntarist interpretation of international law. 'Formalist' judges favoured the literal method of treaty interpretation. In sharp contrast, in the second camp, were judges who formed the minority in the 1966 cases. These judges believed that, given the nature of international relations, a clear distinction between 'political' disputes and 'legal' disputes cannot always be drawn. Consequently, they subscribed to the view that judges are under a duty to decide cases even where they might be political controversial.[271] Accordingly, judges belonging to this second camp believed that a treaty should be interpreted in the light of its purpose and in keeping with the broader progressive development of international law, where such an interpretation was warranted.[272]

Neither the Covenant of the League of Nations nor the Mandate Agreement in respect of South West Africa expressly provided the members with the right to challenge South Africa's performance of its obligations in relation to the mandated territory. According to the majority in the *South West Africa* cases *(Second Phase)*, this lack of express provision was dispositive: 'Rights cannot be presumed to exist merely because it might seem desirable that they should'.[273] In their view, to hold otherwise would require the Court to go beyond the task of interpreting the relevant treaty provisions and to engage in revisionism, even if this led to the outcome that no legal means to supervise the administration of South West Africa would otherwise exist.[274]

In contrast, the minority position in the *Second Phase* decisions, which was best articulated by Judges Tanaka and Jessup, reached the conclusion that the applicants had the standing to institute proceedings against South Africa in respect of its conduct in South West Africa and that this position did not exceed the bounds of treaty interpretation. In Judge Tanaka view:

> What is not permitted to judges, is to establish law independently of an existing legal system, institution or norm. What is permitted to them is to declare what can be logi-

---

[270] ibid, 587.

[271] See eg H Lauterpacht, *The Function of Law in the International Community*, reissued (Cambridge, Cambridge University Press, 2011).

[272] It should be noted that VCLT, Art 31(1) allows both approaches to co-exist. It provides that treaties: 'shall interpreted in good faith in accordance with the ordinary meaning to be given to the terms of the treaty in the context and in the light of the object and purpose'.

[273] *South West Africa* cases *(Second Phase)* (n 142) [91].

[274] The judgment of the majority stated: 'the Court cannot remedy a deficiency if, in order to do so, it has to exceed the bounds of normal judicial action'; ibid, [93].

cally inferred from the *raison d'etre* of a legal system, institution or norm. In the latter case the lacuna in the intent of legislation or parties can be filled.[275]

The need for the continuation of the international supervision of South West Africa, which was recognised in the 1950 *Advisory Opinion on the International Status of South West Africa*,[276] was justified by the UN's assumption of the responsibilities of the League as the leading institution of the organised international community; by its creation of the international trusteeship system in Chapters XII and XIII of the UN Charter; by the respondent's membership of the UN; and by its refusal to enter into a trust agreement in respect of South West Africa.[277] Consequently, in Judge Tanaka's view, the case for the ongoing supervision of South West Africa was not deduced from considerations of: 'mere necessity or desirability but from the raison d'etre and the theoretical construction of the mandates system as a whole'.[278] For Judge Tanaka, treaty interpretation could not be limited to the task of identifying the will of the parties from an examination of the text of the relevant treaty provisions. For him, other factors such as the principle of effectiveness and arguments about social necessity were also factors that must inform the interpretative exercise.[279] This approach orientates the task of construction away from a quest for the intentions of the parties – a strict feature of voluntarism – to a search for the intentions that can be reasonably assumed from all circumstances that exist at the time the act of interpretation is undertaken. Judge Jessup reached the same conclusion.[280] He had occasion to refer to the standpoint adopted by Judge Lauterpacht in his Separate Opinion in the 1955 *Advisory Opinion on the Voting Procedure on Questions relating to Reports and Petitions concerning the Territory of South West Africa*:

> I adopt with emphatic approval what Judge Lauterpacht said in his separate opinion in 1955 on South West Africa about the so-called "clear meaning" rule which to my mind is often a cloak for a conclusion reached in other ways and not a guide to a correct conclusion. Judge Lauterpacht said:
>
> > 'This diversity of construction provides some illustration of the unreliability of reliance on the supposed ordinary and natural meaning of words. Neither having regard to the integrity of the function of interpretation, is it desirable that countenance be given to *a method* which by way of construction may result in a summary treatment or disregard of the principal issue before the Court'.[281]

Despite the progressive interpretations of international law advanced by Judges Tanaka and Jessup in the *Second Phase* cases it is apparent that, at this point in

---

[275] Separate Opinion of Judge Tanaka, ibid, 277.
[276] *Advisory Opinion Concerning the International Status of South West Africa* (n 61).
[277] Judge Tanaka, *South West Africa* cases *(Second Phase)* (n 142) 277.
[278] ibid.
[279] *Advisory Opinion Concerning the International Status of South West Africa* (n 61).
[280] *South West Africa* cases *(Second Phase)* (Separate Opinion of Judge Jessup) (n 142) 355.
[281] *Voting Procedure on Questions Relating to Reports and Petitions Concerning the Territory of South-West Africa* (1955) ICJ Rep 67, 93. (Italics added.)

time, such purposive approaches were, in effect, neutralised by the formalist construction favoured by the majority in the 1966 decisions. Consequently, during the mid-1960s, rather than enlightening States about the progressive direction of international law, the ICJ merely reflected the wider uncertainty that existed in the international community of States regarding the nature of international law and its normative direction during the period under consideration.

XV. THE *SOUTH WEST AFRICA* CASES: SUBSTANTIVE LAW AND THE FORMATION OF CUSTOMARY INTERNATIONAL LAW

In his Separate Opinion in the *South West Africa* cases *(Second Phase)*, Judge Tanaka also considered the merits of the applicants' claims and, in particular, their central substantive contention that the prohibition on racial discrimination was an established CIL principle.[282] The applicants argued that a series of resolutions, adopted by the General Assembly between 1953 and 1963, which repeatedly condemned the South African policy of apartheid and asserted that it was inconsistent with the terms of the UN Charter, were significant in this regard. Moreover, they relied on a host of international instruments, including the Universal Declaration on Human Rights,[283] the Declaration on the Elimination of All Forms of Racial Discrimination[284] and the (then) draft versions of the International Covenants on Human Rights, in support of their core substantive claim. Judge Tanaka readily accepted that the prohibition on racial discrimination was an established CIL principle, according to the requirements set out in Article 38(1)(b) of the ICJ Statute.[285]

Judge Tanaka's conception of the formation of CIL is especially interesting for the present purpose. First, he acknowledged that Article 38(1)(b) does not require that all States must consent to a principle before it can achieve customary status.[286] He then considered whether the resolutions of international organisations could contribute to the formation of CIL to the extent that they are indicative of a general practice accepted as law, as set out in Article 38(1)(b). Judge Tanaka answered this question in the affirmative. He identified the traditional process regulating the formation of CIL as the repetition of specific acts performed by individual States over a considerable period of time, which then steadily lead to the emergence of a customary practice.[287] However, Judge Tanaka suggested that the advent of international organisations – and in particular the UN General Assembly – have enabled participating States to communicate their views about certain practices to the entire membership in a

---

[282] *South West Africa* cases *(Second Phase)* (Separate Opinion of Judge Tanaka) (n 142) 291–93.
[283] UNGA Res 217A(III)(1948), 10 December 1948.
[284] Adopted by the General Assembly on 20 November 1963.
[285] Judge Tanaka, *South West Africa* cases *(Second Phase)* (n 142) 293.
[286] ibid, 296.
[287] ibid, 291.

way that it reminiscent of 'parliamentary diplomacy'.[288] He concluded that such institutional developments have 'accelerated' and 'greatly facilitated' the formation of CIL.[289] Accordingly, Judge Tanaka approved of the extent to which States have the opportunity to participate in the generation of CIL in institutional settings and the clarity of the resultant norms.[290]

Nevertheless, despite this progressive stance, Judge Tanaka acknowledged that the individual resolutions of the General Assembly are not legally binding per se.[291] He indicated that there must be a degree of repetition of the same practice, either in the same organisation or across different organisations for CIL principles to emerge in any given field. Accordingly, Judge Tanaka interpreted the institutional activity of international organisations in the context of the formation of CIL as the repetition of collective acts of will by their members. Consequently, in his view, such collective activity replaces the need for repetitive acts by individual States which characterised the way in which CIL was traditionally established.[292] In his own words:

> Parallel with such repetition, each resolution, declaration, etc., being considered as the manifestation of the collective will of individual participant States, the will of the international community can certainly be formulated more quickly and more accurately as compared with the traditional method of the normative process. This collective, cumulative and organic process of custom-generation can be characterized as the middle way between legislation by convention and the traditional process of custom making, and can be seen to have an important role from the viewpoint of the development of international law.[293]

It is clear that Judge Tanaka's conception of the formation of CIL as a result of State activity within international organisations is consistent with the approach that has been subsequently adopted by the ICJ in cases such as the *Nicaragua* case and the *Nuclear Weapons Advisory Opinion*, as discussed above. However, the focus of the current chapter and the tenor of Judge Tanaka's Separate Opinion in the *Second Phase* of the *South West Africa* cases, prompt the following question: would a progressive Court have been willing to endorse the view that the right of colonial self-determination had acquired CIL status in a similar manner to the way that Judge Tanaka was prepared to hold that the prohibition on racial discrimination had achieved this status in 1966?

In addressing this question it should be noted that, according to Judge Tanaka's reading of the way in which CIL is generated as a result of State activity within international organisations, the General Assembly did produce a series of relevant resolutions which sought to develop the right of self-determination

---

[288]   ibid, 289 (referring to the *South West Africa* cases *(Preliminary Objections)* (n 262) 346).
[289]   ibid, 289.
[290]   In his view, such resolutions constitute authoritative pronouncements regarding the interpretation of the UN Charter by the competent organs of the international community; ibid, 291–92.
[291]   ibid, 292.
[292]   He describes the former as 'manifestations of the collective will of individual participating States', ibid.
[293]   ibid.

within the colonial context during the late-1950s, culminating in the adoption of the Colonial Declaration in 1960. Moreover, it should be recalled that this concerted institutional activity in relation to non-self-governing territories and trust territories was bolstered by the elaboration of the general right of self-determination pursuant to the drafting of the International Covenants. It is notable that, in his Separate Opinion in the *South West Africa* cases *(Second Phase)*, Judge Tanaka was willing to attribute normative significance to the draft versions of the International Covenants and it is apparent that such a willingness to interpret international law in the light of nascent developments would be important in relation to the question of the international legal status of the right of colonial self-determination during the period under consideration. Nevertheless, it should be acknowledged that deciphering the normative significance of the right of colonial self-determination – and the positive obligations associated with the recognition of such a right – would have been much less straightforward than the recognition of the prohibition on racial discrimination – a negative obligation imposed on States. Moreover, while racial discrimination constituted a blatant violation of the UN Charter, colonialism was not prohibited by the Charter even if this condition contradicted the general purposes and principles set out in Articles 1 and 2: colonialism was regulated by Chapters XI and XII of the Charter, which formed a type of *lex specialis*, in this context. Further, it should be recognised that the colonial powers refused to support the key General Assembly resolutions – resolution 1514 and resolution 1541 – and they had fought against the inclusion of the right of self-determination in the International Covenants. In contrast, the entire international community of States – save for South Africa – supported the prohibition on racial discrimination in both General Assembly resolutions and in other international instruments. Accordingly, while progressive developments indicated that an international legal framework dedicated to the task of delivering decolonisation was emerging during the late-1950s and early-1960s, it is suggested that it would be straining teleological interpretations of the relevant international instruments which had been adopted by the mid-1960s to conclude with sufficient certainty that the right of colonial self-determination had achieved the status of CIL by that time.

XVI. FITZMAURICE AND THE FORMALIST INTERPRETATION OF SELF-DETERMINATION

In the *South West Africa* cases *(Second Phase)*, the applicants also argued that South Africa's actions amounted to a violation of the right to self-determination of the people of South West Africa. This issue was not specifically addressed by the Court.[294] Nevertheless, given the focus of this chapter

---

[294] Save for the Separate Opinion of Judge Ad Hoc Van Wyck, *South West Africa* cases *(Second Phase)* (n 142) 166.

and in the light of Judge Tanaka's discussion of the normative direction of international law, it is worth considering the views, expressed extra-judicially, of Sir Gerald Fitzmaurice – one of the judges who was part of the majority in the *Second Phase* decisions in the *South West Africa* cases – concerning the status of the right of self-determination in the colonial context, during the period in question.[295] Writing in the early 1970s, Fitzmaurice argued that it was nonsense to claim that groups or entities, other than States, possessed the right to self-determination.[296] In his view, such groups were incapable of possessing rights as a matter of international law because they lacked international legal personality, and without such personality, legal rights cannot vest in a subject of international law (and neither can international legal obligations be imposed). Further, according to Fitzmaurice, if it is accepted that a given group satisfied the criteria by which its claim to possess the right to self-determination could be established as a matter of international law (ie the criteria for statehood) then its claim has already been 'internationally determined'.[297] Consequently, in Fitzmaurice's view, non-State groups are incapable of possessing the right to self-determination because: (i) the notion of self-determination is only rendered sensible in the context of the creation of a new State; (ii) and it is exhausted by this process. As a result, Fitzmaurice was prepared to accept that only those entities which have achieved statehood are capable of being the holders of international rights and obligations. However, as Berman has rightly pointed out, this approach does not acknowledge the way in which the inter-State system was created, or how it has responded to particular situations when new States were created.[298] Fitzmaurice's approach seems to be premised on the assumption that most States were created at some point in the distant past – either before the founding of international law or in the early days of the international legal system – and that such historical–political processes are beyond the purview of modern international law. Secondly, Fitzmaurice's approach lends itself to a firm belief in the existence of a strict separation between international law and international politics – an approach which recognises that States are merely juridical facts that must be accepted by international law irrespective of when and how they were created.[299] It is clear that this position has major implications for those groups and entities whose international status has yet to be determined as it suggests that international law does not have the authority to regulate such matters. Moreover, by drawing a sharp distinction between political and legal processes, the brand of formalism favoured by Fitzmaurice fails to

---

[295] Fitzmaurice also delivered a Dissenting Opinion in the *South West Africa* cases *(Preliminary Objections)* (n 262) 465; and in the *Namibia Advisory Opinion* (n 11) 220.

[296] See Berman, 'Sovereignty in Abeyance' (n 112) 60.

[297] ibid, 61–62.

[298] ibid, 63–64.

[299] This standpoint is consistent with Fitzmaurice's wider conception of international law as apparent from his understanding of the nature of international legal obligation. See G Fitzmaurice, 'The Foundations of the Authority of International Law and the Problem of Enforcement' (1956) 19 *Modern Law Review* 1.

appreciate the political nature of its own interpretation of particular legal issues, situations and disputes.

XVII. 'DECOLONIZING THE COURT'[300]

In the 1971 *Namibia* case and the 1975 *Western Sahara* case, the ICJ endorsed the principle and right of self-determination, as formulated in the 1960 Colonial Declaration. Moreover, in the latter case, the Court discussed the instrumental role performed by the General Assembly in the evolution of the principle and right of self-determination and in the development of the law of decolonisation, more generally. Nevertheless, it is important to appreciate that, during this period the ICJ was trying to make amends for its decisions in the *Second Phase* of the *South West Africa* cases. Accordingly, in both the *Namibia* case and the *Western Sahara* case,[301] the ICJ went to considerable lengths to demonstrate that it was prepared to engage with legal disputes that were politically controversial and that it was willing to adopt a teleological interpretation of international law, where such an approach was justified. It could be argued that this was the moment when the ICJ found its true role within the United Nations. However, it could also be claimed that the strains exhibited in the *South West Africa* cases during the 1960s were an aberration given that the Court's post-1966 approach was consistent with the one it had followed in its decisions addressing the situation in South West Africa during the 1950s.[302] The corollary of the ICJ's renewed commitment to the progressive interpretation of international law was that it was anxious to align itself with the work of the UN General Assembly in relation to its policy of promoting decolonisation and to the task of bringing colonialism to a speedy end.

According to Crawford, the *Namibia* case signalled a new phase in the development of the ICJ, both in institutional and jurisprudential terms.[303] From an institutional perspective, with regard to the aim of promoting decolonisation, the Court sought to co-ordinate its approach with that of the pioneering work of the General Assembly. Crawford observes that, in the *Namibia* case, the ICJ suggested that 'the subsequent development of international law in regard to non-self-governing territories', which 'made the principle of self-determination applicable to all of them' was largely attributable to the work carried out by the General Assembly in this area.[304] Further, Crawford offers a thorough analysis of the *Western Sahara* case in support of his thesis that the ICJ has consistently supported the principle and right of self-determination as it has been developed and

---

[300] Crawford (n 265) 587.

[301] Also see *Barcelona Traction* case *(Spain/Belgium)* (n 263) 3.

[302] See the 1950 *Advisory Opinion on South West Africa* (n 61) and the 1955 *Case regarding the Voting Procedure on Questions Relating to Reports and Petitions Concerning the Territory of South-West Africa* (n 281).

[303] Crawford (n 265) 589.

[304] ibid, 591 (referring to the *Namibia* case (n 11) [52–53]).

applied by the General Assembly.[305] In particular, he draws our attention to the ICJ's recognition of the discretionary role played by the General Assembly regarding the modalities for the implementation of the right to self-determination in concrete cases. Specifically, in the *Western Sahara* case, the Court observed that 'The right of self-determination leaves the General Assembly a measure of discretion with respect to the forms and procedures by which that right is to be realized'.[306] Furthermore, in the same vein, the ICJ noted that:

> The validity of the principle of self-determination, defined as the need to pay regard to the freely expressed will of peoples, is not affected by the fact that in certain cases the General Assembly has dispensed with the requirement of consulting the inhabitants of a given territory. Those instances were based either on the consideration that a certain population did not constitute a 'people' entitled to self-determination or on the conviction that a consultation was totally unnecessary, in view of special circumstances.[307]

Crawford extracts the general standpoint of international law concerning the processes of decolonisation from the specific approach adopted by the ICJ in the *Western Sahara* case. In so doing, he reveals the way in which the Court has acknowledged the leading role played by the General Assembly in the development of international law relating to decolonisation. Crawford connects a series of passages from the Court's Advisory Opinion in order to capture the modus operandi of the law of decolonisation:

> In relation to any given territory, the specific content of [the self-determination] principle is to be sought, as far as possible, in 'those resolutions which bear specifically on the decolonization of' the relevant territory and in 'the different ways in which the General Assembly resolutions . . . dealt with' that territory as compared with others.[308]

Crawford uses these fragments of the Court's jurisprudence in support of the conclusion that 'the Court has sought wherever possible to align the "*corpus iuris gentium*" [regarding decolonisation] with the policies and practice of the Assembly'.[309] Moreover, he goes beyond the suggestion that the ICJ and the General Assembly achieved an unprecedented degree of co-ordination in an effort to end colonialism to make the startling claim that, in relation to the process of decolonisation:

> the Court's role has been to an extent secondary with the '*corpus iuris gentium*' taking the form, more or less, of an administrative law, a body of rules relating to and supportive of the application of Chapters XI and XII of the Charter by the political organs, and in particular the General Assembly.[310]

---

[305] ibid, 592.
[306] ibid, 591 (drawing on the *Western Sahara* case (n 13) [73]).
[307] *Western Sahara* case (n 13) [59]. See Crawford (n 265) 591–92.
[308] ibid, 592 (drawing on the *Western Sahara* case (n 13) [60]).
[309] ibid, 591 (drawing on the *Namibia* case (n 11) [52–53]).
[310] ibid, 592.

The legal significance of the Colonial Declaration and resolution 1541 were contested by the colonial powers throughout the 1960s; however, they were strongly endorsed by the ICJ during the 1970s. But, by this time, the battles concerning the right of colonial self-determination and the content of the law of decolonisation had been fought and won, the colonial powers having accepted that the right of self-determination had acquired CIL status by virtue of the adoption of the 1970 Declaration on Friendly Relations.

XVIII. CONCLUSION

During the 1970s, the ICJ confirmed that the right of colonial self-determination had attained the status of CIL. However, by this time, the Declaration on Friendly Relations had been adopted by the General Assembly and the colonial powers had accepted the international law relating to decolonisation. For the purpose of the present enquiry it is vital to establish both how and when the customary character of this entitlement was established. Had it attained this status by the time the Lancaster House Agreement was negotiated and the 1965 BIOT Order was enacted? Did it achieve this status as a result of the General Assembly's adoption of the 1960 Colonial Declaration? The evolution of the right of colonial self-determination may be divided into three clear stages. Initially, self-determination was viewed as a political principle that was closely associated with the genesis of independent States. However, the principles and purposes of the UN Charter created the conditions for the development of the normative significance of the principle of self-determination. In the colonial context, the scope for such a development was heightened by the specific provisions of Chapters XI and XII, which recognised the applicability of the broad notion of self-government, and the obligations that were imposed on administering States in respect of non-self-governing territories and trust territories. The second phase in the development of the right to self-determination occurred with the emergence of a normatively muscular conception of self-determination proclaimed as the entitlement of all colonial peoples in the Colonial Declaration which, as the ICJ subsequently observed, together with resolution 1541 and the institutional initiatives that followed the adoption of these General Assembly resolutions, created the framework of the international law of decolonisation. Nevertheless, it is arguable that the terms of the 1960 Colonial Declaration, and the State practice which it engendered, did not lead to the creation of the right to self-determination as a matter of CIL during the early 1960s. While, by this time, colonialism was widely perceived as illegitimate, the refusal of the remaining colonial powers to accept that they were subject to an international legal obligation to effect decolonisation meant that the prerequisites for the formation of CIL could not be satisfied, at least from an orthodox perspective. From a progressive standpoint, it is clear that a strong case for the contemporaneous recognition of a general customary right to colonial self-determination could be constructed. However, it is evident from the strained deliberations of the ICJ in the *South West Africa* cases *(Second Phase)* that it is unlikely that such a groundbreaking argument would have found favour with the ICJ during the period in question.

The uncertainty as to whether the right of colonial self-determination had crystallised as a general norm of CIL by 1965 is important because it means that we cannot assume – as did the 1983 Excision Report produced under the auspices of the Mauritian Legislative Assembly – that the detachment of the Chagos Islands from the colony of Mauritius was necessarily a violation of CIL when the Lancaster House Agreement was concluded and the 1965 BIOT Order in Council was enacted. The next chapter will assess the normative significance of the arguments concerning the application of the right to colonial self-determination in the Mauritian context and the resonance of such arguments for the claims of the Chagos Islanders as a matter of international law.

6

Mauritian Claims of Sovereignty over the Chagos Islands: Mauritian Self-determination

I. INTRODUCTION

THE LAST CHAPTER considered the issue of whether the abstract entitlement to colonial self-determination had acquired the status of customary international law by the time the Chagos Islands were detached from the British colony of Mauritian pursuant to the Lancaster House Agreement negotiated between the UK government and the elected representatives of the Mauritian colonial government in 1965 and the creation of the BIOT via the 1965 BIOT Order In Council. The present chapter examines the resonance of self-determination and the international law relating to decolonisation in the Mauritian context in order to assess the validity of the competing claims to the Chagos Islands advanced by Mauritius and the UK. Such an assessment is necessary because the legal claims of the Chagos Islanders would be markedly different depending on which State can be shown to have a valid claim to exercise sovereign authority over the Chagos Islands as a matter of international law.

In 1946, the UK government identified Mauritius and the Seychelles as non-self-governing territories and it furnished the UN Secretary-General with information in respect of both territories pursuant to the reporting obligations contained in Article 73(e) of the UN Charter.[1] According to the terms of Article 73(b), the interests of the people of a non-self-governing territory are deemed to be of paramount importance and the responsible administering State is bound by a sacred trust in relation to its inhabitants.[2] Consequently, the UK was under an obligation to enable the inhabitants of Mauritius to achieve full self-government. The Mauritian people for this purpose were all inhabitants of the colony of Mauritius, as constituted by British colonial law. Prior to 1965, the Chagos Islands were a lesser dependency of Mauritius; therefore, they consti-

---

[1] See United Nations General Resolution 66(I), 14 December 1946. 74 territories were included in the list annexed to this resolution.
[2] See ch 5.

tuted part of the Mauritian colonial unit. Article 73 did not expressly prohibit the dismemberment of an established non-self-governing territory before full self-government had been achieved. However, it could be argued that the partitioning of a colonial unit in such circumstances would be contrary to the tenor of the provisions of Chapter XI of the UN Charter. It has been contended that the concept of non-self-governing territories presupposed that the sovereign authority, which administering States possessed over such territories, was qualified – it was only valid until the inhabitants of a given non-self-governing territory had attained full self-government.[3] Accordingly, it follows from the temporal constraint placed upon the sovereign authority of administering States in respect of their non-self-governing territories, that they did not have the authority to frustrate the aims declared in Article 73 by dismembering colonial territories as the prospect of decolonisation neared. Nevertheless, the fact that Chapter XI did not prohibit the partitioning of a colonial territory ahead of the achievement of full self-government was deeply problematic given the enduring significance of the *Lotus* principle in international law, which ensures that States retain considerable freedom of action and their liberty remains unconstrained in the absence of a specific international legal principle that would limit this freedom.[4] Notwithstanding the privileged status of this axiom of traditional international law, many international lawyers have argued that developments in international law since the advent of the UN Charter have substantially restricted the capacity of administering States to act freely in relation to their colonial territories.[5] This development is largely attributable to the emergence of the right of self-determination in the colonial context and it has been claimed that, as a result, administering States lost their capacity to alter the territorial parameters of those non-self-governing territories for which they bore international responsibility pending the exercise of that right.

II. COLONIAL SELF-DETERMINATION IN THE MAURITIAN CONTEXT

Paragraph 2 of the 1960 Colonial Declaration proclaimed that: 'All people have the right to self-determination; by virtue of that right they freely determine their political status and freely pursue their economic, social and cultural development'.[6] This conception of self-determination was subsequently echoed in joint Article 1(1) of the International Covenants on Human Rights in 1966.[7]

---

[3] See ch 5.
[4] See *SS Lotus* case *(France/Turkey)* (1927) PCIJ Rep Ser A No 10. See ch 5.
[5] This issue is discussed below.
[6] The Declaration on the Granting of Independence to Colonial Countries and Peoples, UNGA Res 1514 (XV), 14 December 1960 ('Colonial Declaration').
[7] Joint Art 1(1) acknowledges that 'all peoples are entitled to freely determine their political status and freely pursue their economic, social and cultural development'. International Covenant on Civil and Political Rights (1966) 999 UNTS 171; and International Covenant on Economic, Social and Cultural Rights (1966) 993 UNTS 3.

Both sources recognised that the right of self-determination is conferred on 'peoples'. The basic unit for the purpose of the exercise of the right of self-determination must be established before this entitlement can be properly considered. The above-mentioned developments in international law ensured that the meaning of 'people-hood' became increasingly important as the process of decolonisation gathered pace. But while the ICJ clarified much about the nature and scope of the right and principle of self-determination in the 1971 *Namibia Advisory Opinion* and 1975 *Western Sahara Advisory Opinion*, it did not address the concept of people-hood directly in these cases.[8] Consequently, it appears that the notion of people-hood for the purpose of the exercise of the right to self-determination must be considered on a case by case basis.

In the Mauritian context, the Mauritian 'people' for the purpose of exercising the right to self-determination were all the inhabitants of the colony of Mauritius, as constituted by British colonial law. The Mauritian self-determination unit comprised not only of the inhabitants of the island of Mauritius but of all the inhabitants of the colony of Mauritius. Consequently, prima facie, the detachment of the Chagos Islands from the Mauritian colonial unit by the UK amounted to a violation of the Mauritian people's entitlement to national self-determination. This interpretation of the application of the right to self-determination is bolstered by paragraph 6 of the Colonial Declaration, which provides that: 'Any attempt aimed at the partial or total disruption of the national unity and the territorial integrity of a country is incompatible with the purposes and principles of the Charter of the United Nations'.[9] A number of international lawyers, relying upon this provision, have claimed that an administering State is not permitted to dismember a non-self-governing territory for which it is responsible prior to the attainment of independence as such acts would violate the entitlement of self-determination belonging to the colonial people concerned.[10] Paragraph 6 of the Colonial Declaration recognises that the territorial unit for the purpose of exercising the right of self-determination is the established colonial unit, as determined by the applicable municipal colonial law. It assumes that the established colonial unit provides the territorial base for the exercise of their right of self-determination by the colonial people in question. Accordingly, it follows that any

---

[8] See the *Namibia Advisory Opinion* (1971) ICJ Rep 16; and the *Western Sahara Advisory Opinion* (1975) ICJ Rep 12.

[9] This provision was harnessed in Mauritian Legislative Assembly, 'Report of the Select Committee on the Excision of the Chagos Archipelago (No 2 of 1983)' (Mauritius, Mauritian Legislative Assembly 1983) (the '1983 Excision Report') 37. Para 6 refers to 'the partial or total disruption of the national unity and the territorial integrity of a *country*'. However, it was widely understood that a colonial entity would qualify as a country for this purpose. See SKN Blay, 'Self-Determination Versus Territorial Integrity in Decolonization' (1985–86) 16 *New York University Journal of International Law and Politics* 441, 443.

[10] A Rigo Sureda, *The Evolution of the Right of Self-Determination* (Leiden, Sijthoff, 1973) ch 2; J Crawford, *The Creation of States in International Law*, 2nd edn (Oxford, Oxford University Press, 2006) 645; SKN Blay, 'Self-Determination Versus Territorial Integrity in Decolonization' (n 9) 465–66; and TM Franck and P Hoffman, 'The Right of Self-Determination in Very Small Places' (1975–76) 8 *New York University Journal of International Law and Politics* 331.

dismemberment of a colonial territory prior to the achievement of decolonisation would amount to a violation of the right to self-determination because the
societal unit and the territorial unit are assumed to be co-terminous for the purpose of exercising this entitlement.

In the Mauritian context, it has been claimed the beneficiaries of the right of
self-determination were the permanent inhabitants of the island of Mauritius
and its lesser dependencies, which included the Chagos Islands. This claim
extended to the entire territory, which constituted the colony of Mauritius,
during the period prior to Mauritian decolonisation. According to this line of
reasoning, the people of the colony of Mauritius have a valid claim to all the
territory that was deemed to be part of the colony of Mauritius ahead of independence, as a matter of British colonial law. As a result, they have a legitimate
claim to the Chagos Islands. This interpretation of the application of the
Colonial Declaration to the decolonisation of Mauritius achieves a high degree
of consistency between paragraph 2 – the articulation of the right of self-
determination for colonial peoples – and paragraph 6 – the protection of the
territorial integrity of recognised self-determination units. On this reading, the
self-determination unit remains the former colonial unit of Mauritius and, as
the Mauritian State remains entitled to the national territorial integrity of the
colony of Mauritius, the Chagos Islands should be reverted to Mauritius without delay as a matter of international law.

III. THE PRINCIPLE OF *UTI POSSIDETIS JURIS*

The principle that newly independent States have a right to the maintenance of
the territorial parameters of the established colonial unit, as expressed in paragraph 6 of the Colonial Declaration, is bolstered by the principle of *uti possidetis juris*, which was widely endorsed during the processes of decolonisation in
Africa and Asia during the 1960s and 1970s.[11] The principle sought to avoid
fratricidal struggles and external territorial claims by ensuring that: 'new States
will come to independence with the same boundaries they had when they were
administrative units within the territory or territories of a colonial power'.[12]
Independence was deemed to be the critical date for fixing the territorial parameters of the new post-colonial State. Support for the application of the principle
of *uti possidetis* in the African context can be gleaned from Article 3(3) of the
Charter of the Organisation of African Unity (OAU), in which member States
pledged 'respect for the sovereignty and territorial integrity of each State and
for its inalienable right to independent existence'. The principle was implicitly
recognised in resolution 16(1) of the OAU Conference of Heads of State and

---

[11] It should be noted that Mauritius is considered to be part of Africa despite the fact that it is
located a considerable distance from the African continent.
[12] See MN Shaw, 'The Heritage of States: The Principle of *Uti Possidetis Juris* Today' (1996) 67
British Yearbook of International Law 75, 97.

Government held in Cairo in 1964, which declared that member States: 'solemnly . . . pledge themselves to respect the borders existing on their achievement of national independence'.[13]

In the African context, the principle of *uti possidetis juris* became inextricably linked to the principle of territorial integrity which protects an established State's territorial sovereignty.[14] Consequently, it increasingly became known as the doctrine of the inviolability of inherited territorial frontiers. In the *Burkina Faso/Mali* case, the ICJ noted that it had been asked to resolve the dispute by reference to the 'principle of the intangibility of frontiers inherited from colonization'. As a result, it stated that it 'cannot disregard the principle of *uti possidetis juris*, the application of which gives rise to this respect for the intangibility of frontiers'.[15] The ICJ has used these terms interchangeably ever since.[16] In the Court's view, Article 16(1) of the OAU's Cairo Declaration 'deliberately defined and stressed the principle of *uti possidetis juris* contained only in an implicit sense in the [OAU] Charter'.[17]

The process of African decolonisation was driven by the assumption that colonial peoples possessed the right to national self-determination as a matter of international law,[18] and that the colonial powers were under an obligation to realise it. Nevertheless, it was clear that this entitlement would have to operate within a territorial framework and that the balance between the right to territorial continuity and the right to self-determination would be a difficult one to achieve. As noted above, while paragraph 2 of the Colonial Declaration recognised that colonial peoples possessed the right of self-determination, under paragraph 6, the exercise of this right could not undermine the territorial integrity of the national (colonial) unit. Inevitably, the normative tension between these two principles led to practical problems on the ground. In the circumstances, the colonial territorial status quo represented a practical means of giving effect to this right; hence the relevance of *uti possidetis juris*.

While the ICJ has recognised the potential conflict between *uti possidetis juris* and the exercise of the right to self-determination in the African context, it has suggested that

---

[13] OAU AHR/Res16(1). This connection was made by the ICJ in the *Frontier Dispute* case *(Burkina Faso/Mali)* (1986) ICJ Rep 554, 565 (discussed below).

[14] See MN Shaw, *Title to Territory in Africa: International Legal Issues* (Oxford, Oxford University Press, 1986) 183–87; MN Shaw 'Peoples, Territorialism and Boundaries' (1997) 3 *European Journal of International Law* 478; SR Ratner, 'Drawing a Better Line: Uti Possidetis and the Borders of New States' (1996) 90 *American Journal of International Law* 590, 593. Further, see the terms of the UN Charter, Art 2(4); the Declaration on the Principles of International Law concerning Friendly Relations and Co-operation Among States in Accordance with the Charter of the United Nations, UNGA Res 2625(XXV), 24 October 1970; CSCE Helsinki Final Act (1975) *International Legal Materials* 12 1292; *Corfu Channel* case (1949) ICJ Rep 244; and the *Nicaragua* case *(Merits)* (1986) ICJ Rep 14.

[15] *Frontier Dispute* case *(Burkina Faso/Mali)* (n 13) 554, 565.

[16] See eg the *Frontier Dispute* case *(Benin/Niger)* (2005) ICJ Rep 90 [45].

[17] *Frontier Dispute* case *(Burkina Faso/Mali)* (n 13) 565–66.

[18] Shaw, 'The Heritage of States' (n 12) 120.

the maintenance of the territorial status quo in Africa is often seen as the wisest course, to preserve what has been achieved by peoples who have struggled for their independence, and to avoid a disruption which would deprive the continent of the gains achieved by much sacrifice.[19]

However, the rigid interpretation of *uti possidetis juris* followed in Africa was clearly favoured by the international community of States because it was thought that the notion of territorial continuity would promote order and regional and international stability.[20] In addition, it was also attractive to those African political elites which had been primed to lead the newly independent States as it offered principled continuity and sought to stave off irredentist forces and internal conflict.[21]

IV. *UTI POSSIDETIS JURIS* IN THE MAURITIAN CONTEXT

The principle of *uti possidetis juris* has not featured in the arguments between the UK and Mauritius in respect of the sovereignty dispute concerning the Chagos Islands. However, given the salience of this principle in connection with the achievement of decolonisation on the African continent, its significance in the Mauritian context – given that Mauritius is an African State – can hardly be overestimated. It is widely accepted that *uti possidetis juris* can be displaced in situations where affected States agree to vary their territorial boundaries.[22] However, it is important to acknowledge that the principle's presumptive weight is considerable and it will not be rebutted easily. The elected representatives of the Mauritian colonial government consented to the variation of the boundaries of the colony of Mauritius by agreeing to the proposed detachment of the Chagos Islands from Mauritius pursuant to the 1965 Lancaster House Agreement. However, as discussed in chapter four, the claim that their consent

---

[19] *Frontier Dispute* case *(Burkina Faso/Mali)* (n 13) 567.

[20] The continuing attraction of *uti possidetis* was also apparent in relation to the dissolution of the Soviet Union and Yugoslavia during the 1990s. See P Radan, 'Post-Secession International Borders: A Critical Analysis of the Opinions of the Badinter Commission' (2000) 24 *Melbourne University Law Review* 50. See M Weller, 'The International Response to the Dissolution of the Socialist Federal Republic of Yugoslavia' (1992) 86 *American Journal of International Law* 569; and M Craven, 'The European Community Arbitration Commission on Yugoslavia' (1995) 66 *British Yearbook of International Law* 333.

[21] See eg CG Widstrand (ed), *African Boundary Problems* (Uppsala, Scandinavian Institute, 1969).

[22] The Badinter Arbitration Committee was tasked with advising the EC Conference on the legal issues which might arise from the Yugoslavia's constitutional disintegration. In Opinion No 2, 11 January 1992, (1992) *International Legal Materials* 31, 1498, which concerned the question of whether the ethnic Serb populations within Croatia and Bosnia-Herzegovina possessed the right of self-determination in international law, the Badinter Committee was of the view that:

> international law as it currently stands does not spell out all the implications of the right to self-determination. However, it is well established that, whatever the circumstances, the right to self-determination must not involve changes to existing frontiers at the time of independence (*uti posseditis juris*) except where the states concerned agree otherwise.

was obtained by coercion – excising the Chagos Islands from Mauritius was the price to be paid for Mauritian independence – remains plausible. Moreover, agreements to vary territorial boundaries between adjacent States have been invariably negotiated between two (or more) post-colonial States in order to vary a common boundary inherited from a colonial power,[23] or, more recently, by successor States as a result of the dissolution of an independent federal State. However, these two situations are very different from situations where the only parties involved are an administering State and the representatives of a Non-Self-Governing Territory for which it bears international responsibility. Accordingly, it stands to reason that the presumption in favour of the application of the principle of *uti possidetis juris* would be stronger in the latter situation as a consequence of the nature of the relationship between a colonial power and one of its colonial territories.

Nevertheless, it should be acknowledged that *uti possidetis juris* conditions the application of the right to self-determination in the colonial context. These two principles are tied together even when they seem to be pulling in opposite directions. Thus, the principle of *uti possidetis juris* would strengthen the claim that the Chagos Islands are an integral part of the Mauritian self-determination unit. However, the doctrine of *uti possidetis juris* is intimately associated with the exercise of the right to self-determination via the attainment of independence: the scope for the application of the principle of *uti possidetis juris* only arises when the entitlement to self-determination is exercised. But, in the context of decolonisation, the principle carries no significance beyond the realisation of that right through the achievement of independence.[24] If the right to self-determination is not exercisable in a particular setting then the principle of *uti possidetis juris* has no application either. Accordingly, if the right to colonial self-determination was not applicable in the Mauritian context as a matter of customary international law then the principle of *uti possidetis juris* would have no application either: the self-determination argument and the *uti possidetis juris* argument stand and fall together.

V. THE CREATION OF THE BRITISH INDIAN OCEAN TERRITORY

As established earlier in this book, during the early 1960s, the US government entered into discussions with the UK government concerning the establishment of a US military facility in the Indian Ocean. After a joint survey of suitable islands was undertaken, Diego Garcia in the Chagos Archipelago, which formed part of the British colony of Mauritius, emerged as the preferred location for

---

[23] See eg *The Honduras Borders* case*(Guatemala/Honduras)* (1933) 2 *Reports of International Arbitral Awards* 1307.
[24] Nevertheless, the principle retains functional value in relation to the resolution of boundary disputes in the post-colonial context.

this purpose.[25] Both the UK government and US government were concerned that the potential emergence of an independent State of Mauritius would be likely to disrupt the construction of the planned facility and/or interfere with its subsequent operation. Consequently, pursuant to the Lancaster House Agreement, entered into by the UK government and the elected representatives of the colony of Mauritius in 1965, the UK detached the Chagos Islands from Mauritius, via the BIOT Order in Council 1965, in order to create the BIOT. The 1965 Order also excised the islands of Aldabra, Desroches and Farquhar from the British colony of the Seychelles and included them within the new territorial unit, which came into existence on 8 November 1965.[26]

On 16 November 1965, the UK government's UN representative informed the General Assembly's Fourth Committee that the BIOT had been created. Specifically, he stated that:

> The islands had been uninhabited when the United Kingdom Government had first acquired them. They had been attached to the Mauritius and Seychelles Administrations purely as a matter of administrative convenience. After discussions with the Mauritius and Seychelles Governments – including their elected members – and with their agreement, new arrangements for the administration of the islands had been introduced on 8 November. The islands would no longer be administered by those Governments but by a Commissioner. Appropriate compensation would be paid not only to the Governments of Mauritius and Seychelles but also to any commercial or private interests affected. Great care would be taken to look after the welfare of the few local inhabitants, and suitable arrangements for them would be discussed with the Mauritius and Seychelles Governments. There was thus no question of splitting up natural territorial units. All that was involved was an administrative re-adjustment freely worked out with the Governments and elected representatives of the people concerned.[27]

However, the General Assembly was unconvinced by the UK's justifications for the detachment of the Chagos Islands from Mauritius.[28] In December 1965, it adopted a resolution 2066(XX), which strongly criticised the UK's failure to

---

[25] See ch 3.

[26] SI 1965/1920. The Crown's authority to reconstitute its colonial territories, pursuant to its prerogative power of colonial governance, was recognised in the Colonial Boundaries Act 1895.

[27] See the Fourth Committee of General Assembly, 1558th Meeting (XX)(1965) 16 November 1965 [80]. Also quoted by the Divisional Court in *R (Bancoult) v Secretary of State for Foreign and Commonwealth Affairs* [2006] EWHC 1038 (Divisional Court) [29]. See also *Chagos Islanders v Attorney General and HM BIOT Commissioner* [2003] EWHC QB 2222 (High Court) (Ouseley judgment) [27–53].

[28] On the issue of detachment, the General Assembly concerned itself with the detachment of the Chagos Islands from Mauritius rather than the detaching of the islands of Aldabra, Desroches and Farquhar from the colony of the Seychelles. However, it should be acknowledged that the latter process was less controversial from a political perspective. In return for the detachment of the islands of Aldabra, Desroches and Farquhar the UK government undertook to build an airport for the Seychellois government on the island of Mahé; see Ouseley judgment (n 27) [74]. These islands were never evacuated and they reverted to the Seychelles on its accession to independence on 29 June 1976.

observe the provisions of the Colonial Declaration.[29] Given its significance for determining the legality of the excision of the Chagos Islands from Mauritius, it is worth setting out the terms of this resolution in full:

GAR 2066(XX)(1965). Question of Mauritius

The General Assembly

Having considered the question of Mauritius and other islands composing the Territory of Mauritius,

Having examined the chapters of the reports of the Special Committee on the Situation with regard to the Implementation of the Declaration on the Granting of Independence to Colonial Countries and Peoples relating to the Territory of Mauritius,

Recalling its resolution 1514(XV) of 14 December 1960 containing the Declaration on the Granting of Independence to Colonial Countries and Peoples,

Regretting that the administering Power has not fully implemented resolution 1514(XV) with regard to that Territory,

Noting with deep concern that any steps taken by the administering Power to detach certain islands from the Territory of Mauritius for the purpose of establishing a military base would be in contravention of the Declaration, and in particular of paragraph 6 thereof,

1. Approves the chapters of the reports of the Special Committee on the Situation with regard to the Implementation of the Declaration on the Granting of Independence to Colonial Countries and Peoples relating to the Territory of Mauritius, and endorses the conclusions and recommendations of the Special Committee contained therein;
2. Reaffirms the inalienable right of the people of the Territory of Mauritius to freedom and independence in accordance with General Assembly resolution 1514(XV);
3. Invites the Government of the United Kingdom and Northern Ireland to take effective measures with a view to the immediate and full implementation of resolution 1514(XV);
4. Invites the administering Power to take no action which would dismember the Territory of Mauritius and violate its territorial integrity;
5. Further invites the administering Power to report to the Special Committee to keep the question of the Territory of Mauritius under review and to report thereon to the general Assembly at its twenty-first session.[30]

This resolution clearly reaffirmed the Mauritian people's inalienable right to freedom, independence and the integrity of their national territory. In this respect, it stated that the detachment of the Chagos Islands from Mauritian territory would contravene paragraph 6 of the Colonial Declaration. However, the BIOT had already been created by the time the resolution was adopted and the UK government did not change course in response to it. Undeterred, the General

---

[29] UNGA Res 2066(XX)(1965), 16 December 1965.
[30] A/RES/2066(XX) 1387th plenary meeting, 16 December 1965.

Assembly continued to condemn the dismemberment of this non-self-governing territory and the militarisation of Diego Garcia and it adopted a series of resolutions in respect of the situation of Mauritius until Mauritius became independent in 1968.[31]

VI. THE SIGNIFICANCE OF
GENERAL ASSEMBLY RESOLUTION 2066(XX)(1965)

The Mauritian government's position since the early 1980s has been that the excision of the Chagos Islands from Mauritius on the eve of independence amounted to a gross violation of the Mauritian people's right to self-determination, as proclaimed in the Colonial Declaration.[32] The General Assembly reached this conclusion in resolution 2066(XX)(1965). As discussed in the last chapter, although General Assembly resolutions are not generally binding as a matter of international law, they may lead to the crystallisation of customary international law over time and, in highly exceptional cases, they may generate custom directly.[33] Against this background, it is important to consider the legal effects of resolution 2066(XX)(1965) in relation to the status of the Chagos Islands as a matter of international law. However, before addressing this issue, it is worth reflecting on the status of those General Assembly resolutions that do not seek to formulate general principles, as with, for example, the Colonial Declaration, but which are intended to address the implementation of such principles in specific situations.

Castañeda, writing in 1969, analysed the significance of General Assembly resolutions for international law and his work is particularly useful for the present purpose.[34] He distinguished between a condition which underpins the applicable principle of international law – the juridical fact – and the legal consequences which the principle attaches to the existence of the juridical fact – the right or duty which is activated as a result. Castañeda suggested that there are two kinds of General Assembly resolutions. First, there are resolutions which are of a political nature. These resolutions express the opinion of the General Assembly on particular issues and they do not perform a juridical function. Secondly, Castañeda suggested that certain resolutions enumerate juridical facts for the purpose of grounding the applicable principles of international law.[35] This second type of resolution establishes the factual conditions which activate

---

[31] See UNGA Res 2232(XXI), 20 December 1966; and UNGA Res 2357(XXII), 19 December 1967.

[32] This position was articulated in the 1983 Excision Report (n 9) 37. The current view of the Mauritian government is discussed in greater detail below.

[33] See ch 5.

[34] J Castañeda, *Legal Effects of United Nations Resolutions* (New York, Columbia University Press, 1969) 118–30. The timing of Castañeda's work is also instructive as to the status and effect of General Assembly resolutions within the period under consideration.

[35] This approach appears to assume that the applicable principles of international law are to be found elsewhere, in relevant treaties and in customary international law.

the rights and/or duties that have been prescribed by the applicable international law. Consequently, they identify the legal consequences which international law attaches to certain kinds of behaviour.

Castañeda illustrated his thesis by reference to the operation of Article 73 of the UN Charter. The reporting obligation imposed on administering States by Article 73(e) relates to non-self-governing territories, for which they bear international responsibility. As discussed in chapter five, Article 73 does not define the concept of a non-self-governing territory. Accordingly, it does not provide the juridical facts required to activate this international legal obligation. In order for this reporting obligation to be fully functioning, Castañeda thought it was necessary for the competent organ to identify the juridical facts to which this reporting obligation relates and, in his view, this is what the General Assembly did by defining the concept of a non-self-governing territory in General Assembly resolution 1541 (1960).[36] Nevertheless, Castañeda was anxious to stress that this function – the identification of the juridical fact which provides the condition for the operation of the applicable international law – does not mean that the relevant General Assembly resolution is the source of legal rights and/or obligations in question. In Castañeda's view, resolutions are not creative of international law. For him, they establish the factual conditions which must be satisfied for the operation of the principles of international law that would not otherwise be fully activated. Using Article 73 as an example, the reporting obligation contained in Article 73(e) would not be fully operational unless the juridical fact which underpins this obligation – the concept of a non-self-governing territory – is authoritatively defined.

Castañeda's analysis is persuasive but the most interesting thing about his approach is the legal significance that he attached to the General Assembly's determination of juridical facts in particular resolutions. Castañeda claimed that such determinations amounted to legal pronouncements by the competent UN organ and that, as a result, the juridical facts established in relevant General Assembly resolutions were rendered legally definitive. He argued that, in specific cases, as the juridical facts declared in particular resolutions represented the official position of the UN, they would provide the conditions for the activation of the applicable principles of international law in such situations. Consequently, Castañeda asserted that the pronouncements concerning the applicable juridical facts in specific General Assembly resolutions acquired a certain kind of legal validity in the sense that they constituted the only interpretation that the political organs of the UN would take into account when dealing with a particular case. Consequently, Castañeda was suggesting that the General Assembly's capacity to determine the juridical facts in a disputed situation goes beyond its function of establishing the conditions for the activation of the particular legal rights and/or duties. Instead, in his view, it acquired the authority

---

[36] See Castañeda, *Legal Effects of United Nations Resolutions* (n 35) 121. 'Principles which should guide Members in deciding whether or not an obligation exists to transmit the information called for under Article 73(e) of the Charter', UNGA Res 1541(XV)(1960), 15 December 1960.

to determine the legally relevant facts for the application of international law at a general level – even where the conditions for triggering international legal principles are established elsewhere (ie in treaty law or customary international law). Accordingly, for Castañeda, General Assembly resolutions are significant, in terms of the institutional recognition that they offer regarding the legality (or otherwise) of a particular situation, in cases where they have secured considerable support from Member States.

A. Support for Resolution 2066 from UN Members States in the General Assembly

Resolution 2066(XX)(1965) attracted considerable support from members States in the General Assembly. 89 States voted in favour of the resolution and no State voted against it (18 States abstained from voting).[37] Accordingly, resolution 2066 represented the clear expression of the will of the UN membership on the question of the detachment of the Chagos Islands from the British colony of Mauritius. In addition, the language of resolution 2066 must be examined closely in order to decipher its significance, from the perspective of international law. It is notable that the Mauritian question was placed on the General Assembly's agenda for the twentieth session in relation to the implementation of the Colonial Declaration and the terms of Declaration are reinforced at several points in resolution 2066. Specifically, paragraph 2 of the 1965 resolution reaffirmed the Mauritian people's 'inalienable right to freedom and independence' in accordance with the provisions of the Colonial Declaration. This represents a clear reference to the entitlement of colonial self-determination, as expressed in paragraph 2 of resolution 1514(XV)(1960). Further, in resolution 2066, the General Assembly noted, with regret, that the UK had failed to implement the Colonial Declaration in relation to Mauritius. In paragraph 3, it called upon the administering State to take effective measures to ensure that it fully complied with the terms of the Colonial Declaration in the Mauritian context with immediate effect. Moreover, the General Assembly expressed its deep concern that the detachment of the Chagos Islands from Mauritius would amount to a violation of paragraph 6 of the Colonial Declaration, which proclaimed the territorial integrity of established colonial units ahead of the exercise of the right to self-determination. Relying on this provision, in paragraph 4 of resolution 2066, the General Assembly urged the UK to refrain from taking any steps that would lead to the dismemberment of the Mauritian colonial unit.

An examination of the language used in resolution 2066 indicates, prima facie, that it was not drafted in mandatory terms. First, it is notable that the General Assembly expressed the view that the provisions of the Colonial Declaration must be observed in relation to Mauritius in the form of a request.

---

[37] A/RES/2066(XX), 16 December 1965, A/PV/1398.

For instance, in paragraph 3 of the resolution, the General Assembly invited the UK to implement the Colonial Declaration in the Mauritian context. Further, in paragraph 4, it also invited the UK to take no action to dismember the Mauritian colonial unit. Thus, while the General Assembly was clearly alarmed about the situation in Mauritius, it asked the administering State to refrain from taking any steps that would contravene the governing principles of decolonisation.[38] Accordingly, in resolution 2066, the General Assembly represented a serious attempt to persuade the UK to observe the provisions of the Colonial Declaration in relation to Mauritius.

As noted above, the BIOT was created on 8 November 1965 and the UK informed the General Assembly's Fourth Committee of its creation on 16 November 1965. Resolution 2066 was adopted by the General Assembly on 16 December 1965 – after the BIOT had been created and after the Assembly's Fourth Committee had been informed. However, the terms of the resolution are expressed in the future tense. The detachment of the Chagos Islands from Mauritius for the purpose of establishing a military base 'would be in contravention of the [Colonial] Declaration'. Further, in paragraph 4 of resolution 2066, the General Assembly requested that: 'the administering Power take no action which would dismember the Territory of Mauritius and violate its territorial integrity'. This resolution may have been drafted by the time the UK government advised the General Assembly's Fourth Committee of the BIOT's creation. However, the measured tone of resolution 2066 may also be indicative of wider concerns on the part of member States.[39] The future orientation of the resolution afforded the General Assembly a way in which to articulate its opposition to the construction of the planned military base on Diego Garcia. Many States were anxious about the prospective militarisation of the Indian Ocean and this specific issue became the focal point of a number of subsequent General Assembly resolutions concerning the Chagos Islands.[40] The General Assembly maintained its condemnation of the creation and maintenance of military bases on islands in the Indian Ocean after Mauritius achieved independence.[41]

The General Assembly may have been hoping that the UK government (and the US government) would reflect on the wisdom of establishing a military base on Diego Garcia in the face of clear opposition from the international community of States. Consequently, the content of resolution 2066 was evidently

[38] UNGA Res 2066 was substantially informed by the report of C24 produced at the General Assembly's 19th session in 1964 (A/5800/Rev 1), which, in turn, was informed by the report of Sub-Committee 1 on Mauritius, Seychelles and St Helena (A/AC109/L 119).

[39] Compare with UNGA Res 3161(XXVII)(1973) adopted with regard to the island of Mayotte; see below.

[40] In relation to Mauritius, see UNGA Res 2232(XXI), 20 December 1966; and UNGA Res 2357(XXII), 19 December 1967.

[41] In relation to Seychelles, see UNGA Res 2430(XXIII), 18 December 1968; UNGA Res 2592(XXIV), 16 December 1969; UNGA Res 2869(XXVI), 20 December 1971; and UNGA Res 2984(XXVII), 14 December 1972.

informed as much by wider political concerns about the implications of the construction of a US military base in the Indian Ocean as by the decision of a retreating colonial power to partition one of its remaining colonial territories before it had acceded to independence. Further, the qualified way in which the General Assembly set out the terms of resolution 2066 may have also stemmed from the lack of protest from elected representatives of the Mauritian colonial government at the detachment of the Chagos Islands from Mauritius. The knowledge about the dealings between the UK government and the elected representatives of the Mauritian colonial government and the terms of the 1965 Lancaster House Agreement would have been highly restricted during that period.[42] As a result, and in the light of the UK government's statement to the General Assembly's Fourth Committee, UN member States may have been under the impression that Mauritian political leaders were prepared to accept the excision of the Chagos Islands from Mauritian territory. While many States may have had their suspicions about the probity of the terms of any such arrangement there would have been little cogent evidence in the public domain that could be used to confirm them during the period in question.[43]

In the following year, the General Assembly adopted another resolution which addressed the situation of Mauritius. In General Assembly resolution 2232(XXI)(1966), 20 December 1966, the General Assembly was:

Deeply concerned at the [. . .] disruption of the territorial integrity of some [colonial] Territories and at the creation by the administering Powers of military bases and installations in contravention of the relevant resolutions of the General Assembly

[. . .]

Reaffirms the inalienable right of the peoples of these Territories to self-determination and independence;

Calls upon the administering Powers to implement without delay the relevant resolutions of the General Assembly;

Reiterates its declaration that any attempt aimed at the partial or total disruption of the national unity and the territorial integrity of colonial Territories and the establishment of military bases and installations in these Territories is incompatible with the purposes and principles of the Charter of the United Nations and of General Assembly resolution 1514 (XV);

Mauritius was one of 25 colonial territories identified in resolution 2232. But while the General Assembly reiterated its general demands for decolonisation in respect of the territories identified in the resolution, it did not single the Mauritian situation out for particular attention.

---

[42] See ch 4.
[43] However, it should be noted that a number of reputable newspapers including the *Daily Telegraph* (31 August 1964) and *The Economist* (4 July 1964 and 5 September 1964) had reported the UK–US plans to establish a military facility on the island of Diego Garcia. See the 1983 Excision Report (n 9) 30.

C24 prompted General Assembly resolutions on the BIOT question between 1965 and 1967. However, as its remit covers non-self-governing territories and trust territories, it ceased to monitor this issue after Mauritius gained its independence. Is it significant that the General Assembly has not addressed the question of the status of the Chagos Islands since Mauritius acceded to independence? It has been suggested that the General Assembly has a tendency to defer regional conflicts to regional organisations,[44] and it is arguable that this practice is evident in relation to sovereignty dispute over the Chagos Islands.

In 1980, the Organisation of African Unity (OAU) adopted a unanimous resolution calling for the dismantling of the military base and the retrocession of the Chagos Islands to Mauritius. The Non-Aligned Movement (NAM) echoed this demand by adopting a similar resolution in 1983.[45] The African Union, the OAU's successor organisation, has resolved to maintain all OAU resolutions.[46] Further, in 2011, it reiterated its view that the Chagos Islands were excised from the colony of Mauritius in violation of the right of self-determination as expressed in the Colonial Declaration and reaffirmed its support for the Mauritian government's sovereign claim to the Chagos Islands reasserting that the Chagos Islands are an integral part of Mauritius.[47]

B. The Juridical Facts of the Detachment of the Chagos Islands from Mauritius

In the light of Castañeda's analysis of the legal significance of General Assembly resolutions it is useful to identify the juridical facts established in resolution 2066(XX)(1965) for the purpose of considering the UK's international legal obligations in relation to the detachment of the Chagos Islands from Mauritius. First, resolution 2066 confirmed that the Colonial Declaration was applicable to Mauritius and to the question of the detachment of the Chagos Islands from the Mauritian colonial unit. Secondly, it established that the UK, as the responsible administering State, had not fully implemented the provisions of the Declaration with regard to Mauritius. In addition, resolution 2066 indicated the General Assembly's position in the event that the UK decided to detach the Chagos Islands from Mauritius. It indicated that, if the UK took any constitutional steps to excise the Chagos Islands from the colony of Mauritius, in order to create a new territorial unit; or if it took any concrete measures to this end

---

[44] Crawford, *The Creation of States in International Law* (n 10) 619.

[45] OAU Assembly of Heads of State Resolution on Diego Garcia, 4 July 1980, AHG/Res 99 (XVII). NAM adopted its resolution on the Chagos Islands at its Seventh Summit Conference in Delhi on 12 May 1983; see R Aldrich and J Connell, *The Last Colonies* (Cambridge, Cambridge University Press, 1998).

[46] See also African Union Assembly of Heads of State Decision on Chagos Archipelago, AHG/Dec 159 (XXXVI), 12 July 2000.

[47] AU/Res 1(XVI), the Assembly of the African Union, at its 16th Ordinary Session, 31 January 2011.

(eg if it displaced the population of the Chagos Islands; or if the US government began to build a military base on Diego Garcia) such actions would violate the provisions of the Colonial Declaration. However, notwithstanding the terms of resolution 2066, as discussed in the last chapter, the right of colonial self-determination had not acquired the binding character of customary international law by the time the BIOT had been created. Further, the resolution was not drafted in mandatory terms. Consequently, neither resolution 2066(XX)(1965) nor resolution 2232(XXI)(1966) prove that the UK was under an obligation to refrain from detaching the Chagos Islands from Mauritius as a matter of international law.

VII. SOVEREIGNTY OVER THE CHAGOS ISLANDS: THE POSITION OF THE UK GOVERNMENT

The UK government maintains that it is entitled to exercise full sovereignty over the BIOT. However, it has made a vague undertaking to retrocede the Chagos Islands to Mauritius as soon as the military base on Diego Garcia is no longer required for defence purposes. It confirmed this position in a statement to the UK Parliament in 2002.[48] This position is consistent with the terms of the Lancaster House Agreement, which provided, inter alia, that: 'If the need for the facilities on Chagos Islands should disappear the islands should be returned to Mauritius'. As noted in chapter three, while the Mauritian Council of Ministers formally approved the terms of the Lancaster House Agreement, it sought clarification of the terms of the contemplated future retrocession of the Chagos Islands to Mauritian sovereignty.[49] The official record reveals that it was willing to agree to the terms of the Lancaster House Agreement on:

> the understanding that the British government has agreed that [in relation to the condition regarding the reversion of the Chagos Islands to Mauritian sovereignty] there would be no question of sale or transfer to a third party nor of any payment or financial obligation on the part of Mauritius as a condition of the return[50]

The Colonial Secretary responded:

> the assurance can be given provided it is made clear that a decision about the need to retain the islands must rest entirely with the United Kingdom Government and that it would not (repeat not) be open to the Government of Mauritius to raise the matter, or press for the return of the islands on its own initiative.[51]

In a statement to the UK Parliament, made on 11 July 1980, the British Prime Minister, Margaret Thatcher, said:

---

[48] Written Answer of the Foreign Office Minister, HC Deb 15 October 2002, vol 390, col WA 527.
[49] See the 1983 Excision Report (n 9) app O, 62. See ch 3.
[50] ibid, app P, 63.
[51] Telegram dated 19 November 1965. See Excision Report (n 9) app R, 65.

When the Mauritian Council of Ministers agreed in 1965 to the detachment of the Chagos islands to form part of the British Indian Ocean Territory, it was announced that these would be available for the construction of defence facilities and that, in the event of the islands no longer being required for defence purposes, they should be reverted to Mauritius.[52]

Further, in reply to the Mauritian government's sovereignty claim over the Chagos Islands,[53] the representative of the UK government made the following statement to the General Assembly in 2001:

> The British Government maintains that the British Indian Ocean Territory is British and that it has been since 1814. It does not recognize the sovereignty claim of the Government of Mauritius. However, the British Government has recognized Mauritius as the only State which has a right to assert a claim of sovereignty when the United Kingdom relinquishes its own sovereignty. Successive British Governments have given undertakings to the Government of Mauritius that the Territory will be ceded when it is no longer required for defence purposes, subject to the requirements of international law. The British Government remains open to discussions regarding arrangements governing the British Indian Ocean Territory or the future of the Territory. The British Government has stated that, when the time comes for the Territory to be ceded, it will engage in close liaison with the Government of Mauritius.[54]

As noted above, in the statement made to the General Assembly's Fourth Committee on 16 November 1965 the UK government asserted that the Chagos Islands were only attached to the colony of Mauritius for the sake of administrative convenience; that they are not contiguous to the Mauritian territorial unit; and that there were no pre-colonial ties between the Chagos Islands and Mauritius as the two territories were uninhabited prior to the arrival of European colonialism; as a result, they both could be properly labelled *terra nullius*. Consequently, the UK government maintained that Mauritius had no claim to the Chagos Islands by virtue of the exercise of the right of colonial self-determination.

As discussed in chapter three, during the period when the detachment of the Chagos Islands from Mauritius was being planned, the UK government was of the view that the 1965 Lancaster House Agreement was unnecessary for the valid transfer of the Chagos Islands from the British colony of Mauritius to British sovereignty. It claimed that excision could be lawfully achieved unilaterally, by Order in Council.[55] It follows from this standpoint that, as the UK exercised sovereignty over Mauritius before the Chagos Islands were excised from

---

[52] HC Deb 11 July 1980, vol 988, col 314 (cited in the 1983 Excision Report (n 9) 25).

[53] See below.

[54] GAOR, 56th session, 47th plenary meeting, 11 November 2001 UN Doc A/56/PV47, at 38.

[55] This constitutional interpretation has been consistently maintained by the UK government since the 1960s as apparent from official documents and it is important to note that the UK government restated this position in its pleadings for the *Chagos Islanders v UK* case, which was decided by the European Court of Human Rights in 2012; *Chagos Islanders v UK* (2013) 56 EHRR SE15. See ch 2.

that colonial unit, the elected representatives of the Mauritian government did not transfer sovereignty to the Chagos Islands to the UK through the 1965 Lancaster House Agreement. Instead, according to this interpretation, the elected representatives of the Mauritian colonial government merely endorsed the detachment of the Chagos Islands in the 1965 Agreement. Further, according to the UK government, the 1965 Agreement did not constitute a treaty of cession as a matter of international law because the elected representatives of the colony of Mauritius did not exercise full sovereign authority over the territory during the period in question.

VIII. SOVEREIGNTY OVER THE CHAGOS ISLANDS: THE POSITION OF THE MAURITIAN GOVERNMENT

In the 1983 report of the Mauritian Legislative Assembly's Select Committee on the Excision of the Chagos Archipelago, it was noted that the detachment of the Chagos Islands from the colony of Mauritius was: 'in complete violation of [paragraph] 6 of the Declaration on the Granting of Independence to Colonial Countries and Peoples'.[56] It should be recalled that paragraph 6 of the Colonial Declaration provides that: 'Any attempt aimed at the partial or total disruption of the national unity and the territorial integrity of a country is incompatible with the purposes and principles of the Charter of the United Nations'. The 1983 Excision Report also observed that General Assembly resolution 2066(XX) (1965), which confirmed the applicability of the Colonial Declaration – and the terms of paragraph 6 in particular – to the excision of the Chagos Islands from Mauritius pursuant to the creation of the BIOT, was similarly 'flouted' by the UK. The 1983 report concluded that this process violated not only paragraph 6 of the Colonial Declaration but also paragraph 5, which holds that the achievement of independence pursuant to the exercise of the right of colonial self-determination should be effected 'without any conditions and reservations'.[57] Accordingly, the report concluded that:

> Hence, notwithstanding the blackmail element which strongly puts in question the legal validity of the excision, the Select Committee strongly denounces the flouting by the United Kingdom Government [. . .] of the Charter of the United Nations.[58]

The 1983 report was produced by a select committee of the Mauritian Legislative Assembly rather than by the Mauritian government. Nevertheless, the Mauritian

---

[56] 1983 Excision Report (n 9) 4 [11].
[57] ibid, 37. The 1960 Colonial Declaration, para 5, provides that: 'Immediate steps shall be taken, in Trust and Non-Self-Governing Territories . . . to transfer all powers to the peoples of those territories, without any conditions or reservations, in accordance with their freely expressed will and desire, without any distinction as to race, creed or colour, in order to enable them to enjoy complete independence or freedom'. See ch 4.
[58] ibid, 37.

Labour Party, which had been in government since the moment of independence, had been ousted from power in 1982 and the old consensus no longer held sway and the wisdom of the deal – the detachment of the Chagos Islands in return for Mauritian independence – had become a contentious matter in Mauritian domestic politics.[59] Consequently, the claim that the Chagos Islands were excised from Mauritian in violation of the applicable international law soon became the official position of the Mauritian government

In a letter dated 15 August 2001 from the Permanent Mission of the Mauritian government to the Chairperson of the Sub-Commission on the Promotion and Protection of Human Rights, the Mauritian government outlined its position on the question of the Chagos Islands:

> Ever since [the creation of British Indian Ocean Territory] the Government of Mauritius has consistently pressed the United Kingdom Government both bilaterally and internationally for the early and unconditional return of the Chagos Archipelago to Mauritius. Mauritius has never acquiesced in the creation of the so-called British Indian Ocean Territory, which it does not recognize or accept.[60]

This statement reflects the Mauritian government's current position regarding the status of the Chagos Islands. The Mauritian government's revisionist interpretation of the dealings between the UK government and previous Mauritian administrations is understandable given that the detachment of the Chagos Islands from Mauritius was coloured by the available evidence, which suggests that it was the price of Mauritian independence. However, as discussed in chapter three, the historical record does not support the claim that the Mauritian government objected to the excision of the Chagos Islands from the colony of Mauritius, and the subsequent creation of the BIOT, in 1965. The Mauritian demand for the immediate return of the Chagos Islands evolved during the early 1980s. This begs the question whether the lateness of this public claim undermines its veracity? Is the Mauritian government barred from making a claim of sovereignty over the Chagos Islands by virtue of the doctrine of estoppel?

IX. THE ESTOPPEL ARGUMENT

International law has developed a number of requirements that must be established before a valid claim of estoppel can be made. First, a State (or colonial entity) must have made some kind of representation, which is directed at another State, or colonial entity, regarding the existence of a particular state of affairs. In the present context, this requirement can be readily established: the elected representatives of the British colony of Mauritius agreed to the excision

---

[59] This issue is discussed in ch 3.
[60] 17 August 2001, E/CN4/Sub2/2001/39. See also Comments by the Government of Mauritius to the Concluding Observations of the UN Human Rights Committee on the United Kingdom and Overseas Territories, 28 May 2002, CCPR/CO/73/UK/Add.1 and CCPR/CO/73/UKOT/Add.1.

of the Chagos Islands from that colony in the 1965 Lancaster House Agreement. Moreover, the Mauritian representatives were fully aware of the purpose for which the Chagos islands were being detached from Mauritius.[61] Secondly, the applicable international law insists that the material representation must have been made on a voluntary and unconditional basis. According to Bowett, drawing upon the PCIJ's decision in *Serbian Loans* case, the representation must not have been procured as a result of duress.[62] Consequently, it would appear that this requirement for a finding of estoppel can be satisfied in relation to the 1965 Agreement. The available evidence shows that the Mauritian representatives only agreed to the terms of the 1965 Agreement because, in effect, they had no choice: senior representatives of the UK government made it clear to them that the Chagos Islands could be excised unilaterally if they were unwilling to agree to the proposed detachment of the Chagos Islands.[63]

In addition, in order to establish a claim of estoppel, it must be shown that the claimant relied on the representation addressed to it by another State, or entity, and that such reliance led the claimant to act to its detriment. The notion of detrimental reliance is central to the doctrine of estoppel.[64] Nevertheless, it is apparent that the UK government did not actually rely upon the 1965 Agreement in order for it to carry out its policy of detaching the Chagos Islands from the colony of Mauritius; and for the subsequent creation of the BIOT. The BIOT was constituted by the BIOT Order in Council 1965 and the UK government consistently maintained that the Chagos Islands could be excised from the colony of Mauritius unilaterally. Accordingly, on this view, the consent of the elected representatives of the colony of Mauritius was not a prerequisite for the detachment of the Chagos Islands from the colony of Mauritius. In the circumstances, the 1965 Agreement had no material legal effect as a matter of British colonial law. Further, it did not underpin the 1966 UK–US treaty concerning the use of Diego Garcia as the site of a US military facility. In effect, the UK government did not rely on the 1965 Agreement in order to achieve the legal aims it set out to accomplish. Specifically, it did not 'change its position' as a result of the 1965 Agreement.[65]

Even if the UK government did not rely upon the representation made by the elected representatives of the Mauritian colonial government in the 1965 Agreement to its detriment, a valid claim of estoppel could still be advanced if the representation resulted in a benefit to the government of Mauritius.

---

[61] See ch 3.

[62] D Bowett, 'Estoppel before International Tribunals and its Relation to Acquiescence' (1957) 33 *British Yearbook of International Law* 176, 190–93. See the *Serbian Loans* case *(France/Serbia)* (1929) PCIJ Ser A (No 20) 5, 39. The notion of duress for the purpose of a finding of estoppel is broader than that articulated in Art 52 of the 1969 Vienna Convention on the Law of Treaties. For a discussion of the scope of duress in that context, see ch 4.

[63] See ch 3.

[64] See RY Jennings, *The Acquisition of Territory in International Law* (Manchester, Manchester University Press, 1962) 45–50.

[65] See the comments of Judge Fitzmaurice in his Separate Opinion in the *Temple* case (1962) ICJ Rep 23, 62.

Consequently, it is possible to identify certain benefits which accrued to the Mauritian government as a result of the 1965 Agreement. In particular, one could point to the grant of early independence and entry into the international community of States; the payment of £3 million in compensation for the detachment; and the advantages flowing from the internal and external defence treaty which was concluded as a direct result of the 1965 Agreement.[66] In the circumstances, is the Mauritian government vulnerable to the charge that it has enjoyed the benefits gained from the 1965 Agreement but that it is now seeking to deny the legal validity of the 1965 agreement?[67] This point is certainly arguable but the circumstances of the conclusion of the 1965 Lancaster House Agreement and the relative bargaining positions of an administering State and one of its non-self-governing territories indicate that the Mauritian government was not unduly advantaged by the terms of the 1965 Agreement.

Finally, did the Mauritian government acquiesce in response to assertions of sovereign authority over the Chagos Islands by the UK government from 1965 onwards? Acquiescence occurs when a situation is allowed to continue in circumstances where a State, or entity, should have made an objection but failed to do so. In effect, it is the resultant inaction over a significant period of time that amounts to tacit consent to a state of affairs on the part of a directly affected State or entity.[68] In the Mauritian context, given the nature of the 1965 Agreement and in the light of the fact that the Mauritian Labour Party was the government of Mauritius from 1968, when independence was achieved, until 1982, it is not surprising that the Mauritian government chose not to object publicly to the detachment of the Chagos Islands from Mauritius and the UK's continuing exercise of sovereignty over the Chagos Islands during this period. The Mauritian government began to claim sovereignty over the Chagos Islands from the early 1980s and it has maintained this position ever since that time. Against this background, the doctrine of acquiescence does not appear to be applicable to the facts of the sovereignty dispute concerning the Chagos Islands.

The dispute concerning sovereignty over the Chagos Islands has not arisen from one State's unilateral conduct maintained over a significant period of time; and inactivity or silence on the part of the other State. The 1965 Agreement demonstrates that both parties have engaged with the question of the status of the Chagos Islands from the perspectives of British colonial law and international law. Moreover, even if the doctrine of acquiescence were applicable to the sovereignty dispute concerning the Chagos Islands, the period of time which has elapsed between the conclusion of the 1965 Agreement and the first public sovereignty claims advanced by the Mauritian government is a relatively short period of time on which to found claim of acquiescence when it is compared to

---

[66] See ch 3.
[67] International law has been a particularly careful not to reward inconsistent behaviour on the part of States. See the *Temple* case (n 65) 33.
[68] See J Crawford, *Brownlie's Principles of Public International Law*, 8th edn (Oxford, Oxford University Press, 2012) 419–21.

other claims that have been adjudicated by international tribunals.[69] Finally, from 1968 until the early 1980s, it is possible to point to instances when senior representatives of the Mauritian government have publicly endorsed the view that the UK possesses sovereignty over the Chagos Islands. However, it is possible to justify this historical position by reference to the misrepresentations made by the British government concerning its legal authority to detach the Chagos Islands from Mauritius in 1965; and domestic political considerations in post-colonial Mauritius during the 1970s. While international law does not reward States for inconsistent patterns of behaviour it does appreciate that inconsistencies do occur over time. Consequently international tribunals have typically been prepared to take a much more pragmatic view of the patterns of State behaviour and the causes of such behaviour. Against this background, any inconsistencies in the position adopted by the Mauritian government between 1968 and the early 1980s are not sufficient to support the conclusion that it is estopped from asserting its sovereignty over the Chagos Islands. This conclusion is supported by the fact that the significant period of time that had elapsed between the injuries sustained and the instituting of proceedings by Nauru against Australia was not considered to be dispositive by the ICJ.[70]

X. NON-SELF-GOVERNING TERRITORIES AND THE RIGHT TO SELF-DETERMINATION

The ICJ observed in its 1971 *Namibia* case that developments in international law had rendered the principle of self-determination applicable to all non-self-governing territories.[71] However, the General Assembly has not treated all non-self-governing territories in the same way and this was recognised by the Court subsequently in the 1975 *Western Sahara* case.[72] In this case, the ICJ acknowledged that differentiated treatment was justified where the inhabitants of a given non-self-governing territory did not qualify as a 'people' for the purpose of exercising the right of self-determination. In addition, the Court observed that the General Assembly retained a degree of procedural discretion regarding the modalities applicable in relation to the exercise of the right in particular cases.[73] As discussed in chapter five, the ICJ has been content to follow the General Assembly's lead regarding the ways and means by which decolonisation

[69] See I Sinclair, 'Estoppel and Acquiescence' in V Lowe and M Fitzmaurice (eds), *Fifty Years of the International Court of Justice: Essays in Honour of Sir Robert Jennings* (Cambridge, Grotius Publications, 1996) 104.

[70] See *Case Concerning Certain Phosphate Lands in Nauru (Nauru v Australia) (Preliminary Objections)* (1992) ICJ Rep 240. For an overview of the settlement, see A Anghie, ' "The Heart of My Home": Colonialism, Environmental Damage and the Nauru Case' (1993) 34 *Harvard International Law Journal* 445, 472–80.

[71] See the *Namibia Advisory Opinion* (n 8) [53].

[72] See the *Western Sahara Advisory Opinion* (n 8) [59].

[73] Save where democratic consultation was required in accordance with the provisions of UNGA Res 1541. See ibid, [57].

was achieved and thus the exercise of the right to self-determination in concrete cases.[74]

Musgrave examined a number of cases where the General Assembly did not act consistently in the way that it applied the international law relating to decolonisation.[75] He reached the conclusion that the General Assembly did not always treat like cases alike. Musgrave's approach is rooted in the ICJ's observation, in the *Namibia* case, that developments in international law since the 1919 Covenant of the League of Nations have rendered the principle of self-determination applicable to all non-self-governing territories. Clearly, Musgrave believed that the principle of self-determination was applicable to all non-self-governing Territories as a result of the recognition that all colonial peoples are equal – a standpoint that has its origins in the Colonial Declaration. As a result, Musgrave found it difficult to accept the more nuanced approach adopted by the ICJ in the *Western Sahara* case, which recognised that the inhabitants of non-self-governing territories did not necessarily constitute a 'people' for the purpose of the exercise of the entitlement to self-determination.[76] Musgrave claimed that the cases of the Falklands and Gibraltar represent cogent examples of the General Assembly's inconsistent delivery of the right of self-determination and the implementation of the law of decolonisation. However, it is clear that Musgrave placed undue weight on the observation made by the ICJ in the *Namibia* case about the general significance of the principle of self-determination. The *Namibia* case was not directly concerned with the application of the principle of self-determination in relation to a non-self-governing territory; rather, it turned on the fact that obligations owed by South Africa in respect of the mandated territory of South West Africa. In that case, the ICJ was stressing the importance of the evolution of the principle of self-determination for the broader normative trajectory of international law. Consequently, this observation should be viewed as a general comment rather than a peremptory statement about the scope and application of the principle of self-determination in relation to all non-self-governing territories.

The General Assembly's refusal to accept the applicability of the right to self-determination in respect of non-self-governing territories that are, essentially, colonial plantations is comprehensible since it would enable the descendants of colonial settlers – the beneficiaries of colonialism – to become the beneficiaries of decolonisation as well, typically at the expense of other contiguous claimant groups. This approach views the right of self-determination as a corrective entitlement which was developed to bring about the emancipation of oppressed colonial peoples.[77] Consequently, the qualified application of the right to self-

---

[74] See J Crawford, 'The General Assembly, the International Court and Self-determination' in V Lowe and M Fitzmaurice (eds), *Fifty Years of the International Court of Justice: Essays in Honour of Sir Robert Jennings* (Cambridge, Grotius Publications, 1996) 585, 592. See ch 5.

[75] He focused particularly on the cases of the Falklands and Gibraltar. TD Musgrave, *Self-determination and National Minorities* (Oxford, Oxford University Press, 1994) 245–52.

[76] See the *Western Sahara Advisory Opinion* (n 8) [59].

[77] See Blay (n 9).

determination with regard to non-self-governing territories is understandable, despite the fact that the ethical reasons which underpin this approach were not articulated by the General Assembly.

Nevertheless, the argument that colonial self-determination is not an entitlement of the descendants of the colonialists is immaterial in situations where competing claims of self-determination are made by *different* societal groups that have both experienced colonialism. But even in cases where distinct colonial populations have made competing territorial claims the General Assembly has not always followed a consistent approach. The Assembly's decolonisation policy and practice was broadly consistent with the principles articulated in the Colonial Declaration and its implementation of the right of self-determination in concrete cases was remarkably successful. Notwithstanding this level of achievement, it is important to understand why the Assembly chose to depart from its general approach regarding the implementation of the right to colonial self-determination in a small, but significant, number of cases because it enables us to discern the weight that it attached to key considerations for the purpose of bringing about decolonisation. Accordingly, it is suggested that an examination of a range of difficult cases will help to give us a better grasp of the General Assembly's underlying policy preferences regarding the delivery of the right to self-determination in the colonial context. This enquiry may provide us with a more complete understanding of the reasons why the claims of some peoples were favoured while others were overlooked.

XI. THE CONCEPT OF A NON-SELF-GOVERNING TERRITORY

Beyond the exceptional category of mandated and trust territories, which were the product of a particular set of circumstances, the vast majority of colonial territories were classified, or liable to be classified, as non-self-governing territories. The General Assembly whittled away at the list of acknowledged non-self-governing territories in order to bring about decolonisation.[78] As noted previously, the UK government identified Mauritius and the Seychelles as distinct non-self-governing territories at the earliest opportunity and they both acceded to independence, in 1968 and 1976, respectively. In the context of Mauritius, the issue of whether Mauritius achieved independence as a result of the existence of a right to colonial self-determination, which the UK was bound to observe as a matter of customary international law, or whether it was granted by the UK in accordance with its own policy considerations was addressed in the last chapter. This section is not principally concerned with the normative content of the concept of a non-self-governing territory; instead, it explores the way that such a territory can be identified.[79]

---

[78] However, decolonisation was not achieved easily in all colonial territories and, in certain cases it was not forthcoming for a protracted period of time.

[79] The normative content of the concept of a non-self-governing territory was considered in ch 5.

Initially, the General Assembly was prepared to accept that the identification of those colonial territories to which Chapter XI of the UN Charter applied was a matter for the responsible colonial power.[80] However, over time, the General Assembly's policy on this issue changed in response to the intransigence of certain colonial powers. As a result, it began to elaborate the concept of a non-self-governing territory.[81] In particular, it re-examined the nature and scope of non-self-governing territories in resolution 1541(XV)(1960) in tandem with the adoption of the 1960 Colonial Declaration as part of its wider initiative to bring colonialism to a speedy end. The decision to review the essential components of a non-self-governing territory and to consolidate the options available for the achievement of full self-government was also prompted by persistent conceptual difficulties and by the refusal of Spain and Portugal to identify their colonial territories as non-self-governing on a voluntary basis, when they joined the United Nations in 1955. This resistance led to the adoption of resolution 1542(XV)(1960), in which the General Assembly resolved to identify Portugal's colonial territories as non-self-governing territories unilaterally. This act demonstrated that the General Assembly was prepared to identify non-self-governing territories by its own volition, at least as a measure of last resort. Further, the General Assembly maintained that decisions about whether decolonisation had been achieved in concrete cases were matters to be determined by the General Assembly acting in concert with the responsible colonial power.[82] Notwithstanding the General Assembly's strategy to arrogate to itself enough authority to classify a territory as non-self-governing and to decide when a territory ceases to have such a status, the central question for this section is how could decisions about whether a given territory constituted a non-self-governing territory be determined, in situations *other than* where the responsible colonial power or the General Assembly identified a particular colonial territory as non-self-governing? In other words, what was the correct position where the circumstances provide a compelling case for the recognition of a colonial territory as a non-self-governing territory pursuant to Chapter XI of the UN Charter but the General Assembly refused to recognise it as such?

There have been a number of controversial cases concerning the entitlement to the maintenance of established colonial boundaries in the event of decolonisation where the General Assembly struggled with the issue of whether a given colonial territory qualified as a non-self-governing territory. This chapter will examine two such cases – the case of West New Guinea, which is now part of Indonesia, and the case of the Island of Mayotte, which is located in the Comoros Archipelago. The case of West New Guinea is enlightening because it tested the concept of a non-self-governing territory, the strength of claims for the restoration of historical sovereignty in the colonial context and the General Assembly's view of the presumptive entitlements of a post-colonial State during

---

[80] See ch 5.
[81] See eg UNGA Res 742(VIII)(1953), discussed in ch 5.
[82] Crawford (n 10) 622–23.

the height of the period of decolonisation. The case of Mayotte is also instructive because it raises the question of whether processes of democratic decision-making can validate an act of colonial territorial dismemberment. Further, it also provides a useful context in which to study the nature and scope of the concept of people-hood for the purpose of exercising the right to colonial self-determination. These case studies prompt consideration of the issue of whether the BIOT constitutes a non-self-governing territory as a matter of international law; the implications that the recognition of such a status would have for the Mauritian sovereignty claim over the Chagos Islands; and for the international legal obligations that the UK would owe to the exiled inhabitants of the BIOT, if such a status could be established.

There are valid cases when an established colonial unit has been lawfully dismembered pursuant to the process of decolonisation.[83] Such exceptions are permissible, according to the provisions of General Assembly resolution 1541(XV)(1960), where they represent an outcome that has been agreed by the representatives of the affected populations and confirmed by legitimate democratic processes involving the populations in question.[84] However, the disruption of an established colonial unit on the eve of the exercise of the right of colonial self-determination could only occur in highly exceptional circumstances and it can only be justified by the willingness of the affected populations and of all the States involved – including the withdrawing colonial power – to agree to such a course of action. However, it should be noted that compliance with the democratic process is not necessarily a prerequisite for the achievement of independence in the colonial context. In the *Western Sahara* case, the ICJ observed that the UN General Assembly had dispensed with the practice of consulting the affected populations pursuant to the exercise of the right to self-determination where exceptional circumstances justified such an approach.[85] Nevertheless, the ICJ noted that, General Assembly resolution 1541 provides that such a practice was mandatory in relation to a people's decision to integrate or to associate with an independent State.[86]

The orthodox approach to colonial self-determination favoured the maintenance of the territorial integrity of colonial units and the principle of *uti possidetis juris* at the expense of a more nuanced approach to the application of

---

[83] Cases where the principle of *uti possidetis* was not applied could be seen as indicative of the continuing importance of consent in relation to territorial units established on independence. Such cases included the British Cameroons, British Togoland and Rwanda-Urundi. However, the decision to address the question of territorial partition in these cases was determined by the UN acting in concert with the concerned colonial power rather than by the affected nascent African political entities. See GAR 944(X), 15 December 1955 (British Togoland); GAR 1350(XIII) 13 May 1959 (British Cameroons); and UNGAR 1580(XV), 20 December 1960 (Rwanda-Urundi).

[84] Crawford (n 10) 336, believes that partition may be appropriate in order to give effect to the wishes of the people concerned or to ensure international peace and security. See the partition that has occurred in small archipelagos such as the Gilbert and Ellice Islands and the Marshall Islands. See Musgrave, *Self-determination and National Minorities* (n 75) 186–87.

[85] See *Western Sahara* (n 8) [59].

[86] See principles VII and IX, UNGA Res 1541(XV) and the *Western Sahara* case (n 8) [57].

the right to self-determination. By endorsing the continuity of colonial territorial frameworks, the principle of *uti possidetis juris* was widely seen as a significant constraint on the exercise of the right to self-determination since colonial boundaries were typically drawn with little regard to the political, ethnic and cultural cleavages that had previously divided colonial peoples. As noted above, it has been widely claimed that administering States were not permitted to dismember non-self-governing territories prior to their independence since such acts would violate the territorial integrity of colonial self-determination units. Further, it has been argued that 'colonial enclaves' cannot constitute separate units for the purpose of the exercise of the right to self-determination.[87] In this regard, international law appears to condone the assertion, made by certain post-colonial States, that inhabitants of such enclaves constituted part of a wider unit for the purposes of self-determination, which the vestiges of colonialism have prevented from being reintegrated into the pre-colonial unit.[88] In general, the international community of States, acting through the General Assembly, has been reluctant to accept the fragmentation of former colonial units, invariably perceiving State nationalism to be the answer to the challenges of decolonisation.[89] Many States remain mindful of the potential ramifications of condoning the sub-division of territorial units for their own territories.[90] Developing States, in particular, remain deeply wedded to the notion of nation-building and European colonialism remains an emotive issue for them. Consequently, post-colonial political elites have been more concerned with casting off its remnants than assessing the legitimacy of countervailing self-determination claims made by non-European peoples.

XII. THE CASE OF WEST NEW GUINEA

A useful case study is the sovereignty dispute between the Netherlands and Indonesia in respect of the colonial territory of West New Guinea (or West Irian, the preferred Indonesian term) or Netherlands New Guinea (the Dutch colonial designation) between 1954 and 1962. The colonial unit which acceded to independence as the State of Indonesia was administered by the Netherlands. Indonesia was voluntarily identified as a non-self-governing territory by the Netherlands and it was listed as such in General Assembly resolution I(66) (1946).

---

[87] Blay (n 9), and see also Franck and Hoffman, 'The Right of Self-Determination in Very Small Places' (n 10).

[88] However, statements made at the 987th and 988th meetings of the UN Security Council (XVI), 18 December 1961 indicate that such claims are controversial. See DJ Harris, *Cases and Materials on International Law*, 6th edn (London, Sweet and Maxwell, 2004) 220–23; and Q Wright, 'The Goa Incident' (1962) 56 *American Journal of International Law* 617.

[89] See J Castellino and S Allen, *Title to Territory in International Law: A Temporal Analysis* (Aldershot, Ashgate, 2003).

[90] Established States are concerned about the re-emergence of the 'Belgian Thesis', which asserted that the concept of non-self-governing territories should not be restricted to the colonial context.

A. Historical Background

Portuguese mariners and traders established a loose presence in the South Moluccans, an archipelago consisting of about 150 islands in the eastern part of modern day Indonesia. During the seventeenth century, the Dutch East India Company replaced Portuguese traders as the interested colonial power. However, as the Dutch interest was limited to key commercial activities,[91] its authority remained tenuous in much of the East Indies throughout most of the colonial era.[92] The Sultanate of Tidore, situated in the South Moluccans, exercised authority over West New Guinea prior to the arrival of European colonialism.[93] The Dutch established a protectorate over the Sultan's territory during the seventeenth century.[94] In 1848, the Netherlands claimed the western part of the island of New Guinea. It annexed all the territory to the west of the 141 degree east meridian line and incorporated the territory of 'Netherlands New Guinea' into the Dutch East Indies.[95] The Netherlands was primarily interested in acquiring West New Guinea for its abundant natural resources, for potential trading opportunities with local populations and in order to protect its sphere of influence from other competing European colonial powers. Nevertheless, as the interior of West New Guinea comprises dense forests and high mountain ranges, it remained largely untouched by Dutch colonialism and Dutch authority was largely restricted to the coastal areas.[96]

The eastern part of the island of New Guinea, which is now Papua New Guinea, remained unclaimed by European colonial powers until the late-nineteenth century. Expeditions in this region had been undertaken by British explorers but the UK government maintained the view that its colonial responsibilities were already considerable and it had no appetite to extend its colonial reach during this period. However, during the early 1880s, the colonial government of Queensland, Australia, became increasingly anxious about the prospect of a German claim being made to part, or all, of eastern New Guinea. Consequently, in 1883, the Premier of Queensland authorised the annexation of eastern New Guinea on behalf of the UK. However, the UK refused to endorse this claim. Germany subsequently established a protectorate over the north-eastern part of New Guinea in 1884 and it ultimately annexed the territory, which became part of German New Guinea. The UK government changed its policy in response to Germany's actions. In 1884, it authorised the setting up of

---

[91] The Dutch East Indies were historically known as the 'Spice Islands'. See K Suter, *East Timor and West Irian* (London, Minority Group, 1982) 5.

[92] The Dutch East India Company was wound up in 1800 and the Netherlands took over the responsibility of running the Dutch East Indies from that time until the Second World War.

[93] The island of New Guinea is located approximately 100 miles from the South Moluccans at the eastern extremity of modern day Indonesia; Suter, *East Timor and West Irian* (n 91) 9–10.

[94] ibid, 11.

[95] ibid, 10.

[96] ibid, 11.

a British protectorate in respect of the south-eastern part of New Guinea, which was formally annexed as British New Guinea in 1888.[97]

In 1942, Japanese military forces occupied the Dutch East Indies. Indonesia proclaimed its independence on 17 August 1945, at the end of the Second World War. However, the Netherlands refused to recognise the new State and it sought to reclaim the territory, by a variety of means including the use of force, which ultimately proved unsuccessful and resulted in considerable criticism from the international community. Negotiations were held at The Hague with a view to establishing the terms of the transfer of sovereignty of the Dutch East Indies to Indonesia.[98] In the bilateral 1949 Charter of Transfer of Sovereignty, it was agreed that the Netherlands would transfer sovereignty over the Dutch East Indies to Indonesia.[99] However, it was also agreed that the question of the status of West New Guinea would be left open to resolution by negotiation. Consequently, this territory was not included in the transfer of the Dutch East Indies, which was effected on 27 December 1949. Indonesia subsequently asserted that it should succeed to all the territory that comprised the Dutch East Indies as this constituted the territory of the established colonial unit, a territorial unit, which included the territory of Netherlands New Guinea. Negotiations between Indonesia and the Netherlands regarding the status of West New Guinea proved unsuccessful and Indonesia mounted a limited military campaign to seize West New Guinea by the use of force, which ended in failure. The battle at the United Nations was fought tenaciously between 1954 and 1961 and it is that contest which is instructive for the Mauritian–UK dispute regarding the status of the Chagos Islands.

B. The Battles in the UN General Assembly (1954–61)

In 1954, Indonesia took the dispute over the status of West New Guinea to the UN General Assembly. In a bid to get the dispute over West New Guinea (West Irian) on the agenda for the UN General Assembly's ninth session it claimed to the General Committee that:

> West Irian is and always has been – historically as well as constitutionally (legally) – an integral part of the territory of Indonesia; that is to say, also, of the former Netherlands East Indies. [100]

---

[97] The British protectorate was established on the understanding that the costs of running the territory would be met by the Australian colonies. In 1902, colonial responsibility for British New Guinea was transferred to the newly created dominion of Australia, an arrangement which was formalised by the 1905 Papua Act. Australian military forces seized German New Guinea at the outset of the First World War. The territory was subsequently annexed by Australia and this was recognised in the 1919 Versailles Treaty. Papua New Guinea acceded to independence in 1975; ibid, 10–11.

[98] See Rigo Sureda, *The Evolution of the Right of Self-Determination* (n 10) 144.

[99] 69 UNTS 3, and see Rigo Sureda (n 10) app C.

[100] A/2694, General Committee meeting, 9th session 1954, quoted by Rigo Sureda (n 10) 143. This argument is consistent with the doctrine of *uti possidetis juris* as it evolved in relation to 'Third

The matter was placed on the General Assembly's agenda for the ninth session and it was debated during the meetings of the First Committee in 1954.[101] Within this forum, the Netherlands contended that it remained the responsible sovereign authority for Netherlands New Guinea.[102] Further, it claimed that this territory constituted a distinct non-self-governing territory as a matter of international law and it declared its commitment to fostering the conditions necessary to ensure that the Territory's inhabitants would have the chance to achieve full self-government in accordance with the provisions of Chapter XI of the UN Charter. Nevertheless, Indonesia put forward a draft resolution at the ninth session. In effect, it demanded the return of West New Guinea as a means of achieving national reunification. In response, the Dutch representative objected to the discussion of the status of Netherlands New Guinea in the General Assembly on the ground that it lacked the competence to discuss conditions prevailing in a non-self-governing territory.[103] In any event, the Indonesian draft resolution failed to attract enough support in the General Assembly to warrant adoption. The General Assembly was stymied by the fact that, while the Indonesian position attracted significant support from developing States, the Netherlands could rely on the support of Western governments during this period.[104] In addition, there was a degree of uncertainty within General Assembly concerning the scope of its authority to involve itself in political disputes that concerned non-self-governing territories at this time. Consequently, although UN member States had no qualms about discussing the status of West New Guinea in the crucible of the General Assembly they were reluctant to act decisively on such a complex and sensitive issue during this period. In this respect, it is important to remember that the West New Guinea question first came to the attention of the General Assembly in the period before the right to colonial self-determination had been proclaimed.

The status of West New Guinea was, again, the subject of debate in the General Assembly in 1957.[105] The Indonesian representative maintained that Indonesia was simply trying to unify its national territory by seeking to prevent the amputation of West New Guinea.[106] He also insisted that the return of West

World' decolonisation in the 1960s. However, the principle was not raised by Indonesia in this context.

[101] GAOR 9th session, First Committee. The First Committee is concerned with issues affecting international security.

[102] GAOR 9th session, First Committee, 726 meeting [60–64]; see Rigo Sureda (n 10) 77–78. The sovereignty argument is addressed below.

[103] The general standpoint that the General Assembly did not have the authority to interfere in matters concerning non-self-governing territories was consistently maintained by the European colonial powers throughout the 1950s by reference to the domestic jurisdiction argument. See GAOR 9th session (1954), 509th plenary meeting [106–08]; see Rigo Sureda (n 10) 77–78. See ch 5.

[104] See A Cassese, *Self-Determination of Peoples: A Legal Reappraisal* (Cambridge, Cambridge University Press, 1995) 82 and Rigo Sureda (n 10) 149–50.

[105] See United Nations Yearbook 1957, 76–79 cited in Cassese, *Self-Determination of Peoples* (n 104) 82–83.

[106] United Nations Yearbook 1957, 77 cited in Cassese (n 104) 82.

New Guinea to Indonesia would promote regional peace and stability. The Dutch representative reiterated that West New Guinea constituted a distinct non-self-governing territory and that the Dutch government was bound by the obligations contained in Chapter XI of the UN Charter in relation to this Territory.[107] Accordingly, it argued that the issue of whether West New Guinea should be integrated into Indonesia, or not, would be decided by the people of West New Guinea themselves and it reaffirmed that the Netherlands would not transfer the Territory to Indonesia in the absence of a process of democratic decision-making which would establish whether the inhabitants of West New Guinea, in fact, wished to integrate with Indonesia.[108] However, once again, the debate in the General Assembly failed to reach a consensus between member States and no resolution concerning this issue was adopted on that occasion.

In 1961, the Netherlands tabled a draft resolution concerning the status of West New Guinea at the General Assembly.[109] It was inspired by the twin developments that had just occurred in the General Assembly: the adoption of the 1960 Colonial Declaration, which set out the principles by which the General Assembly sought to bring a speedy end to colonialism; and resolution 1541(XV) (1960) which elaborated the concept of a non-self-governing territory and the way that such territories could achieve full self-government.[110] Against this background, the Netherlands proposed a draft resolution that would provide for the holding of a plebiscite in West New Guinea to determine the wishes of the inhabitants of this territory. However, Indonesia objected to the draft resolution on the basis that it amounted to an attempt to partition the national territory of Indonesia. Indeed, during the General Assembly's fifteenth session, the session in which resolution 1514 and resolution 1541 were adopted, the Indonesian representative harnessed the terms of paragraphs 4, 6 and 7 of the Colonial Declaration in support of the view that:

> the integrity of the national territory of peoples which have retained independence shall be respected. This is a rejection of colonial activities which create disputes such as that of West Irian between Indonesia and the Netherlands.[111]

Further, he claimed that: 'the Dutch are perverting this right of self-determination into a justification for an amputation of Indonesian sovereign territory'.[112] At this juncture, it is evident that both sides were anxious to use the language of self-determination to their own advantage. The Dutch draft resolution failed to attract sufficient support from the UN membership and, as a result, it was withdrawn. Certain member States were reluctant to support the proposed resolution because they believed that the adoption of such a resolution would be

---

[107] United Nations Yearbook 1957, 77–78 cited in Cassese (n 104) 82–83.
[108] United Nations Yearbook 1957, 77–78 cited in Cassese (n 104) 83.
[109] UN Doc A/4915, cited in Rigo Sureda (n 10) 145.
[110] See ch 5.
[111] GAOR 15th session (1960), 963rd plenary meeting [55]. The terms of paras 4, 6 and 7 of the Colonial Declaration are set out in ch 5.
[112] GAOR 15th session (1960), 963rd plenary meeting [44].

tantamount to a judgement on Indonesia's claim to West New Guinea.[113] By failing to support either the 1961 Dutch initiative or the 1954 Indonesian draft resolution, it would appear as though the General Assembly was seeking to avoid endorsing the sovereignty claim of either State. However, as will be discussed below, the General Assembly found a way to support the Indonesian claim to West New Guinea in the end.

C. Dutch Resignation and the 1962 New York Agreement

In 1962, at the General Assembly's seventeenth session, the Dutch representative expressed the Dutch predicament in West New Guinea when he said that:

> the Netherlands was faced with the choice between fighting in self-defence [in response to the use of force in the territory by Indonesia] or resigning itself to transfer of the territory to Indonesia without a previous expression of the will of the population. War would have meant exposing the Papuans and their country to death and destruction and many Dutchmen and Indonesians to the horrors of combat – without even providing a sensible solution to the problem. And with a heavy heart, the Netherlands Government decided to agree to the transfer of the territory to Indonesia on the best conditions obtainable for the Papuan population.[114]

In 1962, the US government brokered an agreement between the Netherlands and Indonesia – the New York Agreement – by which West New Guinea was to be transferred from Dutch sovereignty to a UN Temporary Executive Authority (UNTEA).[115] UNTEA handed the territory over to Indonesia on 1 May 1963, pending the holding of a plebiscite to gauge whether the inhabitants of West New Guinea wished to integrate with Indonesia or not. The 'Act of Free Choice' provided for in the 1962 New York Agreement, was conducted by the Indonesian authorities in 1969, with very limited UN oversight.[116] The outcome – that the inhabitants of West New Guinea decided to integrate with Indonesia – was noted by the General Assembly in resolution 2504(XXIV)(1969), which was adopted on 19 November 1969.[117]

However, this exercise amounted to a purported act of self-determination after the fact. In principle, the moment for the genuine exercise of this entitlement should have been while UNTEA exercised authority over West New Guinea rather than after the territory had been handed over to Indonesian

---

[113] See the views of Sudan and India expressed in GAOR 16th session during the 1065th plenary meeting; see Rigo Sureda (n 10) 150.

[114] GAOR 17th session, 1127th plenary meeting, 21 September 1962, at 51. And see Cassese (n 104) 86

[115] The New York Agreement was concluded on 15 August 1962, 437 UNTS 292. See the 1962 UN Yearbook, at 124–27, cited in Cassese (n 104) 84–85. The New York Agreement was noted by the General Assembly in UNGA Res 1752(XVII)(1962) 21 September 1962. The resolution expressed the view that the sovereignty dispute concerning West New Guinea had been resolved.

[116] See Cassese (n 104) 84–85.

[117] The voting record showed that there were 30 abstentions with no negative votes.

sovereignty. Moreover, the choice – whether to remain part of Indonesia or to sever ties with Indonesia – was heavily circumscribed and not in conformity with the options which should have been afforded to the inhabitants of a non-self-governing territory in accordance with the provisions of resolution 1541(XV)(1960).[118] Further, the electoral processes that were used to bring about this outcome were heavily criticised by commentators. In particular, the Indonesian authorities were not prepared to use democratic voting procedures for the purpose of divining the will of the inhabitants of West New Guinea; instead, they used a traditional Indonesian method of indirect consultation (the *musjawarah* system).[119] Commentators castigated the 'Act of Free Choice', as a 'farce',[120] and a 'betrayal of the principle of self-determination'.[121] This process was of dubious validity and legitimacy at the level of principle and in practice. Indeed, in the period leading up to the adoption of resolution 2504(XXIV) (1969), Szudek expressed the fear that the good name of the United Nations would be tarnished by its involvement in this flawed process. In particular, he suggested that:

> It may be better for the UN mission to withdraw rather than to sanction the illegal procedure [. . .] Otherwise an extremely dangerous precedent may be created by the UN in becoming an accessory to the denial of freedom and persecution of a nation which has the same right to independence as all those freed under the law (sic) of the UN Declaration on Decolonization.[122]

Rigo-Sureda's assessment of the way in which the General Assembly dealt with the West New Guinea question is particularly enlightening. First, commenting on Indonesia's claim to West New Guinea, he observed that the Indonesian government was prepared to accept the constituent validity of the Dutch East Indies as a colonial unit for the purpose of State succession.[123] Secondly, Rigo-Sureda noted that Indonesia's claim to West New Guinea was premised on the assumption that, at some point prior to the formal accession to independence, the colonial unit of the Dutch East Indies acquired international status to such an extent that the administering State was prevented from making material changes to its territorial parameters. In this context, Rigo-Sureda asked, when does a colonial authority lose the power to alter the territorial scope of an established colonial unit for which it is responsible? In an attempt to answer this question, he reviewed the discussion of the issue of West New Guinea during the 1954

---

[118]   See Cassese (n 104) 84.

[119]   See the report of the UN Secretary-General Concerning the Act of Self-determination in West Irian, GAOR 24th session, Agenda Item 98, UN Doc A//7723, 6 November 1969, cited in Cassese, (n 104) 85.

[120]   Suter (n 91) 11.

[121]   See Cassese (n 104) 86, referring to T Franck, *Nation Against Nation* (New York, Oxford University Press, 1985) 76–81.

[122]   PA Szudek, 'Crisis in West Papua', *New World* (London, UN Association, 1969) quoted in Suter (n 91) 11.

[123]   Although he does not use the term *uti possidetis juris* this is a clear example of the application of this principle of decolonisation.

debates in the First Committee of the General Assembly regarding the claim, advanced by the Netherlands, that Netherlands New Guinea constituted a distinct non-self-governing territory.

Three arguments were advanced during this discussion of the international status of West New Guinea: (i) the sovereign authority argument; (ii) the administrative argument; and (iii) the ethnic/cultural argument.[124] The consideration of the status of West New Guinea prompted a wider discussion by member States within that forum about whether a colonial unit could be dismembered lawfully prior to the achievement of independence by the inhabitants of that colonial territory. Before considering the views expressed by States during the relevant meetings of the First Committee during the General Assembly's ninth session in 1954, it is worth remembering that this matter was discussed prior to the widespread acceptance of the applicability of the principle of self-determination in the colonial context and before the adoption of the ground-breaking Colonial Declaration in 1960.

D. The Administrative Argument

There was some evidence that the Dutch colonial authorities had given Netherlands New Guinea a distinct administrative status within the Dutch East Indies.[125] However, the territory had not been constituted as a separate colonial unit. Notwithstanding the absence of an observable demarcation between Netherlands New Guinea and the Dutch East Indies, the Netherlands representative argued that both the Dutch East Indies and Netherlands New Guinea were administered from Batavia, the capital city of the Dutch East Indies, for the sake of administrative convenience rather than because the Dutch colonial authorities regarded them as being part of the same colonial unit. In response, the Indian representative observed that the British colonial authorities had administered India, Pakistan and Burma from New Delhi until 1937, when Burma gained its independence by an Act of the UK Parliament.[126] The Indian representative used this example of colonial administrative organisation as a way of questioning the significance of the location of an administrative centre for the identification of the parameters of an established colonial unit. The representatives of those States which participated in the 1954 discussions about the status of West New Guinea sought to establish whether there was any evidence that the Dutch colonial authorities had undertaken any municipal legal act that was indicative of the existence of a constitutional separation between the Dutch East Indies and Netherlands New Guinea. The representative of the Netherlands government could point to no such comparable act. Accordingly, the First

---

[124] These three pivotal arguments subsequently played a role in discussions within the General Assembly regarding the status of the BIOT and also the Mayotte question. See below.

[125] Rigo Sureda (n 10) 146.

[126] ibid, 147.

Committee was not persuaded by the Dutch claim that Netherlands New Guinea had an international status that was distinct from that of the former Dutch East Indies.

E. The Sovereignty Argument

The argument on the question of which State exercised sovereignty authority in respect of West New Guinea after 1949 turned on competing interpretations of the final paragraph of Article 2 of the 1949 Charter of Transfer of Sovereignty, which provided that:

> The status quo of the residency of New Guinea shall be maintained with the stipulation that within a year from the date of the transfer of sovereignty to the Republic of the United States of Indonesia the question of the political status of New Guinea be determined through negotiations between Indonesia and the Netherlands.[127]

The Netherlands argued that Article 2 of the 1949 treaty provided for the maintenance of the status quo regarding West New Guinea. It had previously stated, in an exchange of letters pursuant to the process of drafting the treaty, that:

> the clause in Article 2 of the Draft Charter of Transfer of Sovereignty reading: 'the status quo of the residency of New Guinea shall be maintained' means 'through continuing under the government of the Netherlands'.[128]

In sharp contrast, Indonesia claimed that it was the legitimate successor to the entire territory of the former Dutch East Indies.[129] In particular, it argued that the Netherlands had not exercised sovereignty of West New Guinea since 1949; rather, it had temporary administrative authority in respect of that territory pending its transfer to Indonesia. In the Indonesian government's view, West New Guinea was a component part of the Indonesian State and this had been the case since it acceded to independence on 17 August 1945. Specifically, it claimed that:

> when the people of Indonesia had proclaimed their independence on 17 August 1945, they had set up an independent Republic comprising the former Netherlands East Indies territories.[130]

According to Indonesia, all that remained to be done after the coming into effect of the 1949 Charter of Transfer of Sovereignty was for the former colonial power to hand over the de facto administration of this territory to the successor State, Indonesia. However, it is notable that Indonesia's position does not

---

[127] ibid, 144.
[128] This exchange of letters was included in the 1949 Treaty, app XXIX, quoted, ibid.
[129] It made this sovereignty claim to the General Assembly's General Committee in 1954 in a bid to get the matter on the agenda for the 9th session.
[130] GAOR 9th session, First Committee, 726th meeting [10–11], cited in Rigo Sureda (n 10) 143–44.

appear to accept that sovereignty over the Dutch East Indies had been trans-ferred to Indonesia by the 1949 treaty; instead, it seems to have assumed that 1945 was the de jure date at which Indonesia succeeded to the Dutch East Indies, which included the territory of West New Guinea. However, the better view is that the Netherlands continued to exercise sovereign authority over West New Guinea after sovereignty over the Dutch East Indies had been transferred to Indonesia as a matter of international law and this interpretation was sup-ported by the *travaux* of Article 2 of the 1949 treaty. Further, it is notable that, in 1954 at least, the Netherlands maintained that it could exercise sovereignty over West New Guinea indefinitely.[131] But while the ICJ observed, in the *Western Sahara* case, that an administering State possesses sovereign authority over a non-self-governing territory for which it is responsible,[132] it is also worth point-ing out that such authority is qualified in relation to such territories by virtue of the colonial entitlement to self-determination.[133] This raises the question of whether Netherlands New Guinea constituted a non-self-governing territory during the relevant period. Despite the argument that Netherlands New Guinea constituted a non-self-governing territory after 1949, when it had transferred sovereignty to the Dutch East Indies to Indonesia, it is apparent that the Netherlands made no attempt to identify the territory as non-self-governing with the UN General Assembly, or the UN Secretary-General, for the purpose of complying with its reporting obligations under Article 73(e) of the UN Charter. In such circumstances, it is difficult to avoid the conclusion that Netherlands New Guinea did not constitute a non-self-governing territory in the absence of either: (i) any recognition of the separate constitutional status of Netherlands New Guinea from the Dutch East Indies as a matter of Dutch colo-nial law; or (ii) the formal identification of Netherlands New Guinea as a non-self-governing territory by the Dutch government pursuant to Article 73(e); or (iii) any determination by the General Assembly that Netherlands New Guinea qualified as a non-self-governing territory for the purposes of Chapter XI of the UN Charter.

F. The Ethnic/Cultural Argument

During the discussion of the West New Guinea question in the First Committee of the General Assembly during the ninth session in 1954, the Netherlands contended that the people of West New Guinea were ethnically distinct from the inhabitants of Indonesia.[134] The inhabitants of this territory were pre-dominately Papuans and their cultural practices exhibited a high degree of differentiation from those cultural practices maintained by the Indonesian

---

[131] ibid, 144.
[132] *Western Sahara Advisory Opinion* (n 8) [43].
[133] Crawford (n 10) 613–15. See also Cassese (n 104) 187.
[134] See Rigo Sureda (n 10) 148–49.

population.[135] However, in response, Indonesia advanced a political conception of nationality. In particular, the Indonesian representative argued that ethnic and/or cultural differences were irrelevant to the determination of nationality; instead, he asserted that Indonesian nationality was conferred on all those persons who resided in the territory which was formerly part of the Dutch East Indies.[136]

Rigo Sureda was highly critical of the General Assembly's decision to approve the 1962 New York Agreement, which provided for the transfer of West New Guinea from Dutch sovereignty to UNTEA with a view to transferring it to Indonesia shortly thereafter. He argued that the General Assembly should have examined the issue of whether West New Guinea was a non-self-governing territory by reference to the conditions set out in resolution 742(VIII)(1953) and resolution 1541(XV)(1960) rather than simply condoning the transfer of the territory to Indonesia with the caveat that Indonesia must hold a plebiscite in order to determine the wishes of the inhabitants of West New Guinea within a set time-frame. Specifically, Rigo Sureda observed that:

> the failure of the General Assembly to determine whether West Irian was a Non-Self-Governing Territory or not after the settlement of territorial claims can be interpreted as an implied acceptance of the Indonesian view that the territory was part of Indonesia.[137]

Moreover, as the General Assembly was prepared to assume that West New Guinea was an integral part of Indonesia, there was clearly no need to comply with the established modalities regarding the exercise of the right to self-determination (independence, integration and association).[138] In the end, the General Assembly was unwilling to recognise that West New Guinea constituted a distinct and separate non-self-governing territory for the purposes of decolonisation. Consequently, it was not prepared to accept that the inhabitants of West New Guinea possessed the right of colonial self-determination as a matter of international law.

XIII. THE MAYOTTE QUESTION

Mayotte is a small island in the Comoro Archipelago, which is situated between Madagascar and East Africa.[139] France established a protectorate over Mayotte in 1843. In 1886, the protectorate was extended to incorporate the three other main islands in the Archipelago: Grande Comore, Anjouan and Moheli. The Comoro Archipelago was subsequently annexed by France and it was categorised as a territory *outré-mer*. The Comoros Islands remained a somewhat

---

[135]   Suter (n 91) 12.
[136]   See Rigo Sureda (n 10) 149.
[137]   Rigo Sureda (n 10) 151.
[138]   However, this leaves open the question of how one can explain the 1969 'Act of Free Choice'.
[139]   Mayotte has a land mass of 376 square kms.

neglected Overseas Territory. It was overlooked as a potential candidate for independence in the first wave of African decolonisation during the 1960s. Given the Archipelago's lack of natural resources, the French government thought that it would remain a poor French colony indefinitely. Nonetheless, during the early 1970s, a fledgling Comorian independence movement began to coalesce on the islands of Grande Comore, Anjouan and Moheli. In 1973, the Comorian Local Assembly, which was composed of representatives from the four Comorian islands, voted in favour of the idea of Comorian independence.[140] However, the representatives of the inhabitants of Mayotte – the Mahorais – objected to this development. Despite this opposition, the President of the Governing Council of the Comoro Archipelago and the French government reached an agreement regarding the Accession to Independence of the Comoro Archipelago on 15 June 1973. The UN General Assembly was quick to support this course of action. In resolution 3161 (XXVII)(1973), it called upon France to facilitate the exercise of the Comorian people's right to self-determination by ensuring the Archipelago's accession to independence.[141] To that end, in paragraph 6 of the 1973 resolution, the General Assembly implored the French government to hold a referendum so that this outcome could be achieved by the freely expressed wishes of the inhabitants of the entire Archipelago. Moreover, the General Assembly, took the preventative measures of both 'affirming the unity and territorial integrity of the Comoro Archipelago' (paragraph 4) and requesting that the administering State ensure the preservation of the same (paragraph 5). Clearly, the General Assembly had foreseen that the declared opposition to independence by the Mayotte representatives in the Comorian Local Assembly could generate problems for the future status of the Comoros Archipelago. Further, the General Assembly sought to harness the French government's previously declared commitment 'to respond faithfully to the aspirations' of the Comorians in this context (paragraph 3).[142]

The French government arranged for a plebiscite of the Comoro Archipelago to be held on 22 December 1974. The result was that 95 per cent of the Archipelago's population voted in favour of independence. However, 64 per cent of the inhabitants of Mayotte voted against independence. This outcome left the French government in a predicament. Mayotte held no attraction for France. The island was not of any strategic value, it lacked natural resources and its population was heavily dependent on French aid.[143] Nevertheless, the French

---

[140] The Local Assembly was located in the capital city of the Comoros Archipelago on Grande Comore. However, before 1962, the Territory's capital was situated on Mayotte. See Aldrich and Connell, *The Last Colonies* (n 47) 229.

[141] UNGA Res 3161(XXVII)(1973), para 1 reaffirmed: 'the inalienable right of the people of the Comoro Archipelago to self-determination and independence in accordance with General Assembly resolution 1514(XV)'.

[142] The General Assembly reiterated its standpoint in UNGA Res 3291(XXIX) on 13 December 1974 and it welcomed the plebiscite which was scheduled to be held on 22 December 1974 regarding the status of the Territory.

[143] Aldrich and Connell (n 47) 229.

government felt that it could not ignore the democratically expressed wishes of the Mahorais, as this constituted an act of self-determination in itself. Accordingly, in a statement subsequently made to the General Assembly, the representative of the French government maintained that: 'France seeks no advantage for itself in this matter. It is always willing to grant independence to peoples that desire it, but it cannot oppose the self-determination of peoples'.[144] As a result, on 3 July 1975, the French National Assembly enacted a law which provided that the Comoro Archipelago would be granted independence after a suitable constitution had been drafted and on the condition that each of the Comorian islands was prepared to adopt it. However, the Comorian political leadership were unwilling to wait, or to acquiesce in, any French constitutional measures that would delay independence or place conditions upon it.[145] On 6 July 1975, the Comorian leadership made a unilateral declaration of independence and the Islamic Federal Republic of the Comoros was established. The new State claimed to be the successor to the whole territory of this French non-self-governing territory.

The Comoros applied for UN membership and the General Assembly resolved to admit the Republic of the Comoros to membership of the United Nations via resolution 3385(XXX)(1975), on 12 November 1975. In this resolution, the General Assembly emphasised, 'the necessity of respecting the unity and territorial integrity of the Comoros Archipelago, composed of Anjouan, Grande Comore, Mayotte and Moheli'. The question of the Comorian island of Mayotte attracted considerable attention during the plenary session of the General Assembly at which resolution 3385 was adopted. Many of the representatives of member States which made statements during that meeting were highly critical of the failure of the French government to respect the clearly expressed will of the Comorian people.[146] In this forum, the French representative announced that the French government was making preparations to afford the inhabitants of Mayotte another opportunity to choose whether to belong to an independent Comoros or to remain part of France.[147] To this end, the French National Assembly passed a law on 31 December 1975, which declared that Anjouan, Grande Comore and Moheli were no longer part of the French Republic.[148] Further, it approved for arrangements to be made for the inhabitants of Mayotte to be consulted about whether they wished to join the Comoros or to remain part of France.[149] A referendum was subsequently held in Mayotte on 8 February 1976. The result was that 99 per cent of the island's population voted in favour of remaining part of France. Further, in a second referendum held on 11 April 1976, 80 per cent of the Mahorais expressed the desire to

---

[144] GAOR 2402nd plenary meeting, 12 November 1975, A/PV2402, 815 [6].
[145] It is notable that this position is in accordance with the terms of para 5 of the Colonial Declaration.
[146] See n 144.
[147] ibid, [5].
[148] Musgrave (n 75) 184.
[149] ibid, 185.

become a French Overseas Department.[150] However, the French authorities decided to defer any decision regarding the final status of Mayotte within the French constitutional framework for the time being. Nevertheless, as a result of these referenda Mayotte was classified as a French *collectivité territoriale*.[151]

In these circumstances, the new Comorian State sought to garner international support for its demand that France respect the national unity and territorial integrity of the Comoros Archipelago by ceding sovereignty over Mayotte to the Republic the Comoros with immediate effect. Both the UN General Assembly and the OAU rallied to its cause. In resolution 31/4(1976), 21 October 1976, the General Assembly's criticism of France's conduct in respect of Mayotte was scathing.[152] It is worth quoting from the resolution at length:

31/4. Question of the Comorian island of Mayotte

The General Assembly,

Recalling that the people of the Republic of the Comoros as a whole, in the referendum of 22 December 1974, expressed by an overwhelming majority its will to accede to independence in conditions of political unity and territorial integrity,

Considering that the referendums imposed on the inhabitants of the Comorian island of Mayotte constitute a violation of the sovereignty of the Comorian State and of its territorial integrity,

Considering that the occupation by France of the Comorian island of Mayotte constitutes a flagrant encroachment on the national unity of the Comorian State, a Member of the United Nations,

Considering that such an attitude on the part of France constitutes a violation of the principles of the relevant resolutions of the United Nations, in particular of General Assembly resolution 1514 (XV) of 14 December 1960 concerning the granting of independence to colonial countries and peoples, which guarantees the national unity and territorial integrity of such countries,

1. Condemns and considers null and void the referendums of 8 February and 11 April 1976 organized in the Comorian island of Mayotte by the Government of France, and rejects:

   (a) Any other form of referendum or consultation which may hereafter be organized on Comorian territory in Mayotte by France;
   (b) Any foreign legislation purporting to legalize any French colonial presence on Comorian territory in Mayotte;

[150] See Aldrich and Connell (n 47) 229–30.
[151] This status is a hybrid one between *départements d'outre-mer* (DOMS) and *territoires d'outre-mer* (TOMS). On the phenomenon of departmentalisation, ibid, 24–29. Full integration should not be confused with the self-government option of integration contained in UNGA Res 1541(XV)(1960).
[152] UNGA Res 31/4, 21 October 1976, A/RES/31/4. For the OAU position, see Council of Ministers Resolution on the Comorian Island of Mayotte, 3 July 1976, CM/Res 496(XXVII), as cited in Crawford (n 10) 645.

2. *Strongly condemns* the presence of France in Mayotte, which constitutes a violation of the national unity, territorial integrity and sovereignty of the independent
Republic of the Comoros;

3. *Calls upon* the Government of France to withdraw immediately from the Comorian
island of Mayotte, an integral part of the independent Republic of the Comoros, and
to respect its sovereignty;

The Comorian government, the UN General Assembly and the OAU interpreted
French conduct in respect of Mayotte to constitute a violation of Comorian
sovereignty and its territorial integrity because, in their view, the island constitutes part of the indivisible Comorian self-determination unit. Consequently, in
resolution 31/4, the General Assembly called upon France to transfer Mayotte to
the Comorian Federation.[153] The General Assembly rejected the validity of the
1976 plebiscites and any future referenda organised by France in respect of the
island of Mayotte. In response, the Mahorais made three counter-claims. First,
as the indigenous people of Mayotte, they claimed to be ethnically and culturally distinct from the inhabitants of the other islands in the Comorian
Archipelago. Secondly, they argued that the four islands of the Archipelago constituted a single colonial entity only for the administrative convenience of the
colonial power. As noted above, a French protectorate was established over
Mayotte in 1843 via a treaty negotiated between the island's Sultan and the
French authorities. From the Mahorais perspective, the treaty of protection was
entered into in order to avoid conflicts with the Sultans of the other islands in
the Archipelago.[154] It was claimed that, as no pre-colonial Comorian entity
existed, there was no historical national unit that needed to be reunited. Finally,
the Mahorais argued that the results of the 1976 plebiscites in respect of Mayotte
represented the democratically expressed will of the Mahorais people amount-
ing to the proper exercise of the right of self-determination.[155]

The French government refused to transfer sovereignty over Mayotte to the
Comorian State and it remained unmoved by the protests of the international
community of States through the General Assembly.[156] It argued that Chapter
XI of the UN Charter does not prohibit the dismemberment of a non-self-
governing territory but that Article 73 does acknowledge that the interests of
the people of such a territory are of paramount importance and that administering States are obligated to take due account of the political aspirations of the
inhabitants of such a territory.[157] In addition, the French government contended
that an administering State is not bound to preserve the territorial integrity of a
colonial unit prior to the exercise of the right to self-determination by its inhabitants in accordance with paragraph 6 of the 1960 Colonial Declaration if that

---

[153] ibid.
[154] Aldrich and Connell (n 47) 228
[155] ibid, 228–32.
[156] Musgrave (n 75) 184–86. The General Assembly adopted a resolution every year thereafter
reaffirming its position on the question of Mayotte until 1994. See below.
[157] ibid, 185.

is contrary to the democratically expressed will of the population concerned.[158] It is notable that the French view that its international legal obligations in respect of its Overseas Territories are to be found in Chapter XI of the UN Charter rather than in the Colonial Declaration chimes with the position adopted by the UK government on this issue.[159]

The international community of States considered France to be in breach of Comorian independence. However, the General Assembly's initial approach to the Mayotte question has been complicated by its subsequent treatment of this sovereignty dispute. While, in 1994, in resolution 49/151, the General Assembly reaffirmed the national unity and territorial integrity of the Comoros Archipelago,[160] its tone was notably more conciliatory.[161] The resolution noted the contacts that had been made between the French and Comorian governments pursuant to 'a search for a just solution to the problems of the integration of the Comorian island of Mayotte into the Comoros'. Further, the General Assembly has subsequently deferred consideration of the matter.[162] This change of approach may have stemmed from the ongoing political instability within the Comorian Federation.[163] However, for those directly involved, a major factor influencing the course of this sovereignty dispute was the considerable economic benefits associated with French departmentalisation.[164] The French government has invested heavily in the island's infrastructure and the Mahorais enjoy a standard of living that is substantially higher than that of the inhabitants of the other islands in the Comoros Archipelago.[165] This state of affairs has made the Mahorais increasingly reluctant to contemplate a change to the status quo and it has forced the inhabitants of the other islands to reflect on the wisdom of their choice of independence.[166]

XIV. THE SIGNIFICANCE OF WEST NEW GUINEA AND MAYOTTE FOR BIOT'S STATUS

In both the West New Guinea and Mayotte cases, the General Assembly was presented with a dispute regarding the status of a colonial territory. These disputes were between the former colonial power and the successor State, with the former apparently resisting the process of decolonisation. Accordingly, prima facie, the Netherlands and France were on the wrong side of history and the choice of which party to favour was clear to many UN member States. However,

---

[158] ibid.
[159] See ch 5.
[160] UNGA Res 49/151, 23 December 1994, A/RES/49/151.
[161] ibid, [5].
[162] Crawford (n 10) 645.
[163] See Aldrich and Connell (n 47) 230–32.
[164] The *Statut de Mayotte* 2001 conferred DOM status on the island bringing it within the purview of the French Constitution; see Crawford (n 10) 645.
[165] See Aldrich and Connell (n 47) 231.
[166] Anjouan separatists have sought to use Mayotte as a precedent; see Crawford (n 10) 646.

it could also be argued that the cases of West New Guinea and Mayotte demonstrate that the General Assembly has been willing to endorse the claims of post-colonial States uncritically and it has followed a simplistic approach to the achievement of decolonisation at the expense of the populations most directly affected by the outcome of both sovereignty disputes. Notwithstanding this view, it is clear that the French/Mahorais claim that Mayotte has separate international status from the rest of the Comorian islands is flawed. The Mayotte question became the subject of a series of General Assembly resolutions and French constitutional measures during the mid-1970s: ie after the 1970 Declaration on Friendly Relations had been adopted.[167] As discussed in chapter five, the right of self-determination had acquired the character of customary international law by virtue of the 1970 Declaration. Consequently, France was unable to partition a non-self-governing territory for which it was responsible after this time. Moreover, the Declaration provided that:

> The territory of a colony or other non-self-governing territory has, under the Charter, a status separate and distinct from the territory of the State administering it; and such separate and distinct status under the Charter shall exist until the people of the colony or non-self-governing territory have exercised their right of self-determination in accordance with the Charter, and particularly its purposes and principles.

Accordingly, the temporal scope of the applicable international law meant that France could not dismember the Comoros Archipelago and the Mahorais could not be viewed as a distinct people for the purpose of the exercise of the right to self-determination.

In contrast, the Dutch claim that Netherlands New Guinea constituted a distinct non-self-governing territory for the purposes declared in Chapter XI of the UN Charter was clearly not constrained in the same way as this claim was advanced from 1954 onwards (ie before the right of self-determination had been proclaimed by the General Assembly in the 1960 Colonial Declaration). The Dutch government claimed that Netherlands New Guinea constituted a distinct territorial unit for the purpose of implementing the right to self-determination in 1961. However, as discussed above, the Dutch claim was compromised by the fact that it had not taken any constitutional measures to separate Netherlands New Guinea from the established colonial unit of the Dutch East Indies.

Notwithstanding the weaknesses evident in each of these cases, the claims in respect of West New Guinea and Mayotte fail for different reasons and, in their different ways, both are useful precedents for the purpose of considering whether the BIOT constitutes a valid non-self-governing territory for the purposes of international law.

---

[167] UNGA Res 2625(XXV)(1970).

XV. THE TEMPORAL LIMITS OF
NON-SELF-GOVERNING TERRITORY STATUS

As a matter of contemporary international law, Crawford argues that territorial units created as a result of a decision taken by the responsible administering State to partition an established non-self-governing territory cannot be viewed as valid units for the purpose of exercising the right to self-determination.[168] Moreover, he believes that democratic processes cannot cure or perfect sovereignty claims in situation where an entity, or a State, has been forged through the dismemberment of a recognised non-self-governing territory. Consequently, Crawford suggests that the principle of territorial integrity trumps a claim of self-determination made by the inhabitants of *part* of a non-self-governing Territory. In reaching this conclusion, he relies on the restrictive nature of UN General Assembly practice in relation to the temporal parameters of the concept of non-self-governing Territories.[169] In this regard, it is notable that principle 1 of General Assembly resolution 1541(XV)(1960) provides that:

> The authors of the Charter of the United Nations had in mind that Chapter XI should be applicable to territories which were <u>then</u> known to be of the colonial type

According to resolution 1541, the concept of a non-self-governing territory is only applicable in respect of colonial entities that existed, as such, in 1945.[170] Nonetheless, Crawford is prepared to acknowledge that, in principle, there is no reason, why the concept of a non-self-governing territory should be limited to those colonial territories that existed as constitutionally distinct colonial territories at the moment the United Nations was founded. In particular, he observes that, 'Art 73 expressly refers to after-acquired territories' and, as a result, 'it would be strange if only the characteristics of colonies in 1945 were to be relevant in such cases'.[171] It is well known that the category of non-self-governing territories could also have been expanded in a different way. Article 73 of the UN Charter does not explicitly refer to colonial territories and, during the early 1950s, the Belgian government argued that there was no reason, in principle, why the concept of non-self-governing territories, according to the obligations declared in Chapter XI could not be applied beyond the colonial context.[172] However, the General Assembly was unwilling to embrace such an interpretation.[173] Crawford readily accepts that it is unlikely that the international legal

---

[168] Crawford (n 10) 645.
[169] ibid, 607.
[170] However, it is clear that this formulation would also have been applicable to those colonial territories that were not accepted as colonies by the responsible State at that time (eg the colonial possessions of Spain and Portugal).
[171] Crawford (n 10) 607.
[172] This was the argument advanced by the Belgian government in 1953 and it was one of the vital tenets that underpinned the Belgian Thesis. ibid, 607. See ch 5.
[173] It is clear that the endorsement of the Belgian Thesis would have profound ramifications for many States.

regime which underpins the category of non-self-governing territories will be rendered applicable in non-colonial situations.[174] For the present purpose, there is no need to harness a theoretical argument in order to extend the reach of the concept of non-self-governing territories beyond its intended scope. Chapter XI of the UN Charter and the principles that it generated, directly and indirectly, via a series of General Assembly resolutions – including resolutions 742(VIII) (1953), 1514(XV)(1960) and 1541(XV)(1960) – clearly accepted that colonial status warranted the imposition of international legal obligations on administering States in respect of their non-self-governing territories. These obligations, and the corresponding rights of the inhabitants of such territories, were monitored and elaborated in specific cases through the work of C24, the Fourth Committee, and the General Assembly itself from the early 1960s onwards. Accordingly, the concept of a non-self-governing territory can only be rendered sensible by reference to the existence of an arbitrary relationship founded on relative domination and subordination rather than by reference to a specific historical form of oppression in certain geographical settings and this is confirmed in principle 5 of resolution 1541(XV)(1960).[175] Nevertheless, the geographical separation between the colonial power and the colonial territory – and a particular historical process of territorial acquisition – has been significant with regard to the task of elaborating the category of non-self-governing Territories to the extent that the 'salt-water' test remains a defining feature of the concept of a non-self-governing territory.[176]

For the purpose of the present enquiry – an investigation into whether the BIOT constitutes a valid non-self-governing territory – does not necessitate the assertion that the category of non-self-governing territories should be revised so that it can be rendered applicable in non-colonial situations. The more modest argument is that the temporal scope of the category should be revised in order to encompass colonial territories that were created *after* 1945. First, as noted above, and as Crawford acknowledges, Article 73 of the UN Charter anticipates that colonial territories acquired after the advent of the UN Charter could be classified as non-self-governing territories. Secondly, principle 1 of General Assembly resolution 1541(1960) limits the category of non-self-governing territories to those colonial units that were established at the time the UN Charter that: 'Chapter XI should be applicable to territories which were *then* known to be of the colonial type'. However, it is important to appreciate that, as discussed in chapter five, the overriding aim of resolution 1541 was to try to clarify and elaborate the concept of a non-self-governing territory and the options by which such a territory could achieve full self-government. Consequently, the resolution should be viewed as an important instrument which was designed to prompt reluctant colonial powers to recognise the non-self-governing status of their overseas possessions and to observe the obligations that they owed in respect of

---

[174] Crawford (n 10) 612.
[175] ibid, 606.
[176] This is also apparent from principle 5 of UNGA Res 1541(XV)(1960).

their colonial territories. Given the arguments caused by the notorious Belgian Thesis, the drafters of resolution 1541 were bound to be mindful of the prospect that certain intransigent colonial powers would point to any open-ended phrases contained in the resolution as a means of undermining the exercise. Against this background, it is not surprising that the General Assembly sought to nail-down the scope of the concept of a non-self-governing territory to those territories that conformed to the colonial type and were in existence at the time when the category was first recognised by virtue of the UN Charter. Resolution 1541 should be viewed as a significant step in a series of General Assembly resolutions that sought to realise the obligations contained in Chapter XI of the UN Charter. Seen from this perspective, it is clear that the temporal scope of the concept of a non-self-governing territory was not a pressing concern for the General Assembly at this point in time and it is certainly arguable that the resolution did not constitute an attempt to freeze the category's scope indefinitely; rather, it sought to promote the practical implementation of the concept of non-self-governing territories in the face of ongoing resistance from a number of colonial powers. As a result, the provisions of resolution 1541 should not be viewed as an attempt to define the scope of the category of non-self-governing Territories exhaustively.

XVI. NON-SELF-GOVERNING STATUS AND THE BIOT

The UK government's arguments at the General Assembly in 1965 acknowledged that Chapter XI of the UN Charter would be applicable in respect of the BIOT, if the islands which constituted the territory were inhabited by a permanent population. The position of the UK government was that a territory could only be deemed non-self-governing if it was inhabited by a permanent population in accordance with the provisions of Article 73.[177] The UK government's public position was that the BIOT did not have any permanent inhabitants. To this end, on 16 November 1965, the UK government's representative informed the Fourth Committee that:

> The facts were as follows. The islands in question were small in area, were widely scattered in the Indian Ocean and had a population of under 1,500 who, apart from a few officials and estate managers, consisted of labourers from Mauritius and Seychelles employed on copra estates, guano extraction and the turtle industry, together with their dependents.[178]

Accordingly, the UK government claimed that as Chapter XI had no application in respect of the BIOT, it was under no obligation to observe any of the

---

[177] This orthodox interpretation is confirmed by Crawford, who observes that, according to UN practice, territories cannot be governing or self-governing; in contrast, only peoples/populations can be self-governing (n 10) 606.

[178] 1558th meeting of the General Assembly's Fourth Committee, 16 November 1965 [80].

international legal obligations contained in Article 73 in connection with the territory. This standpoint was apparent from official correspondence within the UK government:

> Our understanding is that the great majority of [those people at present on the islands] are there as contract labourers on the copra plantations on a number of the islands; a small number of people were born there and, in some cases, their parents were born there too. The intention is, however, that none of them should be regarded as being permanent inhabitants of the islands. Islands will be evacuated as and when defence interests require this. Those who remain, whether as workers on those copra plantations which continue to function or as labourers on the construction of defence installations, will be regarded as being there on a temporary basis and will continue to look either to Mauritius or to Seychelles as their home territory [. . .] In the absence of permanent inhabitants the obligations of Chapter XI of the United Nations Charter will not apply to the territory and we shall not transmit information on it to the Secretary-General (cf. The British Antarctic Territory).[179]

This claim was not challenged by the Fourth Committee or by the General Assembly itself. However, the official record shows that officials in the British government knew that the BIOT could qualify as a non-self-governing territory for the purposes of Chapter XI of the UN Charter in 1965, at the moment that its creation was being defended in the General Assembly. The UK government knew there was a permanent population living in the Chagos Islands; nevertheless, it instructed its mission to the United Nations to avoid all reference to it. Its true position was clearly articulated in an internal note of 15 November 1965 – the day before the hearing of the General Assembly's Fourth Committee hearing at which the UK's representative announced the BIOT's creation – in which a well-placed official stated:

> I have no doubt that the right answer under the Charter is that we should [transmit information] for the territory is a non-self-governing territory and there is a civilian population even though it is small. In practice, however, I would advise a policy of 'quiet disregard' – in other words, let's forget about this one until the United Nations challenge us on it.[180]

Official documents show that, during this period and throughout the rest of the 1960s, UK government officials were acutely aware of the fact that the General Assembly possessed the authority to change its position regarding the status of the Chagos Islands. They believed that it was open to the General Assembly to treat the BIOT as a new and distinct Non-Self-Governing Territory rather than maintaining the view that the Chagos Islands remained an integral part of Mauritius, as it had done since the adoption of General Assembly resolution 2066(XX)(1965).

---

[179] 28 July 1965, Foreign Office memorandum from Jerrom, quoted by Laws LJ in *Bancoult 1, R (Bancoult) v Secretary of State for Foreign and Commonwealth Affairs* [2001] 1 QB 1067, [11].
[180] FCO, 1965 quoted in *Bancoult 2* (n 27) [32].

For instance, in a memorandum dated 2 February 1966, Browne, one of the UK's UN representatives, voiced his concern that the General Assembly's approach to the BIOT question could change with serious consequence for the UK. Accordingly, he advised the need for the UK government to take great care in how the matter was presented at the UN. He reported that C24 was solely concerned with the issue of the violation of the territorial territory of the colonies of Mauritius and the Seychelles and:

> not yet on the more serious charge of violating Chapter XI of the Charter itself, although this would come and be much more serious if it became apparent that we were doing so [. . .] [I]t seems to us difficult to avoid the conclusion that the new territory is a non-self-governing territory under Chapter XI of the Charter, particularly since it has and will or may have a more or less settled population, however small. We cannot disclaim Charter obligations to the inhabitants because they are not indigenous, since this would destroy our case on the Falklands and Gibraltar; nor apparently would the facts substantiate a plea that the inhabitants are not permanent – even if (which is not necessarily the case) Chapter XI of the Charter were confined to permanent populations. Therefore we here feel that, however we may present the issue, the United Nations will consider that it does fall under Chapter XI.[181]

Further, the ongoing defensive strategy of the UK government was apparent from a minute written by the Foreign Secretary to the Prime Minister on 25 July 1968 requesting approval for the British response to the US government's decision to proceed with the construction of the military facility on Diego Garcia. In this minute, it was noted that:

> It must be expected that the argument will be put forward in the General Assembly that the interests of the local population are being ignored, and this may receive appreciable support; but we have been able to resist such arguments by pointing out that the inhabitants consist mostly of migrant workers from Mauritius and Seychelles. We have not yet completed arrangements for resettlement of the inhabitants of Diego Garcia or for showing that they remain Mauritian or Seychellois, nor have we consulted the Mauritius Government. Resettlement will involve some small expenses, but it is not expected that there will be any financial difficulty in this. When the arrangements are complete, and they may be complicated by a recently completed survey which found that 128 individuals (about 34% of the total population of 389) are now second generation inhabitants of Diego Garcia, we would propose, as agreed at the time of the creation of the British Indian Ocean Territory, to deny, if necessary, the competence of the United Nations to concern itself with a territory which has no indigenous population.[182]

At no point did officials within the UK government discuss the possibility that Chapter XI of the UN Charter could not apply to the BIOT on the ground that the category of non-self-governing territories was only applicable to colonial entities that existed in 1945. Clearly, from the perspective of the UK

[181] PRO CO 936/947, FDW Browne to CG Eastwood, 2 February 1966 and see MM Ticu, *Chagos: Where International Law Stops* (Utrecht, Utrecht University, 2012) (on file with the author).
[182] Quoted by Ouseley J (n 27) [144].

government, the BIOT was at risk of being classified as a non-self-governing territory if the General Assembly learned of the permanent nature of the Chagossian population.

XVII. CONCLUSION

This chapter has considered the resonance of the right of self-determination in the Mauritian context and, in particular, its significance in relation to the detachment of the Chagos Islands from the British colony of Mauritius pursuant to the creation of the BIOT via the 1965 Lancaster House Agreement and the 1965 BIOT Order in Council. It could be argued that the right of colonial self-determination, as proclaimed in the 1960 Colonial Declaration, was engaged by the dismemberment of Mauritius before it acceded to independence. However, as discussed in the last chapter, it cannot be said with certainty that this right had acquired the binding character of customary international law by the time the Chagos Islands were excised from Mauritius. The right of self-determination had clearly acquired the status of customary international law by virtue of the adoption of the Declaration on Friendly Relations in 1970. However, by that time, the BIOT had already been created and the principle of inter-temporal law holds that the lawfulness of actions must be judged by the law in force at the time they occurred. This standpoint cannot be overlooked no matter how inconvenient it proves to be and irrespective of subsequent developments in international law.

However, this chapter points to a different way forward. Rather than arguing that the Chagos Islands should be reverted to Mauritian sovereignty pursuant to the colonial right to self-determination it contends that the view, which was acknowledged by officials within the UK government at the time the BIOT was established, should be pressed into action: the BIOT was a non-self-governing territory. If the UK government had disclosed the full facts concerning the inter-generational nature of the population of the Chagos Islands to the General Assembly in 1965, the BIOT would have been categorised as a non-self-governing territory from the moment it was created.[183] Nevertheless, it would not follow that the right of colonial self-determination would accrue to the BIOT's permanent population – the Chagos Islanders – in 1965 by virtue of the BIOT's status as a non-self-governing territory as the right had not acquired the character of customary international law by that time. However, the fact that the Chagos Islanders were exiled from the BIOT between 1967 and 1973 meant that many Chagossians still inhabited this non-self-governing territory at the time when the right to colonial self-determination was rendered binding on

---

[183] Although this outcome depends on the argument that the right of colonial self-determination had not acquired the character of customary international law by the time the Chagos Islands were detached from Mauritius and the BIOT was created.

the UK in respect of its dealings with all its remaining non-self-governing territories – including the BIOT – by virtue of the adoption of the Declaration on
Friendly Relations in 1970.

7

The Chagos Islanders and International Law

I. INTRODUCTION

THIS CHAPTER ADVANCES the argument that the British Indian Ocean Territory (BIOT) constitutes a non-self-governing territory for the purposes identified in Chapter XI of the UN Charter and pursuant to the right of colonial self-determination. Consequently, it contends that the UK owes a series of international legal obligations to the Chagos Islanders who constitute the Territory's permanent inhabitants. In addition, the chapter examines the wider influence that international law can exert on the dispute between the Chagos Islanders and the UK government regarding the right of abode in respect of the BIOT via an assessment of the applicable customary international law and treaty law. Moreover, the chapter examines the wider contribution that international law could make to the prospect of resettling the outer Chagos Islands. In particular, it considers the ways in which international law could exert a normative influence on UK policy with regard to this British Overseas Territory. For instance, the UN Human Rights Committee and the UN Committee for the Elimination of Racial Discrimination (CERD) have sought to prompt and engage with the UK government concerning its treaty obligations in respect of the BIOT through their monitoring systems.[1] Accordingly, this chapter harnesses relevant normative and institutional resources in order to determine the extent to which the applicable international law could support a right to a publicly funded resettlement programme that may enable the Chagossians to resettle the BIOT (save for Diego Garcia). This chapter also examines whether the Chagos Islanders constitute an indigenous people in order to examine whether they could secure compensation for the loss of their lands as a result of expulsion via the evolving canon of indigenous rights at the level of international law.

---

[1] See below.

II. THE FEASIBILITY OF RESETTLING THE OUTER CHAGOS ISLANDS

On 3 November 2000 – the same day that the *Bancoult 1* judgment was delivered – the UK Foreign Secretary announced that the government had already commissioned a feasibility study concerning permanent resettlement to the outer Chagos Islands.[2] This preliminary feasibility study on the question of permanent resettlement was produced on 20 June 2000 (Phase 2A) and an independent report was published on 10 July 2002 (Phase 2B).[3] In a written statement on 15 June 2004, the Parliamentary Under-Secretary of State for Foreign and Commonwealth Affairs stated:

> anything other than short-term resettlement on a purely subsistence basis would be highly precarious and would involve expensive underwriting by the UK Government for an open-ended period – probably permanently. Accordingly, the Government considers that there would be no purpose in commissioning any further study into the feasibility of resettlement; and that it would be impossible for the Government to promote or even permit resettlement to take place.[4]

In contrast, the Divisional Court in *Bancoult 2*, reached the conclusion that the decision to discontinue the feasibility study could not justify 'abolishing [the Chagossian public law] right of abode'.[5] The UK government's decision to enact the 2004 Orders amounted to an attempt to override the Chagossian public law right of abode in the BIOT that had been recognised by the Divisional Court in *Bancoult 1*.[6] Such a drastic step suggests that the prospect of permanent resettlement to the outer Chagos Islands was more tenable than the government had publicly acknowledged: if resettlement was not viable, then the *Bancoult* claim could have been resolved legitimately through the feasibility study without resorting to primary legislation in the form of the 2004 Orders.[7] Moreover, the contention that permanent resettlement 'would involve expensive underwriting by the UK Government for an open-ended period – probably permanently' has little traction when evaluated from a broader perspective.[8] The UK government's reluctance to finance any resettlement of the BIOT by the Chagos

---

[2] *R (Bancoult) v Secretary of State for Foreign and Commonwealth Affairs* [2001] 1 QB 1067 ('*Bancoult 1*'); *R (Bancoult) v Secretary of State for Foreign and Commonwealth Affairs* [2006] EWHC 1038 ('*Bancoult 2*') (Divisional Court) [8]; *R (Bancoult) v Secretary of State for Foreign and Commonwealth Affairs* [2006] EWHC 1038 (Divisional Court); [2008] QB 365 (Court of Appeal); [2008] 3 WLR 955; [2009] AC 454 (House of Lords).

[3] *Bancoult 2* (DC), ibid, [84]. Excerpts of the feasibility study were published in (2004) 75 *British Yearbook of International Law* 663; and (2006) 77 *British Yearbook of International Law* 638.

[4] *Bancoult 2* (DC) (n 2) [93].

[5] ibid, [102]. However, it should be acknowledged that the House of Lords decided that the Chagos Islanders had no right of abode in the BIOT. See *Bancoult 2* (HL) (n 2).

[6] See *Bancoult 1* (n 2).

[7] The BIOT Constitution Order in Council 2004 and the BIOT Immigration Order in Council 2004.

[8] This was not an issue raised when considerable sums of money were spent by the UK government in the Falklands; see R Aldrich and J Connell, *The Last Colonies* (Cambridge, Cambridge University Press, 1998) 200–12.

Islanders can be contrasted with its apparent willingness to fund development projects in other British Overseas Territories. It distributes £25 million a year for the development of such territories.[9] Specifically, the UK government contributes 66% of Saint Helena's annual budget (population: 4007) and Montserrat has received approximately £180 million in subsidies since it was struck by a series of natural disasters in 2003.[10] The Falkland Islands (permanent population: 2379) are now self-sufficient; this is largely due to substantial government investment during the 1970s and further subsidies in the aftermath of the 1982 Falklands War.[11] Regarding the issue of resettling the Chagos islanders, the UK government has acted as though it is dealing with the prospect of a new commitment that can be avoided rather than an entrenched legal obligation owed to people it victimised. Any assessment of the feasibility of resettlement is a highly technical exercise but, against a background of UN-inspired decolonisation; the UK government's decision to terminate studies into feasibility prematurely; its disproportionate attempts to introduce primary legislation to prohibit return; and the criticisms made by the Divisional Court in *Bancoult 2*, indicate resettlement is viable prima facie.

The UK government's statement of 15 June 2004 indicates it believed that judicial recognition of a right of abode in the BIOT would attract a legal obligation to publicly fund resettlement. This impression was not lost on Waller LJ in the Court of Appeal in *Bancoult 2*. However, he stated that 'it is quite unclear where the obligation to underwrite comes from [and that] any legal obligation was denied strenuously by [counsel for the government]'.[12] Moreover, on the question of resettlement, Sedley LJ added:

> The prospective cost to the British taxpayer of resettling the next generation of the population (which the British taxpayer paid to remove) is in my view a mare's nest. While resettlement will doubtless be difficult or even impossible without capital expenditure, it is not suggested on either side that the United Kingdom is under any obligation to fund it. As I have said it is the bolting of the door to the Chagossians' home, not the failure to provide transport there or refurbish it, which is in issue.[13]

In this passage, Sedley LJ appears to be echoing the sentiment he expressed in the 2004 *Chagos Islanders'* appeal, when he observed that: 'It may not be too late to make return possible, but such an outcome is a function of economic resources and political will, not of adjudication'.[14] These passages show that the courts have consistently doubted the possibility that English law could bring

---

[9] 6 out of these 14 territories are not self-sufficient. See D Vine, S Wojciech Sokolowski and P Harvey, *Dérasiné: The Expulsion and Impoverishment of the Chagossian People* (draft report, 11 April 2005) 44. On the issue of economic development for the remaining colonies, see Aldrich and Connell, *The Last Colonies* (n 8) ch 3.

[10] *Dérasiné* report (n 9) 45.

[11] ibid, 44.

[12] *Bancoult 2* (CA) (n 2) [97].

[13] ibid, [71].

[14] *Chagos Islanders v Attorney General and HM BIOT Commissioner* [2004] EWCA Civ 997, (CA) [54].

about the realisation of the right of abode in the outer Chagos Islands. Nevertheless, this standpoint does not take into account the applicable international law, as discussed below.

With the assistance of a grant from the Joseph Rowntree Reform Trust, the UK Chagossian Support Association commissioned an independent study into the feasibility of resettlement.[15] It estimated that out of the 800 or so Chagossian families – approximately 5000 individuals or about 400 families – had expressed a willingness to resettle the outer Islands on a permanent basis. Moreover, about 150 families are prepared to return immediately. The report recommended that *Ile de Coin* in Peros Banhos should be the principal focus for the first phase of resettlement. It identified a nearby island, *Ile Pierre*, as a suitable site for an airfield and another, *Ile Anglais*, as a proposed site for a small tourist resort. In a subsequent stage of development, the report suggested that *Ile Boddam* in the Salomon Islands could also be used for the purpose of resettlement. The report concluded that these islands would be sufficient to accommodate the 400 families who expressed an intention to resettle the outer Chagos Islands. In sharp contrast to the UK government's claims arising from the earlier studies, the 2008 report concluded that:

> there are no valid environmental or economic reasons that stand in the way of the resettlement of a relatively small number of Chagossian families on the islands of Peros Banhos and Salomon . . . Furthermore, the absence of any serious estimation of costs or benefits in the earlier studies diminishes the validity of current government claims that resettlement would mean a substantial and open-ended financial liability. In fact, there are clear opportunities for significantly enhancing the incomes of resettled Chagossians and, in the process, securing a level of revenues that would sustain decent living standards for the settlers.[16]

It estimated that the cost of initial resettlement to the public purse would be in the region of £25 million over the first five years. It reckoned that capital expenditure during this period would amount to some £17.5 million with the cost of technical assistance estimated at approximately £7.5 million. The report claimed that this cost is small in comparison with the sums directed at other British Overseas Territories. Further, it claimed that the resettled Chagossian community could benefit from revenue streams generated by commercial fishing and sensitively managed tourism in the relatively pristine Chagos ecosystem. These resources would ensure that the BIOT 'could well become one of the most self-sufficient of those British overseas territories requiring [government]

---

[15] *Returning Home: A Proposal for the Resettlement of the Chagos Islands* (London, Chagos Refugees Group/UK Chagos Support Association, 2008). The report was released on 8 April 2008. It was written without the advantage of site visits but it benefited from relevant professional advice and also consultation with the Chagos Islanders. It did not claim to be an exhaustive study; rather, it aimed to demonstrate that resettlement is feasible and it recommended that the UK government undertake a fully comprehensive study of its own.

[16] ibid, 34. The 2002 feasibility study conducted for the UK government, expressed concerns about the lack of potable water in the outer Chagos Islands and, especially, the impact that climate change would have on the Archipelago given they are less than 2 metres above sea level.

financial support'.[17] Moreover, the public cost of resettlement could be supported, in part, by the European Union through an application for a territorial grant from the European Development Fund.[18]

Despite this positive assessment of the prospect of resettling the outer Chagos Islands, in *Bancoult 2*, the majority in the House of Lords accepted the UK government's argument that resettlement was not feasible. Lord Hoffmann endorsed the view that the 2002 feasibility study that the Chagos Islands could not support the demands of modern commercial agricultural production:

> So there could be no return to gathering coconuts and selling copra. Fisheries and mariculture offered opportunities although they would require investment. Tourism could be encouraged, although there was nowhere that aircraft could land. It might only be feasible in the short term to resettle the islands, although the water resources were adequate only for domestic rather than agricultural or commercial use.[19]

The 2002 feasibility study was commissioned as an initial survey concerning the possibility of resettlement. It was not intended as a comprehensive assessment of the financial costs that would be incurred in the event of resettlement. The study also expressed concerns about the negative impact that the global projections regarding rising sea levels and sea temperatures associated with climate change might have on the Chagos Islands given that they are less than two metres above sea level and bearing in mind that global warming may render these coralline atolls vulnerable to bleaching. Further, it was observed that the Chagos Islands are situated in a virtually pristine ecosystem inhabited by a multitude of rare fauna and florae. Accordingly, the 2002 study concluded that resettlement would have negative environmental consequences for the ecology of the Chagos Islands and potentially for any resettled Chagossians.[20] In Lord Hoffmann's view, these environmental considerations were of paramount importance and the financial costs that would need to be incurred to overcome the risks that they would present to a resettled Chagossian population were prohibitive.[21]

However, if one of the main factors for preventing resettlement of the outer Chagos Islands is the risk of environmental harm to the ecology of the Archipelago then the environmental damage caused by the construction and operation of the US military base on Diego Garcia cannot be overlooked. The construction and periodic upgrading of this massive military base has resulted

---

[17] ibid, 8; and 18–24.
[18] See the Overseas Association Decision (Council Decision 2001/822/EC of 27 November 2001 on the association of the overseas countries and territories with the European Community, [2001] OJ L 314). The Commission confirmed that if the UK government indicated that the BIOT had been resettled the Council could consider modifying the Decision in order to allocate funds to this overseas territory. Written Answer P-3189/06ENS, 5 September 2006 by Commissioner Michel in response to Written Question P-3189/06 by Glenys Kinnock (PSE) (on file with the author).
[19] *Bancoult 2* (HL) (n 2) [23].
[20] C Sheppard and M Spalding, *Chagos Conservation Management Plan* (London, Foreign & Commonwealth Office, 2003).
[21] Lord Hoffmann in *Bancoult 2* (HL) (n 2) [23].

in substantial programmes of dredging undertaken by the US military – without the benefit of environmental risk assessment – which has caused irreparable damage to the coralline atoll. In addition, there have been a number of serious oil leaks which have polluted the waters around Diego Garcia not to mention the greenhouse gases that are produced as a result of the operation of the military base and the negative consequences associated with the nuclearisation of this area.[22] Accordingly, while underlying environmental considerations should be factored into any assessment of the prospect of resettling the outer Chagos Islands it is important that environmental concerns should be examined by a thorough and balanced scientific enquiry into the environmental impact of resettlement rather than as a result of deductions being made as a result of general concerns about the effects of climate change and their potential significance for the ecology of the Chagos Islands.

III. THE BIOT AS A NON-SELF-GOVERNING TERRITORY

Although the General Assembly initially pledged support for Mauritius' claim of sovereignty over the Chagos Islands, its claimed reversionary title is suspect for three reasons. First, since Mauritius acceded to independence the General Assembly has kept silent on the BIOT question. Secondly, the Mauritian government's involvement in the involuntary displacement of the Chagos Islanders, via the terms of the 1965 Lancaster House Agreement and the subsequent arrangements made for the transfer of the Chagossians to Mauritius, and its responsibility for their chronic impoverishment in Mauritius could weaken the legitimacy of the Mauritian claim to the Chagos Islands. Thirdly, the General Assembly's ambivalent responses to the Mayotte question, which is analogous to the BIOT question in certain respects, may suggest that both cases warrant an exceptional approach to the resolution of the principles of self-determination and territorial integrity in the colonial context.

In its report to the General Assembly's Fourth Committee on 16 November 1965, the UK government claimed the Chagos Islands 'had a population of under 1,500 who, apart from a few officials and estate managers, consisted of labourers from Mauritius and Seychelles . . . together with their dependants'.[23] It sought to use this information to draw a distinction between territories inhabited by permanent populations and those without them. It argued that Chapter XI responsibilities only arose where the former exist. As, in its view, the Chagos Islands possessed only a transitory population, the UK government claimed that Chapter XI and the right of self-determination were inapplicable to the BIOT. However, official documents disclosed in the context of the *Bancoult* litigation

---

[22] See PH Sand, 'British-American Legal Blackhole in the Indian Ocean?' (2009) 21 *Journal of Environmental Law* 113; and 'Diego Garcia Legal Black Hole: A Response to Sheppard et al' (2009) 21 *Journal of Environmental Law* 295.
[23] Cited in *Bancoult 2* (DC) (n 2) [29].

show these statements to be disingenuous. The UK government knew there was a permanent population living in the Chagos Islands; nevertheless, it instructed its UN mission to avoid all reference to it. Its true position was clearly articulated in an internal note of 15 November 1965 – the day before the Special Committee session – which stated:

> I certainly hope that it will be possible to avoid giving a supplementary answer on whether we should or should not transmit information to the United Nations in respect of the new British Indian Ocean Territory. I have no doubt that the right answer under the Charter is that we should do so for the territory is a non-self-governing territory and there is a civilian population even though it is small. In practice, however, I would advise a policy of 'quiet disregard'–in other words, let's forget about this one until the United Nations challenge us on it.[24]

It should be acknowledged that, in 1965, the General Assembly had little interest in recognising BIOT's non-self-governing status because these bodies viewed the Chagos Islands as Mauritian territory. However, the coming to light of the UK government's misrepresentations concerning the nature of the Archipelago's population should prompt the General Assembly to re-evaluate BIOT's status, notwithstanding the current absence of its permanent population. Both Mauritius and the Seychelles achieved full self-government via accession to independence. However, if it is accepted that: (i) the UK exercises sovereign authority over the BIOT pursuant to the 1965 BIOT Order in Council; and (ii) at that time, the BIOT was inhabited by a permanent population, it appears that the Territory's status has yet to be formally determined as a matter of international law.

IV. ARE THE CHAGOS ISLANDERS A 'PEOPLE' FOR THE PURPOSE OF EXERCISING THE RIGHT TO SELF-DETERMINATION IN INTERNATIONAL LAW?

In order to argue that the General Assembly should recognise the BIOT's non-self-governing territory status, it must be established that it has a separate status from the former colonial unit of Mauritius.[25] As discussed in chapter five, the right to colonial self-determination had not acquired the character of customary international law by the time the BIOT was created.[26] Consequently, as the UK was not under an obligation to facilitate claim-right in the Mauritian context, it was entitled to detach the Chagos Islands from the colony of Mauritius

---

[24] ibid, [32].

[25] The Declaration on the Granting of Independence to Colonial Countries and Peoples, UNGA Res 1514(XV), 14 December 1960 (the 'Colonial Declaration). Para 6 of the Colonial Declaration proclaimed that administering States were not permitted to dismember colonial units before they could exercise their right of colonial self-determination.

[26] The right of self-determination in the colonial context acquired the status of customary international law with the adoption of the Declaration on the Principles of International Law concerning Friendly Relations and Co-operation Among States in Accordance with the Charter of the United Nations, UNGA Res 2625(XXV), 24 October 1970.

as a matter of British colonial law and such an act was in accordance with the international law in force at that time as well. Nevertheless, as discussed above, the fact that the Chagos Islands supported a permanent population had the effect of rendering the BIOT a non-self-governing territory pursuant to Chapter XI of the UN Charter. Moreover, the fact that a significant proportion of the Chagos Islanders continued to reside in the BIOT until 1973 meant that the entitlement to colonial self-determination was also applicable to the BIOT by virtue of the Declaration on Friendly Relations, which confirmed that this right had acquired the character of customary international law by 1970. However, it should be recalled that, in the 1975 *Western Sahara* case,[27] the ICJ moved away from the general statement it made in the 1971 *Namibia* case, when it had observed that the principle of self-determination was applicable to all non-self-governing territories.[28] Instead, it accepted that the right of self-determination would only apply in those cases where the inhabitants of a non-self-governing territory constituted a 'people'.[29] Accordingly, in the circumstances, a question arises as to whether the Chagos Islanders constituted a 'people' for the purpose of exercising the right to self-determination during the period in question.

As discussed previously, the right of self-determination is conferred on 'peoples'.[30] In an effort to determine which societal groups constitute 'peoples' for the purposes of international law, UN Educational, Scientific and Cultural Organisation experts defined the concept of 'people-hood' as:

> a group of individual human beings who enjoy some of the following features: a common historical tradition, racial or ethnic identity, cultural homogeneity, linguistic unity, religious or ideological affinity, territorial connection, a common economic life.[31]

In addition, for the creation of a distinct group identity such objective criteria must be combined with a subjective group consciousness. Notwithstanding this valuable attempt at clarification, international law has never devised general criteria through which a 'people' could be recognised.[32] The absence of the

---

[27] The *Western Sahara* case (1975) ICJ Rep 12.
[28] The *Namibia* case (1971) ICJ Rep 16 [52–53].
[29] *Western Sahara* case (n 27) [59].
[30] 'Minorities' are not entitled to exercise the right to self-determination; instead, they must rely on more limited cultural rights. The International Covenant on Civil and Political Rights (1966), 999 UNTS 171 (ICCPR), Art 27 specifically addresses the right of minority groups. It provides:

> In those States in which ethnic, religious or linguistic minorities exist, persons belonging to such minorities shall not be denied the right, in community with the other members of their group, to enjoy their own culture, to profess and practise their own religion, or to use their own language.

See P Thornberry, *Indigenous Peoples and Human Rights* (Manchester, Manchester University Press, 2002) 151–81.
[31] International Meeting of Experts on Further Study of the Concept of the Rights of Peoples, 1989, SHS-89/CONF602/7, quoted in P Thornberry, 'The Democratic or Internal Aspect of Self-determination with Some Remarks on Federalism' in C Tomuschat (ed), *Modern Law of Self Determination* (The Hague, Martinus Nijhoff, 1994) 101, 103.
[32] M Koskenniemi, 'National Self-Determination Today: Problems of Legal Theory and Practice' (1994) 43 *International and Comparative Law Quarterly* 241, 260–63.

political will needed to produce such criteria bears testament to the international community's fear that once a test for 'people-hood' is accepted, claims to self-determination by distinct groups will become irresistible, thereby destroying the foundations of the present inter-State system.[33] Therefore, it is perhaps unsurprising that the international community of States has chosen to equate a 'people' with the entire population of an independent sovereign State in an effort to maintain the territorial integrity of existing States.[34] In the colonial context, international law has typically determined the concept of 'people-hood' by reference to the territorial parameters of established colonial entities.[35] For the Chagos Islanders to be able to access the right of self-determination, it must be established that they constitute a separate people rather than a minority group of the wider Mauritian people.[36] The position of the Mauritian government is that the Chagossian community constitutes a Mauritian minority group rather than a distinct self-determination unit.[37] This chapter suggests that distinctive Chagossian ethnic characteristics; the unique *culture des isles* which evolved over five generations on the remote Chagos Islands; the shared consciousness and communal solidarity that developed during this period and was reinforced subsequently by experiences of involuntary displacement and chronic impoverishment, provide cogent evidence of Chagossian people-hood.[38]

In particular, the Chagossian people manifest a strong *communal attachment to their ancestral homelands*. First, it is important to establish the historical extent of their ancestral connection to the islands. By 1900 there were some 426 families (around 1000 individuals) residing in the Archipelago.[39] About 60 per cent were of African-Malagasy origin – descendants of the original slave population – while the remaining 40 per cent heralded from the Indian sub-continent – descendants of indentured labourers brought to the islands after emancipa-

---

[33] Thornberry, 'The Democratic or Internal Aspect of Self-determination with Some Remarks on Federalism' (n 31) 126.

[34] See A Cassese, *Self-Determination of Peoples: A Legal Reappraisal* (Cambridge, Cambridge University Press, 1995) 59–62; R Higgins, 'Judge Dillard and Self-determination' (1983) 23 *Virginia Journal of International Law* 387.

[35] See J Castellino and S Allen, *Title to Territory in International Law: A Temporal Analysis* (Aldershot, Ashgate, 2003).

[36] Regarding the concept of a minority group, see C Brölmann, R Lefeber and M Zieck (eds) *Peoples and Minorities in International Law* (1993) and P Thornberry, *International Law and the Rights of Minorities* (Oxford, Clarendon Press, 1991).

[37] See the statement made by the Mauritian observer at the 17th session of the UN Working Group on Indigenous Populations (WGIP) in 1999 in report of the WGIP on its seventeenth session, 12 August 1999, E/CN4/Sub2/1999/19 [63]. This position was reiterated at the 20th session in 2002: see International Service for Human Rights, Working Group on Indigenous Populations, 20th session (Geneva, 22–26 July 2002) 2.

[38] Chronic impoverishment extends 'beyond economic impoverishment to include material, physical, psychological, social, and cultural impoverishment'; see D Vine, 'The Impoverishment of Displacement: Models for Documenting Human Rights Abuses and the People of Diego Garcia' (2006) 13 *Human Rights Brief* 21, 23.

[39] J Madeley, *Diego Garcia: A Contrast to The Falklands* Report No 54 (London, Minority Rights Group, 1982) 4.

tion.[40] At that time, more than 75 per cent regarded themselves as permanent inhabitants of the islands.[41] It is widely believed that the total Chagossian population at the moment of expulsion was between 1500–1800 individuals.[42] Although the colonial authorities failed to maintain accurate census figures,[43] this estimate is supported by archival research, which showed that there were 2970 births on the Chagos Islands between 1895 and 1965.[44] Secondly, the extent of their communal attachment to the Chagos Islands must be assessed. The *Kreol* word the Chagossian people most often use to describe their removal from the Archipelago is *dérasiné* which derives from *déraciner* in French and is related to 'deracinate' in English. The *Dérasiné* report suggests that the choice of this word has two facets for the Chagossian people. It is capable of meaning 'to uproot' or 'to tear away from one's native land' evidencing the Chagossian people's deep psychological attachment to the Chagos Islands.[45] Further, the word can also be defined as 'to eradicate', a reference to the threat that expulsion poses to their communal survival.[46]

Exile deprived the Chagossian people of their ancestral lands and access to communal territorial resources.[47] However, its impact goes far beyond material losses. Expulsion produced experiences of 'profound cultural and landscape bereavement' that have been transmitted down the generations so that they have become ingrained in the Chagossian psyche.[48] An important manifestation of this loss is the lack of access to ancestral burial grounds. Chagossian social relations manifest a strong inter-generational dimension; traditional practices, which involved visiting, honouring and maintaining ancestral graves, remain culturally significant. The inability of Chagossians to perform such practices since expulsion reinforces the severance of wider cultural connections.[49] The Chagossian people have called their experiences of involuntary displacement *sagren* (from the French *chagrin*) meaning profound sorrow. This term does not merely describe an emotional state; it also refers to a physical condition. As Draebel explains:

---

[40] Vine, 'The Impoverishment of Displacement (n 38) 21.

[41] Madeley, *Diego Garcia* (n 39) 4.

[42] Madeley, ibid, 5, states that, by 1965, the population of the Chagos Islands stood at around 1800 people. Although the Foreign Office contended that only 830 people inhabited the islands in 1971, Madeley argues that 251 *Ilois* families (900–1000 individuals) had already left the Archipelago for Mauritius between 1965 and 1970. This figure is supported by the Mauritian authorities; *Chagos Islanders v Attorney General and HM BIOT Commissioner* [2003] EWHC QB 2222 (HC) ('Ouseley judgment') [41].

[43] Madeley (n 39) 7. The Foreign Office alleged that in 1968 only 128 individuals on Diego Garcia were second-generation inhabitants of the island. It claimed that this figure accounted for 34% of the island's population at the time; see *Ouseley judgment* (n 42) [28].

[44] R Gifford, 'The Chagos Islands – The Land Where Human Rights Hardly Ever Happen' (2004) *Law Social Justice and Global Development Journal*.

[45] *Dérasiné* report (n 9) 48–49.

[46] ibid.

[47] ibid, 178–83.

[48] ibid, 169–71; and 230–31.

[49] ibid, 168–69.

The notion of *le chagrin* has an important place in the explanative system for illness. *Le Chagrin* is in fact nostalgia for the Chagos islands. It is the profound sadness of facing the impossibility of being able to return to one's home in the archipelago. For many people we met, this *chagrin* explains illness and even the deaths of members of the community.[50]

The physical effects of such feelings have long been established.[51] And it is indisputable that *sagren* has contributed materially to the general poor health of displaced Chagossians living in Mauritius and the Seychelles.[52]

During their occupation of the Chagos Archipelago, the Chagos Islanders developed a *distinctive group identity*, which differed markedly from the societal identities found in the islands of Mauritius, Rodrigues and Reunion ('the Mascarenes'). It has been suggested that this *culture des isles* was formed during the nineteenth century and facilitated by the isolated position of the Chagos Archipelago.[53] A wide range of distinctive cultural traditions supports this view. While living in the Chagos Islands, the *Ilois* developed their own Creole dialect, Chagos *Kreol*. Although related and intelligible to Mauritian *Kreol* and *Seselwa* (Seychellois *Kreol*), Chagos *Kreol* has its own distinctive vocabulary and modes of pronunciation.[54] The *espri partaze* ('spirit of sharing') was a significant social practice concerning the sharing of surplus food with neighbours, a practice that reflected the strength of Chagossian social networks.[55] Another important cultural practice was the *sega* music/dance tradition. While this African tradition is popular throughout the islands of the south-west Indian Ocean, each territory typically developed its own traditions. In the Chagos context, the *sega* facilitated weekly gatherings of entire island communities, which bolstered group solidarity by providing a valuable outlet for the transmission of unique social histories.[56] And while Christianity was widely practised in the Chagos Islands, *Tamoule* and Malagasy rituals also formed an important part of Chagossian spiritual traditions.[57] Further, it has been claimed that a unique characteristic of Chagossian society stems from Diego Garcia's early function as a 'colony' for leprosy sufferers from Mauritius. Apparently, female suffers survived longer than their male counterparts and this led to the creation of a predominantly matriarchal society.[58] This unusual phenomenon was subsequently bolstered by low marital rates and a tendency for families to be extended along maternal lines.[59]

---

[50] M Draebel, 'Evaluation des besoins sociaux de la communauté déplacée de l'Archipel de Chagos', December 1997, report produced for the World Health Organization, quoted, ibid, 221.

[51] *Dérasiné* report (n 9) 222.

[52] ibid, 201–24.

[53] ibid, 95.

[54] ibid, 238.

[55] ibid, 232–33.

[56] ibid, 233–35.

[57] Madeley (n 39) 4.

[58] By the end of the eighteenth century the 'colony' comprised 300 individuals; see ibid, 3.

[59] ibid, 4.

The process of exile resulted in the *severe disruption, dislocation and exploitation* of the Chagossian people by successive UK governments. These experiences were exacerbated by the methods used to remove them. First, return voyages of Moulinie & Co (Seychelles) Limited company ships to the Chagos Islands from Mauritius were suspended without notice so that affected Chagossians were left stranded in Mauritius.[60] Secondly, shipments of vital supplies were reduced to such an extent that the welfare of the islanders was compromised, provoking their departure. Thirdly, the Chagossian workers were then summarily informed that the plantations were to be closed and the islands evacuated. Finally, the treatment meted out to Chagossians during their removal represents a grave injustice contrasting with processes of decolonisation experienced throughout Africa and Asia during this period.[61]

The Chagossian people have *experienced oppression and exclusion* in Mauritius and the Seychelles. In the Chagos Archipelago, they had been accustomed to full employment, good housing, rudimentary education and healthcare services and a way of life dependent on barter rather than cash.[62] But, in Mauritius, their existing skills were virtually useless. In addition, at this time an over-populated Mauritius was in a severe recession that caused very high levels of unemployment. The Chagossians suffered structural disadvantages in the employment market,[63] inadequate housing and insufficient knowledge of Mauritian society which meant they were vulnerable to exploitation. Cases of starvation and suicide were not uncommon.[64] By 1977, the lack of a resettlement programme produced spiralling debts, which led to demands for the distribution of the £650,000 paid to the Mauritian government in 1972. However, rampant inflation in the intervening period meant that the value of an already meagre sum was substantially reduced so that displaced Chagossians received paltry cash payments that did little to alleviate their suffering.[65] In 1981, the Sylva report, commissioned by the Mauritian government, found that over 40 per cent of the adult male Chagossian population, were unemployed. Out of 942 Chagossian households, only 65 owned land or houses and most lived in squalid, overcrowded houses, which provided inadequate shelter.[66] Any hopes for a measured resettlement package arising from the 1982 UK-Mauritian compensation agreement were thwarted by the financial indebtedness of the

---

[60] Chagossians occasionally made trips to Mauritius in order to purchase goods, visit relatives or for medical purposes.

[61] For accounts of how they were removed, see *Dérasiné* report (n 9) 97–109; the Ouseley judgment (n 42) [26–50]; and Madeley (n 39) 4–5.

[62] *Dérasiné* report (n 9) 111–14.

[63] ibid, 119–23.

[64] Madeley (n 39) 6.

[65] The fund was distributed between 595 families in 1978. However, the Sylva report (1981) stated that there were 942 *Ilois* families in Mauritius in 1981 (2867 individuals). There were 4959 Chagossian claimants cited in the English private law action in 2003; see the Ouseley judgment (n 42) [99].

[66] Madeley (n 39) 8.

Chagossian community, which again warranted the distribution of the fund in direct cash payments at the expense of structural programmes.[67]

These experiences of oppression and exclusion are ongoing. The quantitative findings of the *Dérasiné* report reveal that in 2002-03: (i) nearly 46 per cent of Chagossians of working age were unemployed; (ii) the average income was $2.15 per day; (iii) 40 per cent of Chagossian households did not have indoor plumbing and 26 per cent were without running water; (iv) 54 per cent were illiterate; (v) 85% claimed that their health-care provision was inadequate; and (vi) substance abuse affected more than 20 per cent of the generation born in exile.[68] Further, 50 per cent of first generation Chagossian refugees said they had experienced social and employment discrimination while 66 per cent had received verbal abuse from dominant societal groups in Mauritius.[69] Material conditions have fuelled social-psychological marginalisation. Although the Chagossian people were at the bottom of a hierarchical plantation society in the Chagos Archipelago, at least they were perceived as the legitimate indigenous people of the islands.[70] In Mauritius and the Seychelles, they were generally viewed as an underclass of foreign outcasts. This characterisation has contributed to the stigmatisation of the Chagossian identity and has intensified existing feelings of isolation, vulnerability and impotence.[71] In the light of the above contextual analysis, it is suggested that the Chagos Islanders satisfy the test of people-hood for the purposes of exercising the right to colonial self-determination.

V. CHAGOSSIAN PERSPECTIVE ON UK SOVEREIGN AUTHORITY IN RESPECT OF THE BIOT

The Chagos Islanders are ambivalent about the Mauritian sovereignty claim to the Chagos Islands. Many Chagossians live in Mauritius and many of the descendants of those who were forced to leave the BIOT between 1967 and 1973 have lived their whole lives in Mauritius. Nevertheless, the decision of the elected representatives of the Mauritian colonial government to agree to the detachment of the Chagos Islands from Mauritius in return for Mauritian independence, which was embodied in the 1965 Lancaster House Agreement; continuing British patronage in the form of a defence treaty which protected Mauritius's external and internal security; and the role of the Mauritian State in the maltreatment of Chagossians, both in terms of the Mauritian govern-

---

[67] Although the concrete houses built on plots of land provided by the Mauritian government between 1982 and 1985 improved housing conditions for some Chagossians, Draebel found that Chagossians continued to live in overcrowded conditions in the poorest and most disadvantaged neighbourhoods. Their housing was typically dilapidated, structurally deficient and lacking in basic sanitary facilities; see the *Dérasiné* report (n 9) 152–55.

[68] These statistics from the *Dérasiné* report are also included in Vine (n 38) 23.

[69] *Dérasiné* report (n 9) 267.

[70] ibid, 138.

[71] Ibid, 236–38.

ment's collusion in the involuntary displacement of the Chagos Islanders from the BIOT and their subsequent chronic impoverishment in Mauritius, have compromised Chagossian support for the Mauritian sovereignty claim.[72] This ambivalence created tension with the Chagossian community in Mauritius. Certain political groups and organisations argued that the Chagossian claims had to be premised on the recognition that the Chagos Islands remained part of Mauritius and that any litigation in the English courts would have the effect of impliedly recognising British sovereign authority over the Archipelago. However, other political leaders, including Olivier Bancoult of the Chagos Refugees Group (CRG) and his lawyers, were of the opinion that the municipal law cases in the English courts could not be viewed as an endorsement of the UK sovereignty claim as a matter of international law, as the UK municipal law and public international law constituted separate and distinct legal systems.[73] Moreover, it has been reported that Bancoult remained undecided about whether it would be more desirable for the Chagos Islands to remain a British Overseas Territory, as the BIOT, and to be classified as a non-self-governing territory for the purposes of Chapter XI of the UN Charter or whether it would be better for the Chagossians if the Chagos Islands were return to Mauritian sovereignty and for autonomous arrangements to be negotiated for the Archipelago with the Mauritian government.[74]

It could be argued that the Chagossian litigation in the English courts did not amount to implied recognition of the UK's sovereignty claim to the Chagos Islands because the CRG, and the other political organisations, which instituted the representative cases in the English courts were not the authorised representatives of an independent State.[75] Further, Chagossian political leaders may argue that the litigation was part of a pragmatic strategy designed: (i) to secure recognition of an entitlement to return to the Chagos Islands within the municipal legal system of the State which currently exercises authority over the Archipelago; and (ii) to claim reparations from the State that was responsible for the involuntary displacement of the Chagossians which would be needed to facilitate the resettlement of the Chagos Islands. However, it is important to recall that the *Bancoult* litigation was grounded in the doctrines of British constitutional law; therefore, it was premised on the assumption that the UK's claim to exercise sovereignty over the BIOT is valid as a matter of international law. In addition, as the Chagos Islanders are the permanent inhabitants of a non-self-governing territory, they have a distinct status from the State that administers

---

[72] See L Jeffery, *Chagos Islanders in Mauritius and the UK* (Manchester, Manchester University Press, 2011) 33–35.

[73] ibid, 45–47.

[74] ibid, 46–47.

[75] Regarding the doctrine of recognition in international law, see I Brownlie, 'Recognition in Theory and Practice' (1982) 52 *British Yearbook of International Law* 197; and J Crawford (ed), *Brownlie's Principles of Public International Law*, 8th edn (Oxford, Oxford University Press, 2012) 143–65.

their territory as a matter of international law.[76] Consequently, as the Chagos Islanders possess a degree of international legal personality for certain purposes, by instituting legal proceedings in the English courts, which were premised on the view that the UK exercises sovereign authority over the BIOT, it could be argued that they have impliedly endorsed the UK's claim to the Chagos Islands and that this endorsement is significant at the level of international law. Further, in *Bancoult 2*, the applicant claimed that the Chagos Islanders were the beneficiaries of the right to self-determination as a matter of international law both by virtue of customary international law and by reference to the applicable treaty law.[77] In that case, it was claimed that the Chagossian community constituted a distinct people for the purposes of the exercise of the right to self-determination. Consequently, it was being claimed that the Chagos Islanders constituted a self-determination unit, which was separate and distinct from the Mauritian people at the level of international law.

VI. CHAGOSSIAN SELF-DETERMINATION AND APPLICABLE HUMAN RIGHTS TREATIES

A. International Covenant on Civil and Political Rights

The UK government ratified the International Covenants on Human Rights in 1976 and they came into force in that year.[78] The instruments of ratification were accompanied by a declaration listing the territories to which the Covenants apply. The list did not include the BIOT.[79]

i. Jurisdiction

The UK government has sought to avoid the application of the International Covenant on Civil and Political Rights (ICCPR) to the BIOT by adopting two different strategies. First, it claimed that the ICCPR is inapplicable because the BIOT was not listed in the territorial 'declaration', which accompanied its instrument of ratification. This argument clearly offends the universality of the Covenant's application under Article 2(1).[80] The Human Rights Committee mon-

---

[76] The Declaration on Friendly Relations, UNGA Res 2625(XXV)(1970) provides that:

The territory of a colony or other non-self-governing territory has, under the Charter, a status separate and distinct from the territory of the State administering it; and such separate and distinct status under the Charter shall exist until the people of the colony or non-self-governing territory have exercised their right of self-determination in accordance with the Charter, and particularly its purposes and principles.

[77] See ch 1.

[78] International Covenant on Civil and Political Rights 1966, 999 UNTS 171 (ICCPR); and International Covenant on Economic, Social and Cultural Rights 1966, 993 UNTS 3 (ICESCR).

[79] Letter of the Director of General Legal Division, Office of Legal Affairs, 29 June 1976, CN193.1976, Treaties-6 (on file with the author).

[80] ICCPR, Art 2(1) provides:

itors compliance with the Covenant and State parties are required to submit periodic reports in order to show how Covenant rights are being given effect.[81] The issue of reservations and the nature of Covenant obligations were addressed in the Committee's General Comments 24 and 31.[82] In General Comment 24, the Committee arrogated to itself the power to determine the validity of claimed reservations.[83] Further, it stated that any reservation to Article 2(1) or the right of self-determination contained in Article 1 would be incompatible with the objects and purposes of the Covenant.[84] Consequently, the declaration is contrary to the Covenant's objects and purposes and, therefore, it cannot constitute a valid reservation. In the present context, these authoritative interpretations of the Covenant are significant and it is notable that the UK government did not seek to rely on the declaration in its exchanges with the Committee on this issue during the Committee's consideration of the government's fifth periodic report in 2001.

Secondly, during this session, the UK government suggested to the Committee that, as the Chagossian people were not in occupation of the territory when the ICCPR came into force, the Covenant did not apply to the BIOT.[85] The inter-temporal principle ensures that the UK could not be held responsible for breaches of Covenant obligations before this date.[86] As such, it could not be responsible for the acts of involuntary displacement that were carried out between 1965 and 1973.[87] Nevertheless, Article 14(2) of the International Law Commission's Articles on

> Each State Party to the present Covenant undertakes to respect and to ensure to all individuals within its territory and subject to its jurisdiction the rights recognised in the present Covenant without distinction of any kind, such as race, colour, sex, language, religion, political or other opinion, national or social origin, property, birth or other status.

Further, General Comment 31(80), 26 May 2004, CCPR/C/21/ rev 1/Add 13 [10] provides:

> State Parties are required by article 2, paragraph 1, to respect and to ensure the Covenant rights of all persons who may be within their territory and to all persons subject to their jurisdiction. This means that a State Party must respect and ensure the rights laid down in the Covenant to anyone in their power or effective control.

[81] ICCPR, Art 40.
[82] General Comment 24, 4 November 1994, CCPR/C/21/Rev 1/Add 6. As the UK has not acceded to the Optional Protocol, it is not open for the Chagos Islanders to bring an individual complaint alleging breaches of the ICCPR by the UK.
[83] ibid, [17–18].
[84] ibid, [9]. The Human Rights Committee stated that a State party must show 'the constitutional and political processes which in practice allow the exercise of the right of self-determination in its periodic reports'. See General Comment 12, 13 March 1984, HRI/GEN/1/Rev 7, 134; 1-2 IHRR 10 (1994).
[85] Summary Record of the First Part of the 1963rd Meeting: UK, 23 October 2001, CCPR/C/SR 1963 [12–14].
[86] The inter-temporal principle holds that actions carried out in one period cannot be judged by the legal standards of another where they have been effectively maintained. See Art 13 of the Articles on the Responsibility of States for Internationally Wrongful Acts, adopted by the International Law Commission 10 August 2001: 53rd session A/56/10. See J Crawford, *The International Law Commission's Articles on State Responsibility: Introduction, Text and Commentaries* (Cambridge, Cambridge University Press, 2002) 131–34.
[87] See P Capps in 'Responsibility for Acts in Violation of International Law in the British Indian Ocean Territory' [12]. Paper presented at the colloquium on 'The Common Law, the Royal Prerogative and Executive Legislation', Centre for Public Law, University of Cambridge, 19 January 2008.

State Responsibility anticipates that the maintenance of any legislative measures violative of the Covenant would attract responsibility because they would evidence the continuing character of a breach of an international legal obligation.[88] Against this background, the original legislative denial of the right of abode – section 4 of the BIOT Immigration Ordinance 1971 – and the subsequent 2004 Orders in Council constitute elements of an ongoing wrongful act that infringed the Chagossian people's Covenant rights for which the UK would be responsible.[89] In its concluding observations, the Committee did not accept the government's temporal argument. It stated that the UK government should: (i) make the right of return practicable; (ii) consider compensating the displaced people for the lengthy denial of the right of abode in the BIOT; and (iii) provide information on the territory in its next periodic report.[90] Despite this recommendation, the UK government chose not to address these issues in its sixth periodic report, produced in November 2006.[91] The report was considered by the Human Rights Committee in July 2008. In its concluding observations, the Committee noted the decision of the Court of Appeal in *Bancoult* 2 and it regretted the failure of the report to provide information concerning the Covenant's application in the BIOT.[92] Accordingly, the Committee reiterated its previous recommendations.[93]

---

[88] Articles on State Responsibility, Art 14 provides inter alia:

(2) The breach of an international obligation by an act of a State having a continuous character extends over the entire period during which the act continues and remains not in conformity with the international obligation.

(3) The breach of an international obligation requiring a State to prevent a given event occurs when the event occurs and extends over the entire period during which the event continues and remains not in conformity with that obligation.

See Crawford, *The International Law Commission's Articles on State Responsibility* (n 86) 135–36. This connection was made by Capps, 'Responsibility for Acts in Violation of International Law in the British Indian Ocean Territory' (n 87). Further, according to the Commentary, at 138, this interpretation would be consistent with the Human Rights Committee's jurisprudence; see *Lovelace v Canada*, Communication No 24/1977, 30 July 1981, A/36/40, 166, 72.

[89] Alternatively, Capps suggests such measures could be deemed elements of a composite wrongful act under Art 15 (n 87). See Crawford (n 86) 141–44.

Art 15 provides that a breach an international obligation may occur where a series of actions and/or ommissions are wrongful when taken together as a composite. In such cases, the breach extends over the entire period that the series in question remain wrongful as a matter of international law.

[90] Concluding Observations of the Human Rights Committee: UK. 6 December 2001. CCPR/CO/73/UK; CCPR/CO/73/UKOT [38].

[91] CCPR/C/GBR/6, 18 May 2007.

[92] CCPR/C/GBR/CO/6, 21 July 2008 [22]. The Committee drew attention to the relevance of ICCPR, Art 12 in this regard. It provides:

1. Everyone lawfully within the territory of a State shall, within that territory, have the right to liberty of movement and freedom to choose his residence.
2. Everyone shall be free to leave any country, including his own.
3. The above-mentioned rights shall not be subject to any restrictions except those which are provided by law, are necessary to protect national security, public order (ordre public), public health, or morals or the rights and freedoms of others, and are consistent with the other rights recognized in the present Covenant.
4. No one shall be arbitrarily deprived of the right to enter his own territory.

[93] It concluded that: 'The State party should ensure that the Chagos islanders can exercise their right to return to their territory and should indicate what measures have been taken in this regard.

Through its reporting system, the Committee seeks to persuade State parties of the need to comply with Covenant obligations through a process of dialogue thereby complementing the narrower range of judicial remedies provided for in Article 2(3). While the Committee's observations on reports are not strictly binding on State parties they do carry weight and thus exert a certain pull towards compliance. In the light of its concluding observations in 2001 and 2008, the Committee has exerted considerable pressure on the UK government to honour its Covenant obligations in the Chagossian context.

ii. Self-determination and Sovereignty over Natural Resources

The 2008 feasibility report alluded to the abundance of natural resources present in the Chagos Archipelago that could be harnessed in a sustainable manner for the benefit of the resettled Chagossian community. Nevertheless, the report does not address the legal issues of sovereignty and ownership of these natural resources. In the High Court, Ouseley J concluded there was no contemporaneous evidence to show that Chagossians had legal rights to the lands they occupied in the Chagos Islands.[94] In addition to the Crown owning all the land in the outer Islands,[95] the UK currently exercises sovereignty over the BIOT. While it could be reasonably assumed that the Crown would be prepared to grant resettling Chagossians plots of land for the construction of residential properties on a leasehold basis, this assumption does not explain why a resettled Chagossian community would be legally entitled to a share in the revenue streams generated by tourism, commercial fishing and other enterprises in the BIOT.

In response, reference could be made to the provisions of the ICCPR. In the context of the right to self-determination, Article 1(1) acknowledges that 'all peoples are entitled to freely determine their political status and freely pursue their economic, social and cultural development'. Further, Article 1(2) declares that such 'peoples may, for their own ends, freely dispose of their natural wealth and resources . . . In no case may a people be deprived of its own means of subsistence'. Finally, Article 1(3) confirms that State parties (including those having responsibility for the administration of non-self-governing territories) shall promote the realisation of this right in conformity with the UN Charter. When these provisions are combined with the customary international law obligation to foster self-determination in all its forms, it could be argued that the UK government is obligated to facilitate progressively the economic development of this dependent people in the event of resettlement. Therefore, it would be required to ensure that an equitable share of any such revenues is directed towards the resettled Chagossian people.

It should consider compensation for the denial of this right over an extended period. It should include the Territory in its next periodic report', ibid.

[94] Ouseley judgment (n 42) [397].

[95] This observation was made by Sedley LJ in *Bancoult 2* (CA) (n 2) [71].

In this context, consideration should also be given to the UN General Assembly Resolution on Permanent Sovereignty Over Natural Resources.[96] In particular, paragraph 1 provides: 'The right of peoples and nations to permanent sovereignty over their natural wealth and resources must be exercised in the interests of their national development and of the well-being of the people of the State concerned'. It has been asserted that the reference to 'the rights of peoples and nations' suggests that the beneficiaries of such rights include dependent peoples; consequently, such peoples possess latent sovereignty over their natural resources.[97] Further, paragraph 7 declares that:

> Violations of the rights of peoples and nations to sovereignty over their natural wealth and resources is contrary to the spirit and principles of the Charter of the United Nations and hinders the development of international co-operation and the maintenance of peace.

It has been claimed that these rights have subsequently acquired the character of customary international law.[98] Accordingly, colonial exploitation of a dependent people's natural resources can lead to actionable claims for reparations once the colonial entity in question has acceded to independence.[99] This was one of the arguments used to great effect by Nauru in its litigation against Australia before the International Court of Justice which resulted in an out of court settlement involving a substantial compensation package.[100] Although decolonisation is not on the horizon for the BIOT, the essence of these arguments could be pressed into action to bolster existing claims for a publicly funded resettlement programme. In the Chagossian context, this line of reasoning gives rise to two distinct claims. First, as a consequence of their (latent) sovereign rights over the BIOT's natural resources, it follows that a resettled Chagossian people would be entitled to a share of the profits derived from commercial fishing ventures, tourism and other commercial activities in the BIOT. Secondly, it could be argued that the environmental damage sustained by the construction and operation of the military base on Diego Garcia constitutes a violation of the Chagossian people's sovereignty over their natural wealth in keeping with paragraph 7.[101] While the second claim would certainly be stronger in the event of decolonisation, given the *Nauru* precedent, the UK government may wish to address such claims now so as to avoid the prospect of them arising in the future.

---

[96] UN GA Res 1803(XVII)(1962), 14 December 1962.

[97] A Anghie, *Imperialism, Sovereignty and the Making of International Law* (Cambridge, Cambridge University Press, 2005) 218.

[98] ibid.

[99] See A Anghie, '"The Heart of My Home": Colonialism, Environmental Damage and the Nauru Case' (1993) 34 *Harvard International Law Journal* 445, 472–80.

[100] *Case Concerning Certain Phosphate Lands in Nauru (Nauru v Australia) (Preliminary Objections)* (1992) ICJ Rep 240. For an overview of the resultant settlement, see ibid, 506.

[101] In particular, the reefs surrounding the island were extensively excavated to provide deep-water anchorage for US navy vessels.

B. International Covenant on Economic, Social and Cultural Rights

The reasoning behind the application of the ICCPR to the BIOT also supports the view that the UK government is obligated to observe the provisions of the International Covenant on Economic, Social and Cultural Rights (ICESCR) in the territory. The ICESCR confers a range of rights salient to the resettlement of the outer Chagos Islands, including a legal commitment to securing adequate and improving standard of living, especially in the domains of employment, welfare provision, housing, healthcare, education and cultural expression. In General Comment 3, the Economic, Social and Cultural Rights Committee stated that a State party would be failing to discharge its minimum obligations under the Covenant if a significant number of individuals were deprived of essential primary healthcare, basic housing and education.[102] In the light of this statement, it could be argued that it would be a prima facie breach of the Covenant if the Chagossian people were allowed to resettle this remote archipelago with its dilapidated infrastructure and with no public money being made available to fund a programme of resettlement. In General Comments 3 and 9, the Committee stated the Article 2(1) obligation that State parties ensure that Covenant rights must be realised 'by all appropriate means' allows for a broad range of measures which extend beyond the enactment of legislation and judicial remedies to include administrative, financial, educational and social measures.[103] Given these authoritative interpretations of the Covenant, it is suggested that the provision of public funding for resettlement is an appropriate way of satisfying the UK government's obligations under this Covenant. The general application of the ICESCR may be more problematic than that of the ICCPR given the alleged programmatic nature of 'second-generation' rights.[104] Nevertheless, the UK government has recognised the interdependence of the International Covenants and that economic and social rights are not inferior to civil and political rights.[105] Although, unlike under the ICCPR, there is no right to a judicial remedy in the ICESCR,[106] in General Comment 9, the Committee indicated that: 'Covenant norms must be recognised in appropriate ways within

---

[102] CESCR General Comment 3, 14 December 1990, E/1991/23 [10]. See ICESCR, Arts 11–13. Art 1 provides for the right of self-determination in the same terms as ICCPR, Art 1.

[103] See General Comment 3, ibid, [5–7]. CESCR General Comment 9, 3 December 1998, E/C 12/1998/24, [2–3]. ICESCR, Art 2(1) provides:

> Each State Party to the present Covenant undertakes to take steps . . . to the maximum of its available resources, with a view to achieving progressively the full realization of the rights recognized in the present Covenant by all appropriate means

[104] For an account of the UK government's approach to this Covenant, see E Bates, 'The United Kingdom and the International Covenant on Economic, Social and Cultural Rights' in R McCorquodale and M Baderin (eds), *Economic, Social and Cultural Rights in Action* (Oxford, Oxford University Press, 2007) 257.

[105] ibid, 278. More generally, see H Steiner, P Alston and M Goodman (eds), *International Human Rights in Context: Law, Politics, Morals*, 3rd edn (Oxford, Oxford University Press, 2007) 275–77 and 313–15.

[106] See ICCPR, Art 2(3).

the domestic legal order, appropriate means of redress, or remedies, must be available to aggrieved individuals or groups, and appropriate means for ensuring government accountability must be put in place'.[107] Consequently, this Comment requires State parties to provide appropriate remedies for breaches of Covenant obligations irrespective of whether such obligations have been incorporated into domestic law. The UK has not incorporated the ICESCR into English law but the government is clearly bound by the legal obligations contained therein regardless of whether they are justiciable. Accordingly, operationalising the Covenant could accelerate the process of resettlement and facilitate the task of rebuilding the infrastructure of the outer Chagos Islands since recognition of such rights should attract the kind of funding currently directed at other British Overseas Territories.

C. International Convention on the Elimination of All Forms of Racial Discrimination

i. Jurisdiction

The UK government ratified the International Convention on the Elimination of All Forms of Racial Discrimination (ICERD) in 1969 and the treaty came into force in that year.[108] Article 6 requires State parties to 'assure to everyone within their jurisdiction effective protection and remedies through the competent national tribunals and other State institutions . . . against any acts of racial discrimination'. There is no evidence of any attempt by the UK government to exclude the application of ICERD in the BIOT via a territorial declaration. Further, the temporal argument used by the UK government in an effort to avoid scrutiny by the Human Rights Committee could have no application in the present context as a considerable number of Chagossians were still in occupation of the BIOT in 1969. Accordingly, the Convention applies to the BIOT and, as Article 6 makes clear, the remedies available for breaches of the Convention are not restricted to judicial remedies.

---

[107] General Comment 9 (n 103) [2].
[108] (1965) 660 UNTS 195.

ii. Discrimination

Article 1(1) of ICERD provides:

> In this Convention, the term 'racial discrimination' shall mean any distinction, exclusion restriction or preference based on race, colour, descent or national or ethnic origin which has the purpose or effect of nullifying or impairing the recognition or enjoyment or exercise, on an equal footing, of human rights and fundamental freedoms in the political, economic, social, cultural or any other field of public life.

Under this article, any refusal to provide public funding for the purpose of resettlement may constitute an exclusion or restriction that impairs the Chagossian people's Convention rights.[109] Further, under Article 5, Chagossians are entitled not to be discriminated against in the recognition and provision of a wide range of rights, including: the right to 'freedom of movement and residence within the border of the State . . . and to return to one's country';[110] rights to housing; healthcare; work; social services; and education.[111] The appropriate comparators for the purpose of assessing claims of discrimination would be members of other ethnic groups subject to the UK's jurisdiction. It is suggested that no other such group has been systematically uprooted from the ancestral homelands in violation of the rights contained in ICERD.[112]

In its 2003 concluding observations on the UK's sixteenth and seventeenth periodic reports, CERD noted that the UK government had not provided information on the implementation of ICERD in the BIOT. It therefore requested that the UK government include information in its next report on the measures taken to ensure the adequate development and protection of the Chagossian people's rights under the Convention.[113] This request indicates that the Committee views resettlement as a necessary condition for satisfactory compliance with the Convention. Further, CERD's specific reference to Article 2(2) in this context indicates that it considers that 'special measures' would be required in order to avoid a situation of discrimination.[114] In the BIOT context, special

---

[109] See N Lerner, *Group Rights and Discrimination in International Law*, 2nd edn (The Hague, Martinus Nijhoff Publishers, 2003) 52–54.

[110] ICERD, Art 5(d)(i)–(ii). It is unclear why a distinction has been drawn between 'State' and 'country' in this context. As a distinct British Overseas Territory, from a constitutional perspective, the BIOT counts as a country for this purpose (and also because it is a non-self-governing territory).

[111] In this respect, State parties guarantee such rights to everyone, without distinction as to race, colour, or national or ethnic origin.

[112] However, it would be wrong to suppose that there is no historical precedent for such processes of deracination. In *Chagos Islanders v Attorney General and H.M. BIOT Commissioner*, (CA) (n 14) [6], Sedley LJ drew a parallel with the clearances of the Scottish Highlands in the eighteenth and nineteenth centuries.

[113] Concluding Observations of the Committee on the Elimination of Racial Discrimination: UK, 10 December 2003, CERD/C/63/CO/11 [26]. The requirement to submit periodic reports is contained in ICERD, Art 9.

[114] ICERD, Art 2(2) provides:

> State parties shall, when the circumstances so warrant, take, in the social economic, cultural and other fields, special and concrete measures to ensure that adequate development and protection of certain racial groups or individuals belonging to them, for the purpose of guaranteeing them

measures might focus on the protection and promotion of the Chagossian people's indigenous status.[115] In the circumstances, it is difficult to see how the UK government's obligations to the BIOT under ICERD could be discharged without the development of a publicly funded resettlement programme.[116]

In its 2010 periodic report, the UK government responded to CERD's concluding observations made in respect of the BIOT in August 2003.[117] First, the government asserted that the Convention does not apply to the BIOT and, therefore, the provisions of Article 2(2) are not engaged in the Territory. Secondly, the UK government observed that many Chagossians had become British citizens by virtue of the terms of the British Overseas Territories Act 2002 and, as a result, many enjoyed the right of abode in the UK – the implication being that any rights that the Chagos Islanders once possessed in relation to the BIOT are now irrelevant.[118] However, in its 2011 concluding observations, CERD remained distinctively unimpressed by the stance adopted by UK government in its latest periodic report.[119] It reiterated its deep concern at the UK's refusal to accept that the Convention is applicable to the BIOT and it regretted that the 2004 BIOT Immigration Order prevented the Chagossians not only from returning to Diego Garcia but also to the outer Chagos Islands on the grounds of national security, which are situated over 100 miles away from Diego Garcia. It indicated that such a ban amounts to a prima facie violation of Article 2 and Article 5(d)(i) of the Convention.[120] CERD concluded that:

> The Committee reminds the State party that it has an obligation to ensure that the Convention is applicable in all territories under its control. In this regard, the Committee urges the State party to include information on the implementation of the Convention in the British Indian Ocean Territory in its next periodic report.[121]

VII. GOOD GOVERNANCE IN BRITISH OVERSEAS TERRITORIES

The 1999 White Paper, *Partnership for Progress and Prosperity: Britain and the Overseas Territories*, set out the FCO's vision for the development of British

the full and equal enjoyment of human rights and fundamental freedoms

[115] See CERD General Recommendation 23, 18 August 1997, A/52/18 Annex V; P Thornberry, 'The Convention on The Elimination of Racial Discrimination, Indigenous Peoples and Caste/Descent-based Discrimination', in J Castellino and N Walsh (eds), *Indigenous Peoples and International Law* (The Hague, Martinus Nijhoff Publishers, 2005) 17; and P Thornberry, 'Confronting Racial Discrimination: A CERD Perspective' (2005) 5 *Human Rights Law Review* 239. The issue of the Chagos Islanders' indigenous status is examined below.
[116] Although ICERD, Art 14 allows CERD to adjudicate complaints lodged by individuals and groups, the UK government has not yet granted CERD jurisdiction to perform this function.
[117] UK periodic report submitted pursuant to Art 9 of ICERD, 9 March 2010, CERD/C/GBR/18-20, Annex IX, 96.
[118] See Annex IX, paras 2 and 3.
[119] CERD 78th session, Concluding Observations, CERD/D/GBR/Co/18-20, 14 September 2011. Art 5(d)(i) refers to: 'The right to freedom of movement and residence with the borders of a State'.
[120] ibid
[121] ibid.

Overseas Territories.[122] It stated that policy would be based on four principles: (i) constitutionality; (ii) autonomy; (iii) self-determination; and (iv) economic development.[123] The promotion of good governance in British Overseas Territories was reiterated in a 2006 White Paper, *Active Diplomacy for a Changing World*.[124] This White Paper stated that one of the ways in which this strategic priority would be satisfied was by ensuring that the UK met its international legal obligations to these territories.[125] In the foreword, Jack Straw, the then Foreign Secretary stated:

> At the heart of any foreign policy must lie a set of fundamental values. For this Government, the values that we promote abroad are those that guide our actions at home. We seek a world in which freedom, justice and opportunity thrive, in which governments are accountable to the people, protect their rights and guarantee their security and basic needs . . . At home, Government and Parliament set out laws and ensure they are enforced. Internationally, we operate as one nation among many. We achieve our objectives by understanding different points of view, by persuasion and negotiation in a framework of international law.[126]

While the Foreign Secretary was careful to maintain a distinction between municipal law and international law in this passage, it is clear that the two systems are porous at a normative level, especially in the context of the protection and promotion of human rights. Moreover, arguably, Straw's value-driven view of international law is consistent with the approach adopted by the constructivist school of thought in international relations.[127] For constructivists, international law is constituted by the shared values of the societies that create it. In particular, international law conditions the conduct of international politics by expressing the prevailing scope of legitimate agency for international actors.[128] It follows from this interpretation that political will may be catalysed by the existence of international legal obligations regardless of whether they are enforceable through formal processes of adjudication. The international legal obligations identified in this chapter are binding on the UK government. Moreover, the values enshrined in these human rights treaties and principles of

---

[122] (Cm 4264, 1999).

[123] These principles were identified in the foreword written by then Foreign Secretary, Robin Cook, ibid, 4–5. Moor and Simpson doubted whether these principles could be applied to the BIOT. They characterised the territory as a British Non-Autonomous Overseas Territory. See L Moor and AWB Simpson, 'Ghosts of Colonialism in the European Convention on Human Rights' (2005) 76 *British Yearbook of International Law* 121, 163–64.

[124] (Cm 6762, 2006). The White Paper identified the security and good government of British Overseas Territories as one of its strategic priorities.

[125] ibid, 39.

[126] ibid, 4–5. However, the next Foreign Secretary, David Miliband, issued a new set of Departmental Strategic Objectives for the period 2008–11, in which the relationship between the UK and its Overseas Territories did not feature expressly. The current position of the UK government in respect of British Overseas Territories is set out in its 2012 White Paper, *The Overseas Territories: Security, Success and Sustainability* (Cm 8374, 2012).

[127] See eg C Reus-Smit (ed), *The Politics of International Law* (Cambridge, Cambridge University Press, 2004).

[128] ibid, 3–5 and 21–23.

customary international law have achieved such a symbolic status in international civil society that their observance is warranted, particularly if the State concerned claims to promote freedom, justice, government accountability and to protect the rights, security and basic needs of the people it governs. The interplay between law and politics at an international level also influences national developments.

In the present situation, this process has been demonstrated by the report of the Inquiry into Good Governance in British Overseas Territories conducted by the House of Commons Parliamentary Committee on Foreign and Commonwealth Affairs.[129] The Inquiry concerned the implementation of the FCO's 2006 strategic priority relating to the good governance of British Overseas Territories. In particular, it focused on standards of governance; transparency and accountability; the application of international treaties, conventions and other agreements; and the application of human rights. The report made a number of key recommendations concerning the BIOT's governance.[130] In the context of resettling the outer Chagos Islands, after a thorough investigation of the evidence,[131] the Committee concluded:

> that there is a strong moral case for the UK permitting and supporting a return to the [BIOT] for the Chagossians . . . The FCO has argued that such a return would be unsustainable, but we find these arguments less than convincing. However, the FCO has told us that the US has stated that a return would pose security risks to the base on Diego Garcia. We have therefore decided to consider the implications of a resettlement in greater detail.[132]

While the Committee chose to emphasise the government's moral obligations to the displaced Chagossians rather than the duties it owes them under international law,[133] its report nevertheless increases the normative pressure on the government to observe such commitments. Moreover, while the UK government has claimed the resettlement presents security risks, the Committee's decision to investigate the matter further shows that it is not prepared to take this claim at face value. Against this background, it is suggested that international law's symbiotic relationship with international politics can generate a degree of traction that is typically unobtainable through municipal litigation; and unavailable from English law in the present case. Consequently, this attribute makes international law a particularly useful resource for those who are currently demanding government succour in connection with the resettlement of the outer Chagos Islands.

---

[129] House of Commons Foreign Affairs Committee, *Overseas Territories*, Seventh Report (HC 2007–08, 147-I). The Inquiry was announced on 5 July 2007. The deadline for written submission was 31 January 2008. Oral evidence was taken between December 2007 and March 2008.
[130] ibid, 138.
[131] ibid, [42–73].
[132] ibid, [69].
[133] Nevertheless, the Committee was mindful of such legal obligations, ibid, [66].

VIII. THE SALIENCE OF INDIGENOUS RIGHTS FOR THE CHAGOS ISLANDERS

A. The Concept of Indigeneity in International Law

The oppression of peoples by European powers led to the practice of labelling all colonial peoples 'indigenous'.[134] However, the concept of indigeneity in contemporary international law has a much more specific meaning. The most comprehensive attempt at a definition was made in the Martinez-Cobo report. It provided that:

Indigenous communities, peoples and nations are those which, having a historical continuity with pre-invasion and pre-colonial societies that developed on their territories, consider themselves distinct from other sectors of the societies now prevailing in those territories, or parts of them. They form at present non-dominant sectors of society and are determined to preserve, develop and transmit to future generations their ancestral territories, and their ethnic identity, as the basis of their continued existence as peoples, in accordance with their own cultural patterns, social institutions and legal system.[135]

Nonetheless, the abstract nature of this and other efforts to capture the essence of indigeneity has led contemporary scholars and the international indigenous movement to avoid formal definitions in favour of devising relevant criteria that assist in the contextual determination of indigeneity.[136]

Thornberry divines four strands of indigeneity: first, association with a particular place, entrenching the idea of indigenous peoples as territorialised societies; second, historical precedence over subsequent societies; third, indigenous societies being not only prior societies but also the first inhabitants of a given territory; and fourth, the cultural distinctiveness of indigenous societies when compared with dominant societal groups.[137] Kingsbury also offers four factors, which he considers to be prerequisite to the attainment of indigenous status: first, the indigenous society identifies itself as a distinct ethnic group; second, it has experienced severe disruption, dislocation or exploitation; third, it can demonstrate a significant historical connection with a particular territorial unit; and, finally, it wishes to retain its distinctive identity.[138] Beyond these factors,

---

[134] B Kingsbury, 'Indigenous Peoples in International Law: A Constructivist Approach to the Asian Controversy' (1998) 92 *American Journal of International Law* 414, 426.

[135] J Martinez-Cobo, *Study of the Problem of Discrimination Against Indigenous Populations*, E/CN4/Sub2/1986/7/Add 4 379].

[136] Another important definition is included in Art 1(1) of Convention No 169 on Indigenous and Tribal Peoples 1989, 1650 UNTS 383. The concept of indigeneity is not defined in the 2007 UN Declaration on the Rights of Indigenous Peoples adopted by the UN General Assembly in UNGA Res 61/295, 13 September 2007. See S Allen and A Xanthaki (eds), *Reflections on the Declaration on the Rights of Indigenous Peoples* (Oxford, Hart Publishing, 2011).

[137] Thornberry also recognised the criterion of self-identification (n 30) 37–40.

[138] Kingsbury, 'Indigenous Peoples in International Law' (n 134) 453–55.

Kingsbury posits additional criteria, which are indicative of indigenous status depending on the circumstances of a given case including: non-dominance in the wider society; a close cultural affinity with a particular place; historical continuity with pre-colonial societies; socio-economic or cultural differences from dominant groups; objective ethnic characteristics; and categorisation as indigenous by dominant societal groups. Daes also offers a number of criteria for the purpose of determining indigenous status, including: priority in time, voluntary perpetuation of their cultural distinctiveness, self-identification as indigenous and experience of subjugation, marginalisation, dispossession, exclusion and discrimination by the dominant society.[139] Thus, at least seven criteria of indigeneity can be distilled from the above formulations: (i) communal attachments to 'place'; (ii) historical precedence; (iii) experience of severe disruption, dislocation and exploitation; (iv) 'historical continuity'; (v) ongoing oppression/exclusion by dominant societal groups; (vi) distinct ethnic/cultural groups; and (vii) self-identification as indigenous peoples. Most communities will not be able to satisfy all criteria; but such approaches create a sliding scale of indigeneity for the purposes of assessment. If a given societal group can establish its status as an indigenous people it will be able to access the evolving canon of indigenous rights in international law.

B. The Concept of Indigeneity in the Chagossian Context

This sub-section assesses whether the Chagossian people can satisfy the concept of indigeneity and thereby access the evolving canon of indigenous rights in international law. To this end, the experiences of the Chagossian people will be measured against each of the seven themes identified above. It should be noted that the following themes have already been discussed in relation to the question of whether the Chagossian constitute a 'people' for the purpose of the exercise of the general right to self-determination, namely: communal attachments to 'place'; experience of severe disruption, dislocation and exploitation; ongoing oppression/exclusion by dominant societal groups; and distinct ethnic/cultural groups. The conception of people-hood in relation to the general entitlement to self-determination and the more specific notion of indigenous people-hood are distinct but they are not necessarily mutually exclusive concepts.

The importance of *self-identification* for societal groups, and for indigenous communities in particular, has long been acknowledged. Article 1(2) of ILO Convention No 169 on Indigenous and Tribal Peoples recognised its importance as a fundamental determinant in the indigenous context.[140] The Chagossian

---

[139] Paper by EI Daes, as reproduced in Working Paper on the Relationship and Distinction between the Rights of Persons belonging to Minorities and those of Indigenous Peoples, 19 July 2000, E/CN 4/Sub 2/2000/10.

[140] It provided that: 'self-identification as indigenous . . . shall be regarded as a fundamental criterion for determining the groups to which the provisions of this Convention apply'.

people identify themselves as indigenous. Chagossian non-governmental organisations have participated in the UN Working Group on Indigenous Populations (WGIP),[141] which has been a major site of the global indigenous movement since the 1980s. In this forum, the Chagossian people have been embraced as indigenous. Accordingly, the Chagossian people's decision to self-identify as indigenous has been reinforced through their acceptance by a movement that has a vested interest in maintaining the integrity of the concept of indigeneity.[142] Moreover, the social ruptures caused by the process of displacement and the subsequent communal experiences of abject poverty, exclusion and ill-treatment in Mauritius and the Seychelles have galvanised Chagossian political identity leading to mobilisation.[143] Involvement in the events that brought about the 1982 UK–Mauritian compensation agreement sharpened the Chagossian political campaign for recognition, rights and compensation. The Chagos Refugees Group, founded in 1983, has been instrumental in promoting the political consciousness of the Chagossian people.[144] It was responsible for instituting the recent litigation against the UK and US governments,[145] a course of action that has been immensely important for the solidarity of the Chagossian people given the deplorable conditions of exile.[146]

The Martinez-Cobo report interpreted the notion of '*historical continuity*' as the continuation for an extended period reaching into the present of one or more of the following factors: (i) occupation of ancestral lands, or at least part of them; (ii) common ancestry with the original occupants of those lands; (iii) culture in general, or in specific manifestations; (iv) language; v) residence in certain parts of the country or in certain regions of the world; and (vi) other relevant factors.[147] Given that the Chagossian people were displaced by the actions of successive UK governments, any failure to maintain those aspects of the notion of 'historical continuity', which involve continuing connections to traditional lands, cannot militate against their claim of indigenous status. Instead attention should be focused on the impressive extent to which the Chagossian people have maintained their core cultural traditions despite their profound experiences of involuntary displacement and chronic impoverishment.

Nevertheless, a major obstacle to securing indigenous status appears to be the criterion of *historical precedence*. The Mauritian government claims that

---

[141] In particular, the Chagos Refugee Group, the Chagos Social Committee, the UK Chagos Support Association and the *Comité Suisse de Soutien aux Chagossiens*. These NGOs have participated in the WGIP's annual sessions (n 37).

[142] See BKR Burman and BG Verghese (eds), *Aspiring to Be: The Tribal/Indigenous Condition* (New Delhi, Konark PVT, 1998).

[143] See Ouseley judgment (n 42) [60–72].

[144] The Chagos Refugee Group represents Chagossians in Mauritius. The Chagos Social Committee, founded in 1997, represents Chagossians in the Seychelles.

[145] The Chagos Social Committee co-sponsored this litigation.

[146] Nevertheless, the twin experiences of exile and chronic impoverishment have inevitably led to a degree of socio-cultural fragmentation; see *Dérasiné* report (n 9) 226–39.

[147] Martinez-Cobo report (n 135) [380].

the Chagossian population does not constitute an indigenous people but rather a national minority of the Mauritian people.[148] Further, it alleges that they cannot possess indigenous status because the Chagos Islands were uninhabited until the nineteenth century.[149] However, the second argument is based on a misunderstanding of indigeneity. The term 'indigenous' relates to a situation in which a people can demonstrate historical precedence over subsequent settler communities rather than original inhabitation of a territorial unit.[150] The fact that the Chagossian people did not inhabit the Chagos Islands from time immemorial does not undermine their claims of indigeneity. But while the Chagossian people began occupying the islands before the United Kingdom acquired derivative sovereignty from France, they were not the first inhabitants of the Chagos Archipelago. As noted earlier, French settlers first occupied the islands. The ancestors of the Chagossian people originally came to the islands as French slaves and, subsequently, as indentured labourers from the Indian sub-continent. Consequently, the historical record appears to sorely test the Chagossian people's entitlement to indigenous status.[151]

From the criteria enumerated above, it appears that the concept of indigeneity is firmly rooted in enduring societal attachments to place. Arguably, it draws much of its intuitive resonance from the notion of prior occupation: if the requirement of historical precedence could be abandoned many established minority groups could be legitimately described as 'indigenous' and thus gain access to the evolving canon of indigenous rights in international law. Clearly, as this criterion performs a vital function in distinguishing indigenous peoples from national minorities, discarding it would inevitably diminish the significance of indigenous status. Nonetheless, the Chagossian people constitute the only societal group with inter-generational attachments to the Chagos Islands. UK Foreign Office documents produced in connection with the *Bancoult* litigation reveal that the UK government covertly appreciated that the inhabitants of the Chagos Islands were entitled to non-self-governing status under Chapter XI of the UN Charter. This represents powerful evidence that the UK government, at the time BIOT was created, understood that no other people had a superior claim to the Chagos Islands. Accordingly, while they are unable to satisfy the criterion of historical precedence, the Chagossian people can satisfy the other criteria of indigeneity; therefore, they can access the canon of indigenous rights in international law.

---

[148]   Report of the WGIP on its 17th session (n 37).
[149]   ibid.
[150]   A Gray, 'The Indigenous Movement in Asia' in RH Barnes, A Gray and B Kingsbury (eds), *Indigenous Peoples of Asia* (Ann Arbor, Association for Asian Studies, 1995) 35, 36–38.
[151]   On the complex relationship between indigenous peoples and modernity, see S Allen, 'The Consequences of Modernity for Indigenous Peoples: An International Appraisal' (2006) 13 *International Journal on Minority and Group Rights* 315.

C. Indigenous Land Rights in the Chagossian Context

As discussed in chapter one, after the decision of the Divisional Court in *Bancoult 1*,[152] the Chagos Islanders brought a representative private law action for compensation against the UK government.[153] The claimants sought, inter alia, compensation and the restoration of their property rights. In particular, they argued that these rights were acquired through prescription or succession under the French Civil Code, which was in force in Mauritius and its lesser dependencies from 1805 onwards, and that such rights were protected by the Mauritian Constitution,[154] which extended to the Chagos Islands. As the nineteenth century progressed, ownership of the coconut plantations in the Chagos Islands was concentrated into fewer hands until Chagos-Agalega Ltd ('the Company') owned all non-Crown lands in the Archipelago. In accordance with established practice, it provided land and houses to the Chagos Islanders. However, pursuant to the planned evacuation of the Chagos Archipelago, the BIOT Commissioner enacted the Acquisition of Land for Public Purposes (Private Treaty) Ordinance No 2, 1967, so that the Crown could purchase all remaining lands in the islands.[155] Under Franco-Mauritian law, rights could be acquired in respect of non-Crown lands that were in the unequivocal possession of persons who could manifest the intention of owning them.[156] Nevertheless, it was necessary for such occupation to endure for a period of 30 years before such rights could be acquired but, once established, they could be transferred or inherited.

In *Chagos Islanders v Attorney General & HM BIOT Commissioner*, Ouseley J was satisfied that the Chagossians exhibited an intention to own the lands they occupied in the Chagos Islands and, as their possession had been uninterrupted, that they had prima facie acquired rights over them.[157] However, he highlighted a number of problems with their claims. First, he observed that as any such land rights could also be acquired by non-Chagossian contract labourers they could not be interpreted as rights arising from group membership.[158] Second, he noted that there was an evidential problem affecting these claims. In order to avail themselves of such land rights, the claimants would need to

---

[152] *R (Bancoult) v Secretary of State for Foreign and Commonwealth Affairs* [2001] 1 QB 1067.

[153] *Chagos Islanders v Attorney General & HM BIOT Commissioner* [2003] EWHC QB 2222 ('Ouseley judgment') (n 42).

[154] In addition, it was argued that the claimants were afforded constitutional protection against the deprivation of property without compensation. See the Mauritian (Constitution) Order in Council 1964.

[155] Acting under this Ordinance, the Crown purchased all the Company's lands in the Chagos Islands for the sum of £660,000. The BIOT Commissioner then granted a lease of these lands to the Company, which was taken over by Moulinie & Co (Seychelles) Ltd in 1968; see *Ouseley judgment*, ibid, at [22].

[156] ibid at [119].

[157] ibid at [385].

[158] ibid at [386].

establish that they, or their predecessors in title, had been in possession of the land since at least 1937.[159] He found that, as many of the properties had been built after 1937, many individuals could not rely on Franco-Mauritian law in this regard. In fact, he stated that the pleadings identified no person as enjoying a right so acquired.[160]

Marcel Moulinie, the de facto manager of the Chagos Islands during the period of the BIOT's evacuation, confirmed in evidence given during these proceedings, that the Chagossians had been living on the Chagos Islands for generations. However, he denied that they owned any lands there.[161] The evidence of a number of Chagossian witnesses supported his assertion that the Company built houses for its workforce; the practice being that individual workers would notify the Company that they wished a house to be built on a certain plot of Company land. The Company would then make the necessary arrangements for it to be constructed using its own builders.[162] Ouseley J interpreted such notification as a request for permission and thus evidence that the claimants were not acting 'as of right', a central requirement in order to found prescriptive claims. In light of this evidence, he decided that workers were service occupiers for the better performance of their employment duties notwithstanding the inter-generational nature of their occupancy.[163] Accordingly, he concluded there was no contemporaneous evidence to challenge the view that Chagossians did not have legal rights to the lands they occupied in the Chagos Islands.[164] Given the unwillingness of English law to recognise Chagossian land claims, the possibility that they may be validated by international law should be considered. If the Chagossian people can establish their status as an indigenous people, they may be able to access the ascendant canon of indigenous land rights. This strategy would enable them to protect and promote their discrete societal identity to greater effect.

While the canon of indigenous rights encompasses a wide array of rights, its most significant contribution vis-s-vis any resettlement process appears to be its potential capacity to bolster Chagossian land claims by securing compensation in the form of monetary awards and/or equivalent lands. It follows from the notion of historical precedence that indigenous peoples were typically situated

---

[159]   The critical date for property claims in this action was fixed at 1967.

[160]   *Ouseley judgment* at [386].

[161]   ibid.

[162]   However, it has been suggested that historically Chagossians chose to build their own houses using Company land and resources and that the Company only started to build houses in the 1960s. See the *Derasine* Report at 93–4 (n 9). The construction of new houses does not mean that families did not occupy the same plots of lands for generations; but this is a question of evidence.

[163]   *Ouseley judgment* at [397].

[164]   Ibid. Section 3, Private Treaty Ordinance 1967, allowed the Crown to purchase lands from if the 'owner or apparent owner agrees to sell such land'. Further, sections 5 and 6 provided that any such sale would overreach the rights of any owners including lessees and beneficiaries. The Court therefore held that any property rights Chagossians may have had were extinguished by this Ordinance. The Acquisition of Land for Public Purposes (Repeal) Ordinance 1983 confirmed that the Crown owns all the land in BIOT. See *Ouseley judgment* at [389–400].

on territorial bases that were severely reduced by colonialism and the onslaught of modern settler States. However, as the Chagos Archipelago constituted *terra nullius* until France occupied it in the late-eighteenth century when French-Mauritian companies first brought the *Ilois'* ancestors to the Chagos Islands, it appears that Chagossian land claims do not conform to the orthodoxy of indigenous land rights. But, before the issue of whether the canon of indigenous rights could support Chagossian land claims can be considered, the extent to which international law recognises indigenous land rights must be established.

ILO Convention No 169 on Indigenous and Tribal Peoples constitutes the existing standard on indigenous rights in international law.[165] Article 14(1) provides that indigenous land rights extend beyond ownership rights to include possessory and use rights over lands traditionally accessed for subsistence and other purposes. Further, Article 14(2) seeks to overcome the absence of State-generated title by requiring States to take all necessary steps to identify and demarcate indigenous lands and guarantee effective protection of their rights of ownership and possession.[166] Accordingly, while Chagos Islanders may not have owned freehold interests in the lands they occupied or held any formal title to them, this does not necessarily undermine their claims to customary title.

Although it appears that Convention No 169 confers extensive land rights on indigenous peoples, it carefully restricts the temporal dimension of these putative entitlements. Article 14(1) limits indigenous land rights to those lands indigenous peoples 'traditionally occupy';[167] a formulation that appears to restrict rights to those lands they currently occupy.[168] Article 16 concerns the removal and relocation of indigenous peoples from their traditional lands. It provides:

> 1. Subject to the following paragraphs of this Article, the peoples concerned shall not be removed from the lands which they occupy.
>
> 2. Where the relocation of these peoples is considered necessary as an exceptional measure, such relocation shall take place only with their free and informed consent. Where their consent cannot be obtained, such relocation shall take place only following appropriate procedures established by national laws and regulations, including public inquiries where appropriate, which provide the opportunity for effective representation of the peoples concerned.

---

[165] Only 20 States have ratified the convention (neither the UK nor Mauritius are parties). Nevertheless, it has been argued that the convention represents customary international law on indigenous rights; see SJ Anaya, *Indigenous Peoples in International Law*, 2nd edn (New York: Oxford University Press, 2004) 61–72. See also the way the convention was applied by the Inter-American Court of Human Rights in *Awas Tingni Indigenous Community of Mayagna v Nicaragua* IACtHR Series C 79 (2001), despite Nicaragua not being a party to it.

[166] ILO Convention No 169, Art 14(2). See also Thornberry (n 30) 355–56; and Daes (n 139) [49–54].

[167] It has been suggested by Thornberry (n 30) 353–54, that the phrase 'traditionally occupy' in Art 14 does not strictly require present day occupation of traditional lands as it extends to relatively recent instances of dispossession.

[168] ibid.

3. Whenever possible, these peoples shall have the right to return to their traditional lands, as soon as the grounds for relocation cease to exist.

4. When such return is not possible, as determined by agreement or, in the absence of such agreement, through appropriate procedures, these peoples shall be provided in all possible cases with lands of quality and legal status at least equal to that of the lands previously occupied by them, suitable to provide for their present needs and future development. Where the peoples concerned express a preference for compensation in money or in kind, they shall be so compensated under appropriate guarantees.

5. Persons thus relocated shall be fully compensated for any resulting loss or injury.

Article 16 appears significant in the Chagossian context. First, Article 16(3) indicates that displacement is not prima facie a permanent condition; indigenous peoples have the right to return to their traditional territories when the reasons for their banishment cease to exist. The value of this provision is enhanced by the finding in *Bancoult 2* that the UK government could not establish a legally valid reason to deny the Chagossian people's right of return to the outer Islands. Secondly, the Chagossian people should be adequately compensated for the confiscation of their traditional lands in keeping with the provisions of Articles 16(4) and 16(5) notwithstanding the possibility of regaining these lands in the future pursuant to Article 16(3). Nonetheless, the significance of Article 16 for the Chagossian people may be compromised by the temporal scope of the land rights contained in Convention No 169. These provisions evidently cover instances of removal and relocation that occurred in the recent past but the extent of its historical reach remains unclear. Consequently, whether Article 16 contemplates a case of systematic displacement initiated nearly 40 years ago is open to question.

Article 26 of the 2007 Declaration on the Rights of Indigenous Peoples addresses the issue of indigenous land rights.[169] It provides:

1. Indigenous peoples have the right to the lands, territories and resources which they have traditionally owned, occupied or otherwise used or acquired.

2. Indigenous peoples have the right to own, use develop and control the lands, territories and resources that they possess by reason of traditional ownership or other traditional occupation or use, as well as those which they have otherwise acquired.

3. States shall give legal recognition and protection to these lands, territories and resources. Such recognition shall be conducted with due respect to the customs, traditions and land tenure systems of the indigenous peoples concerned.

In contrast to Article 14 of Convention No 169, this provision insists that indigenous entitlements encompass lands 'traditionally owned or otherwise occupied or used'. At first glance, this formulation seems to appreciate that indigenous rights may extend beyond the recent past; however, on closer inspection, it merely refers to lands that have been used in a manner consistent with

---

[169] The Declaration represents an important normative development in the context of indigenous rights. However, arguably, most of its key provisions still have the status of *lex ferenda*.

traditional practices and thus does not manifest a retrospective dimension. In addition, this provision does not limit indigenous rights to traditional modes of ownership, occupation or use; it also encompasses rights that have been otherwise acquired. Consequently, Article 26 also recognises instances where indigenous peoples may have acquired rights in modern municipal property regimes. Article 28 provides:

> 1. Indigenous peoples have the right to redress, by means that can include restitution or, when this is not possible, of a just fair and equitable compensation, for the lands territories and resources which they have traditionally owned or otherwise occupied or used, and which have been confiscated, taken, occupied, used or damaged without their free, prior and informed consent
>
> 2. Unless otherwise freely agreed upon by the peoples concerned, compensation shall take the form of lands, territories and resources equal in quality, size and legal status or of monetary compensation or other appropriate redress.[170]

While this formulation is reminiscent of Article 16 of Convention No 169, it manifests a stronger commitment to property rights. By including a reference to restitution this provision reopens the controversy concerning the parameters of indigenous land entitlements.[171] It does not sanction the practice of converting indigenous land rights into monetary compensation in the absence of freely informed prior consent. Nevertheless, the temporal limits of rights contained in Articles 26 and 27 do not favour Chagossian land claims, as they are unable to satisfy the criterion of historical precedence, discussed above. And while Article 26(2) acknowledges that indigenous peoples may have acquired land rights via modern municipal regimes, it is clear that English municipal law does not recognise the validity of Chagossian land claims.

Although the Chagossian people possess indigenous status they may not be able to rely on the canon of indigenous rights for the purpose of establishing their land claims; nevertheless, the possibility that the canon might facilitate the process of resettlement in other key respects should be considered. International law has developed a panoply of rights designed to protect and promote indigenous peoples' traditional way of life. However, as modern States have enveloped

---

[170] The 2007 Declaration also connects the cultural impact of involuntary displacement with the issue of land rights. To this end, Art 8 provides:
1 Indigenous peoples and individuals have the right not to be subjected to forced assimilation or destruction of their culture.
2 States shall provide effective mechanisms for prevention of, and redress for [. . .]
  (b) Any action which has the aim or effect of dispossessing them of their lands, territories or resources;
  (c) Any form of forced population transfer which has the aim or effect of violating or undermining any of their rights.

[171] However, the temporal scope of indigenous land rights was a major obstacle during the process of scrutinising the draft. In particular, settler States, such as Australia, Canada, New Zealand and the United States, became increasingly intransigent on this issue. See the reports of the Commission on Human Rights' inter-sessional Working Group: Office of the UN High Commissioner for Human Rights.

indigenous peoples, the international canon operates within the limits of this societal interrelationship.[172] Once resettled on the outer Chagos Islands, the Chagossian people will not co-exist with other (dominant) societal groups; they will be able to rely on general customary international law and the provisions of the ICCPR and ICESCR. Consequently, while indigenous status currently offers displaced Chagossians a voice in international fora, beyond the a priori possibility of sanctioning land entitlements, it is unclear what additional advantages the indigenous canon could confer on the Chagossian people in the event of resettlement.

IX. CONCLUSION

Although the Divisional Court in *Bancoult 1*, and the both the Divisional Court and the Court of Appeal in *Bancoult 2*, reached the conclusion that the Chagos Islanders possessed a right of abode in the outer Chagos Islands the House of Lords decided otherwise in *Bancoult 2*, as discussed in chapter one. Notwithstanding this conclusion, it is clear that the principles of customary international law and the applicable human rights treaties discussed in this chapter have created international legal obligations which bind the UK regardless of whether or not they were considered to be justiciable or relevant to the *Bancoult* litigation in the English courts.[173] Seventeen territories remain listed as non-self-governing territories. The General Assembly's decision to relist the French Overseas Territories of New Caledonia in 1986 and French Polynesia in 2013,[174] combined with the declaration of a Second UN Decade for the Eradication of Colonialism (2001–10),[175] demonstrate that it remains committed to the task of eradicating colonialism. In particular, these actions show that the General Assembly is still prepared to confer the status of non-self-governing territory on dependent territories in situations where a colonial people have not had the opportunity to exercise their right of self-determination. The coming to light of the UK government's misrepresentations about the nature of the population which inhabited the Chagos Islands in connection with the BIOT's creation; the Mauritian government's role in the impoverishment of the Chagos Islanders in Mauritius; and the applicability of the customary right to self-determination and the human rights treaties examined in this chapter should

---

[172] This is apparent from preambular para 12 of the Declaration, which provides: 'Recognizing also that indigenous peoples have the right freely to determine their relationships with States in a spirit of coexistence, mutual benefit and full respect'. Consequently, many indigenous rights only make sense in this context.

[173] See ch 1.

[174] In UNGA Res 67/295, 17 May 2013, the General Assembly decided to relist French Polynesia as a non-self-governing territory. New Caledonia was relisted by the General Assembly via UNGA Res 41/41A, 2 December 1986. On New Caledonia, see Aldrich and Connell (n 8) 131–37.

[175] Second UN Decade for the Eradication of Colonialism (2001–10), UNGA Res 55/146, 8 December 2000; and UN GA Res 60/120, 8 December 2005.

prompt the General Assembly to revisit the question of the status of the Chagos Islands as a matter of international law. It should recognise the BIOT as a non-self-governing territory and activate the supervisory jurisdiction of the UN Special Committee on the Situation with Regard to the Implementation of the Declaration on the Granting of Independence to Colonial Countries and Peoples. By taking this step the General Assembly would be confirming that the Chagos Islanders constitute the BIOT's permanent population pursuant to the provisions of Chapter XI of the UN Charter, the customary international law concerning the right of self-determination in colonial situations (as identified in the 1970 UN Declaration on Friendly Relations); and the relevant provisions of the applicable human rights treaties, as discussed above. Such recognition would strengthen the normative argument that while the UK currently exercises sovereignty over the BIOT, its authority is qualified; consequently, it is under an international legal obligation to facilitate the exercise of the right of self-determination, which belongs to the Chagos Islanders, and to support their plan to resettle the outer Chagos Islands in accordance with the applicable provisions of international law.

Conclusion

THE UK GOVERNMENT has taken extraordinary steps to avoid the prospect of the resettlement of the outer Chagos Islands. It introduced primary legislation in the form of the 2004 Orders in Council to overturn the Divisional Court's decision in *Bancoult 1*; and it ran up considerable legal costs as a result of its appeals against the decisions of the Divisional Court and Court of Appeal in *Bancoult 2*.[1] It may feel as though its uncompromising strategy was vindicated by the 3/2 verdict in the House of Lords in *Bancoult* 2 and by the refusal by the European Court of Human Rights to consider the merits of the *Chagos Islanders v UK* case. Nevertheless, the UK government has taken other exceptional measures to prevent the resettlement of the Chagos Archipelago, which indicate that it is not confident of the lawfulness of its actions. In 2004, it revised the terms of its declaration made in respect of the optional jurisdiction clause contained in Article 36(2) of the ICJ Statute.[2] This amendment meant that the ICJ's jurisdiction could not be engaged through the optional system with regard to any proceedings instituted against it by a current or former member State of the (British) Commonwealth in relation to a dispute that occurred before 1974. It has been confirmed that this change was made to prevent the Mauritian government from commencing proceedings against the UK at the ICJ over the status of the Chagos Islands.[3]

Further, on 1 April 2010, the UK government established the BIOT Marine Protected Area (MPA), a no-take marine reserve designed to protect the marine ecology that surrounds the Chagos Islands. This MPA extends to 640,000 square kilometres and all marine fishing activities were prohibited in this area from 1 November 2010.[4] The Chagos Islanders protested against this development on the ground that it constituted a disproportionate measure that would have a negative impact on any plan to resettle the Archipelago. Further, the Chagossians suspected that the UK government was using environmental concerns to under-

---

[1] Exceptionally, leave to appeal to the House of Lords was granted on condition that the UK government met Bancoult's legal costs for the appeal.

[2] 5 July 2004, 2271 UNTS 285.

[3] See C Warbrick, 'United Kingdom Materials on International Law' (2004) 75 *British Yearbook of International Law* 804; and A Aust, *Handbook of International Law*, 2nd edn (Cambridge, Cambridge University Press, 2010) 419. Noted by PH Sand, 'The Chagos Archipelago Cases: Nature Conservation between Human Rights and Power Politics' (2013) *Global Community Yearbook of International Law and Jurisprudence* 125 (forthcoming).

[4] See the UK government's 2012 White Paper, *The Overseas Territories: Security, Success and Sustainability* (Cm 8374, 2012).

mine their human rights claims in respect of the BIOT.[5] As a result, the Chagossians challenged the validity of the MPA.[6] Their main contention was that the MPA had been established to serve an improper purpose: it had been created to thwart the resettlement of the outer Chagos Islands. Evidence in support of this allegation was provided by an embassy cable which had entered the public domain by virtue of a Wikileaks disclosure. This cable reported that, Colin Roberts, the then BIOT Commissioner had 'asserted that establishing a marine park would, in effect, put paid to resettlement claims of the archipelago's former residents', in a UK-US meeting held on 12 May 2009.[7] In the light of the cable, Burnton LJ ordered the former BIOT Commissioner and also the former BIOT Administrator to attend court to give evidence about the disclosed cable. However, in giving evidence at a subsequent hearing, these officials followed the UK government's established policy of refusing to confirm or deny whether the contents of the leaked documents were genuine.[8] In the circumstances, as the information was obtained unlawfully, the Divisional Court decided that in the absence of any such confirmation the evidence was inadmissible and the case was dismissed.

The Mauritian government has also protested against the setting up of the BIOT MPA. On 20 December 2010, it commenced arbitral proceedings against the UK as provided for in the 1982 UN Convention on the Law of the Sea. Specifically, it claimed that the declared MPA was incompatible with the terms of the 1982 Convention. Further, it argued that the UK was not competent to establish an Exclusive Economic Zone in the area surrounding the Chagos Islands because it did not qualify as a coastal State for such a purpose.[9] The case is still ongoing at the time of writing.[10]

Many of the legal issues considered in this book are grounded in temporal considerations. As a result, they are governed by the principle of inter-temporal law, which holds that the legality of actions must be judged by the law in force at the time they were conducted. This dimension of this book's enquiry brings into focus the following questions. Had the right to self-determination acquired the status of customary international law by the time the Chagos Islands were

---

[5] It should be recalled that the MPA was established while the *Chagos Islanders v UK* case was still pending at the European Court of Human Rights with regard to alleged violations of the European Convention on Human Rights. However, it should be acknowledged that the UK government made it clear that the MPA's creation was without prejudice to the outcome of that litigation.

[6] *R (Bancoult) v Secretary of State for Foreign and Commonwealth Affairs* [2012] EWHC (Admin) 2115.

[7] Cable No 001156, from US Embassy, London, to US State Department 15 May 2009. See *The Guardian*, 2 December 2010.

[8] *R (Bancoult) v Secretary of State for Foreign and Commonwealth Affairs* [2013] EWHC (Admin) 1502 (Richards LJ and Mitting J).

[9] See I Papanicolopulu, 'Mauritius v. United Kingdom: Submission of the dispute on the Marine Protected Area around the Chagos Archipelago to Arbitration' EJIL Talk!, 11 February 2011: The composition of the arbitration panel was subject to an interesting challenge: see (2012) 51 *International Legal Materials* 350–81.

[10] Sand, 'The Chagos Archipelago Cases: Nature Conservation between Human Rights and Power Politics' (n 3).

detached from the colony of Mauritius pursuant to the terms of the 1965 BIOT Order in Council and the 1965 Lancaster House Agreement? Was the category of non-self-governing territories restricted to those qualifying colonial territories that were in existence when the United Nations was founded (in accordance with paragraph 1 of General Assembly Resolution 1541(XV)(1960))? Was the critical date for the determining the existence of the Chagossian right of abode in the BIOT (as a matter of English law) when the BIOT was constituted by the 1965 BIOT Order, or was it when the 2004 BIOT Constitution Order was enacted?[11] Temporal considerations frequently inform interpretations about the content of the municipal law. However, international law is particularly vulnerable to temporal challenges given the difficulties that often arise in establishing whether binding customary international law has emerged; consequently, it often lacks the temporal markers that characterise the formation of national law. Notwithstanding this difficulty, this book contends that the BIOT constitutes a valid non-self-governing territory and the Chagos Islanders qualify as the Territory's permanent inhabitants for the purpose of the obligations contained in Chapter XI of the UN Charter, despite their 40-year absence. The Chagos Islanders also qualify as the beneficiaries of the entitlement to self-determination in relation to the BIOT because they remained in occupation of the Chagos Islands at the time when this right acquired the status of binding customary international law via the adoption of the 1970 Declaration on Friendly Relations.[12] Moreover, the UK's involuntary displacement of Chagos Islanders and the prohibition on their return constitute violations of the applicable treaty law, as discussed in chapter seven.[13]

The majority of the House of Lords in *Bancoult 2* reached the conclusion that the Chagossians' situation represented a shameful historical injustice, for which the Chagos Islanders have been compensated. In sharp contrast, this book asserts that the violations of international law visited upon the Chagos Islanders are *continuing* violations for the purpose of the establishing State Responsibility, pursuant to the provisions of Article 14 of the Articles on State Responsibility.[14] Further, the meagre level of compensation paid to Chagossians

---

[11] See the Opinions of Lord Hoffmann, Lord Bingham and Lord Mance in the House of Lords in *Bancoult 2* [2008] 3 WLR 955 for different answers to this question, as discussed in ch 1.

[12] Declaration on the Principles of International Law concerning Friendly Relations and Co-operation Among States in Accordance with the Charter of the United Nations, UNGA Res 2625(XXV), 24 October 1970.

[13] As discussed in ch 7.

[14] The Articles on State Responsibility 2001, Art 14 provides inter alia:

(2) The breach of an international obligation by an act of a State having a continuous character extends over the entire period during which the act continues and remains not in conformity with the international obligation.

(3) The breach of an international obligation requiring a State to prevent a given event occurs when the event occurs and extends over the entire period during which the event continues and remains not in conformity with that obligation.

See J Crawford, *The International Law Commission's Articles on State Responsibility: Introduction, Text and Commentaries* (Cambridge, Cambridge University Press, 2002) 135–36. See ch 7.

was offered long after they were exiled to Mauritius. Accordingly, the fact that the chronically impoverished Chagossians took the money cannot be construed as a validation of the UK's involuntary displacement of the BIOT's permanent population. The UK government remains committed to a policy of resisting the resettlement of the outer Chagos Islands and it has devoted considerable resources to this objective in the hope that, in time, the Chagos Islands will pass out of living memory and into the realm of Chagossian folklore thereby becoming an historical injustice to be regretted rather than remedied.

In such circumstances the UN General Assembly has a choice. It can either maintain its support of Mauritius sovereign claim, turning a blind eye to the Mauritian government's preparedness to agree to the excision of the Chagos Islands from Mauritius under the terms of the 1965 Lancaster House Agreement and its role in the impoverishment of the Chagos Islanders during their time in Mauritius. Alternatively, it could change its position as a result of the coming to light of the true nature of the population which inhabited the Chagos Islands when the BIOT was created. By recognising that the BIOT constitutes a valid non-self-governing territory pursuant to Chapter XI of the UN Charter, and for the wider purposes of international law, the General Assembly would be taking the first step towards correcting this travesty of social justice and thus bringing the elimination of the negative effects of colonialism in the Chagossian context one step nearer.

Bibliography

Akehurst, M, 'Custom as a Source of International Law' (1974–75) 47 *British Yearbook of International Law* 47

Aldrich, R and Connell, J, *The Last Colonies* (Cambridge, Cambridge University Press, 1998)

Allan, TRS, 'Human Rights and Judicial Review: A Critique of "Due Deference"' (2006) 65 *Cambridge Law Journal* 671

Allen, S, 'The Consequences of Modernity for Indigenous Peoples: An International Appraisal' (2006) 13 *International Journal on Minority and Group Rights* 315

——, 'Looking Beyond the *Bancoult* Cases: International Law and the Prospect of Resettling the Chagos Islands' (2007) 7 *Human Rights Law Review* 441

——, 'International Law and the Resettlement of the (Outer) Chagos Islands' (2008) 8 *Human Rights Law Review* 683

——, 'The Pitcairn Prosecutions and the Rule of Law' (2012) 75 *Modern Law Review* 1150

—— and Xanthaki, A (eds), *Reflections on the Declaration on the Rights of Indigenous Peoples* (Oxford, Hart, 2011)

American Law Institute, *Third Restatement of Foreign Law* (St Paul, American Law Institute, 1987)

Anaya, SJ, *Indigenous Peoples in International Law*, 2nd edn (New York, Oxford University Press, 2004)

Anderson, B, *Imagined Communities* (New York, Verso, 2002)

Angelo, T and Kessbohm, R, 'The New Constitution of Pitcairn: A Primer' (2009) 7 *New Zealand Yearbook of International Law* 285

Anghie, A, '"The Heart of My Home": Colonialism, Environmental Damage and the Nauru Case' (1993) 34 *Harvard International Law Journal* 445

——, *Imperialism, Sovereignty and the Making of International Law* (Cambridge, Cambridge University Press, 2004)

Aust, A, *Modern Treaty Law and Practice* (Cambridge, Cambridge University Press, 2007)

——, *Handbook of International Law*, 2nd edn (Cambridge, Cambridge University Press, 2010)

Barnwell, PJ and Toussaint, A, *A Short Study of Mauritius* (London, Longmans, 1949)

Bates, E, 'The United Kingdom and the International Covenant on Economic, Social and Cultural Rights' in R McCorquodale and M Baderin (eds), *Economic, Social and Cultural Rights in Action* (Oxford, Oxford University Press, 2007) 257

Berman, N, 'Sovereignty in Abeyance: Self-determination and International Law' (1988–89) 7 *Wisconsin International Law Journal* 51

——, 'But the Alternative is Despair' (1993) 106 *Harvard Law Review* 1792

Besson, S, 'The Extraterritoriality of the European Convention on Human Rights: Why Human Rights Depend on Jurisdiction and What Jurisdiction Amounts to' (2012) 25 *Leiden Journal of International Law* 857

Bingham, T, 'The Rule of Law' (2007) 66 *Cambridge Law Journal* 67

Blay, SKN, 'Self-Determination Versus Territorial Integrity in Decolonization' (1985–86) 16 *New York University Journal of International Law and Politics* 441

Bowett, D, 'Estoppel before International Tribunals and its Relation to Acquiescence' (1957) 33 *British Yearbook of International Law* 176, 190

Brierly, JL, 'International Law in England' (1935) 51 *Law Quarterly Review* 24

Brölmann, C, Lefeber, R and Zieck, M (eds), *Peoples and Minorities in International Law* (Dordrecht, Martinus Nijhoff, 1993)

Brownlie, I, 'Recognition in Theory and Practice' (1982) 52 *British Yearbook of International Law* 197

Burman, BKR and Verghese, BG (eds), *Aspiring to Be: The Tribal/Indigenous Condition* (New Delhi, Konark PVT, 1998)

Caflisch, L, 'Unequal Treaties' (1992) 35 *German Yearbook of International Law* 52

Capps, P, 'Responsibility for Acts in Violation of International Law in the British Indian Ocean Territory' Centre for Public Law, Faculty of Law, Cambridge University, 2007

——, 'The Court as Gatekeeper: Customary International Law in English Courts' (2007) 70 *Modern Law Review* 558

——, *Human Dignity and the Foundations of International Law* (Oxford, Hart Publishing, 2009)

——, 'Lauterpacht's Method' (2011) 82 *British Yearbook of International Law* 248

Cassese, A, *Self-Determination of Peoples: A Legal Reappraisal* (Cambridge, Cambridge University Press, 1995)

Castañeda, J, *Legal Effects of United Nations Resolutions* (New York, Columbia University Press, 1969)

Castellino, J, *International Law & Self-Determination* (The Hague, Martinus Nijhoff, 2000)

—— and Allen, S, *Title to Territory in International Law: A Temporal Analysis* (Aldershot, Ashgate, 2003)

—— and Walsh, N (eds), *Indigenous Peoples and International Law* (The Hague, Martinus Nijhoff Publishers, 2005)

Chan-Low, J, 'The Making of the Chagos Affair: Myths and Reality' in S Evers and M Kooy (eds), *Eviction from the Chagos Islands: Displacement and Struggle for Identity Against Two World Powers* (Leiden, Brill, 2011) 61

Cheng, B, 'United Nations Resolutions on Outer Space: "Instant" International Customary Law?' (1965) 5 *Indian Journal of International Law* 23

Clapham, A, *Brierly's Law of Nations*, 7th edn (Oxford, Oxford University Press, 2012)

Cohn, M, 'Judicial Activism in the House of Lords: A Composite Constitutionalist Approach' (2007) *Public Law* 95

Craig, P, 'Constitutional Foundations, the Rule of Law and Supremacy' (2003) *Public Law* 92

Craven, M, 'The European Community Arbitration Commission on Yugoslavia' (1995) 66 *British Yearbook of International Law* 333

——, *The Decolonization of International Law: State Succession and the Law of Treaties* (Oxford, Oxford University Press, 2007)

Crawford, J, *The Creation of States in International Law*, 1st edn (Oxford, Oxford University Press, 1977)

——, 'Book Review of A Cassese, *Self-Determination of Peoples: A Legal Reappraisal*' (1996) 90 *American Journal of International Law* 331

——, 'The General Assembly, the International Court and Self-determination' in V Lowe and M Fitzmaurice (eds), *Fifty Years of the International Court of Justice: Essays in Honour of Sir Robert Jennings* (Cambridge, Grotius Publications, 1996) 585

——, 'State Practice and International Law in relation to Secession' (1998) 69 *British Yearbook of International Law* 85

——, *The International Law Commission's Articles on State Responsibility: Introduction, Text and Commentaries* (Cambridge, Cambridge University Press, 2002)

——, *The Creation of States in International Law*, 2nd edn (Oxford, Oxford University Press, 2006)

——, *Brownlie's Principles of Public International Law*, 8th edn (Oxford, Oxford University Press, 2012)

Daes, EI, Working Paper on the Relationship and Distinction between the Rights of Persons Belonging to Minorities and those of Indigenous Peoples, 19 July 2000, E/CN4/SUB 2/2000/10

De Jong, HG, 'Coercion in the Conclusion of Treaties' (1982) 15 *Netherlands Yearbook of International Law* 209

De l'Estrac, JC and Prayag, T, *Next Year in Diego Garcia* (Mauritius, Edition Le Printemps, 2011)

Denza, E, 'The Relationship between International Law and National Law' in M Evans (ed), *International Law*, 3rd edn (Oxford, Oxford University Press, 2010)

De Smith, S, 'Mauritius: Constitutionalism in a Plural Society' (1968) 31 *Modern Law Review* 601

Detter, I, 'The Problem of Unequal Treaties' (1966) 15 *International and Comparative Law Quarterly* 1069

Deutsch, K and Foltz, W, *Nation Building* (New York, Atherton Press 1963)

Draebel, M, 'Evaluation des besoins sociaux de la communauté déplacée de l'Archipel de Chagos' (Report produced for the World Health Organization, 1997)

Dworkin, R, 'The Model of Rules' (1967) 35 *University of Chicago Law Review* 14 reproduced in *Taking Rights Seriously*.

——, *Taking Rights Seriously* (London, Duckworth, 1997)

Elias, TO, 'The Doctrine of Intertemporal Law' (1980) 74 *American Journal of International Law* 285

Elliott, M, and Perreau-Saussine, A, 'Pyrrhic Public Law: Bancoult and the Sources, Status and Content of Common Law Limitations on Prerogative Power' (2009) 52 *Public Law* 697

Emerson, R, 'Self-determination' (1971) 65 *American Journal of International Law* 459

Evans, MD (ed), *International Law*, 3rd edn (Oxford, Oxford University Press, 2010)

Evers, S and Kooy M (eds), *Eviction from the Chagos Islands: Displacement and Struggle for Identity Against Two World Powers* (Leiden, Brill, 2011)

——and ——, 'Introduction' in S Evers and M Kooy (eds), *Eviction from the Chagos Islands: Displacement and Struggle for Identity Against Two World Powers* (Leiden, Brill, 2011)

Fastenrath, U, 'Declaration regarding Non-Self-Governing Territories' in B Simma (ed), The Charter of the United Nations: A Commentary, vol II, 3rd edn (Oxford, Oxford University Press, 2012)

Finnis, J, 'Common Law Constraints: Whose Common Good Counts?'(2008) *University of Oxford Law Faculty Legal Studies Research Paper Series*, Working Paper No 10/2008

Fitzmaurice, G, 'The Foundations of the Authority of International Law and the Problem of Enforcement' (1956) 19 *Modern Law Review* 1

Franz, GH (ed), Constitutions of the Countries of the World 12 (Dobbs Ferry, NY, Oceana, 1998)

——, 'The General Principles of International Law Considered from the Standpoint of the Rule of Law (1957) 92 *Recueil des Cours* pt II 68–99

Franck, TM, *Nation Against Nation* (New York, Oxford University Press, 1985)

——and Hoffman, P, 'The Right of Self-Determination in Very Small Places' (1975–76) 8 *New York University Journal of International Law and Politics* 331

Friedmann, WF, 'The Jurisprudential Implications of the South-West Africa Case' (1967) 6 *Columbia Journal of Transnational* Law 1

Gellner, E, *Nations and Nationalism* (Oxford, Blackwell, 1990)

Gifford, R, 'The Chagos Islands–The Land Where Human Rights Hardly Ever Happen' (2004) Law Social Justice and Global Development Journal <http://www2.warwick.ac.uk/fac/soc/law/elj/lgd/2004_1/gifford/>

Goodrich L et al, *Charter of the United Nations: Commentary and Documents*, 3rd edn (New York, Columbia University Press, 1969)

Grant, T, 'Who Can Make Treaties? Other Subjects of International Law' in D Hollis (ed), *The Oxford Guide to Treaties* (Oxford, Oxford University Press, 2013)

Gray, A, 'The Indigenous Movement in Asia, in RH Barnes, A Gray and B Kingsbury (eds), *Indigenous Peoples of Asia* (Ann Arbor, Association for Asian Studies, 1995)

Gross, L, 'The Right to Self-determination in International Law' in M Kilson (ed), *New States in the Modern World* (Cambridge, Harvard University Press, 1975) 139

Halsbury's Laws of England (London, Butterworths, 2003)

Hannum, H 'Rethinking Self-determination' (1993) 34 *Virginia Journal of International Law* 1

Harris, DJ, *Cases and Materials on International Law*, 6th edn (London, Sweet and Maxwell, 2004)

——, *Cases and Materials on International Law*, 7th edn (London, Sweet & Maxwell, 2010)

Hart, HLA, *The Concept of Law* (Oxford, Oxford University Press, 1994)

Harvard Research Draft Convention on Criminal Jurisdiction (1935) 29 *American Journal of International Law Supplement* 443

Hendry, I and Dickson, S, *British Overseas Territories Law* (Oxford, Hart Publishing, 2011)

Higgins, R, *The Development of International Law Through the Political Organs of the United Nations* (London, Oxford University Press, 1963)

——, 'Judge Dillard and Self-determination' (1983) 23 *Virginia Journal of International Law* 387

——, *Problems & Process* (Oxford, Clarendon Oxford University Press, 2007)

Hobsbawm, E, *Nations and Nationalism Since 1780: Programme, Myth, Reality*, 2nd edn (Cambridge, Cambridge University Press, 1992)

Hohfeld, W, 'Fundamental Legal Conceptions as Applied in Judicial Reasoning' (1913) 23 *Yale Law Journal* 16

——, 'Fundamental Legal Conceptions as Applied in Judicial Reasoning' (1917) 26 *Yale Law Journal* 710

International Law Association, 'Statement of Principles Applicable to the Formation of General Customary International Law' (International Law Association, 2000)

Iorns, CJ, 'Indigenous Peoples and Self-determination: Challenging State Sovereignty' (1992) 24 *Case Western Reserve Journal of International Law* 199

Jeffery, L, 'Historical Narrative and Legal Evidence: Judging Chagossians' High Court Testimonies' (2006) 29 *Political and Legal Anthropology Review* 228

——, *Chagos Islanders in Mauritius and the UK* (Manchester, Manchester University Press, 2011)

Jennings, RY, *The Acquisition of Territory in International Law* (Manchester, Manchester University Press, 1962)

——and Watts, A, *Oppenheim's International Law*, vol 1, 9th edn (London, Longman, 1992)

Jowell, J, 'Beyond the Rule of Law: Towards Constitutional Judicial Review' (2000) *Public Law* 671

——, 'Parliamentary Sovereignty under the New Constitutional Hypothesis' (2006) *Public Law* 562

——(ed), *De Smith's Judicial Review*, 6th edn (London, Sweet & Maxwell, 2007)

Kelsen, H, *The Law of the United Nations* (Union, Law Book Exchange, 1951)

Kingsbury, B, 'Indigenous Peoples in International Law: A Constructivist Approach to the Asian Controversy' (1998) 92 *American Journal of International Law* 414

Kirgis, F, 'Custom on a Sliding Scale' (1987) 81 *American Journal of International Law* 146

Knop, K, *Diversity and Self-determination in International Law* (Cambridge, Cambridge University Press, 2002)

Koskenniemi, M, 'National Self-Determination Today: Problems of Legal Theory and Practice' (1994) 43 *International and Comparative Law Quarterly* 241

——, 'The Function of Law in the International Community' (2008) 79 *British Yearbook of International Law* 353

——, 'What is International Law For?' in MD Evans (ed), *International Law*, 3rd edn (Oxford, Oxford University Press, 2010) 32

Kunz, JL, 'Chapter XI of the United Nations Charter in Action' (1954) 48 *American Journal of International Law* 103

Lakin, S, 'Debunking the Idea of Parliamentary Sovereignty: The Controlling Factor of Legality in the British Constitution' (2008) 28 *Oxford Journal of Legal Studies* 709

Lâm, MC, *At the Edge of the State: Indigenous Peoples and Self-Determination* (New York, Transnational Publishers, 2000)

Lauterpacht, E (ed), *Hersch Lauterpacht, International Law: Collected Papers*, vol 1 (Cambridge, Cambridge University Press, 1970)

Lauterpacht, H, *Private Law Sources and Analogies of International Law* (London, Longman, 1927)

——, *The Function of Law in the International Community*, reissued (Cambridge, Cambridge University Press, 2011).

Laws, J, 'Law and Democracy' (1995) *Public Law* 72

Lerner, N, *Group Rights and Discrimination in International Law*, 2nd edn (The Hague, Martinus Nijhoff Publishers, 2003)

Lissitzyn, OJ, 'Territorial Entities other than Independent States in the Law of Treaties' (1968) 125 *Recueil des cours* 1

Lowe, V, *International Law* (Oxford, Clarendon Press, 2007)

Lynch, TP, 'Diego Garcia: Competing Claims to a Strategic Isle' (1984) 16 *Case Western Reserve Journal of International Law* 101

Madeley, J, *Diego Garcia: A Contrast to The Falklands*, Report No 54 (London, Minority Rights Group, 1982)

Martinez-Cobo, J, *Study of the Problem of Discrimination Against Indigenous Populations*, E/CN4/Sub2/1986/7/Add

Mauritius Legislative Assembly, *Financial and Other Aspects of the 'Sale' of the Chagos Islands and the Resettlement of the Displaced Ilois,* Special Report of the Public Accounts Committee for the 1980 (Fourth) Session (Port Louis, Mauritian Government, 1981)

——, *Report of the Select Committee on the Excision of the Chagos Archipelago* (No 2 of 1983) (Port Louis, Mauritian Legislative Assembly, 1983)

——, 'Al-Skeini and Al-Jeppa in Strasbourg' (2012) *European Journal of International Law* 121

Miltner, B, 'Revisiting Extraterritoriality After *Al-Skeini*: The ECHR and Its Lessons' (2012) 33 *Michigan Journal of International Law* 693

Moffett, J, 'Resiling from Legitimate Expectations' (2008) 13 *Judicial Review* 219

Moor, L and Simpson, AWB, 'Ghosts of Colonialism in the European Convention on Human Rights' (2005) 76 *British Yearbook of International Law* 121

Murphy, C, 'Economic Duress and Unequal Treaties' (1970–1971) 11 *Virginia Journal of International* Law 51

Musgrave, TD, *Self-determination and National Minorities* (Oxford, Oxford University Press, 1994)

Nijman, J and Nollkaemper, A (eds), *New Perspectives on the Divide Between National and International Law* (Oxford, Oxford University Press, 2007)

Nolte, G, 'Purposes and Principles (Art 2(7)' in B Simma (ed), *The Charter of the United Nations: A Commentary*, vol I, 3rd edn (Oxford, Oxford University Press, 2012)

O'Connell, DP, 'Independence and Succession to Treaties' (1962) 38 *British Year Book of International Law* 84

Papanicolopulu, I, 'Mauritius v. United Kingdom: Submission of the dispute on the Marine Protected Area around the Chagos Archipelago to Arbitration' EJIL Talk!, 11 February 2011

Peel, E, *Treitel on the Law of Contract*, 12th edn (London, Sweet & Maxwell, 2007)

Radan, P, 'Post-Secession International Borders: A Critical Analysis of the Opinions of the Badinter Commission' (2000) 24 *Melbourne University Law Review* 50

Ratner, SR, 'Drawing a Better Line: *Uti Possidetis* and the Borders of New States' (1996) 90 *American Journal of International Law* 590

Raustiala, K, *Does the Constitution Follow the Flag?* (New York, Oxford University Press, 2009)

Raz, J, 'Legal Principles and the Limits of Law' (1971–72) 81 *Yale Law Journal* 823

——, *Ethnics in the Public Domain: Essays in the Morality of Law and Politics* (Oxford, Clarendon Press, 1995)

——, 'The Problem of Authority: Revisiting the Service Conception' (2006) 90 *Minnesota Law Review* 1003

Reus-Smit, C (ed), *The Politics of International Law* (Cambridge, Cambridge University Press, 2004)

Rigo Sureda, A, *The Evolution of the Right of Self-Determination* (Leiden, Sijthoff, 1973)

Roberts-Wray, KO, *Commonwealth and Colonial Law* (London, Stevens & Sons, 1966)

Rosenstock, R, 'The Declaration of Principles of International Law Concerning Friendly Relations: A Survey' (1971) 65 *American Journal Of International Law* 713

Roth, B, *Governmental Illegitimacy in International Law* (Oxford, Oxford University Press, 2000

Sales, P, and Clement, C, 'International Law in Domestic Courts: The Developing Framework' (2008) 124 *Law Quarterly Review* 388

Sand, PH, 'British-American Legal Blackhole in the Indian Ocean?' (2009) 21 *Journal of Environmental Law* 113

——, 'Diego Garcia Legal Black Hole: A Response to Sheppard et al' (2009) 1 *Journal of Environmental Law* 295

——, *United States and Britain in Diego Garcia* (New York, Palgrave, 2009)

——, 'The Chagos Archipelago Cases: Nature Conservation between Human Rights and Power Politics' (2013) *Global Community Yearbook of International Law and Jurisprudence* 125 (forthcoming)

Schachter, O, 'The Relation of Law, Politics and Action in the United Nations' (1963) 109 *Hague Recueil* 169

Scott R, *Limuria: The Lesser Dependencies of Mauritius* (London, Oxford University Press, 1961)

Sedley, S, 'The Sound of Silence: Constitutional Law Without a Constitution' (1994) 110 *Law Quarterly Review* 270

Shaw, MN, *Title to Territory in Africa: International Legal Issues* (New York, Oxford University Press, 1986)

Shaw, MN, 'The Heritage of States: The Principle of *Uti Possidetis Juris* Today' (1996) 67 *British Yearbook of International Law* 75

——, 'Peoples, Territorialism and Boundaries' (1997) 3 *European Journal of International Law* 478

——, *International Law*, 6th edn (Cambridge, Cambridge University Press, 2008)

Sheppard, C and Spalding, M, *Chagos Conservation Management Plan* (London, Foreign & Commonwealth Office, 2003)

Simma, B (ed), *The Charter of the United Nations: A Commentary*, vol II, 3rd edn (Oxford, Oxford University Press, 2012)

Simmons, AS, *Modern Mauritius: The Politics of Decolonization* (Bloomington, Indiana University Press, 1982)

Sinclair, I, 'Estoppel and Acquiescence' in V Lowe and M Fitzmaurice (eds), *Fifty Years of the International Court of Justice: Essays in Honour of Sir Robert Jennings* (Cambridge, Grotius Publications, 1996) 104

Smith, A, *Ethnic Origins of Nations* (Oxford, Blackwell, 1986)

Snoxell, D, 'Expulsion from Chagos: Regaining Paradise' (2008) 36 *Journal of Imperial and Commonwealth History* 119

Steiner, H, Alston, P and Goodman, M (eds), *International Human Rights in Context: Law, Politics, Morals*, 3rd edn (Oxford, Oxford University Press, 2007)

Suter, K, *East Timor and West Irian* (London, Minority Group, 1982)

Teitel, RG, 'Transitional Justice Genealogy' (2003) 16 *Harvard Human Rights Journal* 69

Thornberry, P, *International Law and the Rights of Minorities* (Oxford, Clarendon Press, 1991)

——, 'The Democratic or Internal Aspect of Self-determination with Some Remarks on Federalism' in C Tomuschat (ed), *Modern Law of Self Determination* (The Hague, Martinus Nijhoff, 1994) 101

——, *Indigenous Peoples and Human Rights* (Manchester, Manchester University Press, 2002)

——, 'Confronting Racial Discrimination: A CERD Perspective' (2005) 5 *Human Rights Law Review* 239

——, 'The Convention on The Elimination of Racial Discrimination, Indigenous Peoples and Caste/Descent-based Discrimination' in J Castellino and N Walsh (eds), *Indigenous Peoples and International Law* (The Hague, Martinus Nijhoff Publishers, 2005) 17

Thorney, A, 'Responsible Government and the Divisibility of the Crown' (2008) *Public Law* 742

Ticu, MM, *Chagos: Where International Law Stops* (Utrecht, Utrecht University, 2012) (on file with the author)

Tomkins, A, 'Magna Carta, Crown and Colonies' (2001) *Public Law* 571

Twomey, A, 'Responsible Government and the Divisibility of the Crown' (2008) *Public Law* 742

UK government, *Partnership for Progress and Prosperity: Britain and the Overseas Territories* (Cm 4264, 1999)

Villiger, ME, *Commentary on the 1969 Vienna Convention on the Law of Treaties* (Leiden, Brill, 2009)

Vine, D, 'The Impoverishment of Displacement: Models for Documenting Human Rights Abuses and the People of Diego Garcia' (2006) 13 *Human Rights Brief* 21

Vine, D, *Island of Shame: the Secret History of the U.S. Military Base on Diego Garcia* (Princeton, Princeton University Press, 2009)

——, 'From the Birth of the *Ilois* to the "Footprint of Freedom": A History of the Chagos and the Chagossians' in S Evers and M Kooy (eds), *Eviction from the Chagos Islands: Displacement and Struggle for Identity Against Two World Powers* (Leiden, Brill, 2011) 11

——, Wojciech Sokolowski, S and Harvey, P, Dérasiné: *The Expulsion and Impoverishment of the Chagossian People* (11 April 2005) (on file with the author)

Warbrick, C, 'United Kingdom Materials on International Law' (2004) 75 *British Yearbook of International Law* 804

Weiss, TG, and Daws, S, *The Oxford Handbook on the United Nations* (New York, Oxford University Press, 2008)

Weller, M, 'The International Response to the Dissolution of the Socialist Federal Republic of Yugoslavia' (1992) 86 *American Journal of International Law* 569

Widstrand, CG (ed), *African Boundary Problems* (Uppsala, Scandinavian Institute, 1969)

Wilde, R, 'Legal "Black Hole" Extraterritorial State Action and International Treaty Law on Civil and Political Rights' (2004–05) 26 *Michigan Journal of International Law* 739

Wright, Q, 'The Goa Incident' (1962) 56 *American Journal of International Law* 617

Index